THE
GREATER MEN AND WOMEN
OF THE BIBLE

THE GREATER
MEN AND WOMEN
OF THE BIBLE

EDITED BY THE REV.

JAMES HASTINGS, D.D.

EDITOR OF "THE EXPOSITORY TIMES" "THE DICTIONARY OF THE BIBLE"
"THE DICTIONARY OF CHRIST AND THE GOSPELS"
"THE DICTIONARY OF THE APOSTOLIC CHURCH" AND
"THE ENCYCLOPÆDIA OF RELIGION AND ETHICS"

ST. LUKE—TITUS

Edinburgh: T. & T. CLARK, 38 George Street

PRINTED IN GREAT BRITAIN BY
MORRISON AND GIBB LIMITED

FOR

T. & T. CLARK, EDINBURGH

LONDON: SIMPKIN, MARSHALL, HAMILTON, KENT, AND CO. LIMITED
NEW YORK: CHARLES SCRIBNER'S SONS

Printed . . . May 1916
Reprinted . . May 1920
„ . . April 1926

INDEX TO CONTENTS.

NAMES AND SUBJECTS.

INDEX TO CONTENTS

TEXTS.

St. Mark.

ST. LUKE.

I.

THE HISTORIAN.

LITERATURE.

Brooke, A. E., *St. Luke: The Historian of the Infancy* (1914), 3.

Brooks, P., *The Light of the World* (1891), 216.

Carpenter, J. E., *The First Three Gospels* (1890), 332.

Conybeare, F. C., *Myth, Magic, and Morals* (1910), 83.

Gibbon, B. J., *Visionaries* (1900), 81.

Harnack, A., *Luke the Physician* (1907), 2.

Haweis, H. R., *The Story of the Four* (1886), 125.

Henson, H. H., *The Value of the Bible* (1904), 69.

McLachlan, H., *St. Luke, Evangelist and Historian* (1912).

Milligan, G., in *Men of the New Testament*: Matthew to Timothy (1905), 29.

Moffatt, J., *An Introduction to the Literature of the New Testament* (1911), 261.

Ramsay, W. M., *St. Paul the Traveller* (1895), 207.

     „   „   *Luke the Physician* (1908), 1.

Redlich, E. B., *St. Paul and his Companions* (1913), 1.

Renan, E., *The History of the Origins of Christianity*: The Gospels, 131, 224.

Weiss, B., *Biblical Theology of the New Testament*, ii. (1883) 291.

Whyte, A., *Bible Characters*: Stephen to Timothy (1901), 72.

Zahn, T., *Introduction to the New Testament*, iii. (1909) 1.

Dictionary of the Apostolic Church, i. (1915) 718 (K. Lake).

Dictionary of the Bible, iii. (1900) 161 (Ll. J. M. Bebb).

     „   „   „   (Single-volume, 1909), 557 (A. J. Maclean).

Encyclopædia Biblica, iii. (1902), col. 2830 (P. W. Schmiedel).

THE HISTORIAN.

It seemed good to me also, having traced the course of all things accurately from the first, to write unto thee in order, most excellent Theophilus.—Luke i. 3.

1. THE Luke to whom the composition of the Third Gospel and of the Acts was unanimously ascribed by the ancient Church is first mentioned by St. Paul in the Epistles of the first and second Roman imprisonments. That the "Luke" whose name is so closely connected with the Third Gospel and the Acts is the Luke mentioned in the Pauline Epistles has never been questioned. According to these Epistles (Col. iv. 14 ; Philem. 24 ; 2 Tim. iv. 11), he was (1) a Hellene by birth, (2) a physician, (3) a companion of St. Paul, (4) a fellow-worker with St. Paul.

2. In ancient times we find that a famous man's place of origin is generally noted, while records of the places where he composed his writings are much more rare. Both Eusebius and the ancient "Argumentum evangelii secundum Lucam" agree in describing Luke as a native of Antioch. But Eusebius is scarcely dependent upon the "Argumentum," since he defines the relations of St. Luke with the original Apostles more accurately than the latter. Rather we are here compelled to assume a common source, which must therefore be of very early date. The fact that this record tells us nothing of the place of composition, but simply fixes St. Luke's native city, speaks in favour of its reliability. The author of Acts is certainly not a native of Palestine, nor does he write for natives of that district. Neither does he write for Macedonians (see Acts xvi. 11). On the other hand, in addition to Antioch and the coastland of Phœnicia and Palestine (especially Cæsarea), he knows Asia well.

ST. LUKE

I.

The Writer of St. Luke's Gospel.

1. At Ephesus, or some place in Asia or Achaia, and about the year 80 A.D., St. Luke wrote his history for the "excellent Theophilus." This is a genuine proper name, not an imaginary *nom de guerre* for the typical catechumen, nor a conventional title for the average Christian reader. Nothing is known of Theophilus, except what may be inferred from St. Luke's language. He was not simply an outsider interested in the faith, but a Christian who desired or required fuller acquaintance with the historic basis of the Christian gospel. He was also a man of rank.

2. St. Luke's chief authority for the Gospel was the work of St. Mark, his late companion in Rome; besides this, he employed for the Lord's life a second source, which he shared with St. Matthew; and, thirdly, he was dependent upon special traditions which had their origin in Jerusalem or Judæa. It is most unlikely that he collected these while he made what was probably only a very short stay in Jerusalem during the first years of Nero's reign, for then they must also have been incorporated in St. Mark; and so far is this from being the case that they go beyond and even correct the conceptions and accounts of the latter Gospel. This material, therefore, must have reached St. Luke at a later period. In all probability it did not reach either St. Luke or St. John in written form, but depended upon the oral tradition of Christians of Jerusalem or Judæa who had wandered from Palestine or Jerusalem at or after the time of the Great War.

¶ God gave men truths in His miraculous revelations, and other truths in the unsophisticated infancy of nations, scarcely less necessary and divine. These are transmitted as " the wisdom of our ancestors," through men—many of whom cannot enter into them, or receive them themselves—still on, on, from age to age, not the less truths because many of the generations through which they are transmitted are unable to prove them, but hold them, either from pious and honest feeling (it may be), or from bigotry or from prejudice. That they are truths it is most difficult to prove, for great men alone can prove great ideas or grasp them.[1]

---

[1] *Letters and Correspondence of J. H. Newman*, i. 205.

¶ It is quite easy to see why a legend is treated, and ought to be treated, more respectfully than a book of history. The legend is generally made by the majority of people in the village who are sane. The book is generally written by the one man in the village who is mad.[1]

3. In the first and second chapters of St. Luke we have a narrative which comes from a Hebrew source, probably from the Virgin Mary herself. The narrator was undoubtedly one who thought in Hebraic fashion, and whose language was saturated with Hebraic imagery. Luke twice points out (ii. 19, 51; cf. i. 66) that Mary kept in memory and pondered significant sayings associated with the childhood and youth of her Son. This is said only of Mary, not of Joseph, though at this time he must have been still alive. In this way Luke indicates that the traditions in Luke i.-ii. were transmitted through her. Who first wrote them down and when they were written we do not know. Nor can any intelligent critic regard the other narrative sections peculiar to Luke as his own fabrications, or as legends which originated outside of Palestine in the second or third generation after Christ. Their striking originality, which could not have been invented, has impressed them upon the mind of the Christian world to an extent scarcely true of any other portion of the whole body of gospel literature.

This narrative Luke has transmitted to us in a form which clearly shows its Hebrew origin, and equally clearly shows that it had been re-expressed in Lukan language and transformed by Luke. It has also been re-thought out of the Hebraic into the Greek fashion. The messenger of God, who revealed to Mary the Divine will and purpose becomes to Luke the winged personal being who, like Iris or Hermes, communicates the will and purpose of God. Exactly what is the difference between the original narrative and the Greek translation it is difficult to say or to speculate; but there was a more anthropomorphic picture of the messenger in Luke's mind than there was in Mary's. Yet we believe that Luke was translating as exactly as he could into Greek the account which he had heard. He expresses and thinks as a Greek that which was thought and expressed by a Hebrew.

[1] G. K. Chesterton, *Orthodoxy*, 82.

¶ Certainly, the most wonderful, the unique, point about the Greek genius, in literature as in everything else, had been the utter absence of imitation in its production. How has the burden of precedent, laid upon every artist, increased since then![1]

4. In using his materials Luke's methods are in the main those of other writers of the same period. They are quite unlike those of modern writers. A writer of the present day seeks to tell his story in his own words and his own way, giving references to, and, if necessary, quotations from, his sources, but carefully avoiding all confusion between traditional fact and critical inference, and certainly never altering the direct statement of the earlier documents without expressly mentioning the fact. The method of antiquity was as a rule almost the reverse. The author of a book based on earlier materials strung together a series of extracts into a more or less coherent whole, giving no indication of his sources, and modifying them freely in order to harmonize them. Sometimes he would select between several narratives, sometimes he would combine, sometimes he would give them successively, and by a few editorial comments make a single narrative of apparently several events out of several narratives of a single event. As a method this is obviously inferior to modern procedure, but even an inferior method can be well or badly used. That Luke used this method is clear from a comparison of the Third Gospel with Matthew and Mark, but on the whole he seems to have used it well, especially if it be remembered that his avowed object was not to "write history" but to provide the historical evidence for the Christian instruction which Theophilus had received.

¶ Shakespeare, according to Carlyle, showed traces of a talent that could have turned the *History of England* into a kind of *Iliad*, almost into a kind of *Bible*. In writing his Gospel, Luke with the Greek element in his nature was long ago doing work Carlyle thought had been left undone until his generation. "A very great 'work,' surely, is going on in these days, no less a 'work' than that of restoring GOD and whatever was Godlike in the traditions and recorded doings of Mankind; dolefully forgotten, or sham-remembered, as it has been, for long degraded and degrading hundreds of years, latterly! Actually this, if you understand it well. The essential, still awful and ever-blessed Fact of all that was meant by 'God and the Godlike' to men's souls is again

---

[1] Walter Pater,

struggling to become clearly revealed; will extricate itself from what some of us, too irreverently in our impatience, call 'Hebrew old-clothes'; and will again bless the Nations; and heal them from their basenesses, and unendurable woes." [1]

5. Passing to the Gospel itself, we are in the fortunate position of finding a preface attached to it, which states very clearly why and how it was written. The Evangelist, so he tells us, had found in existence a number of narratives, embracing the main facts of Christ's life, as these had been handed down by oral tradition. With these narratives in themselves he had no fault to find; but they were manifestly inadequate for those who desired a full and detailed account of the Saviour's ministry. That account he found himself in a position to give, having first carefully investigated all the facts from the very beginning, and so he wrote his Gospel setting forth in order the evangelic tradition.

It might not have been without interest to comment on some of the more outward features of St. Luke's Gospel, such as its historical accuracy, the purity of the Evangelist's own style, and the literary skill displayed in the arrangement of the materials. But these points, after all, are of little account as compared with its loving, gracious, sympathetic heart. Luke is the most evangelic of all the Evangelists. He it is, as Dante remarked long ago, who describes most fully "the meekness and gentleness of Christ."

¶ There is scarcely an anecdote or a parable proper to Luke which does not breathe the spirit of mercy, and of appeal to sinners. The Gospel of Luke is especially the Gospel of pardon, and of pardon obtained by faith. "There is more joy in heaven over a sinner that repenteth than over ninety and nine just persons which need no repentance." "The Son of Man is come not to destroy men, but to save them." Any quantity of straining is lawful to him, if only he can make each incident of the Gospel history a history of pardoned sinners. Samaritans, publicans, centurions, guilty women, benevolent Pagans, all those whom Pharisaism despises, are his clients. The idea that Christianity has pardon for all the world is his alone. The door is open; conversion is possible to all. It is no longer a question of the Law; a new devotion, the worship of Jesus, has replaced it. Here it is the Samaritan who does the good deed, whilst the priest and

[1] Carlyle, *Miscellaneous Essays*, vii. 225.

the Levite pass indifferent by.   There a publican comes out of the Temple justified by his humility, whilst the irreproachable but haughty Pharisee goes out more guilty than before.   Elsewhere the sinful woman is raised by her love for Jesus, and is permitted to bestow on him particular marks of tenderness.   Elsewhere, again, the publican Zacchæus becomes at the first onset a son of Abraham, by the simple fact of his having shown eagerness to see Jesus.   Luke adds the taste for humility.   "That which is highly esteemed amongst men is abomination in the sight of God."   The powerful shall be cast down from his throne, the humble shall be exalted; there, in brief, is the revolution wrought by Jesus. Now, the haughty is the Jew, proud of his descent from Abraham; the humble is the gentle man who draws no glory from his ancestors, and owes everything that he is to his faith in Jesus.[1]

¶ In his charming romance, *Callista*, Cardinal Newman describes the conversion of the perplexed Greek girl, thrown into prison and menaced with extreme peril, as caused by the reading of St. Luke's Gospel.   "She read a few paragraphs, and became interested, and in no long time she was absorbed in the volume. When she had once taken it up, she did not lay it down.   Even at other times she would have prized it, but now, when she was so desolate and lonely, it was simply a gift from an unseen world. It opened a view of a new state and community of beings, which only seemed too beautiful to be possible.   But not into a new state of things alone, but into the presence of One who was simply distinct and removed from anything that she had, in her most imaginative moments, ever depicted to her mind as ideal perfection. Here was that to which her intellect tended, though that intellect could not frame it.   It could approve and acknowledge, when set before it, what it could not originate.   Here was He who spoke to her in her conscience: whose Voice she heard, whose Person she was seeking for. . . . That Image sank deep into her; she felt it to be a reality.   She said to herself, 'This is no poet's dream ; it is the delineation of a real individual.   There is too much truth and nature, and life and exactness about it, to be anything else.'"[2]

II.

THE WRITER OF ACTS.

1. Can it be possible that Luke, the Greek physician of Antioch, the companion and fellow-worker of St. Paul, composed the Third

---

[1] E. Renan, *The Gospels*, 139,   [2] J. H. Newman, *Callista*, 325,

Gospel and the Acts of the Apostles? "If the gospel were the only writing ascribed to his authorship," writes a recent critic, "we should probably raise no objection against this record of ancient tradition; for we have no sufficient reasons for asserting that a disciple of St. Paul could not have composed this work." The difficulty, therefore, is assumed to lie in the Acts of the Apostles. Jülicher feels compelled to regard the ascription of the book to St. Luke as a "romantic ideal." Yet we find that even critics, in spite of their verdict, have actually made, and are still making, considerable strides towards a compromise with tradition. Certain passages are found in the Acts where the author introduces himself into the narrative with the word "we." The more than rash hypothesis that this "we" is a literary forgery has been renounced long ago, and nowadays scarcely a voice is raised even against the hypothesis that this "we" proceeds from the pen of St. Luke, the companion of St. Paul.

2. The main structural feature of the latter half of the book is the presence of four extracts apparently from a diary kept by one of St. Paul's companions (xvi. 10-17, xx. 4, 5-15, xxi. 1-18, xxvii. 1-xxviii. 16). It was customary for distinguished travellers, princes, and generals of the ancient Hellenic world to have short diaries kept by some companion as an aid to memory, in which the stations of the route and perhaps, here and there, notable experiences were cursorily set down. For instance, according to Hermann Diels, the Anabasis of Xenophon is founded on a diary of this description, which Xenophon himself developed into an historical work, inserting all kinds of narratives and speeches. No features of style or diction can be discovered in these passages sufficiently salient to differentiate them from the rest of the Lukan compositions. They contain over fifty words peculiar to, and over seventy specially characteristic of, St. Luke.

Now the author who wrote in the first instance for the "excellent" Theophilus was not unknown to his correspondent. If he, then, in the midst of his text introduced himself with a "we," *after he had begun his book with an "I"* (i. 1), Theophilus would at once know where he was; it would scarcely be fresh news to him that the man who dedicated his book to him was once himself a companion of St. Paul. In these circumstances the literary fault of neglecting to make special mention of this fact at the right place would be quite pardonable; indeed, one might say that this modest expedient for introducing oneself into the course of one's narrative is entirely in harmony with the general objectivity of our author's style throughout his history.

¶ The energetic subjectivity, which has faith in itself, which does not fear to be something particular and definite without any consciousness or shame of its subjective illusion, is unknown to me. I am, so far as the intellectual order is concerned, essentially objective, and my distinctive speciality is to be able to place myself in all points of view, to see through all eyes, to emancipate myself, that is to say, from the individual prison.[1]

3. The Book of Acts was written by a great historian, a writer who set himself to record the facts as they occurred, a strong partisan, indeed, but raised above partiality by his perfect confidence that he had only to describe the facts as they occurred in order to make the truth of Christianity and the honour of St. Paul apparent. His style is compressed to the highest degree; and he expects a great deal from the reader. He does not attempt to sketch the surroundings and to set the whole scene like a picture before the reader; he states the bare facts that seem to him important, and leaves the reader to imagine the situation. Hence, though his style is simple and clear, it often becomes obscure from its brevity; and the meaning is lost, because the reader has an incomplete, or a positively false, idea of the situation.

¶ A historian needs four kinds of capacity. First of all, accuracy, and a desire for the exact truth, which will grudge no time and pains in tracing out even what might seem a trivial matter. Secondly, keen observation, which can fasten upon small points, and discover in isolated data the basis for some generalisation, or the illustration of some principle. Thirdly, a sound and calm judgment, which will subject all inferences and generalisations, both one's own and other people's, to a searching review, and weigh in delicate scales their validity. Fourthly, the historian must have imagination, not indeed with that intensity which makes the poet, but in sufficient volume to

---

[1] *Amiel's Journal* (trans. by Mrs. Humphry Ward), 15.

let him feel the men of other ages and countries to be living and real like those among whom he moves.[1]

4. Sir W. M. Ramsay has advanced a theory to account for St. Luke's introduction to St. Paul which adds a touch almost of romance to the incident recorded in Acts xvi. 9, 10. The position this close student of all matters Pauline adopts is that St. Luke and the man of Macedonia are identical. "When one reads the passage with that idea," he writes, "it acquires new and increased beauty. We can imagine how Paul came to Troas in doubt as to what should be done. As a harbour, it formed the link between Asia and Macedonia. Here he met the Macedonian Luke; and with his view turned onwards he slept and beheld in a vision his Macedonian acquaintance beckoning him onward to his own country. Luke was attracted to Paul; and the vision was taken by Luke, as well as by Paul, for a sign. He left all, and followed his master." It is a striking theory, and it challenges consideration; but it scarcely meets all the facts of the case.

> Here standeth Luke, Physician once, and still;
> Healer of souls whom God delights to save;
> Wise-eyed in helpfulness; in pity brave;
> For all diseases using blessèd skill;
> To halt, maimed, blind, beneficent; until
> From town obscure by Galilean wave
> Flashed forth the Day-Star, born of God, and gave
> New life to suppliants with a sweet "I will."
> At whose appearing Luke was straightly dumb,
> Lost in the greater Light; nor found it hard;
> But knelt and worshippèd; and afterward
> For thy monition, O Theophilus,
> Wrote large his gospel, and for help of us,
> On whom the last days of the world are come.[2]

¶ An interesting detail of Luke's outward life is the old legend that represents him as a painter, and which has led to his being chosen as the patron-saint of so many academies of art. Certain very ancient pictures, notably a Madonna in the Church of S. Maria Maggiore at Rome, are actually claimed as his workmanship. But his influence over Christian art is placed on a surer footing, when we remember how readily painters,

[1] J. Bryce, *Studies in Contemporary Biography*, 148.
[2] E. C. Lefroy, *Sonnets*.

both in early and mediæval times, selected their subjects from the scenes depicted in the pages both of his Gospel and of the Acts.

> Give honour unto Luke, Evangelist;
> For he it was (the aged legends say)
> Who first taught Art to fold her hands and pray.[1]

[1] D. G. Rossetti.

ST. LUKE.

II.

THE COMPANION.

Literature.

Anderson-Berry, D., *Pictures in the Book of Acts,* **161.**

Brooks, P., *The Light of the World* (1891), 216.

Drury, T. W., *The Prison-Ministry of St. Paul* (1911), **175.**

Gibbon, B. J., *Visionaries* (1900), 81.

Grimley, H. N., *Tremadoc Sermons* (1882), **55.**

Harnack, A., *Luke the Physician* (1907), 2.

Haweis, H. R., *The Story of the Four* (1886), 125.

Hort, F. J. A., *Cambridge and Other Sermons* (1898), 252.

McLachlan, H., *St. Luke, Evangelist and Historian* (1912).

Moffatt, J., *An Introduction to the Literature of the New Testament* (1911), 261.

Pratt, S. W., *The Life and Epistles of Saint Paul* (1902), 215.

Ramsay, W. M., *St. Paul the Traveller* (1895), 14.

    ,,   ,,   *Luke the Physician* (1908), 1.

Redlich, E. B., *St. Paul and his Companions* (1913), 1.

Seekings, H. S., *The Men of the Pauline Circle* (1914), 23.

Selwyn, E. C., *St. Luke the Prophet* (1901), 1.

Smith, J., *The Voyage and Shipwreck of St. Paul* (1880), 1.

Weiss, B., *Biblical Theology of the New Testament,* ii. (1883) 291.

Whyte, A., *Bible Characters* : Stephen to Timothy (1901), 72.

Zahn, T., *Introduction to the New Testament,* iii. (1909) 1.

Dictionary of the Apostolic Church, i. (1915) 718 (K. Lake).

Dictionary of the Bible, iii. (1900) 161 (Ll. J. M. Bebb).

THE COMPANION.

Luke, the beloved physician.—Col. iv. 14.
Only Luke is with me.—2 Tim. iv. 11.

BY early tradition, or by putting together incidental indications, we are able to discern that there came from among the men of Antioch one—a physician by profession—who travelled on his missionary journeys with St. Paul, and by and by, before he died, wrote the story of that life of Jesus which lay at the back of all the teaching in which the missionary journeys were engaged.

And yet there is something more; for careful and ingenious study has seemed to make it clear that St. Luke's character as a physician was a genuine and significant thing, and that it remained a strong and influential fact even after he became a missionary. His style, his choice of words, the special events of Christ's life which he selects for his narration, bear marks of the physician's habits of thought and speech; and an exceedingly ingenious comparison of times has made it curiously appear that Luke on several occasions came to Paul just when the great Apostle was most overcome with weakness, or was just recovering from some one of the severe attacks which every now and then broke down his feeble strength. Indeed, we feel in these words from the letter to the Colossians, "Luke, the beloved physician," that Paul is speaking not merely of one who once had been, but of one who now was, in practice of the art of healing. It is a present fact. It is a fact that excites affection. It is as a physician, among other things, that Luke travels with Paul from land to land or shares his long imprisonment at Rome.

¶ Dr. John Brown, of Edinburgh, author of *Rab and his Friends* and *Marjorie Fleming*, was not only a skilful and successful physician, but also a writer whose quality was eminently sanative. He had been richly dowered with the gift of the Healer, and it flowed out from him not more conspicuously

in his professional practice than in the charm of social intercourse
and the cheerful magic of his pen.[1]

I.

THE PHYSICIAN.

1. The companionship between St. Luke and St. Paul was
not at first of long duration. Luke joined Paul at Troas and went
with him into Macedonia, but parted from the Apostle—the
reason is unknown—while yet at Philippi, to join him again
after some years had passed—this time also at Troas. Then he
accompanied Paul from Troas by Miletus and Cæsarea to
Jerusalem, together with a number of companions, including the
Jewish Christian Aristarchus of Thessalonica. In Jerusalem,
where he saw James and the presbyters, but none of the
Apostles (not even Peter), he seems to have stayed only a short
time, for he does not represent himself as having been an eye-
witness of what befell the Apostle here and in Cæsarea. But
when Paul set out as a prisoner on the long voyage to Rome,
we find Luke again in his company. With this exception,
Aristarchus alone of the Apostle's friends voyaged with him.
Paul was an invalid when he began the voyage. Only one day
after the Apostle had begun his voyage he was obliged to land at
Sidon to take advantage of the special care of his friends, having
obtained the permission of his humane commanding officer. In
Malta, where they were compelled to make a considerable stay,
Luke (together with the Apostle) had the opportunity of practis-
ing his medical art (Acts xxviii. 2 f.). In Rome he tarried a
considerable time with Paul, as his physician, and took part in
the work of evangelization (Philem. 24). Yet he did not, like
Aristarchus, share the Apostle's imprisonment (Col. iv. 10).
Besides Jesus Justus, Epaphras, Demas, and others, he there
made the acquaintance of Mark, the cousin of Barnabas
(Col. iv. 10).

While Demas, who is mentioned in both Colossians and
Philemon, along with Luke, deserted the Apostle from sordid
motives in 66, after the Apostle's second arrest, and when his

[1] G. W. E. Russell, *Afterthoughts*, 84.

life was in constant danger, Luke remained faithfully with him.
"Only Luke is with me" (2 Tim. iv. 11)—that is the last we
hear of him. But we know from his works that he survived
the destruction of Jerusalem, and was still at work a good time
afterwards.

Two clouds before the summer gale
In equal race fleet o'er the sky:
Two flowers, when wintry blasts assail,
Together pine, together die.

But two capricious human hearts—
No sage's rod may track their ways,
No eye pursue their lawless starts
Along their wild, self-chosen maze.

He only, by whose sovereign hand
Even sinners for the evil day
Were made—who rules the world He plann'd,
Turning our worst His own good way;

He only can the cause reveal,
Why, at the same fond bosom fed,
Taught in the self-same lap to kneel
Till the same prayer were duly said,

Brothers in blood and nurture too,
Aliens in heart so oft should prove;
One lose, the other keep, Heaven's clue;
One dwell in wrath, and one in love.

Two converts, watching by his side,
Alike his love and greetings share;
Luke the beloved, the sick soul's guide,
And Demas, named in faltering prayer.

Pass a few years—look in once more—
The saint is in his bonds again;
Save that his hopes more boldly soar,
He and his lot unchanged remain.

But only Luke is with him now:—
Alas! that even the martyr's cell,
Heaven's very gate, should scope allow
For the false world's seducing spell.

Ah! dearest mother, since too oft
The world yet wins some Demas frail
Even from thine arms, so kind and soft,
May thy tried comforts never fail!

When faithless ones forsake thy wing,
Be it vouchsafed thee still to see
Thy true, fond nurslings closer cling,
Cling closer to their Lord and thee.[1]

2. If we test what we know of Luke by the historical work which bears his name, we obtain the following results: (1) Luke is never mentioned in the Acts, which is just what we should expect if he himself was the author of the book. On the other hand, Aristarchus is mentioned three times—the man who is named with Luke in the Epistles of St. Paul. What reason, then, can we give for the omission of Luke's name in the Acts? (2) Luke was a physician, and thus belonged to the middle or higher plane of contemporary culture. To this plane we are directed not only by the prologue of the Gospel, but by the literary standard attained in the whole work. The man who could compose speeches like those of Paul in the Acts,—to mention only the most important point,—who also possessed gifts of style and narrative like those of this writer, who knew so well how much to say and could so well arrange his material in accordance with the purpose of his work—this man possessed the higher culture in rich measure.

In the familiar " we " passages, one must recognize how carefully Luke distinguishes between " we " and Paul. Wherever it is reasonably possible, in view of historic and literary truth, he emphasizes Paul and keeps the " we " modestly in the background. Let us take into account the narrative in Acts xxviii. 8–10: "And it was so, that the father of Publius lay sick of fever and dysentery: unto whom Paul entered in, and prayed, and laying his hands on him healed him. And when this was done, the rest also which had diseases in the island came, and were cured (more correctly, " received medical treatment "): who also honoured us with many honours."

[1] J. Keble.

In this passage attention is concentrated on Paul, so long as historic truth allowed; but Paul's healing power by prayer and faith could not always be exercised. Such power is efficacious only occasionally, in suitable circumstances and on suitable persons. As soon as it begins to be exercised on all and sundry, it begins to fail, and a career of pretence deepening into imposture begins. Accordingly, when the invalids came in numbers, medical advice was employed to supplement the faith-cure, and the physician Luke became prominent. Hence the people honoured not "Paul," but "us."

The figures of Paul and Luke walking together through history as the ministers of Christ—the image of theology and medicine labouring in harmony for the redemption of man, for the saving of body, soul, and spirit—are very sacred and impressive.

"Not bread alone" but bread before all else
For these: the bodily want serve first, said I;
If earth-space and the life-time help not here,
Where is the good of body having been?
But, helping body, if we somewhat baulk
The soul of finer fare, such food's to find
Elsewhere and afterward.[1]

¶ John Locke and Thomas Sydenham—the one the founder of our analytical philosophy of mind, and the other of our practical medicine—were not only great personal friends, but were of essential use to each other in their respective departments; and we may safely affirm, that for much in the *Essay on Human Understanding* we are indebted to its author's intimacy with Sydenham. And Sydenham, it is well known, in the dedicatory letter to their common friend Dr. Mapletoft, expresses his obligation to Locke.[2]

The body is the spirit's cell,
But 'tis the avenue as well
Charged, through the finite, to transmit
The message of the infinite.
'Tis by the aid of mortal eyes
That man immortal truth descries;

[1] Browning, *Prince Hohenstiel-Schwangau.*
[2] Dr. John Brown, *Horæ Subsecivæ,* i. 36.

'Tis by the aid of mortal ears
That he immortal tidings hears,
And by the help of every sense
May recognize God's providence.[1]

¶ Able, cautious, and experienced physicians are gifts of God. They are the ministers of nature, to whom human life is confided; but a moment's negligence may ruin everything. No physician should take a single step, but in humility and the fear of God; they who are without the fear of God are mere homicides.[2]

II.

THE FRIEND.

Two causes have been advanced in explanation of our friendships—that of natural affinity, as expressed in Montaigne's eulogy of his friend: "If any man should importune me to give a reason why I loved him, I can but answer, because it was he, because it was I"; and that deeper conviction that there is something of Divine providence in the circumstances which effect the coming together of kindred souls, as Emerson would have it: "My friends have come to me unsought; the great God gave them me." It is in this latter view that the secret of Luke's attachment to and admiration for Paul is to be found. That such a friendship existed, and that it was sustained until the martyrdom of Paul severed the golden bond, is beyond controversy.

1. Foremost among the qualities which equipped Luke for the work of comradeship to which the providence of God had called him was his consecrated culture. Both Luke and Paul had a genuine love of learning, but the scholarship of the one differed in details from that of the other. Paul's mind was of a deeper, more philosophic mould than that of Luke. And Luke's was more artistic. The resultant interplay of mind upon mind must have been to the mutual advantage of each. We owe to the pen of Luke an almost perfect portrait of his friend. And we have but to read the Third Gospel carefully, noting the while the studied use of such characteristically Pauline words as "faith," "mercy," "grace," and "remission," to see the debt that Luke owed to Paul.

---

[1] Ella Fuller Maitland.   [2] Luther.

The accurate scholarship and literary genius of Luke, his rare gift of observation, his careful mode of expression, his capacity for taking pains, which even his easy and polished sentences fail to hide, his refined and sensitive nature, together with his oneness with the high ideals of Paul's ministry, made him peculiarly the man whom the Apostle needed.

Luke had a habit, too, of deliberate self-effacement, and we search in vain for any reference to himself in his writings. He is content to be historian and biographer, but he is careful to make succeeding generations discover for themselves the authorship of this finest biographical fragment in the world.

¶ In society and politics we call those great who have devoted their energies to some noble cause, or have influenced the course of things in some extraordinary way. But in every instance, whether in art, science, or religion, or public life, there is a universal condition, that a man shall have forgotten himself in his work. If any fraction of his attention is given to the honours or rewards which success will bring him, there will be a taint of weakness in what he does.[1]

¶ In his writings Walter Pater shrinks from all definiteness and avoids, by the very habit of his mind, anything like unqualified assertion, employing the impersonal method of parable, or story, or criticism. But throughout, it is a veil which hides nothing that it is profitable for us to know. In Pater's view, such reticence and self-effacing is but a true man's modesty.[2]

2. Under the surface of Luke's narrative of Paul's journeys and labours there moves a current of strong personal affection and enthusiastic admiration for him. Paul is the author's hero. His general aim is to describe the development of the Church; but his affection and his interest turn to Paul, and after a time his narrative groups itself round Paul. He is keenly concerned to show that Paul was in perfect accord with the leaders among the older Apostles, but so also was Paul himself in his letters. That is the point of view of a personal friend and disciple, full of affection, and jealous of Paul's honour and reputation.

The characterization of Paul in Acts is so detailed and individualized as to prove the author's personal acquaintance.

[1] J. A. Froude.
[2] J. A. Hutton, *Pilgrims in the Region of Faith*, 70.

Moreover, the Paul of Acts is the Paul that appears to us in his own letters, in his ways and his thoughts, in his educated tone of polished courtesy, in his quick and vehement temper, in the extraordinary versatility and adaptability which made him at home in every society, moving at ease in all surroundings, and everywhere the centre of interest, whether he is the Socratic dialectician in the agora of Athens, or the rhetorician in its university, or conversing with kings and proconsuls, or advising in the council on shipboard, or cheering a broken-spirited crew to make one more effort for life. Wherever Paul is, no one present has eyes for any but him.

¶ Probably Boswell did not realize how matchless a biographer he was, though he was not disposed to belittle his own performances. But his unbridled interest in the smallest details, his power of hero-worship, his amazing style, his perception, his astonishing memory and the training he gave it, his superb dramatic faculty, which enabled him to arrange his other characters around the main figure, and to subordinate them all to his central emphasis—all these qualities are undeniable.[1]

¶ What we want in a biography, and what, despite the etymology of the title, we very seldom find, is *life*. The very best transcript is a failure, if it be a transcript only. To fulfil its idea, it must have in it the essential quality of movement; must realize the lofty fiction of the divine Shield of Achilles, where the upturning earth, though wrought in metal, darkened as the plough went on; and the figures of the battle-piece dealt their strokes and parried them, and dragged out from the turmoil the bodies of their dead.[2]

3. Throughout the journeyings, it is remarkable with what interest Luke records the incidents from harbour to harbour. He has the true Greek feeling for the sea, a feeling that must develop in every race possessing any capacity for development, and any sensitiveness to the influences of nature, when settled round the Ægean coasts; for the Ægean Sea is so tempting, with its regular winds and regular sunset calm, when the water lies dead, with a surface which looks like oil, dense and glistening and dark, that it seems to invite one to walk upon it.

[1] A. C. Benson.
[2] W. E. Gladstone, *Gleanings of Past Years*, ii.

Repeated examination of Acts xxvii. by experts has shown that, while it could not have been written by a mariner, it must have been written by some gifted man who accompanied Paul on the journey, and who had an appreciation of nature and of the incidents of a sea voyage. If, without recourse to the tradition, we were to ask which one of Paul's travelling companions was most likely to have been the author of the accounts of these journeys, the most probable answer would be, Luke, the physician. If he is, at the same time, the author of the entire work, it was his own notes, which he had written down in the form of a journal during the voyage, that he incorporated in his history. Even the best memory will not retain for decades all such details as changes in the weather and the movements of the sailors in a voyage lasting for months, and no historian would record in a large work such recollections as he might have, simply because he had not forgotten them.

¶ My strongest impression of my father's tastes, writes Dr. Pusey's daughter, was his intense love of the sea. To him, I am sure, it spoke volumes. From my earliest childhood he used to quote the Greek expression of Æschylus, and explain to us children what it meant, "the many twinkling smile of ocean"; and I am sure that it was true to him that—

> Such signs of love old ocean gives,
> We cannot choose but think it lives.

The ocean did live to him in a way I have never observed in any one else. I cannot fully express what I mean; but I used to watch his face as he gazed out at the sea, and feel that it was to him what it was not to others. He often spoke to me in after years of the waves tossing themselves in wild fury against the boundary God had set them. "Thus far and no farther shall thy proud waves go"; likening it to the impotence of human rebellion against the will of God.

He had also a love and enjoyment of beautiful scenery as God's handiwork, His finger tracing all and imparting to them their beauty.[1]

4. A great deal might be said about the special professional life of Luke, the beloved physician, especially as it is linked to the life of the Apostle Paul. As he and Paul are seen travelling

---

[1] *The Story of Dr. Pusey's Life*, 339.

together over land and sea, those two figures taken together represent in a broad way the total care of man for man. Paul is distinctively a man of the soul, a man of the spiritual life. We know him only in his spiritual labours. If he turns aside to tent-making, it is not for the sake of the tents which he can make, but simply that, earning his own living, he may be in true relations to the men whose souls he wants to save. Luke, on the other hand, is physical. His care is for the body. The two together, then, as we watch their figures, climbing side by side over mountains, sleeping side by side on the decks of little Mediterranean boats, standing side by side in the midst of little groups of hard-won disciples—may we not say of them that they may be considered as recognizing and representing between them the double nature and the double need of man? Body and soul as man is, the ministry that would redeem him and relieve him must have a word to speak to, and a hand to lay upon, both soul and body. The two missionaries together make a sort of composite copy of the picture which St. Matthew gives us of Jesus going "about all the cities and villages, teaching in their synagogues, and preaching the gospel of the kingdom, and healing every sickness and every disease among the people."

¶ At a place called Chighakor, one of the minor chiefs came to Mrs. Bishop for medicine, which she gladly gave him. Lingering in her tent, he asked her why she ministered to people unknown to her, without demanding a recompense. This was her opportunity, and she told him the story of Christ, whose anxiety for the physical well-being of the people whom He had come spiritually to save, was so great that He spent His days in going from village to village to heal their disease and rescue them even from death.[1]

¶ When prescribing to his patients, it was Dr. Daniel Rutherford's custom to offer up at the same time a prayer for the accompanying blessing of heaven.[2]

> Beside the unveiled mysteries
> Of life and death go stand,
> With guarded lips and reverent eyes
> And pure of heart and hand.

[1] A. M. Stoddart, *The Life of Isabella Bird*, 228.
[2] J. G. Lockhart, *Life of Scott*, i. 147.

So shalt thou be with power endued
From Him who went about
The Syrian hillsides, doing good
And casting demons out.

That Good Physician liveth yet
Thy Friend and Guide to be;
The Healer by Gennesaret
Shall walk the rounds with thee.[1]

5. From the time that Luke adventured himself with Paul, through weal and woe he remained faithful. He had watched the breaking up of the little band; he had seen his leader grow prematurely old through his exacting labours; and he had guessed the issue of the impending trial before Nero. Yet until the end came he would never be absent for long from the side of the man whom he loved as his own soul. *Only Luke is with me* throbs the human cry of the heart that hungered for the presence of those who felt and understood; but Luke was *with* him in the intenser meaning of that word—*with* him in everything that appertained to the spread of the Redeemer's Kingdom—and for him to desert in the hour of danger not only would have been a violation of trust and honour, a transgression of the most sacred sanctions of life, but would have assumed the proportions of disloyalty to Christ.

Name not as friends the men who by you stand
In pleasant times, when peace and welfare please you;
But him indeed call friend who grasps your hand
In that dark day when want and danger seize you.

¶ O God All-wise, who electing St. Luke to be of the number of Thy four Evangelists didst furnish him with abundance of gifts needful or expedient to so great an end, endowments natural and supernatural, human learning and superhuman wisdom, aptitude and goodwill, knowledge and illumination, intercourse with Saints and inspiration of the Holy Ghost: Grant to us, we beseech Thee, hearing ears and seeing eyes that we may profit by his writings; and following in his footsteps may pass by way of life and death into the kingdom of life everlasting.[2]

---

[1] J. G. Whittier, "The Healer."
[2] C. G. Rossetti, *Called to be Saints*, 455.

JAMES THE LORD'S BROTHER.

I.

BEFORE THE RESURRECTION.

LITERATURE.

Ackworth, J., *Life's Working Creed*, 7.

Adeney, W. F., in *Men of the New Testament*: Matthew to Timothy (1905), 241.

Banks, L. A., *Paul and his Friends* (1898), 169.

Dale, R. W., *The Epistle of James* (1895), 1.

Farrar, F. W., *The Early Days of Christianity* (1891), 265, 280.

Martyn, H. J., *For Christ and the Truth* (1898), 175.

Matheson, G., *The Representative Men of the New Testament* (1905), 227.

Mayor, J. B., *The Epistle of St. James* (1910), p. i.

Moule, H. C. G., *The Secret of the Presence* (1900), 202.

Patrick, W., *James the Lord's Brother* (1906).

Plummer, A., *The General Epistles of St. James and St. Jude* (Expositor's Bible) (1891), 25.

Smith, H. M., *The Epistle of St. James* (1914), 16, 38.

Whyte, A., *Bible Characters*: Joseph and Mary to James (1900), 237.

Dictionary of the Apostolic Church, i. (1915) 628 (W. Montgomery).

Dictionary of the Bible, i. (1898) 320 (J. B. Mayor).

BEFORE THE RESURRECTION.

*Other of the apostles saw I none, save James the Lord's brother.—
Gal. i. 19.*

IT is one of the signs of the inimitable truthfulness and power of
Scripture, that again and again, by a few simple touches, it
enables us to realize the characters of those of whom it speaks.
There are many whose lives, as recorded in Holy Writ, would
occupy only two or three verses, whom, nevertheless, from the
inspired power with which they are delineated, we are enabled to
represent to ourselves in their distinctest personality. Still more
is this the case when we also possess some of their utterances and
writings. And such a picture we can paint of James, one of
the "brothers of the Lord."

I.

THE BROTHER OF THE LORD.

The phrase "brother of the Lord" is used by St. Paul (Gal.
i. 19), and was probably the designation by which James was best
known. The first question connected with James's life is to
ascertain the force of this phrase.

1. Three theories have been held as to the "brethren of the
Lord." (1) According to Helvidius they were the children of
Joseph and Mary, born after Jesus Christ. (2) They were,
according to Jerome, the sons of Alphæus, the cousins of our
Lord, loosely called "brethren." (3) According to Epiphanius
they were the sons of Joseph by a previous marriage. The weight
of opinion is now in favour of the first of these theories.

The chief objections to it are that Jesus commended His
mother to the care of John, not to one of the brothers; that their

conduct in trying to control Him implies that they were older; that tradition favours the theory of Epiphanius as early as the second century; and that it is repugnant to Christian sentiment to suppose that, after the birth of Christ, Mary became the mother of other children. This feeling, so real to us, cannot be attributed with certainty to Jews of the first century. It is uncertain when, or to what extent, Joseph and Mary realized the mystery of the Incarnation.

2. As there was nothing in the announcement made to them which could enable them to realize the astounding truth that He who was to be born of Mary was Very God of Very God, so there is nothing in the subsequent life of Mary which would lead us to believe that she, any more than His Apostles, had realized it before His resurrection. It is hard enough even now to hold together the ideas of the humanity and the divinity of Christ without doing violence to either; but to those who knew Him in the flesh we may safely say it was impossible until the Comforter had come and revealed it unto them. As to what should be the relations between the husband and wife after the birth of the promised Child, there is one thing we may be sure of, viz., that these would be determined, not by personal considerations, but either by immediate inspiration, as the journey to Egypt and other events had been, or, in the absence of this, by the one desire to do what they believed to be best for the bringing up of the Child entrusted to them. We can imagine their feeling it to be a duty to abstain from bringing other children into the world, in order that they might devote themselves more exclusively to the nurture and training of Jesus. On the other hand, the greatest prophets and saints had not been brought up in solitude. Moses, Samuel, and David had had brothers and sisters. It might be God's will that the Messiah should experience in this, as in other things, the common lot of man.

The natural meaning of the language used in the New Testament is that the "brethren" were the children of Joseph and Mary.

¶ Jesus was a son to His mother, an eldest son, too, and maybe, rather likely, of a widowed mother, who leaned upon her first-born in piecing out the small funds, and in the ceaseless care of the younger children. He was a brother to His brothers and sisters, a real brother, the big brother of the little group. He was a neighbour to His fellow-villagers, and a fellow-labourer with the other craftsmen.[1]

¶ The typical human institution of marriage, round which all social existence turns, is transfigured by Christ's appearance. He finds in it the symbol and law of His own relation to man, and so raises it to a higher power, and endows it with a finer force, and a more valid stability, and a deeper significance. And out of this exaltation of marriage there rises a new fabric, a new wonder—the Christian home, with its exquisite ideal of firm and beautiful order, in which all the several parts are given their full value, and the man is at once master yet servant, and the wife is endowed with grace out of her very weakness, as the curse of pain that lay on child-bearing is transmuted by the sweet honour that belongs to it, since she who was highly favoured became a maiden mother. And the children are made holy, even as the type from which we learn how to enter the Kingdom of Heaven by becoming what they are, whose angels behold the face of their true Father who is in heaven.[2]

II.

THE HOME AT NAZARETH.

1. According to either view, James was the son of Joseph, and almost certainly was brought up with his Divine Brother in the humble home at Nazareth.

The life of the household in which he was brought up was one of the utmost simplicity and frugality. The furniture, the meals, and the dress of all the members were of the plainest kind. Luxury was unknown, just as poverty was equally unknown. The necessaries of life were much cheaper in Galilee than in Judæa, and a moderate income sufficed to maintain a family in comfort. Food, clothing, and a house were readily procured by any man prepared to work. Joseph, it may be taken for granted, was diligent in business, and his trade of village carpenter or wright, though doubtless yielding him only a modest competence, was amply sufficient to supply the wants of his family. The sons and daughters of the home would be brought up to assist their

---

[1] S. D. Gordon, *Quiet Talks on Home Ideals*, 113.
[2] H. Scott Holland.

father and mother from their earliest years, and the boys would be set to work as soon as they left school.

¶ The circumstances of Eastern life take away all the sting from the condition of the industrious poor. The wants of life are there reduced to their simplest elements. There is no wasteful luxury, no extravagant display. A little bread, a few dates, a spring of water, a humble cottage, a single change of raiment, are enough to support the honest labourer in dignity and contentment; and these he can earn with ease and certainty. Where there is no envy in the heart, where restlessness and ambition are under due control, such a state of life is not only tolerable, it is endowed with special elements of happiness. There must, we may be sure, have been many who sat around our Lord as they listened to the Sermon on the Mount who could understand from happy personal experience the beatitudes pronounced upon the poor who were also poor in spirit.[1]

2. Whatever means of instruction were within reach of the home at Nazareth, would, we may feel certain, have been eagerly taken advantage of by all its inmates. While accepting, therefore, the view which seems to be best supported, that Jesus and His brothers usually spoke Aramaic, we are surely not bound to suppose that, with towns like Sepphoris and Tiberias in their immediate vicinity, with Ptolemais, Scythopolis, and Gadara at no great distance, they remained ignorant of Greek. In the eyes of the scribes they might "never have learnt letters," since they had not attended the Rabbinical schools at Jerusalem; but the ordinary education of Jewish children and the Sabbath readings in the synagogue would give sufficient start to enable any intelligent boy to carry on his studies for himself; while the example of Solomon and the teaching of the so-called "sapiential" books held up the pursuit of knowledge and wisdom as the highest duty of man.

¶ The love of knowledge is a passion which, once in possession of the mind, can hardly ever be extinguished; it is noble in its nature too, and like other noble passions elevates itself into a kindred with all the virtues of the character.[2]

3. James's father, as St. Matthew tells us (i. 19), was a "just" or "righteous" man, like the parents of the Baptist (Luke i. 6);

[1] F. W. Farrar, *The Early Days of Christianity*, 280.
[2] *The Love Letters of Thomas Carlyle and Jane Welsh*, i. 186.

and this was the title by which James was known during his
lifetime, and by which he is still constantly known.   He is James
"the Just."   The epithet, as used in Scripture of his father and
others (Matt. i. 19, xxiii. 35; Luke i. 6, ii. 25, xxiii. 50; Acts
x. 20; 2 Peter ii. 7), and in history of him, must not be understood
as implying precisely what the Athenians meant when they styled
Aristides "the Just," or what we mean now by being "just."   To
a Jew the word implied not merely being impartial and upright,
but also having a studied and even scrupulous reverence for
everything prescribed by the Law.   The Sabbath, the synagogue
worship, the feasts and fasts, purification, tithes, all the moral
and ceremonial ordinances of the Law of the Lord—these were
the things on which the just man bestowed a loving care, and in
which he preferred to do more than was required, rather than the
bare minimum insisted on by the Rabbis.   It was in a home of
which righteousness of this kind was the characteristic that
James was reared, and in which he became imbued with that
reverent love for the Law which makes him, even more than
St. Paul, to be the ideal "Hebrew of Hebrews."   For him Christ
came "not to destroy, but to fulfil."   Christianity turns the Law
of Moses into a "royal law" (James ii. 8), but it does not
abrogate it.   The Judaism which had been his moral and spiritual
atmosphere during his youth and early manhood remained with
him after he had learned to see that there was no antagonism
between the Law and the Gospel.

¶ New England literature is essentially a product of the
Puritan spirit, though of the Puritan spirit touched, liberalized,
transfigured by new thought and cosmopolitan culture.   Now, all
the great New England writers were men of Puritan ancestry;
and this fact enables us at once to account for their splendid
moral fibre, the strength and nobility of their characters, the
religious element which is so prominent in their works, and their
insistent—often, indeed, over-insistent—didacticism and pre-
occupation at all times with ethical themes.[1]

4. It is certain from the custom prevailing among the Jews of
his rank in life that James would be taught a trade, and it is quite
probable that tradition is correct in saying that he became a
carpenter, like his father.   It may also be supposed that he was

---

[1] W. H. Hudson, *Lowell and his Poetry*, 13.

married.   Marriage was regarded as a duty among the Jews, and St. Paul says (1 Cor. ix. 5) that the brethren of the Lord took their wives with them when they went to visit the churches.

That it was a beautiful household in which he was brought up, well governed, happily trained, we may well believe.   She who was honoured above all women by being privileged to be the mother of Jesus, and to train Him in His childhood, must have been a good mother to all her children.   The presence of her sons, on more than one occasion, with her seems to indicate that the domestic ties were close and warm, that it was a happy, united household till an awful tragedy temporarily scattered it.   But more we cannot say.   That the influence of the Perfect Child shed a radiance of unseen joy and an atmosphere of purity all around Him wherever He went is what we should all have expected. And yet the family may have been slow to perceive its rare significance.   Evidently there was nothing outwardly abnormal about His life and action.   The foolish legends of apocryphal gospels are quite out of harmony with the probability suggested by the silence of the authentic records of Christ's life.

> Something that abode endued
>   With temple-like repose, an air
> Of life's kind purposes pursued
>   With order'd freedom sweet and fair.
> A tent pitch'd in a world not right
>   It seemed, whose inmates, every one,
> On tranquil faces bore the light
>   Of duties beautifully done,
> And humbly, though they had few peers,
>   Kept their own laws, which seemed to be
> The fair sum of six thousand years'
>   Traditions of civility.[1]

¶ Embosomed among soft grey swells, Nazareth was shut out from the world, and offered a sweet seclusion, than which nothing could have been better fitted for the early years of our Lord and His brethren.   There was nothing to distract or disturb in the idyllic isolation of the little valley.   The young child could not see beyond the heights around it, but when the years brought growing vigour and curiosity, He would only need to wander to the top of the village hill to have a wondrous panorama before

[1] Coventry Patmore.

Him. The great plain of Esdraelon lay at His feet, to the south;
then, no doubt, rich in varied growths, to the far-away foot of the
Samaritan hills and the range of Carmel. - To the west His eye
would sweep, over the sinking fringe of the hills of lower Galilee,
to the "Great Sea," where the promontory of Carmel plunges
down into the Mediterranean waters. In the east He had before
Him the great wooded cone of Mount Tabor, then crowned by a
stronghold, but covered on its sides, we may be assured, as it is
to-day, with rich growths of varied green. The caravan track
from Damascus to the coast had run for ages, as it still does, along
Esdraelon, two hours from Nazareth; and over it, when old
enough to stray as far as the heights looking down on the plain,
He would see long strings of camels, each tied to one before, and
all following the humble ass of the turbaned driver, leisurely
pacing east or west, to or from distant Syria, laden with the
wheat or oil or other produce of Western Asia, or bearing back
the varied commodities of Phœnicia, the great trading mart of
those ages. There are no signs of any highway ever having led
up from the great plain to the tableland of Nazareth, and even
now one has to let his native horse climb the steep cliff as it best
can. Indeed, the ascent is only possible to a creature bred in the
country, twisting and winding between rocks, or forcing its way
up slopes distressingly near the perpendicular.[1]

III.

The Unbelief of the Brothers.

In the Nazareth home, then, James did not come to have any
very abnormal idea of his elder Brother. Even after He had
emerged from privacy, and right through His public ministry,
when many hailed Him as a Prophet, and some few secretly
acknowledged Him as the Messiah, James with the other brothers
stood aloof.

1. John, in speaking of the brethren of Jesus, records that
they did not believe on Him, which can mean nothing else than that
they did not believe Him to be the Messiah; and though the
statement is made in connexion with a particular event, whose
chronological place in the life of Christ is not certain, it may
fairly be concluded from it that they continued in the same state

[1] C. Geikie, *Hours with the Bible: The Gospels*, 13.

of unbelief throughout the period of His ministry. It is hardly
to be wondered at that such should have been the case. That
Jesus made a great impression upon His younger brothers during
their boyhood life in Galilee cannot be doubted. They must have
grown up with an unbounded affection and admiration for Him.
And yet the very intimacy of their association with Him, and the
simplicity and naturalness of His life in the home circle, would
make it difficult for them to see in Him the Messiah; and much
as they loved Him, and confident as they must have been of His
honesty and purity of purpose, they could hardly think of one of
their own number, who was of humble extraction like themselves,
and had passed with them through all the simple and homely
experiences of boyhood and youth, as the great Messiah of God, as
the Chosen One who was to deliver Israel from the yoke of the
oppressor and to establish the kingdom foretold by the prophets.
All those difficulties which hindered His townspeople and fellow-
countrymen from recognizing Him as the Messiah must have acted
upon them with double force. The words, "A prophet is not
without honour, save in his own country, and in his own house,"
were spoken by Jesus out of His own experience, and no other
experience was possible in the circumstances.

¶ There is a famous story told concerning James Russell
Lowell. In the days of his youth he spent one memorable summer
vacation in the White Mountain district. One day when enjoying a stroll through the Franconia Notch, he became absorbed in
conversation with a man who was in charge of a sawmill. The
man chatted on, feeding his mill with logs the while. Presently
the poet asked his new acquaintance if he could direct him to a
point from which he could obtain a good view of the "Old Man
of the Mountain." "*Dunno*," replied the man, "*never seed it!*"
Lowell immediately expressed his astonishment that any one
living so near such a marvellous spectacle, which people came
from long distances to see, should never have taken the pains to
gaze upon it. "And how far have you come?" asked the man.
With evident pride the poet answered that he had come from
Boston. "D'you tell?" exclaimed the countryman. "I'd like to
see Boston. Why, just to stand for once on Bunker Hill!
You've been there often, likely?" And James Russell Lowell
confessed with shame and confusion of face that he *never had*![1]

2. It is not simply that Jesus' brethren did not believe in His

[1] F. W. Boreham, *The Golden Milestone*, 113.

Divinity. Nobody, not even Peter or John, did that during His lifetime; they did not believe in *Him*; did not believe that He was the Christ, or even that He was a prophet, a teacher sent from God. They must have known Him too well to have shared the theory of the Jewish authorities—in which they could scarcely have honestly believed—that He was an impostor. But they thought He was a self-deluded dreamer, needlessly courting danger, who ought to be saved from Himself. So they said once that He was "beside Himself," either actually imagining that He must have been out of His mind, or wishing to shield Him from the consequence of His dangerous utterances by intimating that He was not responsible for them; and, on another occasion, they sent a message through the crowd from His mother, as well as from themselves, asking Him to come to them, with the evident intention of rescuing Him. They failed in this act of well-meant but really impertinent interference; and the result was that, apparently, He disowned them, claiming all who did God's will as His brethren, His very nearest relations. The reply was more than a rebuke for the moment. It flashed out a new far-reaching principle of the Kingdom of Heaven. There are ties even closer than blood-relationship.

¶ The man who believes in Christ, who has the spirit of Christ in him, who shows in his life the fruits of that spirit, who, denying himself and taking up his cross, is following Christ in toilsome but loving labour for the salvation of men—he is my brother, and nothing shall hinder me from offering him the right hand of fellowship. I do not care what name they call him by, whether he is a Churchman or Quaker, Universalist or Roman Catholic, he who is united to my Master shall not be divided from me. And when such a man has found a company of people who love him, not because of any brilliancy of wit that has dazzled them, nor because of any tricks of sensationalism that have amused them, but just because of the Christ life that is in him—and want him to live among them and show them how to serve and follow Christ—and when he asks me to come and help to join him in loving bonds as pastor to this people, I shall go, every time! My blessing is not worth much, but, such as it is, God forbid that I should withhold it! And if anybody bids me be cautious, I answer, Yes, I will be very cautious lest I hinder in his work a true servant of Jesus Christ! I will take great care always lest I exalt the letter above the spirit, the dogma above the life. For I would rather make two mistakes on the side of charity than one on the side of bigotry.[1]

3. Any faint hopes which they may possibly have cherished that He might prove Himself to be the Messiah were shattered by the crucifixion. His death was the verdict of God on His claims. However highly they honoured His character, however keenly they resented His unjust sentence, they could not but consider it impossible to hold now that He was the Messiah. The faith even of the Apostles was shattered by His execution, how much more that of the brothers who had never owned His claims! Moreover, the notion of a resurrection was still more foreign to the minds of the brothers than to those of the Apostles.

> There are moments when life's shadows
>   Fall all darkly on the soul,
> Hiding stars of hope behind them
>   In a black, impervious scroll;
> When we walk with trembling footsteps,
>   Scarcely knowing how or where
> The dim paths we tread are leading,
>   In our midnight of despair.[2]

4. They were not with Him during the last scenes : they were not at the Last Supper; they were not in the Garden ; they drew no sword for Him ; they did not follow Him to the Hall of Caiaphas ; they did not defile themselves for the feast by entering the Prætorium ; they did not stand beside the cross ; they did not, so far as we know, visit with sorrowing gifts His tomb.

Yet, strange to say, when next we meet with them they have thrown themselves heart and soul into the struggling fortunes of the Church ! It is after the Ascension. The Eleven have returned from the Mount of Olives, and go to the Upper Room, which is their regular place of meeting in Jerusalem ; and in that Upper Room are not only the Eleven, but also Mary the mother of Jesus and His brethren. From that moment, as a body they disappear, and we hear no more of either Joses or Simon. But Jude lived to travel as a Christian missionary, and to write the Epistle which

---

[1] Washington Gladden, *Recollections*, 263.
[2] F. D. Gage.

bears his name; and James lived to furnish the nearest approach to a bishop which is to be found in the Apostolic Age, and to be for twenty years a main pillar of the persecuted Church.

Whence came this marvellous change?

We have no account of it, we have no means of even conjecturally explaining it, unless the explanation lies in three words of the Apostle Paul. In his relation of the appearances of Christ after His resurrection, he says that He was seen of Cephas, then of the Twelve, then of more than five hundred brethren at once; "then he was seen of James."

James came to believe at last, and was a great personage among those who confessed that Jesus was the Christ. He too discovered how great our Lord was. He does not presume to describe himself as the brother of our Lord, though other men so described him. He is "the servant, the slave, of God and of our Lord Jesus Christ."

¶ By picturing to ourselves the religious history of James, we come to understand the conflicting impressions made upon him by the life of Jesus, his brother. The personal sanctity of that life, drawn from habitual communion with God, no doubt attracted and satisfied him. But those exorbitant pretensions, that arrogation of the title of one sent from God to fulfil the prophecies and bring in the Kingdom of Heaven, must have seemed to him signs of over-weening self-exaltation, and even of madness.[1]

¶ That extreme nearness retards perception is a matter of daily observation. It is just as true of our perception of things as of our perception of persons. One would suppose, for example, that the habitual dwellers in a scene of rare beauty would be peculiarly alive to the attractions of physical nature. The reverse is the case. These are of all people the least responsive to the beautiful. If a stranger comes in among them, he is transfixed, dazzled, by the splendour of the scene; but his enthusiasm rather surprises them. We should suppose, again, that the constant inhabitants of a city would know more about that city than those coming into it from other places. Yet it often happens that a traveller learns more of a town in a week than many of its population learn all through their lives. We should suppose, once more, that those living continuously in a salubrious atmosphere would be free from all illness arising from atmospheric causes. Yet this is not the case. The unvaried presence of one climate is

---

[1] F. Godet, in the *Contemporary Review*, xliv. 68.

like the unvaried application of a somnolent drug—it loses its effect. A change of air will eventually be found beneficial, even though the new air be less balmy than the old. The mind must co-operate with the body to preserve the health of man. It is not enough that an atmosphere is genial; I must feel it to be genial. It must enter into me not only as a draught, but as a joy. And if this joy is to be felt, it must not be an unvaried possession. It must be interrupted to be known; it must be withdrawn to be appreciated; it must be supplanted by a shadow to be valued as a light.[1]

[1] G. Matheson, *The Representative Men of the New Testament*, 233.

JAMES THE LORD'S BROTHER.

II.

AFTER THE RESURRECTION.

LITERATURE.

Ackworth, J., *Life's Working Creed*, 7.

Adeney, W. F., in *Men of the New Testament*: Matthew to Timothy (1905), 241.

Carpenter, W. B., *The Wisdom of James the Just* (1903), 3.

Dale, R. W., *The Epistle of James* (1895), 1.

Farrar, F. W., *The Early Days of Christianity* (1891), 265, 280.

McGiffert, A. C., *A History of Christianity in the Apostolic Age* (1897), 549.

Martyn, H. J., *For Christ and the Truth* (1898), 175.

Matheson, G., *The Representative Men of the New Testament* (1905), 227.

Mayor, J. B., *The Epistle of St. James* (1910), p. i.

Moule, H. C. G., *The Secret of the Presence* (1900), 202.

Patrick, W., *James the Lord's Brother* (1906).

Plummer, A., *The General Epistles of St. James and St. Jude* (Expositor's Bible) (1891), 25.

Smith, H. M., *The Epistle of S. James* (1914), 16, 38.

Stanley, A. P., *Sermons and Essays on the Apostolical Age* (1874), 283.

Whyte, A., *Bible Characters* : Joseph and Mary to James (1900), 237.

Dictionary of the Apostolic Church, i. (1915) 628 (W. Montgomery).

Dictionary of the Bible, ii. (1899) 542 (J. B. Mayor).

Dictionary of Christ and the Gospels, i. (1906) 846 (H. W. Fulford).

AFTER THE RESURRECTION.

James, a servant of God and of the Lord Jesus Christ.—James i. 1.

WITHIN a few weeks after His resurrection, the brethren of Jesus were gathered with His followers in Jerusalem, and evidently belonged to the company of His disciples. In the interval, therefore, they must have become convinced of their Brother's Messiahship. When and in what circumstances their conversion took place, we are not told; but we have a hint of the occasion that led to it, at least in the case of James. In his First Epistle to the Corinthians, St. Paul mentions an appearance of the risen Jesus to James, and separates it from His appearances to Peter, to the Twelve, and to the five hundred brethren, in such a way as to imply that it took place later than the others. This fact at once suggests the conclusion that James was not a disciple at the time of those earlier manifestations, but became such as a result of his own vision of the risen Lord.

I.

THE APPEARANCE TO JAMES.

1. It would seem as if this were among the last of our Lord's appearances during the forty days. The place cannot be determined. It may have been Galilee; it may have been Jerusalem. If James was not in Jerusalem at the Passover, the place was probably somewhere in Galilee, possibly Nazareth. This appearance to James is the only one not made to a known believer. Had any rumours of the resurrection previously reached James? Had he learned that Jesus had appeared to His disciples in Jerusalem? Did his mother inform him that Jesus had indeed risen from the dead and had spoken with the Twelve?

Had his doubts begun to give way? Had they vanished, or was he still in perplexity? Whatever his state of mind, he soon received personal confirmation of the resurrection. His Brother appeared to him. Only the fact is recorded. What would we not give for even a few fragments of the conversation then held? How gentle the blame with which our Lord censured His brother for his unbelief! How deep that brother's self-reproach and shame!—that he of all others should not have recognized the Messiah! that kinsmen and strangers should have had keener spiritual discernment than himself! that he should have been deaf and blind to the evidence that persuaded them!—and such evidence! If he had only weighed it as he should! The interview dispelled for ever his own conception of the Messiah, and rendered him thenceforward a whole-hearted and energetic Christian.

> I looked at life with all-unseeing eyes,
>   Unable to discern the deeper thing
>   Or dive below the surface to the spring,
> Until thou camest as a glad surprise.
> And now to me the smallest bird that flies
>   Twitters a song which seraphim might sing;
>   While roadside flowers a sacred message bring,
> And teach those truths that make the angels wise.
> I cannot tell thee how thy passing touch
>   Had power the underlying thought to show
>   Till all the world was changed because of thee:
> Nor do I care to measure overmuch
>   The why and wherefore: this one thing I know,
>   That I, who once was blind, now clearly see.[1]

2. Some apocryphal writings have supplied details of the appearance of our Lord to James.

The Gospel according to the Hebrews, which Lightfoot speaks of as one of the earliest and most respectable of the apocryphal narratives, is quoted by Jerome (*de Vir. ill.* 2) to the following effect: "The Lord after his resurrection appeared to James, who had sworn that he would not eat bread from the hour in which he had drunk the cup of the Lord till he saw him risen from the dead. Jesus, therefore, took bread and blessed and brake it, and gave it

[1] E. T. Fowler, *Verses Wise or Otherwise*, 162.

to James the Just, and said to him, My brother, eat thy bread, for the Son of Man has risen from the dead." There are other versions of the same story, in which the vow is dated, not from the Last Supper, but from the crucifixion. Possibly the reference to the Last Supper may have arisen from the fact that James shaped his vow after the Lord's words spoken at the Supper, " I will not drink from henceforth of the fruit of the vine, until the kingdom of God shall come."

3. How natural that a brother standing beneath the cross, having heard of the words spoken at the Last Supper, should then at length have thrown in his lot with Jesus and resolved, whether in despairing remorse or with some faint dawning of believing hope, " I too will no more eat bread nor drink wine till the kingdom of God shall come "! How natural also that one of the earliest appearances of the risen Lord should have been made to His repentant brother, and that that brother should from that day forth have united himself to the company of the Apostles, and been chosen by them to preside over the Church in Jerusalem, while they proceeded to carry out their Master's last charge, to preach the gospel to every nation!

4. It is necessary to assume, in the light of subsequent events, that James's conversion was complete and thoroughgoing, and led him to throw himself heart and soul into the service of the Master. He cannot have been a half-hearted disciple. He must have been one of the most zealous, active, and devoted of them all to secure the position which he ultimately held.

¶ Principal Dale said he always divided men into two classes —those who nipped life and those who gripped it. One of the laws of success was that they must be earnest.[1]

II.

AFTER THE ASCENSION.

1. Of James's subsequent history we gather from the Acts and the Epistles of St. Paul that, after the Ascension, he with his brothers remained at Jerusalem in the company of the eleven

[1] *British Weekly*, June 6, 1907.

Apostles and Mary and the other women, waiting for the descent of the Spirit (Acts i. 14), and that within ten years from that time he became the head of the Church at Jerusalem.

We have no information as to when or how he was placed in this position. No title is given to the office he held. There were elders in the Jerusalem Church; but James is never called an elder; nor is the title "bishop" given to him. Still we must not be slaves of words. In point of fact, James held at Jerusalem a position very similar to that of the several town bishops, or pastors, early in the second century, the position of the one pastor of a congregation.

2. There are several references in the New Testament to James after the Ascension.

(1) Eight or ten years after the Ascension (about 38 A.D.) St. Paul paid a visit to Jerusalem and stayed with St. Peter fifteen days, seeing no other Apostle, "save James the Lord's brother." This has given rise to much discussion as to whether James was an Apostle.

(2) In Gal. ii. 1–10 St. Paul describes a later visit to Jerusalem after an interval of fourteen years, i.e. about 51 A.D. At this visit the leaders of the Church, James, Peter, and John, after hearing his report of his first missionary journey, signified their approval of his work, and "gave the right hand of fellowship," agreeing that Paul and Barnabas should preach to the Gentiles and they themselves to the circumcision. St. Paul's second visit to Jerusalem is more fully described in Acts xv. 4–29, where James appears as president of the Council held to consider how far the Gentile Christians should be required to conform to the customs of the Jews. It is James who sums up the discussion and proposes the resolution which is carried.

(3) In Gal. ii. 11–14 Peter's inconsistency in regard to eating with the Gentiles at Antioch is explained by the arrival of "certain from James."

(4) James is seen in the same position of authority in Acts xxi. 18, when St. Paul presents himself before him on his return from his third missionary journey (58 A.D.). After joining in praise to God for the success which had attended his labours, James and the elders who are with him warn St. Paul of the

strong feeling against him, which had been excited among the "myriads of Jewish believers who were all zealous for the law," by the report that he had taught the Jews of the Dispersion to abandon circumcision and their other customs. To counteract this impression, they recommended him to join in a Nazirite vow, which had been undertaken by four members of their community, as a proof that the report was unfounded, and that he himself walked according to the law.

¶ William Wilberforce lived his parliamentary life as a contemporary of William Pitt, Edmund Burke, Charles James Fox, and Richard Brinsley Sheridan. Here was a galaxy of brilliance—the most polished and powerful orators who ever awoke the classic echoes of St. Stephen's! Wilberforce's figure conveyed the inevitable impression of insignificance. Yet when he rose to address the Commons the House instantly crowded. Members held their breaths to listen. The little reformer spoke with an authority rarely wielded by the greatest masters. He was heard in a silence, and with a respect which was never accorded to those illustrious statesmen whose utterances are to this day read in schools and colleges as models of rhetoric. And why? There is only one reason for it. Like Sir Galahad—

> His strength was as the strength 'of ten,
> Because his heart was pure.[1]

3. His relationship to Jesus, and his intimate acquaintance with Him from boyhood, of course made James a marked man among the disciples, and doubtless contributed greatly to his reputation and authority. But such natural advantages do not alone account for the tremendous influence which he wielded for so many years—an influence which he did not share with his brothers. Only because he possessed at the same time the qualities of a leader, and uncommon zeal and devotion, could he acquire the universal credit he enjoyed.

But it was not simply his character as a Christian that contributed to James's influence and authority. His character as a Jew counted for a great deal with the strict Jews of the Mother Church. Though he was converted by a vision of the risen Jesus, as St. Paul was, his conversion produced an entirely different effect upon him. He had apparently passed through

[1] F. W. Boreham, *The Luggage of Life*, 130.

no such experience of the futility of endeavouring to keep the Law, and it was not a sense of the need of justification, or of deliverance from sin and death, that led him to Christ. He was evidently, before his conversion, an uncommonly devout and faithful Jew, and in accepting Christ he never thought of ceasing to be such, or of regarding the observance of the Law as of less importance than before. Rather, like his other Christian brethren, he must have regarded it as of even greater importance; and nothing in the teaching or conduct of Jesus suggested anything else to him. All that we know of him points to an excessive reverence for the Jewish law in all its parts, and a most scrupulous observance of it throughout his life; and in a Church constituted as the Church of Jerusalem was such a tendency naturally promoted greatly his reputation for piety.

How great his influence and authority was we now with difficulty conceive. No doubt if we look at it from the more general point of view, whether of the whole Jewish Christian world, or of the whole Gentile Christian world, it sinks into nothing before the majesty of Peter and of Paul. But place ourselves within the circle of those purely Palestine Christians who still frequented the services of the Temple, and adhered to the usages of the synagogue—confine our view to the horizon of the favoured land, which was the scene of the last expiring struggle of Jewish national life—and we shall find that, to whatever quarter we turn for information, James appears before us as the one authoritative ruler, as the one undoubted representative of the Christian society. If we open the contemporary Christian records of the Acts and Epistles, it is to his decision that the Council of Jerusalem bows—to him, as a pillar of the Church, taking precedence even of Peter and John, that St. Paul communicates the new revelation which had been entrusted to him. If we turn to the later traditions of the Jewish Christians themselves, as preserved in the fragments of Hegesippus or in the Clementine Recognitions and Homilies, he appears before us as the one mysterious bulwark of the chosen people—invested with a priestly sanctity before which the pontificate of Aaron fades into insignificance—as the one universal bishop of the Christian Church, in whose dignity the loftiest claims of the ecclesiastical dominion of later times find their earliest prototype. If we look to the impression produced on the mind of the Jewish people itself, we find that he alone of all the Apostles has obtained a place in their national records.

¶ There are men and women born upon this earth, who, walking lightly, yet print deep, ineffaceable footprints upon the age in which they live. The world is better for them; their breath has purified the atmosphere they existed in. Ignorant of their predestination as they are, every word and act of theirs bears the seal of the Divine Intelligence. They were sent to do the work of the Most High.[1]

III.

THE MARTYRDOM.

1. James, like his namesake the son of Zebedee, died as a martyr. We have two accounts of the last scene, one by Hegesippus written about 160 A.D., the other in Josephus, which is the simpler and more authentic.

(1) The account of Hegesippus is full of improbabilities. It is quoted by Eusebius as follows: The charge of the Church then (after the Ascension) devolved on James the brother of the Lord in concert with the Apostles. He is distinguished from the others of the same name by the title "Just" (righteous) which has been applied to him from the first. He was holy from his mother's womb, drank no wine or strong drink, nor ate animal food; no razor came on his head, nor did he anoint himself with oil, or use the bath. To him alone was it permitted to enter into the Holy Place, for he wore no woollen, but only linen. And alone he would go into the temple, where he used to be found on his knees, asking forgiveness for the people, so that his knees became hard like a camel's, because he was ever upon them worshipping God and asking forgiveness for the people. Accordingly through his exceeding righteousness he was called righteous ("Just") and "Oblias," which being interpreted is "the defence of the people" and "righteousness," as the prophets declared of him. Some of the seven sects, which I have mentioned, inquired of him, "What is the door of Jesus?" and he said that he was the Saviour, where-

[1] Richard Dehan, in *Between Two Thieves.*

upon some believed that Jesus is the Christ. Now the fore-mentioned sects did not believe in the resurrection, or in the coming of one to recompense each man according to his works. But as many as did believe, believed through James. So when many of the rulers believed, there was a disturbance among the Jews and the Scribes and the Pharisees, saying that there was a danger that all the people would look to Jesus as the Christ. They came together therefore and said to James, "We pray thee restrain the people, for they have gone astray in regard to Jesus thinking him to be the Christ. We pray thee to persuade all that have come to the passover about Jesus. For we all listen to thee. For we and all the people bear witness that thou art just, and hast no respect of persons. Do thou therefore stand on the pinnacle of the temple, so that thou mayest be conspicuous and thy words may be well heard by all the people, and persuade them not to go astray about Jesus. For all the tribes have come together with the Gentiles also on account of the Passover." Then the forementioned Scribes and Pharisees set James on the pinnacle of the temple and cried to him, "O thou just one to whom we are all bound to listen, since the people are going astray after Jesus who was crucified, tell us what is the door of Jesus." And he answered with a loud voice, "Why do you ask me concerning Jesus the Son of Man? He is both seated in Heaven on the right hand of Power, and will come on the clouds of heaven." And when many were convinced and gave glory to the witness of James, and cried, "Hosanna to the Son of David," the same Scribes and Pharisees said to each other, "We have done ill in bringing forward such a testimony to Jesus, but let us go up and cast him down that they may fear to believe him." And they cried out saying, "Oh, oh, even the just has gone astray," and they fulfilled that which is written in Isaiah, "Let us take away the just, for he is not for our purpose; wherefore they shall eat the fruits of their deeds." So they went up and they cast down James the Just, and said to one another, "Let us stone James the Just." And they began to stone him, since he was not killed by the fall; but he turned round and knelt down saying, "O Lord God my Father, I beseech thee, forgive them, for they know not what they do." While they were thus stoning him one of the priests of the sons of Rechab, of whom Jeremiah the prophet testifies, cried out,

"Stop! What do ye? The Just is praying for you." And one of them who was a fuller smote the head of the Just one with his club. And so he bore his witness. And they buried him on the spot, and his pillar still remains by the side of the temple (with the inscription), "He hath been a true witness both to Jews and Greeks that Jesus is the Christ." And immediately Vespasian commenced the siege.

(2) The much more probable account of Josephus (*Ant. Jud.* xx. 9, 1) says: During the interval between the death of Festus (probably in the year 62 A.D.) and the arrival of his successor Albinus, the high priest Ananus the younger, being of rash and daring spirit and inclined like the Sadducees in general to extreme severity in punishing, brought to trial James, the brother of Jesus, who is called the Christ, and some others before the court of the Sanhedrin, and having charged them with breaking the laws, delivered them over to be stoned. Josephus adds that the better class of citizens and those who were versed in the law were indignant at this, and made complaints both to King Agrippa and to Albinus, on the ground that Ananus had no right to summon the Sanhedrin without the consent of the procurator; and that Agrippa in consequence removed him from the high priesthood.

Origen (*Cels.* i. c. 47, Lomm. xvii. p. 87) and Eusebius (*H.E.* ii. 23) also cite Josephus as ascribing the miseries of the siege to the Divine vengeance for the murder of James the Just; but this does not occur in his extant writings.[1]

¶ "ΔΙΚΑΙΟΤΑΤΟΣ" is the epitaph inscribed on Lord Aberdeen's monument in Westminster Abbey. The love of justice was, no doubt, strong in him, but, like nearly all attempts to describe a complex human character in a single word, the title of "most just" conveys but a partial idea of what manner of man Lord Aberdeen in truth was. Many have equalled him, perhaps have surpassed him, in devotion to exact justice, who have altogether failed to gain that deep respect and confidence which were invariably given to Lord Aberdeen by those who were brought into close association with him. Nor is the cause of this far to seek, for the existence of a keen sense of justice is quite compatible with the absence of other qualities which Lord Aberdeen also possessed in no common measure; and the possession of which, even had that particular virtue been less strongly developed

---

[1] J. B. Mayor, *The Epistle of St. James.*

in him, would have sufficiently accounted for the influence over others which he obtained.[1]

2. If the traditions are true which say that James was a Rechabite; that is, that he was brought up like John the Baptist, so that from his birth he never drank wine or strong drink, never had his hair cut, and never took a bath, we must conclude that the children in that home of Nazareth were brought up under an austere and rigid discipline. And this makes it the more remarkable that our Lord Himself, when He reached manhood, gave up the severity of His earlier habits, so that men contrasted His way of life with the way of John the Baptist. And perhaps this may also throw light on the unbelief of James and the rest of His brothers. When Christ began to live a life so much freer than theirs, when He broke through the austere restraint which they had associated with the highest forms of righteousness, they would find it difficult to believe that He was really a religious teacher sent from God.

¶ The fact is that purification and austerity are even more necessary for the appreciation of life and laughter than for anything else. To let no bird fly past unnoticed, to spell patiently the stones and weeds, to have the mind a storehouse of sunsets, requires a discipline in pleasure and an education in gratitude.[2]

3. James was a great figure. A strong man, he had the rigidity of his strength; a safe man, he had the natural conservatism which accompanies steadfastness. He had zeal enough to rejoice in the daring radicalism of Peter, and breadth and spirituality enough to sympathize with the grand universalism of Paul; but for himself, he was always place-bound and parochial, and Christianity always remained to him an offshoot, though immeasurably the greatest offshoot, of Judaism.

It is interesting to consider the Epistle of James in connexion with the relationship of the writer to our Lord. There are few direct allusions to the teaching of Christ, and many remarkable omissions. There is no reference to the pre-existence of Christ, to the Atonement, to our Lord's death, or to His resurrection. On the other hand, this Epistle contains more echoes of the

[1] A. Gordon, *The Earl of Aberdeen*, 307.
[2] G. K. Chesterton, *Twelve Types*.

teaching of Jesus than any other New Testament book, except the Gospels, which actually record this teaching. The figurative language of the Epistle recalls our Lord's love of parables. There is a very marked resemblance to the Sermon on the Mount, and it has been pointed out that the similarity is not that of actual quotation but rather that of thought, due to intimate knowledge of our Lord's mind, though not expressed in His words.

¶ The worst of St. James was that when a sermon was preached from his Epistle, there was always a danger lest somebody in the congregation should think that it was against him it was levelled.[1]

[1] W. Hale White, *The Early Life of Mark Rutherford*, 17.

ANANIAS AND SAPPHIRA.

LITERATURE.

Bonar, H., *Light and Truth* : Acts and Epistles (1869), 65.

Dykes, J. O., *From Jerusalem to Antioch* (1875), 165.

Jenks, D., *In the Face of Jesus Christ* (1914), 250.

Lewis, Z. H., *Petros*, 191.

Luckock, H. M., *Footprints of the Apostles as traced by Saint Luke in the Acts*, i. (1905) 134.

Maclaren, A., *The Acts of the Apostles* (Bible Class Expositions) (1894), 55.

    ,,   ,, *Expositions* : The Acts of the Apostles i.–xii. (1907), 172.

Milligan, G., in *Men of the Bible* : Some Lesser-known Characters (1904), 249.

Parker, J., *The City Temple*, ii. (1872) 124 ; iii. (1873) 397.

Seekings, H. S., *The Men of the Pauline Circle* (1914), 127.

Stokes, G. T., *The Acts of the Apostles* (Expositor's Bible), i. (1891) 211.

Whyte, A., *Bible Characters* : Joseph and Mary to James (1900), 187.

Wright, G. F., in *Sermons by the Monday Club*, 17th Ser. (1891), 258.

Dictionary of the Apostolic Church, i. (1915) 54 (W. F. Boyd).

Dictionary of the Bible, i. (1898) 91 (J. A. Selbie).

Preacher's Magazine, iii. (1892) 376 (J. Bennett).

ANANIAS AND SAPPHIRA.

But a certain man named Ananias, with Sapphira his wife, sold a possession, and kept back part of the price, his wife also being privy to it, and brought a certain part, and laid it at the apostles' feet.—Acts v. 1, 2.

To understand fully the sin of Ananias and Sapphira, the two previous chapters must be carefully read. Persecution had driven the members of the Church closer to God and to one another; opposition had, in fact, become a source of strength and a crown of honour. The first result and marvellous proof of that oneness was the so-called "community of goods." The chief way in which at that time a member of the Church expressed his unshaken devotion to the common cause, or his willingness to sacrifice to the last penny for the common weal, was by placing his realized capital at the disposal of the brotherhood. The endangered position of the little community thus tended to inflame the fervour of its charity, and gave a new impetus to that common relief fund which had been started at Pentecost. Many of the poorer converts, on joining the Christian community, would lose all help from Jewish sources, but so heartily did the richer members care for their needs that none were left destitute or in want.

There is nothing of modern communism in all this, but there is a lesson to the modern Church as to the obligations of wealth and the claims of brotherhood, which is all but universally disregarded. The spectre of communism is troubling every nation, and it will become more and more formidable, unless the Church learns that the only way to lay it is to live by the precepts of Jesus and to repeat in new forms the spirit of the primitive Church. The Christian sense of stewardship, not the abolition of the right of property, is the cure for the hideous facts which drive men to shriek, "Property is theft."

The wealthy part of the Church was no doubt made up of two

classes: men who were full of the new spirit, and so hearty in the cause of Jesus that they were forward of their own accord to put all they had into the Church treasury, in order that no lover of Jesus might lack; and men honest enough in their belief, only less enthusiastic or generous, who gave, partly indeed from good-will, but partly also through the force of example or the fear of censure. To whatever extent this latter class existed, it formed a dangerous element. When high-pitched virtue becomes a fashion, men learn to pay to it the homage of hypocrisy.

Of these two classes the writer of the Book of Acts presents us with individual examples—of the former class, in the case of Joseph, or Barnabas, a wealthy Cypriot, who "having a field, sold it, and brought the money, and laid it at the apostles' feet"; of the latter, in the case of Ananias with Sapphira his wife, whose melancholy story is now before us.

¶ Each of us is not only God's workman, but His steward. He has a duty of distribution as well as of accumulation laid upon him. God expects every man to have bestowed so much as well as laboured so much before his time comes.[1]

I.

The Sin of Ananias and Sapphira.

1. "The corruption of the best becomes the worst": so says the proverb, and in the story of the sin of Ananias and Sapphira we have abundant corroboration of its truth. For both must, in the first instance at any rate, have been of a sufficiently generous character.

Ananias had seen what was going on around him, and he had determined that he must not be behindhand in the ministry of love. But ambition to stand well with his fellow-members evidently mingled with the pure spirit of charity, though we do not need to suppose that there was as yet any conscious intention to deceive. Acting, then, on these somewhat mixed motives of charity and ambition, Ananias determined to sell a possession, some farm or other which he had, and hand over the money to the Apostles. He probably meant at first to hand over the whole

[1] R. W. Barbour, *Thoughts*, 91.

price, but with the money in his hand the demon of avarice entered into his heart. And he "kept back part of the price, his wife also being privy to it, and brought a certain part, and laid it at the apostles' feet. But Peter said, Ananias, why hath Satan filled thy heart to lie to the Holy Ghost, and to keep back part of the price of the land? Whiles it remained, did it not remain thine own? and after it was sold, was it not in thy power? How is it that thou hast conceived this thing in thy heart? thou hast not lied unto men, but unto God."

2. The peculiar sin of this pair lay here, that, being tempted by two evil things,—the love of money and the love of applause— they suffered both these unchristian passions to enter and occupy their souls, to fill them up bit by bit, driving out the love of men and the fear of God, till, grown blind and hard and reckless through sin, they plotted in cold blood to cheat the Church and lie to the face of God. Had they been covetous only, they would have kept their property; vain only, they would have given it all. In either case the motive had been a bad one, but in neither case would the offence have grown into a scandal. It was the effort to reconcile two conflicting passions, to be close and seem generous, to keep their gold yet win the credit of giving it, that betrayed these Christians into the first open and shameful breach of Christian morality. Out of the confluence of covetousness with vanity came forth a lie.

3. But they tried to play the hypocrite's part on most dangerous ground just when the Divine Spirit of purity, sincerity, and truth had been abundantly poured out, and when the spirit of deceit and hypocrisy was therefore at once recognized.

The Spirit was vouchsafed during those earliest days of the Church in a manner and style of which we hear nothing during the later years of the Apostles. He proved His presence by physical manifestations, as when the whole house was shaken where the Apostles were assembled — a phenomenon of which we read nothing in the latter portion of the Acts. By the gift of tongues, by miracles of healing, by abounding spiritual life and discernment, by physical manifestations, the most careless and thoughtless in the Christian community were compelled to feel that a supernatural power was present in their midst and resting specially upon the Apostles. Yet it was into such an atmosphere that the spirit of hypocrisy and of covetousness, the two vices to which Christianity was specially opposed, and which the great Master had specially denounced, obtruded itself as Satan gained entrance into Eden, to defile with their foul presence the chosen dwelling-place of the Holy Ghost. The Holy Ghost vindicated His authority therefore, because, as it must be observed, it was not St. Peter that sentenced Ananias to death. No one may have been more surprised than St. Peter himself at the consequences which followed his stern rebuke. St. Peter merely declared his sin, " Thou hast not lied unto men, but unto God "; and then it is expressly said, " Ananias hearing these words fell down and gave up the ghost."

¶ Old piety was wont to say that God's judgments tracked the footsteps of the criminal ; that all violation of the eternal laws, done in the deepest recesses or on the conspicuous high places of the world, was absolutely certain of its punishment. You could do no evil, you could do no good, but a god would repay it to you. It was as certain as that when you shot an arrow from the earth, gravitation would bring it back to the earth. The all-embracing law of right and wrong was as inflexible, as sure and exact, as that of gravitation. Furies with their serpent hair and infernal maddening torches followed Orestes who had murdered his mother. In the still deeper soul of modern Christendom there hung the tremendous image of a Doomsday— *Dies irœ, dies illa*—when the All-just, without mercy now, with only terrific accuracy now, would judge the quick and the dead, and to each soul measure out the reward of his deeds done in the body—eternal Heaven to the good, to the bad eternal Hell.

My friend, it well behoves us to reflect how true essentially all this still is : that it continues, and will continue, fundamentally a fact in all essential particulars—its certainty, I say its infallible certainty, its absolute justness, and all the other particulars, the eternity itself included. He that has with his eyes and soul looked into nature from any point—and not merely into distracted theological, metaphysical, modern philosophical, or other cobweb representations of nature at second hand—will find this true, that only the vesture of it is changed for us ; that the essence of it cannot change at all. Banish all miracles from it. Do not name the name of God ; it is still true.[1]

¶ When Howe received the tidings of the terrible fire which

[1] *Thomas Carlyle, 1795–1835*, ii. 17.

devastated London in September, 1666, he laid to heart the lesson which he, twelve years later, delivered to London itself in the Haberdashers' Hall. "The street shall be built again, and the wall in troublous times" (Dan. ix. 25), was the text. "The judgments of God are audible sermons. They have a voice." He knew something of London, and report had told him of the wild debaucheries with which the city overflowed since 1660. "That the inhabitants of London should be as it were in a conspiracy to destroy London seems very strange. And yet was not that the case?" It was useless for the citizens to be indignant against the supposed authors of the conflagration. They themselves were the true authors. Their sins brought the punishment upon their heads.[1]

II.

SAPPHIRA.

1. A sin which two have arranged is worse than one done singly, for there have been two consciences stifled, and, instead of love warning its dear one against defilement, it plunges both object and subject in the mire.

And Sapphira was "privy to it"—it was a sad revelation of domestic as well as of Church life. They had land. It was very striking indeed that any member of the original Church should have any land at all. It is one thing for a man to have a few coins in his hand, and another to have property in the soil—the soil you cannot burn, the soil that is always there. Ananias and Sapphira, it may be suggested, were perhaps the best-to-do people in the neighbourhood: "They sold a possession."

Hear them talking the case over! They said when they saw all the pieces of silver lying before them, "Really this is too much; I think so: do you concur with me?" And Sapphira said, "Yes." Here in the Church a man and his wife put their heads together to cheat the Cross, to rob the Holy Ghost!

¶ When or wherein the soul is brought but to parley with an objection, then and therein unbelief is at work, whether it be as unto a particular fact or as unto our state. It was so with our first parents in the very entry of their treaty with Satan, in giving a considering audience unto that one question, "Hath God said so?" Our great Pattern hath showed us what our deportment

[1] R. F. Horton, *John Howe*, 79.

ought to be in all suggestions and temptations. When the devil showed him "all the kingdoms of the world and the glory of them," to tempt him withal, he did not stand and look upon them, viewing their glory, and pondering their empire, though he was fully assured that after all he could despise and trample upon the offer, and him that made it; but instantly, without stay, he cries, "Get thee hence, Satan." [1]

2. One can fancy the awed silence that fell on the congregation, and the restrained, mournful movement that ran through it when Sapphira entered. Why the two had not come in company can only be conjectured. Perhaps the husband had gone straight to the Apostles after completing the sale, and had left the wife to follow at her convenience. Perhaps she had not intended to come at all, but had become alarmed at the delay in Ananias' return. She may have come in fear that something had gone wrong, and that fear would be increased by her not seeing her husband in her quick glance round the company.

If she came expecting to receive applause, the silence and constraint that hung over the assembly must have stirred a fear that something terrible had happened, which would be increased by Peter's question. It was a merciful opportunity given her to separate herself from the sin and the punishment; but her lie was glib, and indicated determination to stick to the fraud. That moment was heavy with her fate, and she knew it not; but she knew that she had the opportunity of telling the truth, and she did not take it. She had to make the hard choice which we have sometimes to make, to be true to some sinful bargain or be true to God, and she chose the worse part. Which of the two was tempter and which was tempted matters little. Like many a wife, she thought that it was better to be loyal to her husband than to God, and so her honour was "rooted in dishonour," and she was falsely true and truly false.

¶ The following poem, entitled "A Wife's Farewell to her Husband Going to the Front," shows how honour may be chosen and become the highest loyalty on the part of the wife:—

> How can I let thee go!—and how
>   So bear myself as to conceal
> The pang of grief to which I bow,
>   Only my love and pride reveal.

[1] John Owen, *Of Temptation*, chap. vii.

How can I let thee go! and yet
  I would not bid thee stay. Ah! no,
The claims of honour to forget,
  The call of duty to forego.

Go forth, encompassed by my love,
  Which many waters cannot drown.
May angels guard thee from above,
  And God Most High defend His own.[1]

III.

The Punishment.

1. Scripture authority, including that of our Lord Himself,
represents man as set betwixt a twofold world of invisible moral
influences. The heart of man is as it were a little city or fortress
on the borderland between two nations at war with each other,
and liable to be captured by whichever at that point proves itself
the stronger. "Why hath Satan filled thy heart?" There is a
real, malign Tempter, who can pour evil affections and purposes
into a man's heart. But he cannot do it unless the man opens
his heart, as that "why?" implies. The same thought of our co-
operation and concurrence, so that, however Satan suggests, it is
we who are guilty, comes out in the second question, "How is it
that *thou* hast conceived this thing in thy heart?" Reverently
we may venture to say not only that Christ stands at the door
and knocks, but that the enemy of Him and His stands there too,
and he too enters "if any man open the door."

¶ Watts—the man of that aggressive nineteenth century—
had many wild thoughts, but there was one thought that never
even for an instant strayed across his burning brain. He never
once thought, "Why should I understand the cat, any more than
the cat understands me?" He never thought, "Why should I be
just to the merits of a Chinaman, any more than a pig studies the
mystic virtues of a camel?" He affronted heaven and the angels,
but there was one hard arrogant dogma that he never doubted,
that he himself was as central and as responsible as God.[2]

---

[1] *Church Family Newspaper.*
[2] G. K. Chesterton, *G. F. Watts*, 36.

¶ It is told of the child of a famous painter that, from want of due repression and discipline, he gave way from time to time to paroxysms of violent and vindictive rage, and that in one of these furious moods he kicked and spat at his father. Soon afterwards, downcast and remorseful, he drew near and made his humble confession, "Father, the devil told me to kick you; the spitting was my own idea." [1]

2. With the final fate of Ananias and Sapphira we have nothing whatever to do. Only the time, the place, and the manner of their death were meant for the teaching of the Church—as a protest that the Holy Ghost is in her, and as a warning against hypocrisy. To be false in their hearts, and to thrust this falsehood into their religious worship and pretended service of God in His Church, was the offence for which they died.

The terrible severity of the punishment can be understood only by remembering the importance of preserving the young community from corruption at the very beginning. Unless the vermin are cleared from the springing plant, it will not grow. As Achan's death warned Israel at the beginning of their entrance into the promised land, so Ananias and Sapphira perished that all generations of the Church might fear to pretend to self-surrender while cherishing its opposite, and might feel that they have to give account to One who knows the secrets of the heart, and counts nothing as given if anything is surreptitiously kept back.

¶ The theory of the vow of poverty in the Church took its rise very much from the history of Ananias and Sapphira. That story had a deeper meaning than being a mere lie—it was sacrilege. There was a profession of charity to the Church not kept; an attempt to cheat the Holy Spirit that was in the Church, by vowing more than they meant to perform. St. Peter accepted the vow, but examined them on its sincerity. [2]

¶ Begin thoroughly. It is a thousand times easier to live altogether for Christ than half for Christ. Don't be an amphibian, half in one world, half in another. Be men, through and through, men in Christ Jesus. [3]

[1] Dean Hole, *Then and Now*, 12.
[2] C. A. E. Moberly, *Dulce Domum*, 266.
[3] *The Life of Henry Drummond*, 482.

GAMALIEL.

LITERATURE.

Brooks, P., *Sermons Preached in English Churches* (1883), 243.

Conybeare, W. J., and J. S. Howson, *The Life and Epistles of St. Paul* (1870), 47.

Deane, A., *Friends and Fellow Labourers of St. Paul* (1906), 6.

Farrar, F. W., *The Life and Work of St. Paul* (1897), 23, 59.

Fürst, A., *Christ The Way* (1883), 127.

Gibbon, B. J., *The True Ritual* (1902), 31.

Luckock, H. M., *Footprints of the Apostles as traced by Saint Luke in the Acts*, i. (1905) 151.

Maclaren (A.), *Expositions* : The Acts of the Apostles i.-xii. (1907), 196.

Maurice, F. D., *The Acts of the Apostles* (1894), **61**.

Sabatier, A., *The Apostle Paul* (1891), 48.

Stokes, G. T., *The Acts of the Apostles* (Expositor's Bible), i. (1891) 229 ; ii. (1892) 13.

Taylor, W. M., *Peter the Apostle* (1891), 213.

Tead, E. S., in *Sermons by the Monday Club*, 17th Ser. (1891), 266.

Thackeray, H. St. J., *The Relation of St. Paul to Contemporary Jewish Thought* (1900), 10.

Dictionary of the Apostolic Church, i. (1915) 440 (W. F. Boyd).

Dictionary of the Bible, ii. (1899) 106 (G. Milligan).

Good Words, 1870, p. 856 (C. J. Vaughan).

GAMALIEL.

There stood up one in the council, a Pharisee, named Gamaliel, a doctor of the law, had in honour of all the people.—Acts v. 34.

1. It is strange how a single name here and there out of the great multitude of perished and forgotten names secures remembrance. It is almost as when one stands upon the seashore and looks out across the sea, and here and there upon the surface of the great ocean, all grey and monotonous, there comes one flash of silver; one single wave all by itself leaps up as if it were alive, and burns with a lustre which compels the eye to look at it. You ask yourself why that special wave should have such peculiar privilege, and there is only one answer you can give. It is no larger a wave than the rest, and it is made of no different water from them; it is simply that that wave happened to leap just where the sun was smiting, and so the sun smote it, and it became illustrious. So it is with illustrious men. The sun of history shines on this great sea of human life; and the special career which happens to leap just where the sun is striking catches his glory and seizes men's notice and remembrance. If the man's life is larger than other lives, so much the better—it catches so much more of sunshine. If it is of special fineness, made of more lustrous stuff than other men's, so much the better still—it turns the sunshine into a peculiar radiance. But still the essential thing is that it should leap at the right moment and should be turned the right way. With those conditions even a very common life becomes illustrious; and without them the largest and the finest character melts back into the bosom of the humanity out of which it sprung, unknown, unnoticed, unremembered.

¶ To the judges, philosophers, princelings—these shadows and players who strut and fret their hour upon the stage—of the New Testament age it would have seemed the dream of a disordered

67

brain to forecast their fame and name to after ages as due to one brief moment's meeting with a Galilean carpenter, or a wandering Jewish tent-maker. Yet in this reflected light only do they live, pilloried for ever, some in a sentence, as "Crucified under Pontius Pilate," others set like Felix and Agrippa as the foil and contrast of spurious honour and authority with the true majesty and power of life.[1]

2. Let us turn to the story of a man whose name flashes for a moment as the light of the New Testament history falls upon the life of Jerusalem at the beginning of the Christian Church. The flash is only for a moment, and yet the impression which it leaves is very clear. Gamaliel is peculiarly a representative man, and the nature which he represents is one which appeals peculiarly to our modern life.

In the New Testament Gamaliel appears twice, and each time in a most interesting way. First, he is the teacher of St. Paul, and so we are constantly led to speculate as to what part of the training of his great pupil's character is due to him. In the second place he is the wise counsellor who, when the Apostles were brought for trial before the Sanhedrin, uttered a memorable plea for toleration and delay of judgment.

Let us look at him in each of these rôles.

I.

The Teacher.

1. Gamaliel was the grandson of the great scholar and teacher Hillel, and he belonged distinctly to the same liberal school as his great ancestor. In those days there were two schools or parties among the orthodox religious Jews—the school of Shammai, which was strict and narrow ; and the school of Hillel, which was liberal and free. Gamaliel was of the school of Hillel. His learning was so eminent, and his character so revered, that he is one of the seven who alone among Jewish doctors have been honoured with the title of "Rabban." As Aquinas, among the Schoolmen, was called *Doctor Angelicus*, and Bonaventura *Doctor Seraphicus*, so

---

[1] A. Rudman.

Gamaliel was called the "Beauty of the Law"; and it is a saying of the Talmud, that "since Rabban Gamaliel died, the glory of the Law has ceased." He was a Pharisee; but he was not trammelled by the narrow bigotry of the sect. He rose above the prejudices of his party. Our impulse is to class him with the best of the Pharisees, like Nicodemus and Joseph of Arimathæa. Candour and wisdom seem to have been features of his character; and this agrees with what we read of him in the Acts of the Apostles, that he was "had in honour of all the people." He died eighteen years before the destruction of Jerusalem, about the time of St. Paul's shipwreck at Malta, and was buried with great honour. Another of his pupils, Onkelos, the author of the celebrated Targum, raised to him such a funeral-pile of rich materials as had never before been known, except at the burial of a king.

¶ What were the Rugby, the Uppingham school-books compared with the personality of an Arnold, a Thring? What were the Balliol traditions compared with the influence of a Jowett? What a story is that of Da Feltre of Mantua in the fifteenth century! Villari says of him: "His success in so immoral an age was entirely owing to the nobility and generosity of his mind. . . . For a long time his pupils were distinguished by a loyalty of character in strong contrast with the general corruption." He believed evidently in Joubert's maxim: "Make truth lovely and do not try to arm her; mankind will then be far less inclined to contend with her." [1]

2. The Rabbinical schools assembled as a rule in their own buildings; but they met on special occasions within the precincts of the Temple itself—usually, perhaps, at the time of the great feasts, when the normal attendance of pupils would be swelled by the presence of pilgrims temporarily sojourning in the city. The teacher sat on a raised bench, so his hearers were quite literally "at his feet." Of all the instruction given, the basis was the Law; the text itself was repeated until the pupils knew it by heart, and then the amplifications and interpretations given by Rabbinical tradition were expounded. To a great extent the method of teaching was catechetical, and not unlike that employed by Socrates. Knotty points would be put forward, apparently conflicting traditions compared, hard cases of conduct discussed.

[1] J. Brierley, *Faith's Certainties*, 24.

Questions were asked of the pupils, and they were encouraged to question their teacher freely in turn.

¶ It is a good thing to ask questions. It was the occupation of the child Jesus in the midst of the doctors. Towards the close of his life Dr. Thomas Guthrie wrote a beautiful letter to his daughter congratulating her on her first approach to the table of the Lord. The letter simply overflows with intense affection and fatherly counsel. And it contains this pertinent passage: "I saw an adage yesterday, in a medical magazine, which is well worth your remembering and acting on. It is this wise saying of the great Lord Bacon's: WHO ASKS MUCH, LEARNS MUCH. I remember the day when I did not like, by asking, to confess my ignorance. I have long given up that, and now seize on every opportunity of adding to my stock of knowledge. Now don't forget Lord Bacon's wise saying!"[1]

3. From Jewish sources we learn something of the character of Gamaliel's teaching. Almost alone of the Rabbis, he encouraged his pupils to read Greek literature, which the others regarded as a dangerous study. So to Gamaliel possibly was due the fact that St. Paul could quote Cleanthes with such effect in his speech on Mars' hill. And in many ways he showed his liberality towards the heathen. They, he urged, should be allowed in harvest-time the same rights of gleaning as the Jews possessed, and he bade his pupils give their salutation of "Peace be with you" to them, even when they were on their way to some idolatrous feast.

¶ A friend wrote of John Mackintosh: "However widely a man differed in opinion or sentiment from himself, it seemed he did not care to dwell on the difference, but rather to open his mind fairly to take in whatever of good or true he had to teach. This open-mindedness in one so earnest and fixed in his own mind, was very remarkable; and the whole seemed so evenly balanced, that while he was not only fair, but sympathetic towards all men, there appeared no symptom of that weakness and uncertainty of thought often visible in those whose sympathies are stronger than their heads."[2]

4. Gamaliel in his capacity as teacher laid in St. Paul the foundations of modes of thought and reasoning, the influence of

---

[1] F. W. Boreham, *The Luggage of Life*, 235.
[2] N. Macleod, *Memorials of John Mackintosh*, 74.

which moulded the Apostle's whole soul and can be traced all
through his Epistles. Analogy, allegory, illustration, form the
staple elements of Eastern logic, and in their use St. Paul was
elaborately trained in Gamaliel's classes, and of their use his
writings furnish abundant examples. If we were to specify the
three effects which the teaching and example of Gamaliel may be
supposed to have produced on the mind of St. Paul, they would
be as follows—candour and honesty of judgment, a willingness to
study and make use of Greek authors, and a keen and watchful
enthusiasm for the Jewish law.

¶ Baur and the Tübingen school find it so difficult to reconcile
Gamaliel's attitude in Acts v. with the persecuting spirit afterwards shown by Saul, then his pupil, that they pronounce the
whole passage unhistorical. But do pupils never in later years
diverge from their teachers' doctrines? And may not special
circumstances have arisen in connexion with the appearance of
Stephen which called forth a fanatic zeal in Saul little in accord
with his early training? [1]

II.

THE COUNSELLOR.

The life of the early Christians was the poetic childhood of
the Church in her earliest innocence. It was marked by simplicity,
by gladness, by worship, by brotherhood. At home, and in their
place of meeting, their lives were a perpetual prayer, their meals
a perpetual love-feast and a perpetual eucharist. In the Temple
they attended the public services with unanimous zeal. In the
first impulses of fraternal joy many sold their possessions to
contribute to a common stock. The numbers of the little community increased daily, and the mass of the people looked on them
not only with tolerance, but with admiration and esteem.

The events which followed all tended at first to strengthen
their position. The healing of the cripple in Solomon's porch;
the bold speech of Peter afterwards; the unshaken constancy with
which Peter and John faced the fury of the Sadducees; the
manner in which all the disciples accepted and even exulted in

[1] G. Milligan, in Hastings' *Dictionary of the Bible*, ii. 106.

persecution, if it came in the fulfilment of their duties; the power with which they witnessed to the resurrection of their Lord; the beautiful spectacle of their unanimity; the awful suddenness with which Ananias and Sapphira had been stricken down; the signs and wonders which were wrought by the power of faith; the zeal and devotion which marked their gatherings in Solomon's porch —caused a rapid advance in the numbers and position of the Christian brothers.

1. The popularity of the Apostles, and the enthusiastic admiration of the multitude, stirred the envy of the Sadducees. Annas the high priest, who was regarded as their leader, was too determined a man to brook with patience the hateful doctrine which seemed now to be always on their lips. Undismayed by his previous failure, he made up his mind to a second arrest; before, they had laid hands only on St. Peter and St. John; now they proceed to take all the Apostles, and instead of locking them up in the precincts of the Council chambers, they put them this time in the public prison.

The Sanhedrin met at dawn to try them; but when they sent for them to the prison they found that the Apostles were not there, but that, delivered by "an angel of the Lord," they were calmly teaching in the Temple. In the deepest perplexity, the Sanhedrists once more despatched the Levitical officer to arrest them, but this time without any violence, which might lead to dangerous results. They offered no resistance, and were once more placed where their Lord had once stood—in the centre of that threatening semicircle of angry judges.

Their defence made a very strong and adverse impression upon the Council; something they said seems to have stung them to the quick. It is described by a remarkable figure, for which we have no English equivalent; every word they spoke went deeper and deeper, till "they were sawn asunder"; it is repeated in describing the effect of St. Stephen's speech, and in both cases the result was the same—it filled them with rage and fury.

¶ A friend of mine was once talking to an old family butler about a son of the house who had lately taken Orders, and gone to be a curate in a colliery village. The old man said, "Mr. Frank has got himself into sad trouble by preaching against drunkenness ; now 'e should 'ave stuck to the doctrine, sir. That would 'ave done no 'arm ! " [1]

2. The Council was upon the point of proceeding to extremities, when it was saved from the guilt of bloodshed by the interposition of Gamaliel. It was, no doubt, the weight of authority attaching to his name, combined with his great popularity, that gained him a hearing at a crisis when the whole Court was in a tumult of excitement and anger. What influenced him to stand up in the face of such opposition, and offer advice which went in the very teeth of his brother councillors' determination, we can only conjecture.

As soon as Gamaliel had calmed the excitement, he had the prisoners removed, and then began his condemnation of what the Court had resolved upon. Appealing to history in support of more moderate counsels, he pointed out how other pretenders had arisen, trading on the Messianic expectations which then existed all over Palestine, and especially in Galilee, and how they had been all destroyed without any action on the part of the Sanhedrin. He instanced two cases : Judas, who lived in the days of Cyrenius and the taxing under Augustus Cæsar ; and Theudas, who some time previous to that event had arisen, working upon the religious and national hopes of the Jews, as the persons now accused before them seemed also to be doing. Here surely, Gamaliel argued, was sufficient encouragement to induce them to wait the order of Providence. If, like their predecessors, these men were mere revolutionary agitators, they would probably share their fate ; if, however, they had right on their side, all opposition would certainly be useless, possibly it might recoil upon themselves with disastrous results. If the work were of men, it would fall to pieces ; if it were of God, no human power could cause its destruction.

¶ In this speech of Gamaliel there is one thing which seems to call for special remark. There is an apparent discrepancy between him and Josephus as to the insurrection of Theudas. A person of that name is spoken of by the Jewish historian as having headed an insurrection ; but, then, the date of his rising was some years subsequent to that of the events which we have now been

[1] A. C. Benson, *Along the Road*, 128.

reviewing. Hence, many would infer that the account given in the Acts is erroneous. But that is far from being a just conclusion; for, apart altogether from the consideration of the question of Luke's inspiration, Josephus was just as likely to be wrong as he was. Nay, the history of Josephus, as Alford remarks, "teems with inaccuracies"; so that we have no right to argue that, because he says one thing and Luke another, therefore Luke must be wrong. Moreover, Josephus himself, speaking of a time which might very well accord with that referred to here, says, "Now at this time there were ten thousand other disorders in Judea, which were like tumults, because a great number put themselves into a warlike posture, either out of hopes of gain to themselves or out of enmity to the Jews." Once more, the name Theudas was by no means uncommon; and it may very well have been that a person called by it may have been the leader of one of those tumults to which, in the passage which I have just quoted, the historian has referred.[1]

3. Gamaliel's plea was not so much a plea for systematic tolerance as for temporary caution. The day of open rupture between Judaism and Christianity was indeed very near at hand, but it had not yet arrived. His advice was due neither to the quiescence of Pharisaic fatalism, nor to a "fallacious *laisser aller* view of the matter, which serves to show how low the Jews had sunk in theology and political sagacity if such was the counsel of their wisest." There was time, Gamaliel thought, to wait and watch the development of this new fraternity. To interfere with it might only lead to a needless embroilment between the people and the Sanhedrin. A little patience would save trouble, and indicate the course which should be pursued. Gamaliel was sufficiently clear-sighted to have observed that the fire of a foolish fanaticism dies out if it be neglected, and is only kindled into fury by premature opposition. Let those who venture to arraign the principle of the wise Rabbi remember that it is practically identical with the utterance of Christ, "Every plant, which my heavenly Father planted not, shall be rooted up."

Gamaliel's argument, based as it was upon prudential principles pure and simple, was unanswerable; and it appears that the Sanhedrists thought so, for they agreed to act upon his advice. It was necessary, however, that their dignity should be maintained,

[1] W. M. Taylor, *Peter the Apostle*, 224.

which they feared would hardly be the case if the trial issued in nothing; accordingly it was proposed as a compromise, which Gamaliel accepted, that the prisoners should be flogged and then released, with a strict admonition to be more careful in future.

¶ Fools rush in through the doors; for folly is always bold. The same simplicity which robs them of all attention to precautions deprives them of all sense of shame at failure. But prudence enters with more deliberation. Its forerunners are caution and care; they advance and discover whether you can also advance without danger. Every rush forward is freed from danger by caution, while fortune sometimes helps in such cases. Step cautiously where you suspect depth. Sagacity goes cautiously forward while precaution covers the ground.[1]

4. We see from the numerous notices of Gamaliel in the Talmud, and from the sayings there ascribed to him, that he was a man of exactly the character which we should infer from the brief notice of him and of his sentiments in the Acts of the Apostles. In both these sources we see a humane, thoughtful, high-minded, and religious man—a man of sufficient culture to elevate him above vulgar passions, and of sufficient wisdom to see, to state, and to act upon the broad principles that hasty judgments are dangerously liable to error; that there is a strength and majesty in truth which needs no aid from persecution; that a light from heaven falls upon the destinies of man, and that by that light God "shows all things in the slow history of their ripening."

(1) Gamaliel was a man who believed in God. This was not a mere faith *about* God; he believed *in* God. To him evidently surrounding all that man does—behind it and before it and working through it—there is God. And with God are the final issues and destinies of things. Work as man will, he cannot make a plan succeed which God disowns; work as man will, he cannot make a plan fail which God approves. That is a noble and distinct faith. It is stepping across the line between fear and courage, between restlessness and peace, between intolerance and charity, when a man thoroughly, heartily, enthusiastically enters

---

[1] B. Gracian, *The Art of Worldly Wisdom*, 46.

into that faith, when he comes to believe that with all his heart and soul.

No coward soul is mine,
No trembler in the world's storm-troubled sphere:
 I see Heaven's glories shine,
And faith shines equal, arming me from fear.

O God within my breast,
Almighty, ever-present Deity!
 Life—that in me has rest,
As I—undying Life—have power in Thee!

Vain are the thousand creeds
That move men's hearts: unutterably vain;
 Worthless as withered weeds,
Or idlest froth amid the boundless main,

To waken doubt in one
Holding so fast by Thine infinity;
 So surely anchored on
The steadfast rock of immortality.

With wide-embracing love
Thy spirit animates eternal years,
 Pervades and broods above,
Changes, sustains, dissolves, creates, and rears.

Though earth and man were gone,
And suns and universes ceased to be,
 And Thou wert left alone,
Every existence would exist in Thee.

There is no room for Death,
Nor atom that his might could render void:
 Thou—Thou art Being and Breath,
And what Thou art may never be destroyed.[1]

(2) And yet we want to know what it is to believe in God and to trust Him for the great results of things. It is not to rest in idleness. Gamaliel worked. Nobody can doubt that Gamaliel went back from the Sanhedrin meeting to teach with all his might that

[1] Emily Brontë, "Last Lines."

Christianity was wrong. He had his thoughts, and he upheld them. He said, "This is the truth"; only, as he said that, he must have said also to his scholars—"There are some men here in Jerusalem—earnest, brave, enthusiastic, woefully deluded, as I think—who are asserting that not this which I tell you about the Messiah, but something else quite the opposite is true. They are asserting that the Christ has come, and that His reign has begun. I think these men are wrong. I give you my reasons. By and by you will see their fanaticism wither and dry up because no life of God is in it. But now let them alone. Believe your truth, assert it, prove it, live it: so will you do your best to kill this folly." That was Gamaliel. That is the true spirit always. To hold your truth, to believe it with all your heart, to work with all your might first to make it real to yourself and then to show its preciousness to other men, and then—not till then, but then—to leave to God the question of when and how and by whom it shall prevail; that is the true life of the true believer.

¶ Belief in God is only made our very own by our meeting the work of daily life trusting in what we believe, trying it, proving it and finding by proof that the facts we have known as bits of history which belonged to us became, when acted on, bits of our own lives, certainties inseparable from ourselves.[1]

¶ God will not have His work made manifest by cowards. Trust thyself: every heart vibrates to that iron string. Accept the place the Divine Providence has found for you; the society of your contemporaries, the connexion of events. Great men have always done so, and confided themselves childlike to the genius of their age, betraying perception that the Eternal was stirring at their heart, working through their hands, predominating in all their being. And we are now men and must accept in the highest mind the most transcendent destiny.[2]

(3) Gamaliel believed that God was the only life of this world, that all which did not live in Him must die. We do not know whether he became a Christian before he died, whether, in this life, he ever saw that the light which these poor prisoners adored was the true light, and gave himself to Christ. The legends say that he did. History seems to say that he did not. But at least we know that, if we have rightly read his character and story, he

---

[1] E. Thring, *Teaching, Learning, and Life*, 58.
[2] Emerson.

made the Christian faith more possible for other men, and he must somewhere, sometime—if not here, then beyond—have come to the truth and to the Christ Himself.

Ye, that the untrod paths have braved,
  With heart and brain unbound;
Who ask not that your souls be saved,
  But that the Truth be found;
Whose fiery cross is borne unseen,
Whose meek brows, bleeding but serene
  With only thorns are crowned;
Who, still and steadfast, stand for Right,
Though none acclaim and none requite:

Who learn how little is the sum
  Of all that Truth can teach,
And where the serried boundaries come
  That bar your utmost reach;
For whom no sage, no saint, can find
A clue to aught that lies behind;
  For whom the preachers preach
Only to leave ye at the door
That opens to their knock no more:

Who, listening in the trackless night,
  Hearing no bugle-call,
Still fight, undaunted, the good fight,
  And never fail or fall;
Who, standing on an inch of ground,
Feel the Infinities around,
  Yet dare to face it all,
And keep the life ye hold in trust
Safe from besetting moth and rust.

Life—tragic mystery of Man—
  Strange tale of joy and grief!
Chaff for the errant winds to fan,
  A bubble bright and brief,
That floats and shines and bursts unseen,
And leaves no trace where it has been;
  Like thistle-down and leaf,
That in soft airs of autumn dance,
The helpless sport of Fate and Chance.

Ye, who can see the case so clear,
   And scorn to cringe and moan,
Who follow humbly, without fear,
   The soul's behest alone;
Content to suffer for the sake
Of faithful manhood, and to make
   A loftier stepping-stone,
A straighter way, a smoother street,
For tread of unborn children's feet.

Ye, whom the children's sorrows rend,
   And who despise the smart,
Who walk uprightly to the end
   With an undoubting heart,
To take the guerdon of your pain—
Death, with no hope to live again—
   Ye have the better part,
Salt of the world, that keeps it sound!
Kings that shall yet be throned and crowned.[1]

[1] Ada Cambridge, *The Hand in the Dark*, 63.

STEPHEN.

I.

THE DEACON.

LITERATURE.

Anderson-Berry, D., *Pictures in the Book of Acts*, 110.

Banks, L. A., *Paul and his Friends* (1898), 26.

Brooke, S. A., *Short Sermons* (1892), 141.

Dykes, J. O., *From Jerusalem to Antioch* (1875), 207, **231**.

Farrar, F. W., *The Life and Work of St. Paul* (1897), 65, 76.

Lee, F. T., *The New Testament Period and its Leaders* (1913), 203.

Liddon, H. P., *Christmastide in St. Paul's* (1889), 157.

Luckock, H. M., *Footprints of the Apostles as traced by Saint Luke in the Acts*, i. (1905) 161.

Maclaren, A., *The Acts of the Apostles* (Bible Class Expositions) (1894), 73.
    „   „ *Expositions* : The Acts of the Apostles i.–xii. (1907), 212.

Meyer, F. B., *Paul* (1910), 35.

Moulton, W. F., *The Old World and the New Faith* (1896), 59.

Purves, P. C., *The Divine Cure for Heart Trouble* (1905), 262.

Rowland, A., in *Men of the New Testament* : Matthew to Timothy (1905), 261.

Sabatier, A., *The Apostle Paul* (1891), 39.

Seekings, H. S., *The Men of the Pauline Circle* (1914), 85.

Stokes, G. T., *The Acts of the Apostles* (Expositor's Bible), i. (1891) 246.

Symonds, A. R., *Fifty Sermons* (1871), **133**.

Westcott, B. F., *Peterborough Sermons* (1904), **339**.

Whyte, A., *Bible Characters* : Stephen to Timothy (1901), 9.

Wright, D., *The Power of an Endless Life* (1897), 226.

Christian World Pulpit, lxxiv. (1908) 20 (F. B. Meyer).

Churchman's Pulpit : St. Stephen, St. John the Evangelist, The Innocents, xiv. 88 (G. A. Smith), 91 (L. Hughes), 93 (H. A. Coit), 96 (H. P. Liddon), 103 (A. O. Johnston), 107 (R. C. Trench).

Dictionary of the Bible, iv. (1902) 613 (A. Grieve).

THE DEACON.

And they chose Stephen, a man full of faith and of the Holy Spirit.—
Acts vi. 5.

STEPHEN was such a martyr that we have almost forgotten that
he was anything else. The blaze of glory in which his life closed
hides from our vision the train of virtues that kindled it, and
hundreds thrill with the story of his martyrdom who consider his
long speech before the Council a tiresome repetition of Old
Testament history. But this want of emphasis, as we might call
it, or want of proportion, with which most of us treat the story of
Stephen, is not due to the Scriptures themselves. For a time
even though the Book in which the story lies is called the Acts
of the Apostles, the Apostles disappear, and the whole crisis
of which Stephen is the chief factor and which culminates in the
conversion of Saul, and the opening of the world to the Church,
and her mission to the Gentiles, is achieved without one of them
being present. Stephen stands alone to our view. Even the
deacons who have been ordained with him for this special service
are withdrawn, and Stephen stands alone. It is comparable with
only one other great loneliness in all Scripture: " I have trodden
the winepress alone; and of the people there was no man with
me." " And they all left him and fled." But you will remember
what He said: " The cup that I drink ye shall drink; and with
the baptism that I am baptized withal shall ye be baptized."
These words were first of all fulfilled in Stephen.

Now this loneliness of his is not due to any divergence or
branching off of the current of the Church's life. There is, as we
all know, a loneliness of the eddy—cut off from the main current
and turning and returning upon itself, always by itself; but
Stephen's loneliness was not of that kind. His ministry and his
career were the channel down which the main current of the
Church's life was carried swiftly to wider fields, when all the

ordinary, recognized receptacles of that life were still holding their contents stagnant. Stephen is the central figure between Jesus and Paul. Let us illustrate with another metaphor. Let us think of a prism—that three-sided bar of glass on which, if you cast a pure undivided sunbeam or ray of light, it will, by passing through it, be broken up into its component parts and colours, beautiful, full of radiance of various sorts. Stephen was such a prism in the Church life. On the one side of him you have the pure clear unbroken peace of the Church's childhood, steadfast faith and pure joy, the unbroken peace of the early days of Christianity, all simple and white as can be, but yet unconscious of its true character ; and on the other side of Stephen you have that same life, but broken, scattered and bleeding, yet bleeding so as to show its heart.

I.

The Election.

Stephen is introduced to us in connexion with a quarrel about the distribution of Church funds.

1. The work of the Apostles at Jerusalem had been growing so rapidly that they found it impracticable, at length, to give their personal attention to the distribution of charities among needy Christians, which had come to be a large and important responsibility. Many of these were Greek-speaking Jews, as they were called, or Hellenists, who had come from the various provinces around, as distinguished from the native or Palestinian Jews. A fund had been provided toward the support of the more needy converts among both these classes. Some complaint having arisen that there had been unfairness in the distribution by those who had been appointed to the work, that the widows, especially, of the Hellenists or Greek-speaking Jews were being neglected in the daily ministrations, the Apostles took steps not only to remove all grounds of complaint, but at the same time to relieve themselves of the burden of looking after the distribution of alms altogether. They proposed that the Christian people of Jerusalem should select seven men, in whom they had full confidence, to have charge of the whole business, in order that they themselves

might be left free to give their undivided attention to the work of preaching the gospel.

In asking the community to make the selection, they insisted upon these qualifications: they must be careful to select only those who were well spoken of for unimpeachable honesty, who combined learning and wisdom with a sound judgment, and who were, as became all who were to hold office in the Church, thoroughly religious-minded men.

The seven elected were Stephen, Philip, Prochorus, Nicanor, Timon, Parmenas, and Nicolas, a proselyte of Antioch. The appointment of these seven, partly because of their zeal and power, and partly because of the great freedom secured for the Apostles, led to marked successes in the progress of the Church. Not only was the number of disciples in Jerusalem greatly multiplied, but even a large number of the priests became obedient to the faith.

¶ The elect are nowhere elected for themselves. They are chosen as handers on of the good gifts to their fellows. No man invents, discovers a thing for his profit alone. He cannot do it if he would. The laws of his own nature and of the world outside him compel him to be a purveyor. His discovery becomes at once the property of mankind. A Newton, a Kepler, explore the heavens, and the new light they draw thence enlightens the world. Watt and Stephenson find the uses of steam as a force generator, and all the continents are covered with railways. Marconi wins the secret of wireless telegraphy, and ships at sea are rescued by it from the devouring fire and the engulfing wave. And the saint, finding in his soul a new experience of God, a glorious access of spiritual power, can keep no movement of it to himself. He becomes to his fellows a centre of warmth and light; the hungry multitude rushes to feed upon the divine bread he dispenses.[1]

2. The first and most prominent name in the list of deacons is that of Stephen, of whom it is expressly stated that he was "full of faith and of the Holy Spirit."

Devout expositors of Scripture have recognized in his name a prophecy of his greatness. Stephen is Stephanos, a garland or crown, in the Greek language. Garlands or crowns were given by the ancient Greeks to those who rendered good services to

[1] J. Brierley, *Faith's Certainties*, 228.

their cities, or brought fame to them by winning triumphs in the great national games. And Stephen had his name divinely chosen for him by that Divine Providence which orders all things, because he was to win in the fulness of time an imperishable garland, and to gain a crown of righteousness, and to render highest services to the Church of God by his teaching and by his testimony even unto death.

Stephen's character and abilities, as indicated in the narrative, were evidently of a high order. Up to this time his name had not occurred in Christian history. Although it is not certain that he was a Hellenist, there seems to be considerable ground for the belief that he was. He must have been a diligent and independent student of Scripture, for when at length he appears for a brief interval upon the stage, it is with fully matured views, which were, in many respects, far in advance of his contemporary Christians.

As the tradition that he had been one of the seventy disciples is valueless, we know nothing of the circumstances of his conversion to Christianity. His recognition, however, of the glorified figure which he saw in his ecstatic vision, as the figure of Him who on earth had called Himself "the Son of man," makes it probable that he was one of those who had enjoyed the advantage of hearing the living Jesus, and of drawing from its very fountainhead the river of the water of life. We would fain know more of one who, in so brief a space of time, played a part so nobly wise. But it was with Stephen as it has been with myriads of others whose names have been written in the Book of Life; they have been unknown among men, or known only during one brief epoch, or for one great deed. For a moment, but for a moment only, the first martyr steps into the full light of history. Our insight into his greatness is derived almost solely from the record of a single speech and a single day—the last speech he ever uttered, the last day of his mortal life.

¶ Stephen reminds us of a cloud, not specially distinguishable from its companions, which has helped to form the leaden covering of the sky during an overcast afternoon; we had not noticed it, indeed, the sun had set without even touching it; but when the orb of day has passed beneath the horizon, the cloud catches its departing rays, and becomes saturated and steeped with fire. See how it burns with glory! Its very heart is turned to flame! For a few moments the light remains, and it is gone! So Stephen caught for a brief space the glory of the departed Lord, and, reflecting it, was transformed into the same image.[1]

> The sweetest song was ever sung
> May soothe you but a little while:
> The gayest music ever rung
> Shall yield you but a fleeting smile.
>
> The well I digged you soon shall pass:
> You may but rest with me an hour:
> Yet drink, I offer you the glass,
> A moment of sustaining power,
>
> And give to you, if it be gain,
> Whether in pleasure or annoy,
> To see one elemental pain,
> One light of everlasting joy.[2]

II.

THE ACCUSATION.

1. Stephen's work was not confined to the distribution of alms, to which duty he had been specially called, important as that duty was. In addition to his qualifications for that office, he possessed gifts which fitted him for preaching and for performing miracles—functions which were characteristically apostolic. In this sphere he was remarkably successful, and became conspicuous because of his effectiveness and power. Many converts were won to Christ through his efforts.

It seems that the foreign-born Jews in Jerusalem had synagogues of their own, named from their respective provinces, whenever their numbers were sufficient to maintain them. To these synagogues the visiting Jews from the different countries represented would naturally resort. It was here, mainly, that Stephen preached. After he had given utterance, in setting forth the claims of Christ, to views which ran counter to some of the Jewish prejudices of his hearers, he was challenged by their

[1] F. B. Meyer, *Paul*, 35. [2] A. E., *Collected Poems*, 265.

leaders to public disputation. But it soon became evident that they were no match for him. His power and skill as a controversialist were such that they were speedily discomfited.

2. Foiled in argument, the Hellenists of the synagogues adopted the usual resource of defeated controversialists who have the upper hand. They appealed to violence for the suppression of reason. They first stirred up the people—whose inflammable ignorance made them the ready tools of any agitator—and through them aroused the attention of the Jewish authorities. Their plot was soon ripe. There was no need to secure the services of the Captain of the Temple to arrest Stephen at twilight, as he had arrested Peter and John. There was no need even to suppress all semblance of violence, lest the people should stone them for their unauthorized interference. The circumstances of the day enabled them to assume unwonted boldness, because they were at the moment enjoying a sort of interregnum from Roman authority. The approval of the multitude had been alienated by the first rumour of defective patriotism. When every rank of Jewish society had been stirred to fury by false witnesses whom these Hellenists had suborned, they seized a favourable moment, suddenly came upon Stephen, either while he was teaching in a synagogue, or while he was transacting the duties of an almoner, and led him away, apparently without a moment's pause, into the presence of the assembled Sanhedrin.

Everything was ready; everything seemed to point to a foregone conclusion. The false witnesses were at hand, and confronted their victim with the charge of incessant harangues against "this holy place" (the expression seems to show that the Sanhedrin were for this time sitting in their famous "Hall of Squares") and against the Law. In support of this general accusation, they testified that they had heard him say that Jesus —"of Nazareth," as they indignantly added to distinguish Him from others who bore that common name—"shall destroy this place, and shall change the customs which Moses delivered unto us." It is evident that these false witnesses made some attempt to base their accusation upon truth. There was good policy in this, as false witnesses in all ages have been cunning enough to see. Half truths are often the most absolute of lies.

¶ Part of the truth, as often happens in answer to a question, may be the foulest calumny. A fact may be an exception; but the feeling is the law, and it is that which you must neither garble nor belie. To tell truth, rightly understood, is not to state the true facts, but to convey a true impression; truth in spirit, not truth to letter, is the true veracity.[1]

¶ One morning about two o'clock, two men came knocking loudly at the door of Dr. Kidd's house. When it was opened by the servant, they said they had come from a poor dying woman who implored Dr. Kidd, through them, to see her before she died, as she had something on her mind she could tell to no one but himself. Like himself, the simple-hearted man that he was, he rose immediately, nothing surprised, as he had so often before been the recipient of such confessions. The men took him to the Gallowgate, and into one of its low courts, where was a stair leading down to a cellar. On reaching the top of the stair they tripped him up, so that he fell headlong, and lay stunned for some time, while the scoundrels had some persons brought to witness his emerging from a place of ill-fame! "False witnesses did rise up; they laid to my charge things that I knew not."[2]

3. It is certain that if Stephen had not used the very expressions with which they charged him, he had used others not unlike them. It is his immortal glory to have remembered the words of Jesus, and to have interpreted them aright. Against the Moral Law—the great Ten Words of Sinai, or any of those precepts of exquisite humanity and tenderness which lie scattered amid the ceremonial observances—he is not even falsely accused of having uttered a word. But Stephen did not at all intend to confine his argument to this narrow range. Rather the conviction came upon him that now was the time to speak out—that this was the destined moment in which, even if need be to the death, he was to bear witness to the inner meaning of the Kingdom of his Lord. That conviction—an inspiration from on high—gave unwonted grandeur and heavenliness to his look, his words, his attitude. His whole bearing was ennobled, his whole being was transfigured by a consciousness which illuminated his very countenance. It is probable that the unanimous tradition of the Church is correct in representing him as youthful and beautiful; but now there was

[1] R. L. Stevenson, *Truth of Intercourse.*
[2] J. Stark, *Dr. Kidd of Aberdeen,* 124.

something about him far better than youth or beauty. In the spiritual light which radiated from him he seemed to be over-shadowed by the Shechinah, which had so long vanished from between the wings of the Temple cherubim. While the witnesses had been delivering their testimony, no one had observed the sudden brightness which seemed to be stealing over him; but when the charge was finished, and every eye was turned from the accusers to a fixed gaze on the accused, all who were seated in the Sanhedrin—and one of the number, in all probability, was Saul of Tarsus—"saw his face as it had been the face of an angel."

In the sudden hush that followed, the voice of the high priest was heard putting to the accused the customary and formal question: "Are these things so?"

¶ What was the power of St. Stephen's face on which was riveted the gaze of the council? What? why, the angels are God's messengers; they see the face of the Father; they catch some expression of the uncreated beauty. Once on earth *that* had been seen in its real loveliness; no mere earthly attractiveness of exactly-chiselled feature, but the beauty of the Face which revealed, to those who gazed on the Incarnate, a Sinless Soul. Once it had awed the multitudes, subdued the intrusive band in the garden of Olives, flashed on Peter and melted him to penitence, gazed on the Magdalene and wakened her to heavenly love; now the likeness of its loveliness was seen on the face of the martyr, because in his soul was Jesus the crucified. Like Jesus in suffering, His martyr was like Him in unearthly beauty—"His face was like the face of an Angel." [1]

¶ Did you ever notice that when the Jews said that Stephen blasphemed Moses, the Lord put upon him the same glory that He put upon Moses, and his face shone? [2]

> Crimsoning the woodlands dumb and hoary,
>   Bleak with long November winds and rains,
> Lo, at sunset breathes a sudden glory,
>   Breaks a fire on all the western panes!
>
> Eastward far I see the restless splendor
>   Shine through many a window-lattice bright;
> Nearer all the farm-house gables render
>   Flame for flame, and meet in breathless light.

[1] Canon Knox Little, *Manchester Sermons*, 221.
[2] *Reminiscences of Andrew A. Bonar*, 146.

Many a mansion, many a cottage lowly,
 Lost in radiance, palpitates the same,
At the torch of beauty strange and holy,
 All transfigured in the evening flame.

Luminous, within, a marvellous vision,—
 Things familiar half-unreal show;
In the effluence of Land Elysian,
 Every bosom feels a holier glow.

Faces lose, as at some wondrous portal,
 Earthly masks, and heavenly features wear;
Many a mother like a saint immortal,
 Folds her child, a haloed angel fair.[1]

III.

THE DEFENCE.

The defence of Stephen was a speech delivered by a Jew, and addressed to a Jewish audience. We are apt to judge the Scriptures, their speeches, arguments, and discussions, by a Western standard, forgetting that Orientals argued then, and argue still, not according to the rules of logic taught by Aristotle, or by the methods of eloquence derived from the traditions of Cicero and Quintilian, but by methods and rules essentially different. What would satisfy Westerns would have seemed to them utterly worthless, just as an argument which now seems pointless and weak appeared to them absolutely conclusive. Parallels, analogies, parables, mystical interpretations were then favourite methods of argument, and if we wish to understand writers like the authors of the books of Scripture we must strive to place ourselves at their point of view, or else we shall miss their true interpretation. Let us apply this idea to Stephen's defence, which has been often depreciated because treated as if it were an oration addressed to a Western court or audience.

1. Stephen's defence is really one of the finest things in that Book of splendours—the Word of God. Carelessly reading it, one might take it for an epitome of the history of his people, and

[1] J. J. Piatt.

might imagine that, ere he had reached the application of it, Stephen, suddenly pricked by the apparent indifference and definite hostility of his audience, had thrown the rest of his speech to the winds and had poured over them a lava torrent of burning, scorching invective that had blistered and burned until they could bear the agony no more, and with one horrid, blood-curdling shout had, after a moment's pause, cast themselves upon him, and had halted not until he lay dead under a shower of stones.

True, the end came suddenly, but when we study the speech word by word, we find Stephen had by three parallel lines crept up to the enemy's weak spot, and then with a mighty climactic rush had hurled himself upon it. Notice the three parallel lines of attack:

(1) What relation has locality to the acceptable worship of God? His accusers said that he had spoken against "this holy place." Now Abraham had acceptably worshipped God, yet no possession had he in that land save for a burial-place. Moses saw in a lonely spot in the wilderness a bush burning yet not consumed, and from the heart of it came a voice, "Put off thy shoes from off thy feet, for the place whereon thou standest is holy ground." Although David had captured Jerusalem, yet he was not allowed to build a temple there, the tabernacle meanwhile being pitched in various parts of the land. Even Solomon, who built the Temple, said: "But will God in very deed dwell on the earth? behold, heaven and the heaven of heavens cannot contain thee; how much less this house that I have builded!" And what saith the prophet Isaiah many years later? Stephen tells us: "The heaven is my throne, and the earth the footstool of my feet: what manner of house will ye build me? saith the Lord: Or what is the place of my rest?" Therefore it is the Presence and not the place that makes worship acceptable.

> "Where is the Sanctuary of God?"
>   "Where two or three in My name have met,
> There is the Sanctuary of God."
>
> "Just 'two or three'? Nay, that may be
>   In garret grim or on moorland free,
> And there no Sanctuary I see."

"Where two or three in My name have met,
    There am I." " Yea, Lord, indeed
There is the Sanctuary of God."

(2) What relation has the Mosaic economy to time? Was
it permanent or transitory? His accusers said that he had
"blasphemed Moses." Stephen calls them to behold the evolu-
tion of true religion. Abraham had been called from his own
country—an idolatrous land—and brought into a strange land,
yet there he erects his altar. Then comes the covenant, with its
seal of circumcision. Next, when the performance of the promise
is nearly due, there arises another great leader who is to bring
them—now grown a great company—out of Egypt into the Land
of Promise. This was another great act of faith, yet Moses
points to a coming and yet greater Leader, for "this is that
Moses, which said unto the children of Israel, A prophet shall
God raise up unto you from among your brethren, like unto me."
As Moses brought in one economy, so his successor was to bring
in another. Thus from the altar of Abraham, which smoked
whilst dawn stained the sky, and blazed at dewy eve a beacon
light on the heights of Mamre, to the elaborate service of the
tent of meeting in the wilderness was a step ; and from the tent
that at the motion of the pillar of cloud could be taken down, to
the temple that crowned the rocky heights of Moriah, with its
stately fabric and splendid ritual, was another ; yet as these were
all material, and "the Most High dwelleth not in houses made
with hands," there must be still another step. And in that
dazzling moment when Stephen stood on that mount of spiritual
exaltation we so seldom climb, and saw with keen vision the
greatness of that step, doubtless the Paraclete brought to his
memory the words of the Lord Jesus : "The hour cometh, when
neither in this mountain, nor in Jerusalem, shall ye worship the
Father. . . . God is a Spirit : and they that worship him must
worship in spirit and truth."

To assert, then, the permanence of Moses and his economy
was to deny what he himself had said and what the history of
their nation had proved. Therefore he could not have " blasphemed
Moses" in thus speaking the truth, for no blasphemy is of the
truth.

¶ Blasphemy is an artistic effect, because blasphemy depends on a philosophical conviction. Blasphemy depends upon belief, and is fading with it. If anyone doubts this, let him sit down seriously and try to think blasphemous thoughts about Thor. I think his family will find him at the end of the day in a state of some exhaustion.[1]

(3) In thus treating him, the preacher of the truth, with contumely and cruelty, they were manifesting the continuity of that generation which had ever been the curse of their race from its beginning, when "the patriarchs, moved with jealousy against Joseph, sold him into Egypt." And here Stephen adds one more of his significant phrases—"and God was with him."

As Joseph had suffered for speaking the truth, so Moses suffered for doing the same. Let him slay the Egyptian, but let him not dare to remonstrate with a Hebrew. "Sirs, ye are brethren; why do ye wrong one to another?" For these words Moses had to flee into Midian. Yet again God was with him, and the Angel of the Lord, the pre-Incarnate Messiah, as his hearers understood the expression, appeared unto him. Yet again, although this great leader had brought them out from their bondage and the land of their slavery, they turn against him whilst he is absent talking with this selfsame "angel which spake to him in the mount Sinai." Nay, they turned away from God Himself, from His service, and from His worship.

Did his eye light upon the crafty Caiaphas and the hoary Annas, and did he realize what this generation had now done? They made much of the Moses their fathers had rejected, but what of Him whose coming Moses had foreseen and prophesied? They had crucified Him! And in a moment the three parallel lines of argument met in one mighty shock. The thunder of his voice rolled and reverberated through Gazith whilst the lightning of his eyes lighted to their dim depths their false hearts: "Ye stiffnecked and uncircumcised in heart and ears, ye do always resist the Holy Ghost: as your fathers did, so do ye. Which of the prophets did not your fathers persecute? and they killed them which shewed before of the coming of the Righteous One; of whom ye have now become betrayers and murderers; ye who received the law as it was ordained by angels, and kept it not."

[1] G. K. Chesterton, *Heretics*.

¶ "Who art Thou?" we answer to His cry of sharp pain, when, through His grace, this sense of "otherness" is brought home to us for the first time, and we find that in betraying, despising and resisting our conscience we have all along been betraying, despising and resisting our God, as real actors in that supreme tragedy which the historical Passion of Christ but symbolizes and makes visible to our imagination. Even when we are not crucifying Him afresh by flagrant sin, we are ever tormenting and persecuting Him by negligence, by recklessness, by skirting the edge of sin's precipice, so that He is never at rest or free from anxiety.[1]

2. A denunciation so scathing and so fearless, from the lips of a prisoner whose life depended on their will, might well have startled them. He could hardly have addressed them in words more calculated to kindle their fury. The very terms in which he characterized their bearing, being borrowed from their own Law and Prophets, added force to the previous epitome of their history; and to call them uncircumcised *in heart and ears* was to reject with scorn the idle fancies that circumcision alone was enough to save them from God's wrath, and that uncircumcision was worse than crime. To convict them of being the true sons of their fathers, and to brand consciences, already ulcerated by a sense of guilt, with a murder worse than the worst murder of the prophets, was not only to sweep away the prestige of an authority which the people so blindly accepted; it was to arraign his very judges and turn upon them the tables of accusation. And this he did, not only in the matter of their crucifixion of the Messiah, but also in the matter of disobedience to that Law ordained by angels of which they were at that very moment professing to vindicate the sanctity and the permanence.

¶ Robertson was never violent, never "in a passion" when he spoke, but each word fell like a sledge-hammer upon its point and on its victim. I have been told that once, when he found it necessary to denounce a man for a dastardly and wilful crime, his words had all the awfulness of a judicial sentence; that the hardened sinner writhed under them as if under a whip. To this, I think, he alludes in a letter, when he says, " Once in my life I felt a terrible might. I knew, and rejoiced to know as I spoke, that I was inflicting the sentence of a coward and a liar's hell." [2]

[1] George Tyrrell.
[2] S. A. Brooke, *Life and Letters of the Rev. F. W. Robertson*, 352.

3. The members of the Sanhedrin were roused to fury. The most excitable of Western nations can hardly imagine the raging passion that maddens a crowd of Eastern fanatics. Barely able to continue the semblance of a judicial procedure, they expressed the agony of hatred which was sawing their hearts asunder, by outward signs which are almost unknown to modern civilization —by that grinding and gnashing of the teeth possible only to human beings in whom "the ape and the tiger" are not yet quite dead.

To reason with men whose passions had thus degraded them to the level of wild beasts would have been worse than useless. The flame of holy anger in the breast of Stephen had died away as suddenly as the lightning. It was a righteous anger; it was aimed not at them but at their infatuation; it was intended not to insult but to awaken. But he saw at a glance that it had failed, and that all was now over. In one instant his thoughts had passed away to that heaven from which his inspiration had come. From those hateful faces, rendered demoniac by evil passion, his earnest gaze was turned upward and heavenward. There, in ecstasy of vision, he saw the Shechinah—the Glory of God—the Jesus "standing," as though to aid and receive him, "at the right hand of God." Transported beyond all thought of peril by that Divine epiphany, he exclaimed as though he wished his enemies to share his vision: "Behold, I see the heavens opened, and the Son of man standing on the right hand of God." At such a moment he would not pause to consider, he would not even be able to consider, the words he spoke; but whether it was that he recalled the Messianic title by which Jesus had so often described Himself on earth, or that he remembered that this title had been used by the Lord when He had prophesied to this very Sanhedrin that hereafter they should see the Son of Man sitting on the right hand of power, certain it is that this is the only passage of the New Testament where Jesus is called the Son of Man by lips other than His own.

But those high words were too much for the feelings of his audience. Stopping their ears as though to shut out a polluting blasphemy, they rose in a mass from both sides of the semi-circular range in which they sat, and with one wild yell rushed upon Stephen. There was no question any longer of a legal decision. In their rage they took the law into their own hands, and then and there dragged him off to be stoned outside the city gate.

¶ This vision of Jesus does not present Him as seated in colossal calm, like those sublime Egyptian statues that look out with folded hands, as if having finished their work, across the desert sands. The great truths of Christ's session at God's right hand were not those which the prisoner before the council most needed. What he needed he received in the shape, as well as at the moment, required. The seated Jesus has risen to His feet, as if intent to watch and help His servant. It is the attitude of service, of priestly ministry, of readiness to succour. It expresses true interest in what is going on down there in the council, and is the attitude which says, "The Lord shall help thee, and that right early." [1]

> He heeded not reviling tones,
> Nor sold his heart to idle moans,
> Tho' cursed and scorn'd, and bruised with stones:
>
> But looking upward, full of grace,
> He pray'd, and from a happy place
> God's glory smote him on the face. [2]

[1] A. Maclaren.   [2] Tennyson, "The Two Voices."

STEPHEN.

II.

The Martyr.

LITERATURE.

Armitage, W. J., *The Church Year* (1908), **16.**

Brooke, S. A., *Short Sermons* (1892), 141.

Dykes, J. O., *From Jerusalem to Antioch* (1875), **231.**

Knowlton, W. H., in *Sermons on the Gospels* : Advent to Trinity (1896), 50.

Lee, F. T., *The New Testament Period and its Leaders* (1913), 203.

Liddon, H. P., *Christmastide in St. Paul's* (1889), 157, 175.

Luckock, H. M., *Footprints of the Apostles as traced by Saint Luke in the Acts*, i. (1905) 195.

Maclaren, A., *The Acts of the Apostles* (Bible Class Expositions) (1894), 73.
      „   „ *Expositions* : The Acts of the Apostles i.–xii. (1907), 226.
      „   „ *Last Sheaves* (1903), 242.

Meyer, F. B., *Paul* (1910), 35.

Moulton, W. F., *The Old World and the New Faith* (1896), **59.**

Punshon, W. M., *Sermons*, i. (1882) 303.

Purves, P. C., *The Divine Cure for Heart Trouble* (1905), 262.

Rowland, A., in *Men of the New Testament* : Matthew to Timothy (1905), 261.

Seekings, H. S., *The Men of the Pauline Circle* (1914), 85.

Stokes, G. T., *The Acts of the Apostles* (Expositor's Bible), i. (1891) 322.

Symonds, A. R., *Fifty Sermons* (1871), 133.

Westcott, B. F., *Peterborough Sermons* (1904), 339.

Wordsworth, C., *Primary Witness to the Truth of the Gospel* (1892), 104.

Christian World Pulpit, lxxiv. (1908) 20 (F. B. Meyer).

Churchman's Pulpit : St. Stephen, St. John the Evangelist, The Innocents, xiv. 91 (L. Hughes), 96 (H. P. Liddon), 103 (A. O. Johnston), 107 (R. C. Trench).

Examiner, April 6, 1905 (J. H. Jowett).

THE MARTYR.

And they stoned Stephen, calling upon the Lord, and saying, Lord Jesus, receive my spirit.—Acts vii. 59.

THE apology of Stephen, as it is reported in the seventh chapter of the Acts of the Apostles, struck the keynote of Christian freedom, traced out the fair proportions of the Catholic Church, while the actual martyrdom of Stephen taught men that Christianity was not only the force which was to triumph, but the power in which they were to suffer, and bear, and die. Stephen's career was a type of all martyr lives, and embraces every possible development through which Christ's Church and His servants had afterwards to pass,—obscurity, fame, activity, death—fixing high the standard for all ages.

The illegality of the proceeding is beyond dispute, for, on the admission of the chief priests themselves, the Sanhedrin had no power to put to death; but it is not necessary to view it at all in the light of a judicial action. It was an outbreak of mob violence on the part of the leaders of the nation, which could easily be disavowed, if necessary, by the Council. But they probably felt assured of their safety, for there is every reason to believe that this took place during the interregnum which ensued on the recall of Pilate.

I.

STEPHEN'S DEATH.

1. The scene of Stephen's murder is sometimes located in the Valley of Jehoshaphat, near the brook Kedron, under the shadow of Olivet, and over against the Garden of Gethsemane. To that spot the gate of Jerusalem called the Gate of St. Stephen now leads. Another tradition assigns the open country north-east of

Jerusalem, on the road to Damascus and Samaria, as the place consecrated by the first death suffered for Jesus Christ. It is, however, according to the usual practice of Holy Scripture to leave this question undecided, or rather completely disregarded and overlooked. The Scriptures were not written to celebrate men or places, things temporary and transient in themselves, and without any bearing on the spiritual life. They were written for the purpose of setting forth the example of devotion, of love, and of sanctity presented by their heroes, and therefore they shroud all such scenes as that of Stephen's martyrdom in thickest darkness.

Stephen was hurried by the mob to some spot outside the Holy City, and then they proceeded in regular judicial style so far as their fury would allow them. The place, the mode of death, the first stone thrown by the witnesses, were all in exact accordance with ancient precedent and express Mosaic statute. By such formalities they sought to represent their bloody work as a solemn vengeance of national law upon a blasphemer of Jehovah.

¶ Lightfoot describes how a crier preceded a doomed man, proclaiming his crime, till the place of execution was reached; where, after he was stripped of his clothes, the two witnesses threw him violently down from a height of twelve feet, flinging upon him two large stones. If death did not at once ensue, the whole multitude lent their assistance.

We usually picture to ourselves St. Stephen as perishing beneath a deadly hail of missiles, rained upon him by an infuriated mob, before whom he is flying, just as men are still maimed or killed in street riots; and we wonder, therefore, when or where St. Stephen could have found time to kneel down and commend his spirit to Christ, or to pray his last prayer of Divine charity and forgiveness under such circumstances as those we have imagined. The Jews, however, no matter how passionate and enraged, would have feared to incur the guilt of murder had they acted in this rough-and-ready method. The witnesses must first strike their blows, and thus take upon themselves the responsibility for the blood about to be shed if it should turn out innocent. The culprits, too, were urged to confess their sin to God before they died. Stephen may have taken advantage of this well-known form to kneel down and offer up his parting prayers, which, displaying his steadfast faith in Jesus, only stirred up afresh the wrath of his adversaries, who thereupon proceeded to the last extremities.[1]

[1] G. T. Stokes, *The Acts of the Apostles*, i. 334.

2. Stephen's death was his last act of imitation of his Lord. The account of it is obviously modelled on that of Jesus. The two sayings on his lips are two recorded in St. Luke's Gospel, and the fact has been made an argument against the historical value of the narrative. But why should not the martyr have sought to die like his Lord, as well as the writer to make him die so? Possibly the place of the crucifixion was the place of the martyrdom, and, if so, the remembrance of the other sufferer would fill the dying man's heart. And if the resemblance of Stephen's words to our Lord's on the cross is noticeable, the differences also are worth observing. Christ prayed to God; Stephen, to Jesus. Christ said "I commit"; Stephen said "Take." The Lord died because He willed, and voluntarily, by a true act of will and power, gave His life into the Father's hands. That absolute voluntariness of His death is essential to its value as the sacrifice for the world's sin, and must never be obscured. But the servant says "receive," or "take," as knowing that his Lord has the keys of death, and as asking to be released. That martyr death was a Christ-copying act of forgiving love. Jesus, in His dying prayer for His murderers, said, "They know not what they do"; Stephen is silent as to the degree of knowledge and criminality, for it was not his to read hearts. Christ could infallibly determine degrees of guilt; His servant does not try, but he has learned forgiving charity from Jesus, and, first of many thousands, has spent his last breath in prayer for his murderers.

¶ When Dr. Joseph Parker was quite a young lad, he was accustomed to hold arguments with infidels outside the great iron works on Tyneside. One day an infidel challenged him upon this great passage, and said, "What did God do for Stephen?" insinuating that if there had been a God, He would have interposed to rescue him from the hands of his foes. Dr. Parker always said he believed that it was given to him in the same hour what he should say, and he answered, "What did God do for him? He gave him the power to pray for the forgiveness of those who stoned him." It was a great answer.[1]

3. "When he had said this, he fell asleep." We need quiet ere we can sleep. This man at one moment had his ears stunned

[1] F. B. Meyer.

with the fierce yells of the cruel mob, and his body tortured with the sharp, rough stones, and the next moment, how far he was from it all! What a calm ensued on the wild fury! "He fell asleep," and they might do what they liked with the corpse; Stephen was at rest.

¶ The Christian sleep of death does not seal the spirit in torpor. Seen from this side, death is sleep; seen from the other side death is awaking—waking to an intenser life than was ever experienced before; to a keenness of vitality compared with which the highest consciousness of existence and effort that we have ever known is but as the stirrings of a sleeper. "The drowsy pipe of half-awakened birds" does not contrast more with the full-throated notes with which they welcome the sun than does life here at its fullest and keenest with life yonder, with which, when we awake in Christ's likeness, we shall be satisfied.[1]

4. This is the only narrative with any fulness of detail of any death in the New Testament, save one. There is scarcely a hint as to how any of the Twelve passed away except the traitor. It is not recorded with what death Peter at last glorified God. We read in a sentence of one of the two to whom Christ had promised that they should drink of His cup, and be baptized with His baptism—"Herod killed James, the brother of John, with the sword." On the career of one who fills a larger space in the history of the Church than any other of them the curtain falls before the final sentence is pronounced and shuts out from our view the procession to the headsman's block on the Ostian Road. In the solitary instance of Stephen is there anything approaching to a description of a dying scene. Is it wrong to infer from this that in the New Testament greater importance is attached to the manner of a man's life than to the manner of a man's death; that in his conquering temptation in living, even more than in his triumphing over fear in dying, is the power of the grace of Christ displayed?

> For now "the former things have passed away,"
> And man, forgetting that which lies behind,
> And ever pressing forward, seeks to find
> The prize of his high calling. Send a ray

[1] A. Maclaren, *Last Sheaves*, 249.

From art's bright sun to fortify the day,
And blaze the trail to every mortal mind.
The new religion lies in being kind;
Faith stands and works, where once it knelt to pray;
Faith counts its gain, where once it reckoned loss;
Ascending paths its patient feet have trod;
Man looks within, and finds salvation there.
Release the suffering Saviour from the Cross,
And give the waiting world its Radiant God.[1]

5. "And devout men buried Stephen, and made great lamentation over him." They were not disciples, but probably Hellenistic Jews, perhaps from the synagogue whose members had disputed with Stephen and had dragged him to the Council. His words or death may have touched them, as many a time the martyr's fire has lighted others to the martyr's faith. Stephen was like Jesus in his burial by non-disciples, as he had been in his death.

Foremost and nearest to His throne
By perfect robes of triumph known,
And likest Him in look and tone,
    The holy Stephen kneels,
With steadfast gaze, as when the sky
Flew open to his fainting eye,
Which, like a fading lamp, flash'd high,
    Seeing what death conceals.

Well might you guess what vision bright,
Was present to his raptured sight,
Even as reflected streams of light
    Their solar source betray—
The glory which our God surrounds,
The Son of Man, th' atoning wounds—
He sees them all; and earth's dull bounds
    Are melting fast away.

He sees them all—no other view
Could stamp the Saviour's likeness true.
Or with His love so deep embrue
    Man's sullen heart and gross—
"Jesu, do Thou my soul receive:
Jesu, do Thou my foes forgive:"
He who would learn that prayer, must live
    Under the holy Cross.

[1] E. W. Wilcox, *Poems of Experience*, 54.

He, though he seem on earth to move,
Must glide in air like gentle dove,
From yon unclouded depths above
    Must draw his purer breath;
Till men behold his angel face
All radiant with celestial grace,
Martyr all o'er, and meet to trace
    The lines of Jesus' death.[1]

II.

THE VALUE OF HIS DEATH.

The events which followed upon Stephen's death are instructive in many ways. But they teach us more especially one of the principles of God's government of the world. They teach us that, so far as this sphere of existence, at any rate, is concerned, evil is permitted to exist and to triumph, only that sooner or later, in one way or another, good may be brought out of it.

1. There can be no doubt that the death of Stephen must have appeared at the moment to those first Christians as marking a great triumph of evil. The withdrawal of a man of such power and activity from this earthly scene, where his peculiar capacities were, as it seemed, so greatly needed; the high-handed violence which precipitated his death; the evident resolve of the leading minds in Jerusalem to exterminate Christianity—all that might well have inspired widespread alarm and discouragement.

At first, indeed, it might have seemed that the only consequence of Stephen's death would be the outbreak of a general persecution, which might stamp Christianity out of existence. The Sanhedrin, now thoroughly aroused against the disciples of Christ and their religion, determined to suppress the new sect altogether. Accordingly a general proscription of the sect was issued. Meetings were broken up, men and women were arrested and imprisoned, and Christians were persecuted throughout the land, even to distant cities. In consequence of this persecution, a great body of disciples fled from the city, most of them scattering through Judæa and Samaria, but many of them going much

---

[1] J. Keble, *The Christian Year* (St. Stephen's Day).

farther, even to Phœnicia, Cyprus, and Antioch in northern Syria.
The Apostles themselves seem to have continued in Jerusalem,
evidently considering it their duty to remain at the headquarters
of their work.

Yet all these events, disheartening as they must have been to
Christian believers at the time, turned out, providentially, to be
the most effective means of extending a knowledge of the new
religion. Wherever these persecuted believers went, they continued to bear their testimony to the faith as before, and many
were converted to it, not merely of Jews and Jewish proselytes,
but some even from the ranks of the Gentiles. But for the death
of Stephen and the subsequent persecution, these pioneers of the
faith would perhaps have been content to stay at home, basking
in the moral sunshine that their religion had brought to them,
enjoying and fondling it in private, while making no effort for the
spiritual well-being of others at a distance. Now the dangers
which awaited Christians in Jerusalem, the stir and ferment
which had been created by the words and the sufferings of
Stephen, the spectacle of his tranquil, saintly death, have all had
their effect. The Church of Jerusalem has gone into exile, and
almost every one of its members is perforce a missionary.

> By Heaven directed, by the world reviled,
> Amidst the wilderness they sought a home,
> Where beasts of prey and men of murder roam,
> And untamed Nature holds her revels wild.
> There on their pious toil their Master smiled,
> And prospered them, unknown or scorned of men,
> Till in the satyr's haunt, and dragon's den,
> A garden bloomed, and savage hordes grew mild.
> So, in the guilty heart, when heavenly grace
> Enters, it ceaseth not till it uproot
> All evil passions from each hidden cell;
> Planting again an Eden in their place,
> Which yields to men and angels pleasant fruit,
> And God Himself delighteth there to dwell.

2. Such, then, was the effect on the Church. But what of
Saul, what of the young Pharisee at whose feet the witnesses had
cast their raiment and who had taken a leading part in the
persecution?

Saul goes on persecuting, arresting, imprisoning, accusing. But there is something significant, something to arrest attention, in his feverish activity. Men often try to crush a conviction which is taking shape within them, and which they dread to recognize, by talking or acting violently in an opposite direction. They hope that the conscience will obey the tongue or the arms, or that, at least, its voice will be silenced amid the din of work. But Saul has heard that speech before the Sanhedrin; and he knows that it was not answered by arguments, but only by stones. Saul has marked the bearing of the martyr in his last moments, while he himself stood by keeping the raiment of them that slew him. Let us be patient with him. He will make a few more Christian homes desolate, and then he will be on the road to Damascus.

It has ever been the faith of the Church that Saul was the fruit of Stephen's prayers. "Si Stephanus non orasset, Ecclesia Paulum non haberet," was one of its sayings. The quenching of Stephen's light was the kindling of a yet brighter lamp for the illumination of the world.

> It does not die,
> That Prayer rejected.
> Like a hovering dove
> It is drawn up towards the invisible flight
> Of benedictions, breathings of pure Love,
> The Angels of the Earth, continually
> Streaming above us, potent, unsuspected.
> Yet, as the Mother's prayer not unfulfilled
> Could float upon the night,
> It enters where she neither knew nor willed.
>
> On a mean bed
> A boy lies reading,
> His candle-end
> Flickers on the gloom.
> Darkness is round, has always been around him,
> Drunkenness, lies, dishonesty;
> But the persistent Life within him said,
> "Come forth out of this tomb!"
> And he all blind followed where it was leading.
> In his lone night the Mother's Prayer has found him,
> And he immediately
> Knows there is light somewhere, somewhere a friend.[1]

[1] Margaret L. Woods, *Collected Poems*, 20.

III.

STEPHEN'S CHARACTER.

1. Stephen is described by certain significant phrases.

(1) He was a man "*full of faith.*" It was faith in the highest degree. While others showed timidity and were in danger of wavering, he stood firm as a rock against every withering blast of error and storm of unbelief. His supreme trust was in Christ, in whom he confided with all his heart, and to whom he clung as the only One who could help and save. He was a man of faith, in whom that marvellous faculty, which is the eye of the soul, was fully developed, by which he saw, strange paradox as it may appear, the Invisible, just as some animals have the strange power of seeing in the dark.

There's a star overseas like a dew-drop new-hung on a bud
    that uncloses;
There's a fire in the turrets of heaven; there's a flush on the
    breast of the sea;
And the gates of the sun-rise are filled with a flame as of
    myriad roses,
That kindles ineffable vistas, a world re-created for me.

There's a hill in its vestment of dew-fall that kneels like a
    priest to the altar;
Low bird-cries resound in the silence, frail tendrils reach forth
    to the light;
The fields flower-breasted are fragrant, and fresh the faint
    breezes that falter:—
Life's faith in the future is perfect, life's dream of eternity
    bright!

If ours were the faith of the petals unfolding, the nest and its
    treasure,—
The faith all revealed and illumined, the faith that alone
    makes us free,—
What divine understanding were ours of the sun-light that
    flows without measure,
Of the silver of moon-light that rings down the resonant floor
    of the sea!

What divine understanding for life; for the world how
  majestic a meaning;
What truths by the way-side; in martyrdom, poverty, pain
  what delight;
What poems in the midnight; what visions revealed that the
  darkness was screening,
As like fire-tinged incense the dawn-mists flush deep round
  the knees of the night!

O, beware! for the safety we cherish is false:—we are blind!
  we are soothless!—
Have we learned how the fields are made fruitful?   Are we
  aimed to life's ultimate goal?—
O for faith to accept for our lives not an ecstasy less, not a
  truth less,
Than the world and the senses afford us, than are sphered in
  the scope of the soul![1]

(2) He was not only "full of faith," but also "*full of the Holy
Spirit.*"   And rich in privilege as the life of faith is, this is a
higher step in Christian attainment.   For while faith is the hand
of the soul clasping God, or the eye of the soul looking unto
Jesus; to be "full of the Holy Ghost" is to enjoy the actual
presence of God in the heart.   Faith is a great gift of the Holy
Spirit, but to be "full of the Holy Ghost" is to possess the fulness
of His spiritual gifts.

          I believe in Thee!
            Life's Lord, Life's Giver,
            For aye and ever
Source and Fountain of boundless sanctity,
Pouring high sapience and wisdom royally
Down on Thy suppliant people, the blest, the free.
Thou who art fain to hallow all men, oh, hallow me,
          My God, I believe in Thee.[2]

(3) It is no wonder, then, that Stephen is described as being
"*full of grace,*" as reflecting in his life the life of Christ in all its
singular charm of gentleness and strength.   And with grace he
had "*power,*" a strong word in the Greek, which we have carried

---

[1] G. C. Lodge, *Poems and Dramas*, ii. 155.
[2] E. Hickey, *Later Poems*, 52.

into English, in a term which deals with the science of forces, "dynamics," and in the expression "dynamite," a material which possesses great explosive force.

> Grant us such grace that we may work Thy Will
>   And speak Thy words and walk before Thy Face,
> Profound and calm, like waters deep and still:
>   Grant us such grace.
>
> Not hastening and not loitering in our pace
> For gloomiest valley or for sultriest hill,
>   Content and fearless on our downward race.
>
> As rivers seek a sea they cannot fill
>   But are themselves filled full in its embrace,
> Absorbed, at rest, each river and each rill:
>   Grant us such grace.[1]

(4) Stephen was a man "*full of wisdom.*" This was a necessary qualification on the part of men who were called to the conduct of affairs. Their chief duties were administrative. We usually think of Stephen as a beautiful and lofty character, standing on a pedestal above others in true nobility of life, in a spirit of detachment from mundane affairs. But we do well to remember that he was specially selected on account of his discretion, because of his aptitude for practical business and his capacity for work.

Stephen, as the record of his trial shows, was possessed of marvellous intellectual powers, coupled with wonderful facility of expression and utterance. His eloquence, when he stood before his judges, was irresistible. They "were not able to resist the wisdom and the spirit by which he spake." His adversaries could not understand it, but Stephen, like Micah, might have said, " I truly am full of power by the Spirit of the Lord," as his burning thoughts followed one another, "in fit words and heavenly eloquence."

¶ The first and highest rule of all deed and speech, the more necessary to be followed the higher and more numerous our posts, is: an ounce of wisdom is worth more than tons of cleverness. It is the only sure way, though it may not gain so much applause.

[1] Christina G. Rossetti, *Verses*, 114.

The reputation of wisdom is the last triumph of fame. It is enough if you satisfy the wise, for their judgment is the touch-stone of true success.[1]

(5) We might also say that Stephen was a man *full of love.* His triumph over force was the triumph of forgiving love. It is the very royalty of victory when love pours its rain of forgiveness upon the place where cruelty and wrong have stained our lives, and washes out the stain. No nobler thing is known on earth than the soul which forgives and forgets an injury, or remembers it only to use it as a means of redeeming the injurer. For that is the magnificence of God's triumph over us. We refuse His love; we neglect His voice; we set aside His education. Unmoved, His love soars serene above our wrongs, and if it punishes, as it often must, punishes with the unwavering tenderness that regenerates our hearts, burning up all our chaff, and gathering, in the harvest of eternity, our wheat into His garner.

> Triumphant Love! Now comes apace
> Thy flood-tide, that will leave no trace
> Of Time and Death, dead, hand in hand.
> Half-rooted in the desolate sand,
> Heart-shapen, blooms Thy garb of grace,
>
> Till, by Thy waves, that conquer space,
> The robe of that sweet flower's embrace
> Be freed from Time's cold rocky strand,
>   Triumphant Love.
>
> Sole King of an immortal race,
> Though men thy mortal name debase!
> Thy feet upon the rock now stand,
> Thy wings the infinite have spanned!
> Unveil Thy power, reveal Thy face,
>   Triumphant Love![2]

2. Stephen stood the supreme test that can be applied to any life. He was " faithful unto death." We may not feel with Bishop Woodford, that " if he had failed in the trial, humanly speaking, Christianity would have failed." We cannot tell

[1] B. Gracian, *The Art of Worldly Wisdom*, 54.
[2] A. Matheson, *Maytime Songs*, 13.

whether Stephen realized that for a brief hour the world's destinies had rested with him. But of this we are sure, that a great crisis had come, that as—

Once to every man and nation comes the moment to decide,
In the strife of Truth with Falsehood, for the good or evil side,

so it came to Stephen. He was more than conqueror through Him that loved him.

3. It was Jesus who, from the cross as from a pulpit, taught to Stephen the law of devout living; and it was Jesus, too, who, when His scholar had well learned that rule and fully practised it, rose from His throne to crown him. Before us we too have the same Unchanged One to gaze at; nor can the long procession of succeeding saints hide Him from our eyes. He who for the joy set before Him endured the cross, has set open to us also the gates of everlasting life. From beside the throne of God He beckons to us as He beckoned Stephen. Stephen, by His grace, followed and entered in, but, entering, did not break the bridge or shut the gate behind him. Martyrs we may not be unto blood; but witnesses, and sufferers, too, for Christ we all must be. In our lives, if not in our deaths, we surely need great Stephen's steadfast courage, and his clear-eyed faith, and his heaven-piercing hope, and his Godlike charity. After such life, death shall be sweet as a falling on sleep, and beyond it are the crown laid up, and the conqueror's palm, and the welcoming Lord.

Fear not, O little flock, the foe
Who madly seeks your overthrow,
   Dread not his rage and power:
What though your courage sometimes faints,
His seeming triumph o'er God's saints
   Lasts but a little hour.

Be of good cheer; your cause belongs
To Him who can avenge your wrongs,
   Leave it to Him our Lord.
Though hidden yet from all our eyes,
He sees the Gideon who shall rise
   To save us, and His word.

As true as God's own word is true,
Nor earth nor hell with all their crew
　Against us shall prevail.
A jest and byword are they grown;
God is with us, we are His own,
　Our victory cannot fail.

Amen, Lord Jesus, grant our prayer!
Great Captain, now Thine arm make bare;
　Fight for us once again!
So shall Thy saints and martyrs raise
A mighty chorus to Thy praise,
　World without end.　Amen.[1]

[1] *Gustavus Adolphus' Battle-Song* (Lyra Germanica, 17).

PHILIP THE EVANGELIST.

LITERATURE.

Baker, E., *The Revivals of the Bible* (1906), 146.

Bourdillon, F., *Short Sermons* (1904), 19.

Burrell, D. J., *The Cloister Book* (1909), 58.

Davis, W. H., in *Sermons by the Monday Club*, 17th Ser. (1892), 296.

Farrar, F. W., *The Life and Work of St. Paul* (1897), 144.

Goulburn, E. M., *The Acts of the Deacons* (1867), 213.

Hiley, R. W., *A Year's Sermons*, iii. (1897) 275.

Hooton, W. S., *Turning-Points in the Primitive Church* (1910), 58, 68.

Horton, R. F., *The Hidden God* (1905), 127.

Lee, F. T., *The New Testament Period and its Leaders* (1913), 221.

Luckock, H. M., *Footprints of the Apostles as traced by Saint Luke in the Acts*, i. (1905) 212.

McGarvey, J. W., *Sermons* (1894), 122.

Mackintosh, H. R., *Life on God's Plan* (1909), 102.

Maclaren, A., *Expositions* : The Acts of the Apostles i.–xii. (1907), 236 ; xiii.–end (1907), 222.

Maurice, F. D., *The Acts of the Apostles* (1894), 96, 110.

Milligan, G., in *Men of the Bible* : Some Lesser-known Characters (1904), 237.

Morrison, G. H., *The Footsteps of the Flock* (1904), 324.

Moulton, W. F., *The Old World and the New Faith* (1896), 61.

Noble, F. A., *Typical New Testament Conversions* (1901), 137.

Stokes, G. T., *The Acts of the Apostles* (Expositor's Bible), i. (1891) 346, 398.

Taylor, W. M., *Peter the Apostle* (1891), 230.

Twitchell, J. E., in *Sermons by the Monday Club*, 17th Ser. (1892), 284.

Vaughan, C. J., *The Church of the First Days* (1890), 157, 177, 484.

Dictionary of the Apostolic Church, i. (1915) 373 (C. L. Feltoe).

Dictionary of the Bible, iii. (1900) 836 (H. Cowan).

PHILIP THE EVANGELIST.

Philip the evangelist, who was one of the seven.—Acts xxi. 8.

PHILIP the Evangelist, also called Philip the Deacon, must be carefully distinguished from Philip the Apostle. There are many interesting things told us in the Gospels about Philip the Apostle during the lifetime of his Master. But after our Lord's ascension to Heaven we are not told a word about him. He is mentioned along with the rest of the Apostles who met together to choose a successor to Judas; he was present on the day of Pentecost when the Holy Ghost came down upon the Twelve; and then he passes out of history. But Philip the Evangelist is a very different man.

The life of this Philip, as recorded, is a very remarkable one. It is divided into two unequal parts: one full of conspicuous service, one passed in absolute obscurity. Like the moon in its second quarter, part of the disc is shining silver and the rest is invisible. Let us put together the notices of him.

I.

IN SAMARIA.

The account of Philip's character and life is given in a very brief form in Scripture, but it is full of encouragement to us, because we cannot all expect to be a Paul, and very few of us expect even to be a Stephen; but might not all of us be a Philip?

1. The Evangelist bears a name which makes it probable that he was not a Palestinian Jew, but one of the many who, of Jewish descent, had lived in Gentile lands and contracted Gentile habits and associations. We first hear of him as one of the seven who

were chosen by the Church, at the suggestion of the Apostles, in order to meet the grumbling of that section of the Church called Hellenists, who complained that their people were being neglected in the distribution of alms. He stands in that list next to Stephen, who was obviously the leader.

These seven were never called "deacons" in the New Testament, though it is supposed that they were the first holders of that office. It is instructive to note how their office came into existence. It was created by the Apostles, simply as the handiest way of getting over a difficulty. They were appointed to deal with a temporary difficulty and to distribute alms when necessary; and their office dropped when it was no longer required, as was probably the case when, very soon after, the Jerusalem Church was scattered.

2. Philip was the next after Stephen to give a decided impulse to an enlarged conception, among the early Christians, of the scope of the gospel. Stephen had made a brief but notable campaign, for the times, of progressive ideas, declaring boldly against the exclusive spirit of the Jews; repudiating their claim to a monopoly of the Divine favour; setting forth clearly the true relation of Judaism to Christianity—the former designed to be of but temporary duration, the latter intended to be permanent. In the advanced views which he advocated, he may properly be regarded as the precursor of the Apostle Paul, the great champion of an open-door Christianity for the whole world. But if the first martyr was the forerunner of the great Apostle in the realm of progressive ideas, Philip was his precursor in the application of the same, both in zealous missionary operations and, especially, in opening the door of the Church to non-Jewish believers.

¶ From Wesley's death up to that time the impulse for foreign evangelization had come from one moving spirit, and the responsibility for supporting such enterprises rested on one man's shoulders. Dr. Coke was the Atlas upbearing the burden. Small in stature, but small in nothing else, warm-hearted, wide-minded, of indefatigable energy, he was the sole superintendent of missions, and the principal, if not the only, collector of subscriptions; for while the preachers made annual collections in the chapels he went his rounds from door to door. The shores washed by the Atlantic were well acquainted with him, for he had crossed the ocean eighteen times, but the Eastern Indies knew him not. Ceylon and Java were beckoning him. He resolved to visit them. The Conference at first withheld consent. He was sixty-seven; the voyage was perilous; the work at home would suffer by his absence. But, bursting into tears, and exclaiming, "You will break my heart," his sorrow won his reluctant brethren over, and they allowed him to go, little thinking that they would see his face no more.[1]

3. The preaching of the liberal-minded Stephen not unnaturally stirred up the more narrow and conservative Jews. They were inflamed against him. To them he seemed to be the setter forth of dangerous, heretical views, views which threatened the very existence of the Jewish faith. The outcome of all was, first, the martyrdom of Stephen, then a persecution of all bearing the Christian name. In consequence, many of the Christians fled from Jerusalem. But so filled were they with the love of Christ, and with zeal for His cause, that they continued to bear witness for Him and to preach wherever they went. Among those who thus went forth was Philip. He went into Samaria, perhaps to the city of that name.

The Samaritans were a peculiar people. They were neither Jews nor Gentiles, though they were descendants from both—*i.e.* from colonists from the East whom the Assyrian king had placed in the land of Israel when the leading inhabitants of the country were carried into captivity at the time of the fall of Samaria in 721 B.C., and from the Jews whom the king permitted to remain.

At first these colonists continued, in their new home, the idolatrous practices in which they had been reared, but later they partially embraced the worship of Jehovah as the recognized God of the land. They accepted the law of Moses and practised the Jewish rite of circumcision. The Pentateuch constituted their only Scripture, and they had a temple of their own and temple services on Mount Gerizim. But although their religion and their worship were perverted by the admixture of foreign elements, and they were isolated from their distinctively Jewish neighbours by a feud which had continued for many generations, there was still not a little which they had in common with them in the matter of religious worship, and they looked for the same Messiah. Yet,

[1] E. J. Brailsford, *Richard Watson*, 62,

notwithstanding their partial Hebrew descent and their partial acceptance of the tenets of Judaism, they were rigidly excluded from the Jewish Church, and were even denied the privileges accorded to the heathen of becoming proselytes to the Jewish faith.

Enough has been said to show that a strict Jew of the high orthodox school would have had a vast deal of prejudice to surmount in carrying to Samaria the tidings of the Kingdom of God and the gracious offers of the gospel. But Philip the Evangelist did not belong to this school. His circumstances, his position, and his office would all give him wider sympathies than were to be found among Pharisees and Hebrews of the Hebrews.

¶ When Henry Ward Beecher came to Brooklyn there was no place for coloured men and women in the theatre except the negro pen; no place in the opera; no place in the church except the negro pew; no place in any lecture hall; no place in the first-class car on the railways. The white omnibus of Fulton Ferry would not allow coloured persons to ride in it. They were never allowed to sit even in the men's cabin on the boats. He invited Fred. Douglass, one day, in those times, to come to church here. "I should be glad to, sir," said he; "but it would be so offensive to your congregation." "Mr. Douglass, will you come? and if any man objects to it, come up and sit on my platform by me. You will always be welcome there."[1]

4. Philip had been chosen for the office of a deacon because he was full of the Holy Ghost; and now the gift of the Holy Ghost seems to have been imparted to him in larger measure, for he was able to work miracles. This gift, added to the great earnestness of his preaching, drew multitudes to listen to his ministry. Thus the faith in Jesus Christ, instead of being stamped out, increased with wondrous power. Instead of being only a server of tables, a distributer of alms-money, Philip became an Evangelist, a teacher of the gospel to a whole city. They were astonished at the miracles he wrought, they were overpowered by his telling words; unclean spirits cried out with a loud voice and came out of many that were possessed of them; many that were afflicted with palsies and that were lame were healed. The word "gospel" means good news, and no wonder that there was a great joy in that city.

[1] N. D. Hillis, *Lectures and Orations by Henry Ward Beecher*, 221.

¶ The Ways of the Lord are unsearchable, but He reveals them to those that fear Him, and whatever may be manifest to any other, this I am certainly persuaded of, that through all these things the Gospel of Truth shall go on to prosperity, and though the day be dark and gloomy and the wrath of the wicked be great, yet the bound is sure beyond which they cannot pass, and though we that remain alive to this day were all dissolved and were all rolled together in the dust, yet that Life and Power in which we have believed and that Everlasting Truth of which we have testified and for which we have suffered, shall never be extinguished or rooted out, but it shall find other persons to declare it from generation to generation while the sun and moon endure.[1]

5. Among those who professed to be converted to the faith, and received baptism at his hands, was Simon Magus or Simon the magician.

This Simon is never named again in the New Testament; but a multitude of legends, more or less improbable, have gathered round his name, and fancy seems to have run wild in the marvels it attributed to him. So powerful was his influence, it was said, that he was able to convert human beings into brute beasts; that he could make lifeless statues speak; that he claimed to be able to fly, and exhibited his power in the presence of Nero, but was arrested in his flight by the prayer of St. Peter; that he was buried alive at his own express desire in the firm assurance that he would burst the bands and rise from his grave. He has been designated "the hero of the romance of heresy"; and we may judge of the wildness of his heresy from a single sentence in one of the Early Fathers, who has summed up his extraordinary claims in the few words: "He was glorified by many as God, for he taught the people that it was he who appeared to the Jews as God the Son, who had come down to Samaria as the Father, and had come to other nations as the Holy Ghost."

We find him in the sacred narrative at a city of Samaria, the inhabitants of which country were said to have been a most simple-minded and credulous folk, especially susceptible to impressions from anything of a supernatural character. It was an age, we must remember, when thaumaturgy was a rôle of the

[1] Francis Howgill.

time. Our Lord Himself had prepared men for a great development of deception and imposture ; false Christs and false prophets were to arise and, if it were possible, deceive even the very elect. Simon was the foremost among them ; he had been trained in the art of magic or sorcery in its degenerate form, and had no difficulty in gaining a complete mastery over the Samaritans by the charms and spells which he practised.

In the midst of his wonder-working he was suddenly interrupted by the arrival of Philip the Evangelist, whose signs and miracles completely eclipsed all that he had done. Indeed, he was so impressed by their superiority that, in the hope of becoming initiated into the secret, he was baptized, and joined himself to Philip's company.

6. That Simon's adherence to Philip implied no real change of heart is made clear by what followed. The church at Jerusalem, on hearing of Philip's success, sent down Peter and John to report upon this latest extension of the Christian Kingdom, and to confirm the new believers. When Simon Magus saw that by the laying on of the Apostles' hands the Holy Ghost was given—the gift being probably accompanied by outward signs—he attempted to bargain for that gift for himself, that by the imposition of *his* hands these powers might be conferred.

The proposal was in the highest degree dishonouring to God. It put the operations of the Holy Ghost on a level with the deceptions of men ; it proposed to make merchandise of that which was the richest gift of the Divine goodness ; it wanted to turn to individual aggrandisement that special blessing which God has bestowed upon the Church to assist its progress in the world. Therefore Peter was utterly shocked by the blasphemy of the man, and exclaimed, with holy indignation, "Thy silver perish with thee, because thou hast thought to obtain the gift of God with money."

We are surprised, perhaps, that Philip should have baptized Simon. It may have been that in his eagerness to gain over such an influential convert, he was less circumspect than he should have been ; or that, if he had doubts of his sincerity, in that spirit of charity which has inspired the Church from the beginning, which permits us to bury a sinful man with words of hope and blessing, Philip accepted Simon on his own profession, and refused himself to sit in judgment upon him.

But where Philip was gentle, because he had no proof of his insincerity, Peter was severe, because there was no longer any doubt: "Repent therefore of this thy wickedness, and pray the Lord, if perhaps the thought of thy heart shall be forgiven thee. For I see that thou art in the gall of bitterness and in the bond of iniquity." But there was no true response to the appeal; no manly confession of his sin; no compunction for the deception with which he had bewitched the people; no publican's prayer and broken-hearted cry for forgiveness; nothing but a slavish fear of threatened punishment; not a hint that a word of supplication to the God of mercy crossed the threshold of his own lips; and he passes out from the sacred story like the ghost in Hamlet, "unhousel'd, disappointed, unaneled."

7. Like John the Baptist before our Lord, Philip withdraws behind the scenes when the two Apostles come upon the stage. There is something very touching in this willingness to be eclipsed, which it were an injustice to the character of the Evangelist to pass over. Philip might have naturally felt that he had borne the burden and heat of the day in Samaria, and that the success which the Apostles met with there was owing to their finding all things made ready to their hand. He had dug the soil, and thrown in the seed, and watered it, until the field was white to the harvest; and now it remained for St. Peter and St. John only to put in the sickle, and mow down the corn. Their doing so seems to have been watched by him without any of that grudging jealousy which mere nature in such circumstances must have prompted. Philip's aim in his ministry was just the reverse of Simon's aim in his sorcery. The latter sought popularity and influence for himself; the former sought to attract men to the Saviour. And, accordingly, any increase in the knowledge, any confirmation in the faith of the Saviour, was to Philip a matter of pure joy, because he sought the people's souls, and not their suffrages.

> Down the furrow strides the sower—
> From his hand the live seeds leap—
> In his heart the hope of harvest
> Little knowing who will reap!

Harvest comes in, teeming—teeming—
  Golden stalk and laden ear,
But the sower's sleeping—sleeping
  In the earth he held so dear!

So through life, if I am sowing,
  What to me the toil or gain?
If my brothers reap the harvest
  I shall not have lived in vain![1]

¶ "Great poets," says the author of Thalaba, "have no envy;
little ones are full of it!"[2]

II.

ON THE WAY TO GAZA.

1. Philip had no special Divine command either to flee to, or
to preach in, Samaria, but "an angel of the Lord," and afterwards
"the Spirit," directed him to the Ethiopian statesman. God
rewards faithful work with more work. Samaria was a borderland
between Jew and Gentile, but in preaching to the eunuch Philip
was on entirely Gentile ground. So great a step in advance
needed clear command from God to impel to it and to justify it.

Philip might well wonder why he should be taken away from
successful work in a populous city, and despatched to the lonely
road to Gaza. But he obeyed at once. He knew not for what
he was sent there, but that ignorance did not trouble or retard
him. When the Angel of the Lord said: "Go toward the south,"
this is the simple record which follows: "And he arose and
went."

¶ Time was when God spake to His people in dreams and
visions of the night; who shall say that He does not speak in like
manner now? God has so many voices! He speaks in nature;
He speaks through conscience to the inner man; He speaks in the
notes of the church bell. He speaks in the Scriptures and by
the Holy Spirit. All good impulses and high aspirations are as
Voices of God. The vital question is not how He speaks, but
shall we straightway heed Him?

[1] P. J. O'Reilly, *Harvest.*
[2] J. G. Lockhart, *Life of Scott,* iii. 45.

If He bids us remain in Samaria, so be it. If He bids us go down to Gaza by the way that is desert, so be it. The habit of heeding is the pathway of life; and the secret of character is to run when He bids us.

> I said, "Let me walk in the field";
>   He said, "Nay, walk in the town."
> I said, "There are no flowers there";
>   He said, "No flowers, but a crown."
>
> I said, "But the skies are black,
>   There is nothing but noise and din."
> And He wept as He sent me back,
>   "There is more," He said; "there is sin."
>
> I said, "But the air is thick,
>   And fogs are veiling the sun."
> He answered, "Yet souls are sick,
>   And souls in the dark undone."
>
> I said, "I shall miss the light,
>   And friends will miss me, they say."
> He answered me, "Choose to-night,
>   If I am to miss you, or they."
>
> I pleaded for time to be given;
>   He said, "Is it hard to decide?
> It will not seem hard in heaven
>   To have followed the steps of your Guide."
>
> I cast one look at the field,
>   Then set my face to the town.
> He said, "My child, do you yield?
>   Will you leave the flowers for the crown?"
>
> Then into His hand went mine,
>   And into my heart came He,
> And I walked in a light divine,
>   The path I feared to see.[1]

¶ I like the hopefulness of Philip, as he advances to his new task. Remember, he had just been imposed upon by a bad man at Samaria, when Simon the Sorcerer, a kind of false Christ,

[1] George MacDonald.

had tried to buy the Holy Spirit. That was a bitterly disappoint-
ing case, yet Philip went on evangelizing just the same. He
would not throw up his mission in disgust because Simon had
turned out a sham; here he is, a few days later, guiding an earnest
man to the Redeemer. One meets persons occasionally who have
never been able to get over some glaring instance of hypocrisy in
a professing Christian. For the remainder of their life it forms the
favourite arrow in their quiver. They produce the well-worn
anecdote in season and out, and make it the basis of extremely
dismal conclusions as to the sincerity and trustworthiness of
Christians as a body. Now in this there is very little sense. The
merchant who has been defrauded once does not feel called upon
to suspect each new customer till he proves himself honest. Now
and then we have a wet summer, but it is only foolish persons
who go about saying that the fine old-fashioned seasons are gone
for ever. An exception is exceptional. This or that instance of
religious inconsistency counts for one, but it counts for no more
than one. If it makes a great noise, that is because it is so
unusual. When a railway accident happens, the papers are full
of it, and nervous people vow they will never set foot in a train
again; yet thousands of trains are running safely all the time. So
we ought not to allow an isolated case of religious breakdown,
which certainly may occur, to bulk too largely in our thoughts.
Consider rather the unnumbered multitudes whose lives from day
to day are being made beautiful through faith in the Son of God.
Whatsoever things are true, honourable, lovely, and of good report
—think on these things.[1]

2. Gaza has always been the gateway of Palestine. Invader
after invader when passing from Egypt to Palestine has taken
Gaza in his way. It is still the trade route to Egypt, along which
the telegraph line runs. In the days of Philip it was the direct
road for travellers from Jerusalem to the Nile and the Red Sea.
There were then, and there are still, two great roads leading from
Jerusalem to Gaza, one a more northern road, through villages and
cultivated land, the other a desert road, through districts inhabited
then as now by the wandering Arabs of the desert alone. Strange
as it might seem, Philip, a lone man, obliged to go on his feet, was
directed to take this latter route.

When he arrived at the point where the road from Jerusalem
fell into that by which he had come from Samaria, he saw a

[1] H. R. Mackintosh, *Life on God's Plan*, 103.

chariot, in which was a person of some consequence. Luke's "Behold!" suggests the sudden sight of the great man's cortège in the distance. No doubt, he travelled with a train of attendants, as became his dignity, and would be conspicuous from afar. Philip, of course, did not know who he was when he caught sight of him, but Luke tells his rank at once, in order to lay stress on it, as well as to bring out the significance of his occupation and subsequent conversion. He was an Ethiopian by birth, a eunuch, and treasurer of Candace, Queen of the Ethiopians, whose centre of government was Meroë on the Upper Nile, Candace being the name of the dynasty.

3. Now this eunuch for whose help Philip had come was seeking God. He was not by birth a member of the Jewish race; but by choice he had become, so to speak, an associate-member, or, in more technical language, a proselyte of the gate. He had travelled over a thousand miles to worship at Jerusalem. Then he had turned home again, perhaps a little disappointed, anyhow with his mind in something of a maze. Possibly he had heard stray rumours about a certain Jesus, crucified a few months earlier, whose followers were making a great stir by persistently claiming that He had risen from the dead. But the stories were far from clear. And now on his way home he held open before him the scroll of the prophet Isaiah, and was reading it attentively. He was reading aloud, for Orientals rarely, if ever, read in silence, even when alone.

4. No sooner had Philip caught sight of the stranger than he seems to have realized the object of his mission; a second Divine impulse hurried him forward to go and speak to him; and, when he heard the particular passage he was reading, it quickened his keenest interest. Without waiting to go through any preliminaries, or to make any explanations, Philip broke in on him with the question: "Understandest thou what thou readest?" The prompt answer was: "How can I, except some one shall guide me?" Thereupon "he besought Philip to come up and sit with him."

So the chariot rolled on, and through the silence of the desert the voices of these two reached the wondering attendants, as they plodded along. The Ethiopian was reading the Septuagint translation of Isaiah, which, though it missed part of the force of the original, brought clearly before him the great figure of a Sufferer, meek and dumb, swept from the earth by unjust judgment. He understood so much, but what he did not understand was whom this great tragic Figure represented. His question—"Of whom speaketh the prophet this? of himself, or of some other?"—goes to the root of the matter, and is a burning question to-day, as it was all these centuries ago on the road to Gaza. Philip had no doubt of the answer. Jesus was the "lamb dumb before his shearer."

¶ How afraid we all are of religious talk! How we pride ourselves on our reserve, and how ready we are to freeze up any warm, eager soul who is not quite so taciturn as we are! There was an Indian gentleman who once came to this country because he had been filled with an insatiable desire to learn all he could about immortality, and he supposed people in England could tell him something. He went to London, and to his neighbour at table one evening he said: "I should like to know what you think about immortality." He received the answer, "Ah! in this country we don't talk about these subjects at dinner"; and that was the end.[1]

5. "And Philip opened his mouth, and beginning from this scripture, preached unto him Jesus." If only we had the notes of that sermon, delivered with a chariot for pulpit, and to an audience of one, and filled, as we shall see, with such persuasive power! What were Philip's arguments and illustrations and appeals? How did he set Jesus livingly and compellingly before this man who an hour ago had heard no more than His name, and perhaps not even that? In all probability he would tell him first of the Resurrection; then, as the background of that, snatches from the story of Christ's life, and some of His most gracious parables, and perhaps a few of His best-remembered sayings. Yet whatever else he told him, he would inevitably tell him of the cross. With such a text he could not help that, and Philip was the last man that would wish to help it. No preacher can be true to the Word and leave out the cross. No preacher can leave out the cross who would be faithful to man's need, or

[1] H. R. Mackintosh, *Life on God's Plan*, 107.

just to his frailty, or compassionate to the wounds of conscience. And rest assured that if Philip *had* kept silence about Calvary— its meaning, its issues, its glory—then the gleam of interest would soon have faded from the hearer's eyes, and his eager face have lost its quiver of expectancy. But so it was that by the strong pleading of the outward voice, and the gracious power of the Spirit inwardly, the Ethiopian was brought to look to the Crucified, to desire Him, to reach out empty hands of longing after Him; until, as the chariot rolled on its unconscious way, then and there he yielded himself to the new constraining Presence, and began to love a Saviour he had never seen.

> Begin from first where He encradled was
> In simple cratch, wrapt in a wad of hay,
> Between the toilful ox and humble ass,
> And in what rags, and in how base array,
> The glory of our heavenly riches lay,
> When Him the silly shepherds came to see,
> Whom greatest princes sought on lowest knee.
>
> From thence read on the story of His life,
> His humble carriage, His unfaulty ways,
> His cancred foes, His fights, His toil, His strife,
> His pains, His poverty, His sharp assays,
> Through which He passed His miserable days,
> Offending none, and doing good to all,
> Yet being maliced both of great and small.
>
> Then shalt thou feel thy spirit so possessed,
> And ravished with devouring great desire
> Of His dear self, that shall thy feeble breast
> Inflame with love, and set thee all on fire
> With burning zeal, through every part entire,
> That in no earthly thing thou shalt delight,
> But in His sweet and amiable sight.[1]

6. On the swift conversion followed, as swiftly, an eager confession of new faith. Everywhere in that day, of course, as in heathenism still, the obvious and natural mode in which a man could signify his personal belief in Jesus was an open and deliberate submission to the rite of baptism. None of the

[1] E. Spenser.

elements of publicity were lacking now; one can see the officers
and servants of the retinue crowding round to watch and comment
and remember.   In some pool or streamlet by the wayside the
sacrament took place, and the new disciple took the words of
Christian confession on his lips.   There might have been reason,
to one of less breadth of mind than Philip, for hesitating, in the
circumstances, to perform the rite; but he did not hesitate a
moment, and so another step was taken towards opening the door
of the gospel to all classes and conditions of men.

¶ As is well known, the answer to the eunuch's question
(v. 37) is wanting in authoritative manuscripts.   The insertion
may have been due to the creeping into the text of a marginal
note.   A recent and most original commentator on the Acts
(Blass) considers that this, like other remarkable readings found
in one set of manuscripts, was written by Luke in a draft of the
book, which he afterwards revised and somewhat abbreviated into
the form which most of the manuscripts present.   However that
may be, the required conditions in the doubtful verse are those
which the practice of the rest of the Acts shows to have been
required.   Faith in Jesus Christ the Son of God was the qualification for the baptisms there recorded.[1]

7. "And when they came up out of the water, the Spirit of
the Lord caught away Philip; and the eunuch saw him no more,
for he went on his way rejoicing."   Whether by a sudden inward
summons to depart, like that by which he had been commanded
to come, or by a miraculous withdrawal, such as God could
employ, in this or any other case, at His pleasure, further communication was precluded between the convert and his evangelist.
The work was done for which Philip came; the work of faith with
power, the work of an abiding conversion, the work of love and
hope and great joy: the Ethiopian saw him no more; and it
mattered not; he stayed not to seek or to murmur; "for he went
on his way rejoicing."   He disappears for ever from the page of
sacred history, but tradition says that he became the inaugurator
of a great religious movement in his own country, which continued
for generations.

And "Philip was found at Azotus."   When next he was seen,
it was there, twenty miles northward from Gaza; and passing

[1] A. Maclaren.

through, he evangelized all the cities, proclaimed his glad tidings in every place through which he journeyed, till he came to Cæsarea. Two cities lying on or near his route were Lydda and Joppa. These we find Peter visiting in the course of the next chapter; in the former he healed the paralytic Æneas, in the latter he raised Dorcas or Tabitha from the dead. It appears, therefore, that Philip prepared the way for the Apostles in the cities which lay along the coast-line of Palestine, as he had formerly done in Samaria.

¶ How interesting the meeting and greeting and passing of those ships in the desert—Philip and the Ethiopian officer. Only a look and a voice, then light, brotherhood and joy. Philip had something to give, and there was something the officer longed for. One had the joy of giving, the other of receiving; each went on his way rejoicing, a better man.[1]

III.

At Cæsarea.

1. We know but little of the further work of Philip. According to tradition, Cæsarea was his birthplace, and here he eventually made his permanent home. The details of his work would be interesting, as would the details of the evangelistic work of any of the early gospel preachers; but we can only leave it to imagination to fill out the picture.

Cæsarea is noted in Church history as being the place where, by the conversion of Cornelius, the door of faith was first formally opened to the Gentiles. Our Evangelist having taken up his residence in the place some time previous to this great event, it may surprise us that he was not in any way employed in it. But a subordinate minister of the Church, however eminent his gifts or great his success, would not have been in place here. The formal admission of the Gentiles, as distinct from the sporadic conversion of individual Gentiles here and there, was to be transacted by an Apostle.

2. Philip remained in Cæsarea for twenty years; and we do

[1] M. D. Babcock, *Thoughts for Every-Day Living*, 65.

not hear a word about him all that time. But at last Paul and his companions, hurrying to keep the Feast at Jerusalem, found that they had a little time to spare when they reached Cæsarea, and so they came to "the house of Philip the evangelist," and spent "many days" with him. It is specially mentioned, though without any incident to be explained by it, that Philip had four virgin daughters endowed with the gift of prophecy. When Joshua was giving his final charge to the people of God, he expressed before them: "As for me and my house, we will serve the Lord." Philip the Evangelist had made the same determination, and he had carried it out. He had let his light shine before men, and his family did the same thing, giving themselves up to the service of God and adorning the doctrine of God their Saviour. There was no envy in Philip's heart of the younger brother that had so outrun him. He was quite content to share the fate of pioneers, and rejoiced in the junior who had entered into his labour. "One soweth and another reapeth"; he was prepared for that, and rejoiced to hear about what the Lord had done by his brother, though once he had thought it might have been done by him.

And there was one sitting by who did not say very much, but who had his ears wide open; his name was Luke. In Philip's long, confidential conversations he no doubt got some of the materials for his account of the early days of the Church in Jerusalem, materials which have been preserved for us in the Book of Acts.

3. Of the closing period of Philip's life we know nothing certainly, although there would seem to be some grounds for the tradition that in the unsettled conditions existing in Judæa about 65 A.D., due to the breaking out of the great Jewish war, he, like many other Jewish Christians, probably left Palestine and found a home elsewhere. As to whether he suffered martyrdom, or died a quiet and natural death, tradition is divided.

4. The life and experience of Philip, as in the case of others of the early Christian leaders, are full of suggestion.

(1) In him, for example, we have a notable instance of the good which a consecrated layman may accomplish. A similar possibility of usefulness, even if not in precisely the same sphere,

is open to any consecrated layman to-day. He may make his life as successful as that of Philip, if he will.

(2) Another thing which impresses us in the narrative is his instant obedience, upon all occasions, to the voice of the Spirit, and this even though the way may not have seemed clear before him at the time. It was enough for him to know that he was bidden to go in a certain direction, and this promptness of response was the secret of his success. As he went forward, the way opened before him, step by step, added light was given as it was needed, and the work which was waiting for him was made plain.

¶ " My own life—my own struggles—and sins—and sufferings," said Meynell, stooping towards the sick man, and speaking each word with an intensity behind which lay much that could never be known to his questioner. " A good man, Bateson, put it once in this way, ' There is something in me that asks something of me.' That's easy to understand—isn't it ? If a man wants to be filthy, or drunken, or cruel, there is always a Voice within—it may be weak or it may be strong—that asks of him to be— instead—pure and sober and kind. And perhaps he denies the Voice, refuses it—talks it down—again and again. Then the joy in his life dies out, bit by bit, and the world turns to dust and ashes. Every time that he says No to the Voice, he is less happy —he has less power of being happy. And the Voice itself dies away—and death comes. . . . But now, suppose he turns to the Voice and says, ' Lead me—I follow ! ' And suppose he obeys, like a child stumbling. Then every time he stretches and bends his poor weak will so as to give It what It asks, his heart is happy ; and strength comes—the strength to do more and do better. It asks him to love—to love men and women, not with lust, but with pure love ; and as he obeys, as he loves—he *knows*, he knows that it is God asking, and that God has come to him and abides with him. So, when death overtakes him he trusts himself to God—as he would to his best friend."[1]

(3) But especially interesting and instructive is the relation of Philip to the New Testament movement and its progress in those early times. His broad-minded disregard of the national and religious prejudices of the Jewish people, as illustrated in both the incidents recorded of him was, at the time, a real con- tribution to the progress of the cause. The time had not yet

[1] Mrs. Humphry Ward, *The Case of Richard Meynell*.

come for an open rupture with Judaism, but things were working
that way.   There was a constant introduction of broader ideas
among Jewish Christian people, and a loosening of the prejudices
in which they had been reared.   This, in due time, was bound to
bring about the inevitable separation.   Philip is to be thought of
as one of the pioneers in promoting these enlarging conceptions,
and in boldly acting in accordance with them as opportunity
presented.

> All honour to you!—ye who made the road
>   Whereon we walk rejoicing.   Ye have known
> The fiercest combat, and the cumbrous load
>   Upon the path with brambles overgrown;
> But, nothing daunted, with your care and toil
>   Ye cleared a way for Freedom's holy feet,
> And scattered seeds upon the wayside soil
>   Which since have yielded blossoms fair and sweet.
> And we, who follow after, walk with ease
>   Because of that wild travail full of tears,
> We hear the songs of Freedom on the breeze,
>   And see her triumph in the nearing years.
> The Dawn ye witnessed breaks to golden Day—
>   All honour to you—ye who made the Way![1]

[1] Rose E. Sharland, *Voices of Dawn*, 42.

SIMON THE SORCERER.

LITERATURE.

Dykes, J. O., *From Jerusalem to Antioch* (1875), 247.
Furneaux, W. M., *The Acts of the Apostles* (1912), 109.
Goulburn, E. M., *The Acts of the Deacons* (1867), 234.
Hobhouse, W., *The Spiritual Standard* (1896), 31.
Hooton, W. S., *Turning-Points in the Primitive Church* (1910), 62.
Luckock, H. M., *Footprints of the Apostles as traced by Saint Luke in the Acts*, i. (1905) 204.
Maclaren, A., *The Acts of the Apostles* (Bible Class Expositions) (1894), 82.
Maurice, F. D., *The Acts of the Apostles* (1894), 96.
Moore, A. L., *God is Love* (1894), 266.
Potter, H. C., *Sermons of the City* (1880), 234.
Rackham, R. B., *The Acts of the Apostles* (1901), 112.
Stokes, G. T., *The Acts of the Apostles* (Expositor's Bible), i. (1891) 346.
Thorne, H., *Notable Sayings of the Great Teacher*, 90.
Woods, H. G., *At the Temple Church* (1911), 56.
Dictionary of the Bible, iv. (1902) 520 (A. C. Headlam).
Preachers' Monthly, vii. (1884) 39 (H. R. Raymond).

SIMON THE SORCERER.

There was a certain man, Simon by name, which beforetime in the city used sorcery, and amazed the people of Samaria, giving out that himself was some great one.—Acts viii. 9.

SIMON of Samaria, Simon Magus as he is generally called, is the central figure of an episode in the Acts which, brief as it is, has attracted men's attention in almost every age of Christianity. Although only once mentioned in the New Testament, he had a considerable place in the Christian literature of the first three centuries. We may leave, for the present, the legends which gathered round his name, and consider the New Testament incident—the meeting of Simon with St. Peter.

I.

THE SIMON OF THE BOOK OF ACTS.

1. Simon, according to Justin Martyr, was born at the Samaritan village of Gitta, now Kuryet Jit, and by another account he is said to have been educated at Alexandria. He certainly had picked up ideas which were not Samaritan: the occult learning of his time, its black arts, and those endless speculations on the hidden powers of nature, the spiritual emanations from the Godhead, and the like abstruse and profitless subjects, which, under the name of Gnosticism, were, for two centuries after, to be the plague of the Christian Church. Thus equipped, he had returned to astonish his countrymen.

2. The Samaritans, like the Jews, were eagerly looking for the coming of a Messiah. In this they only shared a characteristic of their time. The whole East at this time, we are told by the historian Suetonius, was flooded with Messianic expectations, and

the expectations produced a harvest of false Christs. But apart from such special ideas, there was, in the decay and exhaustion of the old pagan religions, a greatly increased demand among men for religious teachers, to tell them something of the truth, to heal their diseases of spirit and mind as well as of body, to open up some channel of intercourse with the spiritual world, and, in a word, give them some knowledge of God. The class of "prophets," "seers," and "magi," who answered to this demand had always existed in the East, but now they were especially abundant. The developments and intermixture of Greek philosophy and Oriental religion had given them most varied characters. They appeared sometimes as exorcists, healers, wonder-workers; sometimes as astrologers or spiritualists. Some really tried to fill the place of philosophers and moral teachers; others claimed to be prophets and to possess a Divine inspiration. A few of the class may have been great men with more or less sincerity, like Apollonius of Tyana, whose biography was put forward in a later generation to compete with the Gospels. But the temptation to gain and cheat was too powerful, and the majority were nothing else than pretenders, quacks, and charlatans. Some were learned in astrology and the learning of the East, and the magi of Chaldæa had an honourable reputation. But the boundaries between true and false science, as between religion and superstition, had not yet been clearly marked out, and so the word *magus* had already acquired its evil associations of magic and sorcery.

> Thousands there are who have their first estate
>   Inviolate maintained without transgression;
> But there are thousands who have risen irate
>   Against authority; to such regression
> Seems never granted, but upon their pate,
>   The consequences of their indiscretion,
>   Their vile revolt,
>   Their treacherous and treasonable fault,
> Must one day fall: till then, their course pursuing,
> They work assiduously for man's undoing.
>
> 'Tis such who in defiance of divine
>   And wholesome laws respond to all who call them.
> Men count their baneful influence benign,
>   And as their spiritual guides instal them;

> Tho' they be but a brood of viperine,
>   Who men deceive in order to enthral them.
>   What soul could guess
>   How false, how mischievous, how merciless,
> Are all their diabolic machinations!
> And how pernicious their communications![1]

¶ During the early centuries there was a wide and current belief in the existence of demons. There was also a corresponding belief in demoniacal possession. Though this form of insanity still occurs at the present day, cases of it are rare, owing to the fact that wide circles of people have lost all belief in the existence and activity of demons. But the forms and phases in which insanity manifests itself always depend upon the state of general culture, and the ideas current in the social environment, so that whenever the religious life is in a state of agitation, and a firm belief prevails in the sinister activity of evil spirits "demon-possession" still breaks out sporadically.[2]

3. As the counterfeit of the true, these false prophets were among the most dangerous enemies of Christianity; and the distinction between the true and the false had to be sharply drawn once for all. The Lord had warned His disciples against false prophets and false Christs, and in the Acts we find the class convicted and judged in the persons of Simon Magus and Barjesus. Simon, as his name "the Magus" and his position in Christian tradition show, was in the first rank of these pretenders. By his skill in magic he had acquired quite a sovereignty over the Samaritans. His claim to be "some great one" was probably a Messianic pretension. But he aspired still higher. Besides being a *magus*, he was a philosopher; and he had elaborated a hierarchy of Divine emanations (*i.e.* successive mediators between God and man) which he called Powers. Of these powers he professed to be himself the chief, giving himself the name of "the great power of God." It is in view of such theories about powers that the Apostles assert the superiority of Christ to all such orders of being. St. Paul calls Christ "the power of God"; in the Acts the Divine power is generally associated with the Holy Spirit.

[1] J. Boyd, *The Story of the Glory*, 290.
[2] A. Harnack, *Expansion of Christianity*, i. 153.

In short, the Samaritans regarded Simon as a sort of incarnation of the highest power in the Deity. That he magnified himself to the extent of the most audacious blasphemy may be gathered from several passages in the Fathers. Justin tells us that "almost all the Samaritans, and a few also among other nations, acknowledged and worshipped him as the first God"; while Irenæus implies that he recognized a plurality of persons in the Godhead, and claimed to be himself an incarnation of all of them, and to have appeared among the Samaritans as the Father, among the Jews as the Son, and among people of other religions as the Holy Ghost.

¶ We cannot prevent hypocrites arising; it is only a proof that true religion is worth having. You took a bad half-sovereign the other night, did you? Did you say, "All half-sovereigns are worthless, I will never take another"? Not so, you became more careful; but you were quite sure there were good half-sovereigns in currency, or else people would not make counterfeit ones. It would not pay anybody to be a hypocrite, unless there were enough genuine Christians to make the hypocrites pass current.[1]

4. It was in the middle of this success that Philip came to Samaria.

The Lord Himself had preached to the Samaritans at Sychar (about seven miles from Samaria) for two days, and the conversation of the Samaritan woman showed their strong Messianic convictions. Philip went down to their capital, the old Samaria, which had been rebuilt by Herod the Great on a magnificent scale and called after Augustus—in Greek *Sebastos*—Sebaste. Here like a herald he proclaimed the Messiah, *i.e.* the establishment of the Kingdom of God. This Kingdom was neither the Jewish ecclesia nor the rival Samaritan ecclesia, but a new ecclesia which bore the name of Jesus, who had been anointed as its Messianic King or Christ. Philip confirmed his words by working many signs of healing. The superstition of the Samaritans made them specially liable to "amazement," or, as the A.V. implies, to "being bewitched" by a power they could not understand. Accordingly the miracles were necessary in order to overthrow the power and influence which Simon had acquired over them by his false miracles. Those of Philip were real, and the result was corresponding. The attention of the whole population was won; the healings caused great joy;

---

[1] C. H. Spurgeon, *Barbed Arrows*, 134.

the people at once believed that Philip's words must likewise be true, and many began to carry their belief into action by being baptized. It is surprising that no opposition was offered by Simon. But in fact he himself was deeply impressed by the real spiritual power of Philip and by his signs, which altogether eclipsed his own. He believed and was baptized, and became a disciple of Philip as of a superior master. The nature of his faith was soon to be tested and laid bare.

What led him to believe we are left to conjecture; whether it was only that he saw his followers gradually disappearing, and that the miracles wrought by Philip impressed him by their superiority to his own sorceries, or whether some deeper feeling moved him for a time, we can perhaps hardly decide. As far as we can answer these questions, his motive was chiefly a love of power and of gain, and perhaps an intellectual interest in religion. Simon was dabbling in philosophical speculations; he saw in the gospel something which seemed capable of being fitted into his system with a little necessary distortion; he saw performed every day miracles of healing which made his own achievements seem petty and trifling. He was smitten with discontent and envy, perhaps not unmingled with admiration and reverence. Good and evil feelings struggled for the mastery within him; there may have been self-disgust, the recognition of what was higher, and a longing after better things, as well as the grosser thought of future profit and the desire of greater notoriety, which no doubt was strongest; for why should he stop short at being called "the power of God" and not win worship as an actual deity? At all events, he professed his belief and submitted to the rite of baptism; and, having been thus enrolled in the ranks of the Christian Church, he continued with Philip, wondering at, or "bewitched by" (the word is a strong one), the miracles which he wrought.

¶ I once thought that almost all that could pray movingly and fluently and talk well of religion had been saints. But experience hath opened to me, what odious crimes may consist with high profession; and I have met with divers obscure persons whom I have found to have long lived a truly godly and sanctified life. I more plainly perceive the difference between the Church as congregate or visible, and as regenerate or mystical; and between sincerity and profession; and that a credible profession is proof sufficient of a man's title to Church admission; and that the profession is credible at the bar of the Church, which is not disproved. I am not for narrowing the Church more than Christ Himself alloweth us; nor for robbing Him of any of His flock. I am more sensible how much it is the will of Christ that every man be the chooser or refuser of his own felicity, and that it lieth most on his own hands, whether he will have communion with the Church or not; and that if he be an hypocrite it is himself that will bear the loss.[1]

5. The Apostles were not long in visiting the new Church, and in completing the work which Philip had begun. They conferred upon the new converts the gift of the Holy Ghost by the laying on of hands. This gift, we must suppose, made itself visible by outward effects, as in Jerusalem on the day of Pentecost, and afterwards in the Church of Corinth. They spoke with tongues or prophesied. When Simon saw miraculous powers not only exercised, but actually communicated to others, his curiosity and his cupidity were roused.

Such a scene stirred in him also that which was deepest in his heart. The deepest thing in him was neither the burden of an evil and unspiritual life, nor the yearning after God, nor the gladness of a pardoned sinner. It was just what it had always been—ambition, the lust after spiritual power. As he gazed, amazed, on the sublimest exhibition of spiritual power which he or any other man had ever seen—the descent of the Holy Ghost on the souls of men, so as to master their bodily organs as well, and to lift the whole man into an ecstasy of devotion—the one desire which leapt up in him and sprang to his lips was that he too might possess power like an Apostle, to give power like this to men. But there was in unhappy Simon, as there had been in Balaam of old, a baser passion than even ambition. To him spiritual power was valuable because he could turn it to profit; take captive the silly by it, and wheedle them out of their money. What will win gold is worth gold. What can be sold may also be bought. To one who had affected to traffic in what is super-human till he had ceased to believe in what is really Divine, the two Apostles were only cleverer magicians than himself. They

[1] Richard Baxter.

possessed some more potent formulæ. They could work upon some mightier spirit than he knew. If they were like himself, they might be bribed to share their secrets with him and enter into profitable partnership. Thus, in presence of the holiest, the unholiest in Simon came to light. "Give me also this power," he exclaimed, "that on whomsoever I lay my hands, he may receive the Holy Ghost."

¶ I remember, says Goldwin Smith, when I was for some months giving help to my father as a deputy in the Collector's office, hearing one of the larger distillers say with almost unnecessary frankness: "Mr. Collector, your authorities pay those inspectors in my place twelve hundred a year, do they not?" "Yes," said my father. "Well," said the distiller, "if I wanted to send out a few thousand gallons of whiskey without paying the tax, I could certainly afford to give those inspectors a much larger salary for omitting to make record of that portion of my product."[1]

> Curst be the gold and silver which persuade
> Weak men to follow far-fatiguing trade.
> The lily-peace outshines the silver store,
> And life is dearer than the golden ore.
> Yet money tempts us o'er the desert brown,
> To every distant mart, and wealthy town:
> Full oft we tempt the land, and oft the sea,
> And are we only yet repaid by thee?
> Ah! why was ruin so attractive made,
> Or why fond man so easily betrayed?
> Why heed we not, whilst mad we haste along,
> The gentle voice of peace, or pleasure's song?
> Or wherefore think the flowery mountain's side,
> The fountain's murmurs, and the valley's pride,
> Why think we these less pleasing to behold,
> Than dreary deserts, if they lead to gold?[2]

6. But St. Peter saw straight into his heart; he read there the lust of power and fame and money. With burning words he rebuked him, "Thy silver perish with thee, because thou hast thought to obtain the gift of God with money. Thou hast neither part nor lot in this matter: for thy heart is not right before God.

---

[1] *George Palmer Putnam, 1814–1872*, p. 347.
[2] W. Collins, "Persian Eclogues."

Repent therefore of this thy wickedness, and pray the Lord, if perhaps the thought of thy heart shall be forgiven thee. For I see that thou art in the gall of bitterness and in the bond of iniquity."

The other Simon's fiery rebuke flashed a terrible beam into the dark caves of this dark soul. The crime of crimes, in St. Peter's eyes, was to think of "the gift of God" as purchasable with money, and that not merely because such a misconception darkened the freedom of the gift, but because it ignored the one condition of obtaining it, which St. Peter proceeds to lay down in the words which shut Simon out from it: "Thou hast neither part nor lot in this matter" (which is to be taken as defined by the context—namely, the gift in question): "for thy heart is not right before God." The right heart, which comes through faith, is the condition. Money cannot buy the gift any more than it can purchase sunshine; but the faith which purifies the heart is sure to receive it.

¶ Money never did, and never could, create religion. Your capitalist may endow religious institutions. To see the way he is run after by religious societies, to observe the part which finance plays in the Church organizations, one might easily imagine that here the gold bag is omnipotent. But come to realities and we find where we are. You cannot, by any alchemy, extract prayer from a dollar bill or a banknote. All the gold in the world could never produce a genuine religious aspiration. The noblest emotions were never born in that atmosphere, and where it prevails they do not thrive. It was not money that started Christianity, or gave us the New Testament. They are not Stock Exchange values.[1]

¶ With money you can buy the canvas and the oil, but not the artistic eye which interprets and appreciates the picture; you can buy the poem, but the living and inspiring poetry is not for sale; you can rent the garden, but cannot bribe the flowers to whisper their tender messages. After all, it is but a very little way that money can go; it can do nearly everything in the market-place or among the dust of cities, but what do the angels know of your currency, your bills of exchange, your promissory notes, and your intricate conveyancing of estates? Not one of the great redemptions of life can be wrought out with money: death takes no bribe; the grave will not sell its victories for

[1] J. Brierley.

gold; you may buy the Bible, but you cannot buy the Holy Ghost; you may pay for the masonry, but no money can put you in possession of the Spirit of the altar.[1]

7. The terrible " imprecation " launched at the cowering quack is to be taken in connexion with the urgent call to repentance, which would avert the otherwise certain doom. St. Peter speaks doubtfully, but the doubt concerned the possibility not so much of forgiveness as of Simon's repentance. For his heart was full of " the bitter gall " of sin and fast bound with " the chain of his iniquity " (a reminiscence of Isa. lviii. 6). Such is the meaning of the English translation. The first expression, however, is taken from Deut. xxix. 18, where the Israelite whose heart turns away from God is among the people as " a root that beareth gall and wormwood," *i.e.* " a root of bitterness." And as the Greek is literally " thou art for " or " unto," the rendering of the R.V. margin [" will become "] is the best. St. Peter sees—and sees most truly—that Simon's sin will be a root of bitterness and gall to the Church and a fetter of iniquity, impeding its free course.

Like Pharaoh, Simon was frightened but not reformed. His words recall Exod. viii. 28, " Entreat the Lord for me." The denunciation by one in whom he recognized a power above his own terrified him. And, not recognizing that penitence is a personal matter between the soul and God, he thought that he could pray by deputy. But he must not be condemned unfairly. One man cannot rise so high as another. The lofty nature loathes sin, and goes to God to escape it. The poorer nature fears judgment, and goes to God to escape it. The prayer of the latter will be less spiritual than that of the former, and yet God may accept it.

With this incident Simon disappears from the New Testament, according to the Bezan text, " weeping loudly."

¶ The element of fear is one of the great primal passions, and to all those deep basic human elements the gospel makes its peculiar appeal. And the fears of men must be excited. The music cannot be all bass; but the bass note must not be absent, or the music will be ruined.

There are still those who, far from being cowards, may, like Noah, be " moved with fear " to the saving of their houses.

[1] Joseph Parker.

Cardinal Manning tells in his Journal how, as a boy at Totteridge, he read again and again of the lake that burneth with fire. "These words," he says, "became fixed in my mind, and kept me as boy and youth and man in the midst of all evil. I owe to them more than will ever be known to the last day." And Archbishop Benson used to tell of a working man who was seen looking at a placard announcing a series of addresses on "The Four Last Things." After he had read the advertisement he turned to a companion and asked, "Where would you and I have been without hell?" And the Archbishop used to inquire whether, if we abandoned the legitimate appeal to human fear, we should not need some other motive in our preaching to fill the vacant place.[1]

II.

The Traditionary Simon.

1. The earliest authority is Justin Martyr, who was himself a Samaritan, and lived less than one hundred years later than Simon. He tells us that Simon was a Samaritan, of the village of Gitta; he came to Rome in the time of Claudius Cæsar; by the power of the demons he worked miracles, and was honoured in Rome as a god, so that a statue was erected in his honour by order of the Senate and people, between the two bridges, bearing the inscription SIMONI DEO SANCTO. Almost all the Samaritans and a few of other nations honour him as the first god. He took about with him a woman called Helena, whom he is said to have called the first conception which came forth from him. He is described as God above "all rule and authority and power."

¶ As regards one part of this story an interesting discovery has been made. In the year 1574 there was dug up in the place indicated by Justin, namely, in the island of the Tiber, a marble fragment, apparently the base of a statue, with the inscription SEMONI SANCO DEO FIDIO. It is now generally agreed that Justin mistook a statue dedicated to a Sabine deity for one dedicated to Simon.[2]

2. Justin also represents him as the originator of heresy, and the founder of the heretical sect of the Simonians. During the

[1] F. W. Boreham, *Mushrooms on the Moor*, 165.
[2] A. C. Headlam, in Hastings' *Dictionary of the Bible*, iv. 520.

second century, all the information, as far as we know, that existed about Simon, was derived from the Acts of the Apostles and the writings of Justin. But during the second and fourth centuries a great mass of legendary matter accumulated round his name. In the Patristic literature, the Clementine literature, and the legendary *Acts of Peter and Paul*, its growth may be traced, until at the close of the fourth century we find in the *Apostolic Constitutions* what we may call the completed legend, combining the stories from the Clementine literature with those derived from the apocryphal *Acts* and the narrative in the Acts of the Apostles. He is represented, with increasing details, as the opponent of St. Peter, who follows him from place to place, disputing with him and exposing his pretensions at Cæsarea, Tyre, Laodicea, Antioch, and Rome. In the *Acts of Peter and Paul*, St. Paul is connected with St. Peter in resisting Simon. By one account Simon undertakes to fly over Rome, but by the prayers of St. Peter he falls and is killed. By another he ordered his disciples to dig a grave and bury him, saying he would rise on the third day. They did as they were ordered, " but he remained away even to the present day. For he was not the Christ."

3. How far there is an actual historical basis for the idea that Gnosticism was directly or indirectly derived from him may be doubtful. His system exhibits all the elements which go to make up Gnosticism ; especially we may notice that there we first find the idea that the highest God was not the Creator of the world ; but then such tendencies and ideas were in the air. The same influences of dualism and syncretism which worked in his case would work also in others. But, anyhow, Simon was the one clear instance of a heretic mentioned in the New Testament. It was natural, therefore, to represent him as the typical arch-heretic, the originator of heresy, and the place which Justin assigned to him at the head of his heretical genealogy was one in which his position was uncontested.

4. Samaria was a country in which a sort of bastard Judaism came in contact with the old Syrian and Phœnician religions and the newer Hellenic paganism. All these different elements are present in Simon's system. That the relation of himself and Helena is a reminiscence of the Syrian male and female deity is

equally natural, whether Helena be a real person (as is probable) or only the personification of an idea. The fact that in one account—that of the *Recognitions*—she is called *Luna* (a translation of σελήνη), makes the parallel to the Sun and Moon worship, the Baal and Astarte, more close. Simon represents an almost pre-Christian Gnosticism, and it is significant that only here do we find this very repulsive dualistic element. Simon represents the impostor of the period, whose claims are even more improbable than those of Apollonius of Tyana or Alexander of Abonoteichus. His mind is a medley of Hellenism, Judaism, and Orientalism; out of this he forms a system, in which he himself occupies the first position. The influence of Christianity and then the opposition to it give a certain vitality and force to the ideas he suggests, and in other hands they become fertile and prolific. Later Gnostics were more definitely Christian. The founders of the sects never claimed Divine honours for themselves. They discarded more extravagant features. But they shared with Simon the fundamental doctrine that the Creator of the world was an inferior and, perhaps, a malevolent deity.

¶ There are some curious coincidences between the legends of Faust and Simon Magus. In the Clementine *Homilies* Faustus is the father of Simon, and Simon by his magical power changes his father's face into the exact image of his own.

The hero of the Faust legend is supposed to have been a certain Dr. Faust, of Knittlingen, who died in 1540. The legend appears first in a written form in 1587, and was obviously the result of a fertile imagination. It is quite possible that in building up the story reminiscences direct or indirect of the legend of Simon Magus may have come in. The following are points of resemblance : (1) firstly and most clearly the introduction of Helena in both ; (2) the name Faustus ; (3) the *homunculus* ; (4) in Simon Magus himself we may have a suggestion of Mephistopheles. This connexion may be due to direct literary influence, or we may have here two different versions of a theme which has been common at various times, the contest between Religion and Magic—a contest which we have to believe is far older and more universal than was once thought.[1]

5. Interest in Simon has been revived in modern times by the theory of Baur that he was not an historical character, but repre-

---

[1] A. C. Headlam, in Hastings' *Dictionary of the Bible*, iv. 527.

sents the Apostle Paul. On this view the contest between Simon
Peter and Simon Magus really represented the original conflict of
Peter and Paul. Wherever Simon Magus occurs we should read
Paul. At first it was clearly understood who this person designated as Simon the Samaritan really was, but as the two parties
more and more came together the original meaning was forgotten,
and hence we find, even in a book like the Acts of the Apostles,
written in a conciliatory interest, fragments of the old contest still
embedded. But we have to recognize that the whole of our
accepted history of early Christianity is really a conventional
ecclesiastical legend, and the real history of the period must be
disentangled from the Clementine literature. It is marvellous
with what ingenuity the parallel was worked out when once the
idea was started. Simon called himself the great power of God.
Paul claims that he lived by the power of God (2 Cor. xii. 9,
xiii. 4). When Simon offers money to buy the power of conferring the gift of the Holy Ghost, this is an allusion to Paul, who
by his contributions for the poor saints at Jerusalem was attempting to obtain the apostleship. Peter telling Simon that he has
neither part nor lot in this matter, is really Peter telling Paul
that he has not the κλῆρος τῆς ἀποστολῆς.

It seems very doubtful whether Simon of the Clementine literature is ever intended to represent Paul; nor is there any Pauline
teaching put into Simon's mouth. The above passages, which are
all the more important quoted, are hardly sufficient to establish
the theory that Simon is Paul. The author or compiler of the
Clementines really starts from the belief that the Simon of the
Acts, whom Peter combated, was the source of all heresy, and so
he makes his favourite Apostle travel from place to place combating
in the person of Simon the false Marcionite teaching of which he
was believed to be the originator. This will explain the whole
situation, and is much less far-fetched than the explanation which
finds Paul everywhere.

III.

The Sin of Simon.

1. The memory of Simon's proposal has been preserved apart
from the Scripture record, for his name has been branded all

through the Church's history in connexion with an unhallowed traffic in holy things. The purchase of any spiritual office or dignity, or any corrupt presentation to an ecclesiastical benefice for money or reward, is accounted "simony," though an attempt by such means to procure the gift of ordination itself more exactly corresponds with the sin of which Simon was guilty.

Simon's first error, or, more truly, sin, was his entire blindness to all but the outward miraculous effects of the Spirit—a blindness which was possible only if evil desires and selfishness had become dominant.

His next fault was consequent on the first. If the influence of the Spirit was only what he thought it, of course it could be communicated without regard to moral conditions. His own words might have struck him as involving the impossibility of his request. The very name "Holy Ghost," which he pronounces without thought of its meaning, might have taught him that its reception needed some preparation in whosoever received it, and that it was not communicated by the mere touch of hands.

His last error was the degrading supposition that this power could be bought. If he was ready to buy, he doubtless meant to sell. So he has, deservedly enough, the dishonour of having stood godfather to the crime, often repeated in its grossest form, and called after him, simony.

¶ John Hus writes: "This year lying, lascivious, avaricious men, who by their evil deeds disowned Christ and derided the true path of Christ, have robbed the people by false indulgences, imagining strange speeches and absolutions, and granting remittance of all sins and punishments. And these men having the support of the masters (of the university) robbed the people all the more boldly, and lied as much as they could."[1]

2. The sin has, indeed, taken different shapes. Simony, throughout the Middle Ages, was a common vice against which some of the more devout popes strove long and vigorously. In England, and according to English law, simony means still the purchase of spiritual office or spiritual functions. It would be simoniacal for a bishop to receive money for conferring holy orders or for appointment to a living. It would be an act of

[1] Count Lützow, *The Life and Times of Master John Hus*, 189.

simony for a man to offer or give money to attain either holy orders or a living. Simony, however, is a much more extensive and far-reaching corruption than the purchase of ecclesiastical benefices. Simony can take subtler shapes and can adapt itself to conditions very different from those which prevail under an established Church. Every one recognizes, in word at least, the scandalous character of money traffic in Church offices. Even those who really practise it hide from themselves, by some device or excuse, the character of their action. But the simoniacal spirit, the essence of Simon's sin, is found in many quarters which are never suspected. What is that essence? Simon desired to obtain spiritual power and office, not in the Divine method, but in low, earthly ways. Money was his way because it was the one thing he valued and had to offer; but surely there are many other ways in which men may unlawfully seek for spiritual office and influence in the Church of Christ. Many a man who would never dream of offering money in order to obtain a high place in the Church, or would be horrified at the very suggestion, has yet resorted to other methods just as effective and just as wrong. Men have sought high position by political methods. They have given their support to a political party, and have sold their talents to uphold a cause, hoping thereby to gain their ends. They may not have given gold which comes from the mine to gain spiritual position, but they have all the same given a mere human consideration, and sought by its help to obtain spiritual power; or they preach and speak and vote in Church synods and assemblies with an eye to elections to high place and dignity.

¶ Christians have found that they might trade with the belief that there is a Holy Spirit, a Spirit of truth, a heart-purifying, heart-regenerating Spirit, which He will renew in us day by day. And always when they have done so, this belief that the gift of God may be purchased with money, that money is the all-conquering divine power, has been discovered to be dwelling in them. It was the awful revelation of this simony in the hearts of the rulers of the Church, taking then the form of the sale of indulgences, which produced the Reformation of the sixteenth century. Forgiveness, it was seen, was in the highest sense the gift of God. Indulgence was a gift of the devil. It must have been his suggestion that they could buy such a gift of God. This is one instance; there are multitudes more in earlier and later times, in all countries and in all religious communities.[1]

¶ In Dante's *Inferno*, the Simonists are found in the third chasm. The heart of Dante seems almost too full for utterance when he comes in sight of them. To him they are, as it were, a more hateful species of panders and seducers than those he has just left; and they lie beneath the vile flatterers "that call evil good, and good evil; that put darkness for light, and light for darkness." It is they who have prostituted the things of God for gold and silver, and made "His house a den of thieves." They are all fixed one by one in narrow round holes, along the sides and bottom of the rock, with the head downwards, so that nothing more than the feet and part of the legs stands out. The soles of them are tormented with flames, which keep flickering from the heels to the toes, and burn with a brightness and intensity proportioned to the different degrees of guilt. Dante is carried down by his Guide to the bottom of the chasm; and there finds Pope Nicholas the Third, who, with a weeping voice, declares his own evil ways, and those of his successors Boniface the Eighth and Clement the Fifth.

"I know not if here I was too hardy, for I answered him in this strain: 'Ah! Now tell me how much treasure our Lord required of St. Peter, before he put the keys into his keeping? Surely he demanded nought but "Follow Me"! Nor did Peter, nor the others, ask of Matthias gold or silver, when he was chosen for the office which the guilty soul had lost. Therefore stay thou *here*, for thou art justly punished.'"[2]

---

[1] F. D. Maurice, *The Acts of the Apostles*, 108.
[2] J. A. Carlyle, *Dante's Inferno*, 217, 225.

CORNELIUS.

LITERATURE.

Binney, T., *St. Paul : His Life and Ministry* (1866), 108.

Brooke, S. A., *Sermons,* ii. (1875) 36.

Clark, F. E., in *Sermons by the Monday Club,* 17th Ser. (1891), 326.

Dykes, J. O., *From Jerusalem to Antioch* (1875), 347.

Fairweather, D., *Bound in the Spirit* (1906), 180.

Horton, R. F., *Lyndhurst Road Pulpit* (1893), 257.

Lewis, Z. H., *Petros,* 245, 255.

Luckock, H. M., *Footprints of the Apostles as traced by Saint Luke in the Acts,* ii. (1905) 1.

Maclaren, A., *The Acts of the Apostles* (Bible Class Expositions) (1894), 129.

  „   „ *Expositions* : The Acts of the Apostles i.-xii. (1907), 295.

Matheson, G., *The Representative Men of the New Testament* (1905), 296.

Milligan, G., in *Men of the New Testament* : Matthew to Timothy (1905), 277.

Noble, F. A., *Typical New Testament Conversions* (1901), 210.

Stokes, G. T., *The Acts of the Apostles* (Expositor's Bible), ii. (1892) 92.

Wakinshaw, W., *John's Ideal City* (1915), 159.

Williams, J. P., *The Duty of Exercise,* 72.

Dictionary of the Apostolic Church, i. (1915) 259 (W. F. Boyd).

Dictionary of the Bible, i. (1898) 499 (A. Grieve).

CORNELIUS.

There was a certain man in Cæsarea, Cornelius by name, . . . a devout man, and one that feared God with all his house.—Acts x. 1, 2.

CORNELIUS will always be of special interest to us as almost the first, if not actually the first, Gentile convert admitted into the Church of Christ.

The Church was at first in appearance only a Jewish sect; but the great stride is now taken which carries it over the border into the Gentile world, and begins its universal aspect. If we consider the magnitude of the change, and the difficulties of training and prejudice which had to be encountered in the Church itself, we shall not wonder at the abundance of supernatural occurrences which attended it. Without some such impulse, it is difficult to conceive of its having been accomplished.

In this narrative we see the supernatural preparation on both sides. God, as it were, lays His right hand on Cornelius and His left on Peter, and impels them towards each other. Philip had already preached to the Ethiopian, and probably the anonymous brethren in Acts xi. 20 had already spoken the word to pure Greeks at Antioch; but the importance of Peter's action here is that by reason of his Apostleship, his recognition of Gentile Christians becomes the act of the whole community. His entrance into the house of Cornelius ended the Jewish phase of the Church.

¶ To Peter, as to every other Jew, it was quite a familiar idea that the Gentiles should come one day to worship God and believe in His Messiah; but it had never yet occurred to him, or to almost any other Jew, that this could happen unless by the Gentiles first becoming Jews. By training, Peter was a Jew of the intensely national school. In spite of their faith in Christ, he and the bulk of Palestine believers had remained, up to this point, Jews still. To such men the division which God had set up betwixt the two portions of mankind did not seem at that time a temporary party-wall (as St. Paul afterwards described it), intended to be taken down after it had served its purpose, in order that wider room might be made for both in one new temple. It was a fence of permanent and hopeless exclusion for all beyond, of permanent inclusion for all within. God had, as they believed, limited His grace for ever to the covenant of circumcision. All men who had not been brought near by that covenant and consecrated by its rites, were unclean and profane. It followed that the Church, or assembly of such as believed in Jesus Christ, could not be a wider communion than the followers of Moses, but a narrower. It formed a lesser fold inside the fold of Judaism. It was a more retired and safe shrine, to which you could only pass through the fore-court of the law. Any man might, it was felt, get into the fellowship of Jesus, and all men, it was hoped, would some day do so; still, to the great world of uncircumcised heathen sinners, access could lie only through that preliminary apparatus of cleansing which God had prepared in the Abrahamic covenant and the Mosaic ritual.[1]

¶ Did it ever strike you that Cornelius is our *father*? You never thought, perhaps, that you were so nearly related to him; but it is even so. He was a Gentile, and in him the Gentiles were formally admitted to the Church. He is the father of the Gentile branch of it. But we are Gentiles; and we, therefore, were, so to speak, "in the loins" of Cornelius when Peter received him. He is our Abraham. What Abraham was to the Jew, Cornelius is to us. The Jews gloried in the patriarch, looking up to their Abraham with love to his memory and reverence for his character. We have no reason to be ashamed of our father Cornelius. We may thank God for such a spiritual ancestor. When we think of him, however, we must do so with shame as well as exultation, for there is reason to fear that he, before his conversion and knowledge of Christ, was essentially and in fact a better Christian than some of us.[2]

I.

The Man.

i. The Roman Soldier.

Cornelius was a centurion, that is, a commander of the sixth part of a cohort, or the sixtieth part of a legion—6000 men.

---

[1] J. O. Dykes, *From Jerusalem to Antioch*, 359.
[2] T. Binney, *St. Paul: His Life and Ministry*, 126.

Hence, he would have the command of one hundred soldiers. His band was called the Italian—Italy being the country from which the cohort was chiefly gathered.

We know very little of his history, but his name indicates that he belonged to one of the noble families of Rome. The Romans knew no more honourable name than that of the Cornelian house; some of their most famous men had sprung from that stock, and doubtless when this descendant of the family entered the army, his dreams would be of achieving on the field of battle still greater glory to add to the lustre of the family name. Little did he think of the kind of fame he was to gain, as little perhaps as Peter thought of becoming a fisher of men those long summer days when he dragged the Lake of Galilee with his fisherman's net.

1. That Cornelius was a soldier was both in favour of and against his becoming a Christian. It was in his favour because he was a man accustomed to discipline.

The world of unregenerate man at the time of our Lord's appearance had become utterly selfish. Discipline of every kind had been flung off. Self-restraint was practically unknown, and the devil and his works flourished in every circle, bringing forth the fruits of wickedness, uncleanness, and impurity in every direction. The army was the only place or region where in those times any kind of discipline or self-restraint was practised. For no army can permit—even if it be an army of atheists—profligacy and drunkenness to rage, flaunting themselves beneath the very eye of the sun. And as the spiritual result we find that this small measure of pagan discipline acted as a preparation for Christianity, and became under Divine guidance the means of fitting men like Cornelius of Cæsarea for the reception of the gospel message of purity and peace.

¶ Why did the Medieval Church initiate orders of sacred knighthood—knights of the temple, knights of St. Mary, knights of St. John? It was because the Medieval Church wanted a section of her sons to be soldiers in spirit and to transfer the qualities of war into the paths of peace. Why has our modern Christianity instituted a Salvation Army? It is because Cornelius is still needed among the Christians—because in peace as well as in war there are wrongs that await redressing. Why does our twentieth century inaugurate in every town a Boys' Brigade? It is because we want Cornelius in the midst of us. It is because we desire that from an early age our youthful generation should learn to associate religion with manliness, to connect the cross of Christ with all that is brave and heroic and noble, and to plant in civil life those very seeds which in the sphere of the warrior made for military glory.[1]

2. On the other hand, Cornelius was exposed to all the temptations of a soldier's life. It cannot have been easy for him to maintain his high ideals, to keep true to the God he worshipped, in the atmosphere of a soldier's barracks. His life had been spent in war—in the service of an empire whose aims were *not* Messianic. He had breathed the atmosphere of the camp rather than the air of Calvary, had heard, not sermons on the mount, but ribald jests on the highway.

> A soldier,
> Full of strange oaths and bearded like the pard,
> Jealous in honour, sudden and quick in quarrel,
> Seeking the bubble reputation
> Even in the cannon's mouth.[2]

¶ It was an early dream of F. W. Robertson of Brighton, the son, grandson, and brother of gallant officers in the British army, that he might serve his Lord and Master as a soldier. The temptations to which he would be exposed in the army were strongly set before him, but he could not believe that they were any real barriers against his entrance into it; on the contrary, with his usual desire for some positive outward evil to contend with, he imagined that it was his peculiar vocation to bear witness to God, to set the example of a pure and Christian life in his corps, to be as he said "the Cornelius of his regiment."[3]

ii. The Devout Man.

By and by this man, as the captain of a regiment, was ordered to Cæsarea. He was sent there to represent the fact of Roman conquest, to exercise a military surveillance over the district. But, all the time that he was keeping military watch over Judæa,

---

[1] G. Matheson, *Representative Men of the New Testament*, 314.
[2] Shakespeare, *As You Like It*, ii. vii. 149.
[3] S. A. Brooke, *Life and Letters of the Rev. F. W. Robertson*, 8.

Judæa kept moral watch over him. He came to represent Rome's conquest of Israel; he ended by representing Israel's conquest of Rome.

Cornelius may have at the time counted his lot a hard one when despatched to Palestine as a centurion, for it was a province where, from the nature of the warfare prevalent, there were abundant opportunities of death by assassination at the hands of the Zealots, and but few opportunities of distinction such as might be gained in border warfare with foreign enemies. But the Lord was shaping his career, as He shapes all our careers, with reference to the highest spiritual purposes. He led Cornelius, therefore, to a land and to a town where the pure worship of Jehovah was practised and the elevated morality of Judaism prevailed.

Cornelius is represented to us as "a devout man," "one that feared God with all his house," "who gave much alms to the people," and who "prayed to God always."

1. He was *a devout man,* a man of serious and reverent spirit, of an earnest turn of mind, conscientious up to his light, seeking with all his heart to be true to the best within him. By birth and training he must have been a pagan. When he worshipped his father's gods at Rome he was serious in his worship; he bowed down reverently, humbly, and devoutly, and we may be sure that when he embraced the pure worship of God, the Father of our Lord Jesus Christ, he would become not less but more devout. He belonged to the same class of men as Nathanael and Nicodemus. He was conscious of the existence of higher powers, and of the obligation to worship. To him there was mystery in life; there were powers beyond him; and before these he bowed his head and worshipped. May not this have been the secret of his finding out the true God? He lived up to the best he knew; and when Providence placed him in Cæsarea, where he must have found some faithful worshippers, he found the light after which he had been seeking.

¶ He, therefore, is the devout man, who lives no longer to his own will, or the way and spirit of the world, but to the sole will of God; who considers God in everything, who serves God in everything, who makes all the parts of his common life parts of piety, by doing everything in the Name of God, and under such rules as are conformable to His glory.[1]

2. Cornelius was more than devout: *he feared God with all his house.* He was one of those men who make the fear of God the basis of all their actions, who make that the touchstone by which they test their conduct, the law by which they regulate their lives, the motive that determines their whole course of action. Like the psalmist he could say, " I have set Jehovah continually before me."

The fear of the Lord may mean two things. It may mean the fear which springs from dread, the fear which, traced back to its source, is the consequence of guilt, the fear which, were it possible, would make us hide ourselves from God, the fear that Felix felt when Paul reasoned with him of righteousness, temperance, and judgment to come. Or it may mean the fear which springs from love, the veneration, reverence, obedience a son renders a father, which is mingled with the apprehension of his displeasure incurred by misconduct—a restraining, wholesome, praiseworthy fear.

To Cornelius the fear of God was of the latter kind. It had its origin in a right motive. It was the fear which held in reverence God's holy character, and never would bow before Him without a sense of deep unworthiness and sinfulness, a fear which led him to own God's authority over his life, and to do His will from the heart fervently, ungrudgingly, and willingly. He did not suffer the customs and usages of those around him to determine his conduct; he did not suffer social sanction to usurp the place of Divine. In all things he sought to be well-pleasing unto God, setting himself daily in the light of His law that he might the more easily see his own mistakes and sins; and he was spurred to effort by the fear lest he should lose God's approbation. On this wise and sure foundation he built the house of his life. In this fear of God he exercised all his household. Cornelius had a church in his home. His children, his servants, his guests were all taught the fear of the Lord.

It was the influence of Cornelius himself that brought all that household at Cæsarea under the fear of God. It was his personal influence, his devout, earnest, godly character that wrought the

---

[1] William Law.

change. He, the master of the house, himself feared God, and so all his house were taught the secret.

¶ The genius of Michael Angelo made the Sibyls splendid on the ceiling of the Sistine from the magnificence of proportion quite as much as from the softness of colour; proportion is the secret of lasting charm. It is holy fear that is the principle of proportion in the relation of the creature—the fallen creature—to his Creator. To see GOD in suffering is, by grace, to have a proportionate affection; by it we are restrained, by it we are awed and solemnized, by it we act as men should in the felt presence of their Maker, by it we learn, in fact, our proper place.[1]

3. Cornelius was *a liberal man*: "he gave much alms to the people." That was the form his liberality took. He had learned the compassion of Christ for the needy, he had learned one of the secrets of Christian living—to give.

"Give," Christ said, "and it shall be given to you." What shall be given for giving? Goods, money, material things? No. Jesus knew what He was saying; to give these hoping to receive again is not giving at all. "Do not even the publicans the same?" No, give these if you have them, but first give the willing heart, give yourself, give your love, give your help to a neighbour, be the good Samaritan; spend, hoping to receive nothing again, and great will be your reward in heaven. Cornelius had learned that lesson.

¶ Let us remember always that for a worthy contribution to life, the discipline of the heart is more even than that of the brain. And that is a discipline of which we can all partake. You may take no place in the ranks of learning or of science; none can prevent you entering the lists of love and of service. The learning may in the end prove out of date; love never grows old, never misses its aim. The soul that is fired with faith and hope carries everywhere its instant benediction. It shines in the countenance and radiates health by a glorious contagion. It is like the Alps. The Alps do not know you, never heard your name. But just because they are Alps — their snowy summits catching the sunlight, their glorious air charged with force; their immortal beauty shining in upon the soul—just by being that, what a boon are they, all unknowing, to the fever-worn travellers who look upon them! Oh, for more Alpine souls! The soul never grows for itself; it grows that others may climb on it to the heights.

[1] W. J. Knox Little, *The Witness of the Passion*, 50.

It gives all it receives—gives without knowing it is giving. Yes, we are here to give, and to taste its blessedness. Our contribution may seem of the poorest, but the universe would not be complete without it. No one else can offer it. The Spirit of Holiness, striving in His eternal struggle to shape this rude world into a kingdom of light, looks for our co-operation, for our contribution. Shall we offer aught less than our best ? [1]

4. To his devoutness, godliness, and liberality, the centurion added this other distinguishing mark of a Christian character : *he prayed to God alway.* It was the secret of all his goodness ; he communed with God, he was a man of prayer. Nor was it an occasional exercise. He prayed to God alway, like Job, of whom we read, " Thus did he continually." It was the root of the whole matter. The prayer of faith brings down God into our lives, and that means the answer to all our needs.

> Wherefore if anywise from morn to morn
> I can endure a weary faithfulness,
> From minute unto minute calling low
> On God who once would answer, it may be
> He hath a waking for me, and some surprise
> Shall from this prison set the captive free
> And love from fears and from the flesh the soul.[2]

iii. The Earnest Seeker.

Cornelius, as we have seen, was devout, God-fearing, liberal, and prayerful, but he was more than that—he was an earnest seeker after the truth. It seems indubitable that at the time the vision came to him he was in deep spiritual anxiety, craving clearer light from God. He knew of the coming and preaching and wonders of the holy Man of Galilee. He could not fail to have heard of a new sect that everywhere declared this Man to be the promised Saviour. The neighbouring country was at the moment ringing with Peter's name. In his own town there dwelt a deacon and evangelist of the Church. But these new revelations from the Jehovah of Israel, who had (it was said) visited His people at last to raise up for them an horn of salvation, were revelations

---

[1] J. Brierley, *Religion and To-day*, 271.
[2] F. W. H. Myers, *Poems*, 68.

of mercy for the elected and covenanted nation, the circumcised sons of Abraham. For himself, a Gentile foreigner, was there any word of hope and peace from the one great God of heaven? Will God hear his prayers, or accept his offerings? Or must he, after all, if he would have life, forsake his nationality, his profession and his friends, to enter by the strait door of circumcision into that narrow alien fold of Judaism? It was while the heart of the centurion was wrestling with these doubts and questionings that the light came to him.

> I labour groaning. Comes a sudden sheen!—
> And I am kneeling at my father's knee,
> Sighing with joy, and hoping utterly.[1]

¶ It's not only a great flight of confidence for a man to change his creed and go out of his family for heaven's sake; but the odds are—nay, and the hope is—that, with all this great transition in the eyes of man, he has not changed himself a hairbreadth to the eyes of God.[2]

II.

THE VISIONS.

i. Cornelius' Vision.

The answer to the centurion's prayers was given in the form of a vision, about the ninth hour of the day. Cornelius was undoubtedly engaged in prayer when suddenly he beheld in his mind an angel of God coming unto him and addressing him by his name. Cornelius felt affrighted at the vision, and could only ask: "What is it, Lord?"

The message was encouraging. His prayers had been accepted, and the desire of his heart for more and fuller light was granted. But the fuller light was to come through human instruments, hence he must send to Joppa for the possessor of the keys who would open the door of the Kingdom to him, and admit him into the secrets of God's household. The instruction to send for Peter tested Cornelius' willingness to be taught by an unknown Jew,

---

[1] G. MacDonald, *Poetical Works*, ii. 265.
[2] R. L. Stevenson, *Travels with a Donkey*.

and his belief in the Divine origin of the vision. The direction given by which to find this teacher was not promising. A lodger with a tanner by the seaside was certainly not a man of position or wealth. But military discipline helped religious reverence; and without delay, as soon as the angel "was departed" (an expression which gives the outward reality of the appearance strongly), Cornelius' confidential servants, sympathisers with him in his religion, were told all the story, and before nightfall were on their march to Joppa.

¶ The vision appeared to Cornelius in the manner corresponding to his spiritual susceptibility, and it came at the hour of prayer. God's angels ever draw near to hearts opened by desire to receive them. Not in visible form, but in reality, "bright-harnessed angels stand" all around the chamber where prayer is made. Our hours of supplication are God's hours of communication.[1]

ii. Peter's Vision.

Meanwhile, as the messengers were still upon their journey, Peter himself had been undergoing a special Divine preparation to qualify him for the new work to which he was to be called.

1. It was drawing on towards the noon hour. The time was at hand when the body was to be refreshed with food and the soul cheered and strengthened by communion with God. The Apostle went up to the flat roof of the house where he was staying to offer prayer. He was there in retirement, with no eye upon him save the Divine eye, to render his thanks and make his supplications. A sudden hunger seized him, but lingering, he fell into a trance. Shut out from the world by his trance, and shut in with the Spirit, the heavens were opened to his gaze. He saw a vessel, or a great sheet, as near as he could describe it, knit at the four corners, and let down out of the skies to the earth. In it were all manner of creatures—beasts, creeping things, fowls of the air. On the descent of this vessel or sheet there came a voice calling on him to kill and eat. He was hungry. His hunger gave shape to the imagery under which he was to learn his all-important lesson.

Hardly any other form in which the instruction could have

[1] A. Maclaren.

been communicated would have been so effective. For the Jews, especially Jews of the strict class to which Peter had always belonged, were exceedingly careful about what they ate. Very naturally, therefore, the Apostle, not yet broadened out to the full dimensions of the love and aim of the Great Teacher, shrank back and said he must not do it. This was not the kind of repast of which he felt at liberty to partake. "Not so, Lord; for I have never eaten any thing that is common or unclean." The distinction between things clean and unclean instituted in the ceremonial law had been abolished on the coming of Christ; but Peter had not yet risen up into sympathy with this idea. This was why he had to be put to school to the vision he beheld and trained out of his race pride and narrowness. "Not so, Lord." He was too dainty and delicate in his tastes. The great commission which he had heard was: "Go ye therefore, and make disciples of all the nations"—no distinctions—"baptizing them"—without distinction—"into the name of the Father and of the Son and of the Holy Spirit; teaching them to observe all things whatsoever I commanded you; and lo, I am with you all the days, even unto the consummation of the age." But this was not enough to liberate his mind and conquer his prejudices. In his view of men there were still distinctions of clean and unclean. Then there came a second voice: "What God hath cleansed, make not thou common." After this had been done thrice, the vessel disappeared. But the great words, the significant words, the key words of the whole disclosure, still lingered: "What God hath cleansed, make not thou common."

2. Taken by itself, this vision might hardly have been quite intelligible to Peter. It might on reflection have indicated no more to him than some approaching change in the laws which regulated food. But the providence of God soon helped him to a clue. He was still meditating on the meaning of what he had seen, when he heard the three strangers approach the outer gate of the entrance court, and call to know if one Peter were lodging there. Hurrying down the outside stair, which led from the roof to the court without passing through the house, Peter himself met and admitted the men. In the light of their message and the dealings of God with their master, Peter felt instinctively

that he was meant to read the true lesson of his ecstasy. So read, it was not hard to interpret it aright. He saw that in the abolition of that symbolical distinction betwixt clean animals and unclean, betwixt what might and might not be eaten, there was also enclosed the abolition of all such unreal distinctions as had hitherto divided before the face of God the Gentile from the Hebrew.

¶ We had a vast party at Earlham, and a remarkable day, a perfectly harmonious mixture of High Church, Low Church, Lutheran, Baptist, Quaker! It was a time which seemed to pull down all barriers of distinction, and to melt us all into one common Christianity. Such a beginning warrants us to expect much.

At five we adjourned to Earlham Hall to dinner, when we sat down thirty-four in number—a mixture of different sects and persuasions. Words fail to express the delightful harmony of our feelings. Soon after the cloth was removed, our dear friend Elizabeth Fry [Joseph John Gurney's sister, who had come from London for the occasion] knelt down, and in a most sweet and impressive manner implored the Divine blessing upon the company present, and for the general promotion of truth upon earth. On her rising, the Secretary, Joseph Hughes (a Dissenting minister) observed in a solemn manner: "Now of a truth I perceive that God is no respecter of persons, but that in every age and nation those who fear Him and work righteousness are accepted of Him"; and the conversation, becoming general, flowed on in a strain which assuredly had less in it of earth than of Heaven.[1]

III.

The Meeting.

1. The event for which the preceding steps had been a preparation took place on the third day after the vision of Cornelius, on the second day after that of Peter. The scene shifts back to the officers' quarters in the barracks at Cæsarea. The good centurion had calculated quite correctly the length of time likely to be consumed by the journey of his messengers and their return. He allowed one night for rest at Joppa, as well as for Peter to make his arrangements to accompany them; and

[1] A. J. C. Hare, *The Gurneys of Earlham*, i. 229.

because the distance exceeded an average day's march, he supposed
the party to have spent another night on the road. This delay
was made all the more requisite by a circumstance which
Cornelius could not anticipate. Conscious that the Divine
summons to Cæsarea and his vision on the housetop must be
precursors of some very momentous transaction, by which the
future relations of Jew and Gentile within the Church were to be
affected, Peter adopted the precaution of taking witnesses along
with him. No fewer than six of the believing Jews of Joppa
were selected to be his companions, in order that their evidence
might afterwards confirm to the whole Jewish Church whatever
indications of His will the Lord should grant. The party, thus
increased to the number of ten, did not actually reach Cæsarea
till towards three o'clock on the afternoon of the second day. By
that time Cornelius was fully expecting them.

2. The description of the meeting of Peter and Cornelius is
very graphic. Fully alive to the importance of the occasion, the
centurion had gathered round him his kinsmen and near friends.
And as the Apostle approached the outer gate of his quarters, he
at once hastened to meet him, and falling down at his feet
" worshipped " him. The word used does not necessarily point to
religious worship, and may indicate only an act of profound
homage ; but that Peter felt the respect thus shown to him
excessive is proved by his vigorous protest: " Stand up ; I
myself also am a man." And then, in opposition to the traditional
interpretation of the law forbidding intercourse with Gentiles, the
Apostle entered the house along with Cornelius, and, in answer to
the inquiry why he had been sent for, learned from the centurion's
own lips the story of the Divine answer to his prayers, in
accordance with which he had despatched his messengers to Joppa.
" And thou hast well done," so Cornelius courteously continued,
" that thou art come. Now therefore we are all here present in
the sight of God, to hear all things that have been commanded
thee of the Lord."

3. Peter's sermon is, on the whole, much like the other addresses
of his which are abundantly reported in the early part of the
Acts. The great business of the preachers then was to tell the

history of Jesus. Christianity is, first, a recital of historical events, from which, no doubt, principles are deduced, and which necessarily lead on to doctrines; but the facts are first.

But the familiar story is told to Cornelius with some variation of tone. And it is prefaced by a great word which crystallizes the large truth that had sprung into consciousness and startling power in Peter, as the result of his own and Cornelius' experience. He had not previously thought of God as "a respecter of persons," but the conviction that He was not never blazed with such sunclearness before him as it did now. Jewish narrowness had, unconsciously to himself, somewhat clouded it; but these four days had burned in on him, as if it were a new truth, that "in every nation" there may be men accepted of God, because they "fear him and work righteousness."

Having started with the statement of what he had come to "perceive" concerning the impartial love of the common Father for the people of all nations, the Apostle went on to preach Jesus to the centurion and his assembled friends as the One who was anointed of God with the Holy Spirit; who was clothed with miraculous powers and filled with tenderest compassion; who was slain and hanged on a tree (of which things he and others were witnesses); who charged His followers to announce Him to the world as the appointed Judge of all, and as the foretold Saviour through whose name every one that believeth may receive remission of sins.

4. Cornelius may have known little of the prophets, but he knew the burden of sin. He did not know all that we know of Jesus, and of the way in which forgiveness is connected with His work, but he did know now that it was connected, and that this Jesus was risen from the dead, and was to be the Judge. His faith went out to that Saviour, and as he heard he believed. Therefore the great gift, attesting the Divine acceptance of him and the rest of the hearers, came at once. There had been no confession of their faith, much less had there been baptism, or laying on of Apostolic hands. The sole qualification and condition for the reception of the Spirit which John lays down in his Gospel when he speaks of the "Spirit which they that believe on him should receive," was present here, and it was enough. Peter

and his brethren might have hesitated about baptizing an un-circumcised believer. The Lord of the Church showed Peter that He did not hesitate.

So, like a true disciple, Peter followed Christ's lead, and though " they of the circumcision " were struck with amazement, he said to himself, " Who am I, that I should withstand God ? " and opened his heart to welcome these new converts as possessors of " like precious faith," as was demonstrated by their possession of the same Spirit.

5. As he enters the portals of the Christian life Cornelius fades from our view; his form is lost in the crowd, and we see him no more.   But he leaves behind him the impression of a man —brave, upright, generous, humble, courteous, a man who, because he was faithful to the light he had, received the crowning blessing.

> Unheard by all but Angel ears
> The good Cornelius knelt alone,
> Nor dream'd his prayers and tears
> Would help a world undone.
>
> The while upon his terraced roof
> The loved Apostle to his Lord
> In silent thought aloof
> For heavenly vision soar'd.
>
> Far o'er the glowing western main
> His wistful brow was upward raised,
> Where, like an Angel's train,
> The burnish'd water blazed.
>
> The saint beside the ocean pray'd,
> The soldier in his chosen bower,
> Where all his eye survey'd
> Seem'd sacred in that hour.
>
> To each unknown his brother's prayer
> Yet brethren true in dearest love
> Were they—and now they share
> Fraternal joys above.

There daily through Christ's open gate
They see the Gentile spirits press,
Brightening their high estate
With dearer happiness.

What civic wreath for comrades saved
Shone ever with such deathless gleam,
Or when did perils braved
So sweet to veterans seem ? [1]

[1] J. Keble, *The Christian Year* (Monday in Easter Week).

DORCAS.

LITERATURE.

Adeney, W. F., *Women of the New Testament* (1899), 209.

Austin, A. B., *Linked Lives* (1913), 181.

Dickinson, C. A., in *Sermons by the Monday Club*, 17th Ser. (1891), 318.

Elmslie, W. G., *Memoir and Sermons* (1890), 108.

Joynt, R. C., *Bible Readings for Class and Home* (1914), 71.

Lewis, Z. H., *Petros*, 229.

Luckock, H. M., *Footprints of the Apostles as traced by Saint Luke in the Acts*, i. (1905) 258.

Mackay, W. M., *Bible Types of Modern Women* (1912), 33.

Maclaren, A., *Christ's Musts* (1894), 179.

    „   „   *Expositions* : The Acts of the Apostles i.–xii. (1907), 288.

    „   „   *Last Sheaves* (1903), 231.

Milligan, G., in *Women of the Bible* : Rebekah to Priscilla (1904), 225.

Morrison, G. H., *The Footsteps of the Flock* (1904), 331.

Salmond, C. A., *For Days of Youth* (1896), 54.

Taylor, W. M., *Peter the Apostle* (1891), 244.

Williams, I., *Female Characters of Holy Scripture* (1890), 311.

Christian Age, xlii. (1892) 354 (A. H. Bradford).

Christian World Pulpit, viii. (1875) 211 (N. H. Axtell); xxxvi. (1889) 269 (T. C. Hill) ; lxxxiv. (1913) 334 (H. Jeffs).

Preacher's Magazine, xvi. (1905) 32 (C. O. Eldridge).

Preachers' Monthly, v. (1883) 252.

DORCAS.

Now there was at Joppa a certain disciple named Tabitha, which by interpretation is called Dorcas: this woman was full of good works and almsdeeds which she did.—Acts ix. 36.

THE Book of Acts holds a unique place in the Bible. It tells us what occurred immediately after Christ's accession to His throne, and in this history we see how He was to conduct His government in the world which He had redeemed by His death. There was at that time introduced into human affairs a new, Divine power, which was to work with tremendous effect in renovating the human race. This new force was to turn men from sin to righteousness. It is for this reason that the raising of Dorcas to life is of such vital importance in the sacred history. It is one of the seals of the new government, a witness to the power of the new King, whose greatest claim was that He held in His hands the issues of life and death.

¶ The last words of George Fox (founder of the Society of Friends) were:
"All is well, all is well—the Seed of God reigns over all, and over death itself. Though I am weak in body, yet the power of God is over all, and the Seed reigns over all disorderly spirits." A little later he said, and they were his last words, "Never heed; the Lord's power is over all weakness and death."[1]

I.

1. The name "Dorcas," so familiar to us through those very useful societies in our modern churches which bear it to-day, is only the Greek translation of the Aramaic "Tabitha," which was the actual name of the woman disciple at Joppa whose story is narrated in the Acts of the Apostles. The Septuagint translates the

[1] F. W. Marvin, *The Last Words of Distinguished Men and Women*, 101.

Hebrew equivalent wherever it occurs in the Old Testament as a common noun meaning "gazelle" by the same Greek word. Still Dorcas is the familiar name to us of the Western Church, and with that name the story must always be associated. A Christian community had been formed in the busy seaport of Joppa, no doubt after the pattern of the Mother Church at Jerusalem. In both places St. James's ideal of "pure religion and undefiled before our God and Father" was aimed at, viz., "to visit the fatherless and widows in their affliction, and to keep himself unspotted from the world." Mary the mother of Mark seems to have been a sort of patroness of the church at Jerusalem. At all events, the brethren used to meet for prayer at her house. Dorcas appears to have been a woman of good social position at Joppa; but her service was rendered in the old-fashioned forms of almsgiving and the work of her needle. She is the type of the homeliest, simplest, and yet most directly practical form of woman's work.

2. Not much is told about Dorcas personally, but what is told is of such a kind that we may conjecture more. Little things have a significance in combination. Thus we can fill in the meagre outline that is given us, till the picture grows into completeness.

When she first comes before us it is at Joppa, apparently a lonely woman, but whether maid or widow we are not told. And we can imagine how in her loneliness Dorcas might, like so many similarly situated, have grown hard and selfish, or have given way to mourning at the bitterness of her lot. But she did neither. She was a disciple, and longed to be of use. And her zeal found an outlet in the "good works" and "almsdeeds," of which, as the sacred historian tells us, she was "full."

> My hastening life admonishes
>   My often-faltering soul to try
> And yet perform some goodly work,
>   Ere, with the years, desires fly.
>
> What, in a world where cries for help
>   Must ever sound till sin shall cease,
> Can be a goodlier work than this,—
>   Griefs to assuage, and joys increase?

To fill with light some sunken eyes
   Where reason struggles with despair:
To bring sin's pallid prisoners forth
   Into the free and wholesome air:

To cheer the oppressed with righteous words,
   And aid them with a labouring arm:
The slaves of tyrant ignorance
   To rescue, and then shield, from harm:

To offer cups of water pure
   From rocky truth's cool, plenteous well,
To souls confused with feverish woes
   Unspoken and unspeakable.

To set ablaze some signal-fire
   Of zealous thought, till in affright
The careless slumberers start and rise,
   And rally round the true and right.

Let me remeditate the truth,
   That Christ did for and with us bleed,
Then, " He is good that doeth good,"
   Shall be my dear and honoured creed.[1]

II.

1. The special charm of Dorcas's charities lies in the fact that she worked for the poor with her own hands. She is celebrated for her " good works " as well as for her " almsdeeds." If the latter means her gifts, the former would point to her personal actions. Perhaps she remembered her Lord's commendation, " I was naked and ye clothed me," and thought that, if it was true that in clothing the poor she clothed Christ, she would do it with no other hands than her own, for it might be that she would, in spirit at least, draw virtue from the hem of His garments while she made them.

¶ Probably Dorcas had been a fine sewer as a girl; but in her girlish days it would be fancy work. The fancy work never became real work till the pity of Jesus touched her womanly

[1] T. T. Lynch, *The Rivulet*, 11.

heart. She was not a speaker; she never addressed meetings. I dare say she envied the ladies who could speak. But she learned that there was a service quite as good as that, and that was the service of a consecrated needle.[1]

2. Dorcas was "a woman of a loving heart." It is said that "prosperity gains friends but adversity tries them." It was not so with Dorcas. Adversity was to her the sole passport to friendship. The house of Dorcas was Joppa's "cave of Adullam." Wherever need or sickness, poverty or death, were stretching out pale and piteous hands, there was always one hand ready to grasp them and lift them up. It was the hand of Dorcas. In the meeting, while the others were preaching and praying, Dorcas would be silent; but when the meeting was over you would have seen her in her little home busy late and early, working there coats and garments by which she clothed the widows and orphans of Joppa. Thus, without knowing it, she became a kind of pioneer in Christian work, and made herself famous in the Church as the founder of "Dorcas societies."

¶ Shall I tell you what I saw the other day? It made me laugh, and yet it made me sad. I saw, in one of your parks, a poor little ragged boy, who was evidently hungry, and who was anxious to appeal successfully to the pity of the public. He was met by a tall, lean, clean man, who set his long, bony fingers together stiffly and impressively, and lectured the child in very suitable language. I overheard him say, "This is not proper. You ought to have been at school; you should not be prowling about here in this way; there are places provided for such as you, and I earnestly advise you to get away from this course of life." Every word he said was grammatically correct, and socially very true. As he was delivering his frosty lecture to the poor lad, there came a boy—a school-boy hastening to school—who was carrying a large lump of bread and butter in his hand, which he was eating as school-boys only can eat; and when he saw the poor ragged child, he pulled his bread and butter in two, put one-half into the boy's hand, and went on. "Not every one that SAITH unto me, Lord, Lord, shall enter into the kingdom of heaven." That boy, who gave his bread and butter away, will stand a better chance than the ninety-nine legally upright, who apparently need no repentance![2]

[1] G. H. Morrison, *The Footsteps of the Flock*, 333.
[2] Joseph Parker.

3. When Dorcas died, it was felt by the whole of Joppa that she had died too soon. Not until then did the Apostles of the Church know what a treasure they had had in her. When the box was broken the odour of the precious nard filled the house. It soon appeared that the lonely woman had won for herself a loving affection which could not have been surpassed had she been the mother of the whole community of the faithful. The widows she had relieved came together, each feeling that she had a property in the heart of their dead friend. They sent for Peter in their bereavement. They sang her praises. They exhibited her works. It is all a touching, impressive lesson of the abiding influence of a true heart.

> If I might guess, then guess I would
> That, mid the gathered folk,
> This gentle Dorcas one day stood,
> And heard when Jesus spoke.
>
> She saw the woven seamless coat—
> Half envious, for His sake:
> "Oh, happy hands," she said, "that wrought
> The honoured thing to make!"
>
> Her eyes with longing tears grow dim:
> She never can come nigh
> To work one service poor for Him
> For whom she glad would die!
>
> But, hark, He speaks! Oh, precious word!
> And she has heard indeed!
> "When did we see Thee naked, Lord,
> And clothed Thee in Thy need?"
>
> The King shall answer, "Inasmuch
> As to My brethren ye
> Did it—even to the least of such—
> Ye did it unto Me."
>
> Home, home she went, and plied the loom,
> And Jesus' poor arrayed.
> She died—they wept about the room,
> And showed the coats she made.[1]

[1] G. MacDonald, *Poetical Works*, i. 314.

III.

Probably the friends of Dorcas expected nothing more than Peter's sympathy and counsel.   At the same time, they can hardly have failed to hear of the miracle he had just been enabled to work on the paralysed limbs of Æneas, and may consequently have nourished a secret hope that even for Dorcas some cure was possible.   At any rate they sent for him, and the urgency of their need may be taken as excusing the urgency of their message: "Delay not to come on unto us."   Nor did Peter hesitate.   At once he arose, and went to them.

1. There are close resemblances between the raising of Tabitha and the raising of Jairus' daughter.   Peter had never forgotten that memorable hour, and *now* he could not follow his Lord too closely.   Peter had been boastful and self-willed and impetuous once; he had loved to suggest and dictate and take the lead.   But *now*, with all the past graven on his heart, his passion is to follow in Jesus' steps.   Had Jesus put all the mourners from the room ?   Then Peter must be alone with Tabitha.   Had Jesus taken the maiden by the hand, and given her back again to her rejoicing friends ?   Then Peter will present Tabitha alive.   The one point of difference is this : Peter knelt down and *prayed*.   In that one clause there lies the difference between the work of Jesus and that of His disciple.   For the power of Peter was delegated power.   It was Christ who was working, and to Christ he must cry.   But Jesus was acting in His inherent sovereignty.   In His own right He was Lord of life and death.   He has the keys of death and of Hades.

¶ In the physical system we owe everything to the sun.   The earth is just a receiver of its light and heat, and by receiving and transmuting it has become what it is.   All its power comes from above.   And we expect to get more and more out of the sun by better uses of it.   We hear of receivers in tropical countries which, by collecting and concentrating its rays, are being used as creators of mechanical energy.   All the forces indeed that are stored in the earth are sun forces.[1]

2. One of the most remarkable things about the Gospels is

[1] J. Brierley, *Faith's Certainties*, 150.

that so many women of whom we know little more than the names have had their names immortalized as the founders of departments of Christian service and Christian liberality inspired by their example. But we should do injustice to womankind in general, and to the women of the old Jewish Church in particular, if we took it for granted that the charities which blossomed in the life of such a saint as Dorcas were entirely new flowers of grace quite unknown to the world before the time of Christianity. We may be permitted to suppose that the model housewife Penelope, spinning among her women while her husband Ulysses is on his travels, would find some garment to spare for the poor swineherd's widow. Almsgiving, we know, was about the principal duty of the pious Jew in the time of our Lord. It takes a prominent place as a manifestation of righteousness in the so-called " Psalms of Solomon," a Pharisaic work of the times just before the advent of Christianity.

Still, while we make full allowance for these facts, not in any degree attempting to minimize them in order to exalt Christianity, but rather honouring them most ungrudgingly, we may go on and observe how much the gospel of Jesus Christ deepens and quickens the motive for charity. If so much kindness is seen in the world and in Judaism, how much more should be found in the Church of which brotherly love growing out of the love of God in Christ is to be the characteristic note!

3. Dorcas in some quarters to-day may be regarded as an old-fashioned type of woman, and yet, surely, the noblest type of woman is the woman who is most womanly; and there is nothing more womanly than the exercise of those specific feminine gifts in the name, and for the sake, of Christ, for the help of those who are in deep need.

¶ By the raising of Dorcas, God meant to set a mark of honour on the love that was displayed. I think He would guard the Church against undue estimation of preaching, apostles, miracle-working, deeds of show, gifts; and teach us that beyond all is love. So He singles out not an apostle, not a martyr, but this gentle, kind, womanly life, and crowns it with grandeur and glory, makes it conqueror of death, encircles it with a halo of most wonderful, Divine, loving care.[1]

[1] *Professor W. G. Elmslie, D.D.*, 116.

When Dorcas worked to clothe the poor,
 A neighbour or a friend
Sometimes came tapping at the door,
 A little help to lend;
Then Dorcas said, "Come in, my dear;
All willing hands are welcome here."

A friendly light was in her eyes,
 And pity on her tongue,
Her words were mild as well as wise;
 And round her room there hung
Nice things to make the children glad,
And warm ones for the old and sad.

And everybody in the town
 Knew Dorcas, as she went,
In any weather, up and down,
 On doing good intent;
And blest her for her cheerful face,
The kindest woman in the place.

But tender-hearted Dorcas died;
 New tears the widows shed;
For, "Who such garments can provide,
 Now she is gone?" they said;
Dorcas, who by the pleasant sea
Had spent her life so usefully.

She died: they bore her as was meet,
 With many a heavy sigh,
A little further from the street
 And nearer to the sky:
Now in a spacious upper room
She waits the low and narrow tomb.

"O Peter, can she live again?
 This is a grievous day."
Said he, "Submit, and not complain;
 But I will kneel and pray:
'Lord, on Thy sorrowing people smile;
Give Dorcas back a little while.'"

She came: "But not for long," she said;
    "For God will others raise
Whose lovingkindness, in my stead,
    His gracious name shall praise;
I heard a voice in Paradise
Say, 'Lovingkindness never dies.'"

And Dorcas in her daughters lives,
    Industrious and kind;
For help her good example gives
    To willing hand and mind.
Lord, in our hearts her spirit stir:
She followed Thee; we follow her.[1]

[1] T. T. Lynch, *The Rivulet*, 164.

BARNABAS.

LITERATURE.

Adeney, W. F., in *Men of the New Testament* : Matthew to Timothy (1905), 303.

Bartlett, J. S., *Sermons* (1870), 138.

Boyd, A. K. H., *The Graver Thoughts of a Country Parson*, ii. (1865) 72.

Brooke, S. A., *Short Sermons* (1892), 129.

Brown, J., *Sermons with Memoir* (1892), 234.

Clifford, J., *The Gospel of Gladness* (1912), 172.

Deane, A., *Friends and Fellow Labourers of St. Paul* (1906), 37.

Farrar, F. W., *The Life and Work of St. Paul* (1897).

Greenhough, J. G., *The Apostles of our Lord* (1904), 253.

Harper, F., *Echoes from the Old Evangel* (1899), 58.

Howson, J. S., *The Companions of St. Paul* (1874), 1.

Jenks, D., *In the Face of Jesus Christ* (1914), 436.

Keble, J., *Sermons for the Christian Year* : Saints' Days (1877), 234, 242.

Lee, F. T., *The New Testament Period and its Leaders* (1913), 234.

Mackay, W. M., *Bible Types of Modern Men* (1910), 89.

Maclaren, A., *Expositions* : The Acts of the Apostles i.–xii. (1907), **323, 343**.

      ,   „   „   „   „   xiii.–end (1907), 91.

     „   „ *Last Sheaves* (1903), 219.

Newbolt, W. C. E., *Words of Exhortation* (1900), 92, 105, 245.

Ryley, G. B., *Barnabas* (1893).

Seekings, H. S., *The Men of the Pauline Circle* (1914), **33**.

Smith, W. M., *Giving a Man another Chance* (1908), 11.

Stuart, J. G., *Talks about Soul-Winning* (1900), 82.

Vince, C., *The Unchanging Saviour* (1875), 263.

Whyte, A., *Bible Characters* : Joseph and Mary to James (1900), **227**.

Wordsworth, J., in *Sermons for the People*, New Ser., v. (1906) 27.

Young, D. T., *Neglected People of the Bible* (1901), 201.

Christian World Pulpit, xviii. (1880) 324 (J. Kelly).

Church Pulpit Year Book, ii. (1905) 153.

Churchman's Pulpit : St. Barnabas, St. John the Baptist, xiv. 438 (J. S. Bartlett).

Examiner, May 25, 1905 (J. H. Jowett).

Homiletic Review, lvii. (1909) 69 (J. Silvester).

Literary Churchman, xvii. (1871) 215.

BARNABAS.

Our beloved Barnabas and Paul, men that have hazarded their lives for the name of our Lord Jesus Christ.—Acts xv. 25, 26.

1. SCRIPTURE narratives are remarkable for the frankness with which they tell the faults of the best men. This has nothing in common with the cynical spirit in historians, of which this age has seen eminent examples, which fastens upon the weak places in the noblest natures, like a wasp on bruises in the ripest fruit, and delights in showing how all goodness is imperfect, that it may suggest that none is genuine. Nor has it anything in common with that dreary melancholy—which also has its representatives among us—which sees everywhere only failures and fragments of men, and has no hope of ever attaining anything beyond the common average of excellence. But Scripture frankly confesses that all its noblest characters have fallen short of unstained purity, and with boldness of hope as great as its frankness teaches the weakest to aspire to, and the most sinful to expect, perfect likeness to a perfect Lord. It is a mirror which gives back all images without distortion.

The interest of such a revelation lies in this, that it gives us an encouragement to do our best with our own lives, by showing us that much may be done by secondary characters and by ordinary means. We cannot expect to reach the glory of St. Peter, St. Paul, and St. John, but we may have more hope of treading in the footsteps of St. Andrew, as shown in the Gospels, or St. Barnabas, as portrayed in the Acts. The description here given is that of a simple character, not of one specially distinguished for strength or commanding personality, for eloquence or dialectic skill.

2. Barnabas has been in a measure eclipsed, or at least overshadowed, by his more distinguished colleague and fellow-soldier. That is not surprising. Paul was much the greater man of the

two in intellectual power and perhaps in force of character. With Paul the fine moral and spiritual qualities were united with the gifted mind, the eloquent tongue, the originating genius, and the boundless energy which belong to the makers of history. Such men inevitably go to the front and win the leading place in the world's regard. At first in the Acts of the Apostles, when the two men are spoken of together, Barnabas is placed first. That was evidently the position assigned to him by those who sent them forth. The Church had not then discovered which was the greater man. But the course of events proved it, and Barnabas quietly fell back into the second place, and before long was allowed to drop out of the story.

Yet no one can read the story of Barnabas without seeing that he is one of the saints who have been pressed out of their proper place. Unintentionally they have been dwarfed in history by the greater prominence and wider reach, in visible influence, of some of their comrades. The mental intensity and greatness of Paul, together with the consequently large and permanent publicity of his work, have unfortunately lessened both the recognition and the estimate of the services of Barnabas. It ought not to have been so. The life and work of Paul ought to have been as added light on the lustre of Barnabas. For a true judgment of Paul cannot but aid in giving to Barnabas his proper value; while, at the same time, the right estimate of Barnabas will assign to Paul only additional and more evidently deserved honour. The two are inseparable in some of the most important events in the history of the Church of Christ. They were, in their union and comradeship, involved in such momentous crises of the brotherhood in Christ, and together had so to determine the direction of the Church's action at important turning-points, as to make it more than desirable to judge neither of them apart from the other, but each in his dependence on his brother, for a right valuation of their work in the Lord. They have been regarded almost as moving in separate circles, and as coming only for a little time into influential relationship with each other, Barnabas being but the satellite of Paul. They were, rather, for the most important part of their lives, as twin stars having concentric revolution, of different colour and size, certainly, but therefore all the more interesting in their nearness and companionship, and all the more suggestive to devout thought because of their action and reaction on one another.

¶ Barnabas is one of those minor characters of Scripture, who at once gain and lose by their proximity to a greater figure. He gains doubtless much from his relation to the gigantic figure of Paul, for it was in company with him that his best work was done. And yet, perhaps, he suffers more; for the friend with whom he walks is so colossal that we forget all when we see him. A mountain in Scotland would be a hillock in Switzerland. A Thames in England would be an obscure rivulet if it poured itself into the Amazon.[1]

¶ And then, when at last we reached the summit of that monster mountain, which summit was like the bottom of an inverted cone situated in the centre of an awful cosmic pit, we found that we were at neither top nor bottom. Far above us was the heaven-towering horizon, and far beneath us, where the top of the mountain should have been, was a deeper deep, the great crater, the House of the Sun. Twenty-three miles around stretched the dizzy walls of the crater. We stood on the edge of the nearly vertical western wall, and the floor of the crater lay nearly half a mile beneath. This floor, broken by lava-flows and cinder-cones, was as red and fresh and uneroded as if it were but yesterday that the fires went out. The cinder-cones, the smallest over four hundred feet in height and the largest over nine hundred seemed no more than puny little sand-hills, so mighty was the magnitude of the setting.[2]

I.

THE SON OF EXHORTATION.

Joseph, who by the apostles was surnamed Barnabas (which is, being interpreted, Son of exhortation).—Acts iv. 36.

1. We cannot read the Bible with the least degree of attention without observing what great importance is everywhere attached to names. In the Old Testament, the name of a person, being frequently taken from some leading incident in the course of his previous life, is found to convey this incident to us and, as it were, to concentrate it in a single word. We find names connected

[1] W. M. Mackay, *Bible Types of Modern Men*, 89.
[2] J. London, *The Cruise of the Snark*, 121.

with events far more frequently than is the case with us; we find them changed from time to time, in order that they may become more fully descriptive of their owner, and impress his history on the mind. And above all, we find this usage expressly sanctioned by Almighty God Himself, in His giving new names to many of His servants, descriptive of His own will and regard concerning them. It was not, we may reverently believe, without a deep purpose in the Divine counsels that God commanded a name already given by man to be exchanged for another, which should be an earnest and a witness of His goodwill to His faithful servants. "Neither shall thy name any more be called Abram, but thy name shall be Abraham; for a father of many nations have I made thee." "As for Sarai thy wife, thou shalt not call her name Sarai, but Sarah"—that is, Princess—"shall her name be." "Thy name shall be called no more Jacob, but Israel: for as a prince hast thou power with God and with men, and hast prevailed." In all these cases, of Abraham, of Sarah, and of Jacob, we see that the giving of a new name is made a pledge to them of mercies yet future, it might be yet distant, but secured to them by this title-deed of God's favour and gracious purposes towards them. In the New Testament the giving of a new name to the Apostle Simon—"I also say unto thee, that thou art Peter"—"thou shalt be called Cephas, which is by interpretation, A stone"—sets before us his office as the first and zealous preacher of Christ to the Gentile Church. The name "sons of thunder," given by our Lord to St. James and St. John, tells of their fervour in His cause, their jealousy for His honour, and, it may be, the mighty effect which their mission should have on the hearts of men. Saul the persecutor becomes the Apostle Paul, the "little one," "less than the least of all saints," yet through the grace of Christ labouring more abundantly than all. We observe the change in the case of Barnabas. It is not by the name Joseph, but the surname added by the Apostles, "Barnabas, the son of exhortation," that we bring him to our remembrance. It is difficult for us to point with confidence to the exact occasion on which this name Barnabas was given, or to the particular circumstances which led to its being given; nor is it indeed possible or necessary to enter now on the various opinions given by Christian writers on the subject. But we may without any difficulty trace, even in the short record of Barnabas given to us in the Acts of the Apostles, a singular degree of correspondence between his character and his name.

Notwithstanding the presence of miraculous gifts in the Church, and the ministration of Apostles, the need of gentle and tenderly helpful hearts must have been very great in the young community, if the manifold grace of God was to be adequately shown. And very deep and hallowed must Joseph's service of Christ and the Church have been for him to be known as the first believer, after the ascension of our Blessed Lord, who is recorded to have had a new Christian name. This renaming with a religious name had been begun by Christ Himself; and Peter, who was the notable instance of this, must have felt less worthy of his sacred and almost august name than Joseph was of his more tender and gracious nomination.

¶ Dick Sunshine was not his real name; at least so they said. But the thing that they called his real name did not describe him a scrap; it seemed to abandon all attempt at description as hopelessly impossible; but when you called him Dick Sunshine it fitted him like a glove. That is the immense advantage that nicknames possess over real names. Of all real things, real names are the most unreal. There is no life in them. They stand for nothing; they express nothing; they reveal nothing. They bear no kind of relationship to the unfortunate individuals who are sentenced to wear them, like meaningless badges, for the term of their natural lives. But nicknames, on the other hand, sparkle and flash; they bring the man himself vividly and palpitatingly before you; and, without more introduction or ado, you know him at once for what he is.[1]

2. On three occasions in the history of the Apostolic Church we find Barnabas exhorting new converts to the faith of Christ—fulfilling his function as a son of exhortation. The first occasion was when he was sent by the Apostles from Jerusalem to Antioch, in Syria, to investigate the work which had been done among the Gentiles by the ministry of some of the disciples who had been scattered abroad upon the persecution that had arisen about Stephen. The second occasion was when, in company with Paul, he came to Antioch, in Pisidia, on the first missionary journey of

[1] F. W. Boreham, *Mushrooms on the Moor*, 85.

the great Apostle of the Gentiles. The third occasion was on their return journey, when they confirmed the souls of the disciples in the various places which they had visited.

(1) Barnabas came to Antioch in some doubt about the work, the tidings of which had reached Jerusalem. It was a new and unexpected occurrence, this conversion of a multitude of Gentiles. They did not know what to make of it at Jerusalem—it does not appear that the tidings of the formal opening of the door of faith to the Gentiles by the Apostle Peter at Cæsarea had yet reached the Mother Church—and Barnabas came down, with instructions, perhaps, to keep things all right, to see that things were properly managed; but when he saw the work, all misgiving vanished, and he was glad; and instead of interfering in any way, he furthered the work by his exhortations. He was a large-hearted, liberal-minded man, and sympathized with every genuine spiritual move-ment. Wherever he saw the hand of God really at work, he was ready to co-operate and rejoice. We read, "When he came, and had seen the grace of God, he was glad, and exhorted them all, that with purpose of heart they would cleave unto the Lord."

(a) The first thing that strikes one about this all-sufficient directory for Christian life is the emphasis with which it sets forth "the Lord" as the one object to be grasped and held. The sum of all objective religion is Christ—the sum of all subjective religion is cleaving to Him. A living Person to be laid hold of, and a personal relation to that Person—such is the conception of religion, whether considered as revelation or as inward life, which underlies this exhortation. Whether we listen to His own words about Himself, and mark the altogether unprecedented way in which He was His own theme, and the unique decisiveness and plainness with which He puts His own personality before us as the Incarnate Truth, the pattern for all human conduct, the refuge and the rest for the world of weary ones; or whether we give ear to the teaching of His Apostles; from whatever point of view we approach Christianity, it all resolves itself into the Person of Jesus Christ.

¶ If Barnabas had been like some of us, he would have had a very different style of exhortation. He would have said, "This irregular work has been well done, but there are no authorized teachers here, and no provision has been made for the due administration of the sacraments of the Church. The very first thing of all is to give these people the blessing of bishops and priests." Some of us would have said, " Valuable work has been done, but these good people are terribly ignorant. The best thing would be to get ready as soon as possible some manual of Christian doctrine, and in the meantime provide for their systematic instruction in at least the elements of the faith." Some of us would have said, " No doubt they have been converted, but we fear there has been too much of the emotional in the preaching. The moral side of Christianity has not been pressed home, and what they chiefly need is to be taught that it is not feeling, but righteousness. Plain, practical instruction in Christian duty is the one thing they want." Barnabas knew better. He did not despise organization, nor orthodoxy, nor practical righteousness, but he knew that all three, and everything else that any man needed for his perfecting, would come, if only the converts kept near to Christ, and that nothing else was of any use if they did not.[1]

(b) He also exhorted them to be resolute. It was to be the settled purpose of their heart to continue with the Lord. It was not to be a fitful, impulsive thing, a thing of wind and tide merely; it was to be a steadfast continuance. The purpose was to be deliberate and deep. Nothing else will enable any one to continue with the Lord. There might be some in Antioch who were caught up in the sweep of a great movement, and had not duly considered what it was to be the Lord's. It requires resolution and perseverance to be true to the Lord. Those who do not purpose in their hearts to continue with the Lord are sure to drop off when the immediate impulse that moved them to associate themselves with Him has spent its force. There are those who are easily moved, and very ready to form and express resolutions to be the Lord's; but they are soon drawn back to the world or turned aside. They do not really purpose in their hearts. The best sign in some cases is when people cease to resolve, and substitute a steady course of action for fitful and inconstant resolution. It is resolute action, resolute continuance with the Lord, that is wanted.

¶ As in some great symphony the theme which was given out in low notes on one poor instrument recurs over and over again embroidered with varying harmonies, and unfolding a richer music till it swells into all the grandeur of the triumphant close, so

[1] A. Maclaren.

our lives should be bound into a unity, and in their unity bound to Christ by the constant renewal of our early faith, and the fathers come round again to the place which they occupied when as children they first knew Him that is from the Beginning to the End one and the same.[1]

¶ The writer of this testimony was for many months engaged in a civil capacity on the fortifications near Gravesend, whose erection Gordon was superintending, and thus speaks of what he knew. The "superb confidence in himself" which he noted and admired in the hero was associated with unusual Christian humility. It is more than probable that something of Gordon's fixed resoluteness arose from the fact that he came to no decision but in implicit reliance on the Divine direction. Here we have what has very lately been described as the "insubordinate" element in General Gordon's character. The same fixed unchangeable quality—"insubordinate" to human dictation—is plainly evident in Saul of Tarsus, whom no warnings, no prayers, lamentations, or tears, could bend from *his* purpose when he went bound in the spirit to Jerusalem.[2]

(2) Let us now consider the second occasion on which we see Barnabas as an exhorter of young converts. It was at Antioch in Pisidia, in Asia Minor. He had arrived there after a perilous journey from the sea-coast with the great Apostle of the Gentiles. They had attended the synagogue on the first Sabbath after their arrival. St. Paul had preached to the assembled congregation, and after its dispersion, we read, "Many of the Jews and of the devout proselytes followed Paul and Barnabas: who, speaking to them, urged them to continue in the grace of God." This after-meeting sprang from the felt and clearly expressed needs of the new converts. It was sought by the converts themselves, for the purpose of obtaining fuller and more detailed instruction than could be got from a public address to a large and more mixed audience. It afforded them the opportunity of putting questions and having doubts and difficulties removed. It gave the Apostles the opportunity of applying the Word to the needs of various single cases.

There were two parts in the work of this after-meeting. There was instruction and there was persuasion. The persuasion was the practical application of the instruction. Now what did

---

[1] A. Maclaren, *The Secret of Power*, 121.
[2] A. E. Keeling, *General Gordon, Hero and Saint*, 63.

Paul and Barnabas persuade their followers to do? They persuaded them to continue in the grace of God. They had received the forgiveness of sins that was preached to them through Jesus. They were now justified from all things from which they could not be justified by the law of Moses, and they were exhorted to continue in the grace of God. Now what is to continue in the grace of God? It is to hold fast the salvation that the grace of God brings, to practise what the grace of God teaches, to look for what the grace of God leads us to expect, to be what the grace of God would have us to be. This is continuance in the grace of God. "By the grace of God I am what I am," wrote the great Apostle to the Corinthians, "and his grace which was bestowed upon me was not in vain; but I laboured more abundantly than they all" (*i.e.* all the Apostles): "yet not I, but the grace of God which was with me." St. Paul wrote thus of his position and work as an Apostle, but in principle his words apply equally to the position and life of every Christian.

> My stock lies dead, and no increase
>   Doth my dull husbandry improve.
> O let Thy graces without cease
>   Drop from above!
>
> The dew doth ev'ry morning fall,
>   And shall the dew out-strip Thy dove?
> The dew, for which grass cannot call,
>   Drop from above.
>
> Death is still working like a mole,
>   And digs my grave at each remove;
> Let grace work too, and on my soul
>   Drop from above.
>
> Sin is still hammering my heart
>   Unto a hardness void of love;
> Let suppling grace, to cross his art,
>   Drop from above.
>
> O come! for Thou dost know the way.
>   Or if to me Thou wilt not move,
> Remove me where I need not say,
>   Drop from above.[1]

[1] George Herbert.

(3) The third and last occasion on which we find Barnabas exercising his peculiar gift as an exhorter was on the return journey from Derbe—the extreme limit of St. Paul's first great missionary journey. We read (Acts xiv. 21, 22): "When they had preached the gospel to that city, and had made many disciples, they returned to Lystra, and to Iconium, and to Antioch, confirming the souls of the disciples, exhorting them to continue in the faith, and that through many tribulations we must enter into the kingdom of God." The exhortation is twofold. It is to continuance in the faith and to preparedness for manifold troubles.

(*a*) Continuance in the faith is just continuance in the belief of the gospel. There are many influences adverse to continuance in the belief of the gospel. They are inward and outward. They are moral and intellectual. They are different at different times, in different places and circumstances. Whatever they are to us, we must not let them rob us of our faith in the gospel. We must hold fast the faithful Word as we have been taught. The preservation of a good conscience is necessary to continuance in the faith. The putting away of a good conscience leads in many cases to the shipwreck of faith. The discernment of the true grounds of faith, the refusal to permit inappropriate tests to be applied to it, and the domain of faith to be invaded by intruders who have neither the authority nor the qualifications to speak concerning the things with which it is conversant, are necessary as safeguards against the assaults to which the faith of many is exposed and to their continuance in the faith.

(*b*) "Through many tribulations we must enter into the kingdom of God." The tribulations are such as are common to man, and they are such as are special to the believer. They include those things which the Christian has to suffer immediately for Christ's sake, for righteousness' sake. Paul and Barnabas spoke, doubtless, of what was before the particular disciples whose souls they confirmed by exhorting them to continuance in the faith, and by telling them that through much tribulation they should enter the Kingdom of God; but the way into the Kingdom is ever the pathway of tribulation. Tribulation is the disciple's portion in the world. "Enter ye in at the strait," or, in more modern English, "the narrow gate." Narrow is the gate, and restricted or crushed in, is the way that leadeth unto life, said our Saviour in the

Sermon on the Mount. Christ, in the very terms in which He exhorted His hearers to enter by the gate and tread along the way, taught this, and on different occasions He insisted on the necessity of cross-bearing and self-denial in order to discipleship, and fully prepared His disciples for all they were to meet with in and from the world. He would have all His disciples fully and fairly count the cost. In the same spirit and with the same end in view—viz., the strengthening, the confirming, the establishment of the disciples whom they were addressing, the fortifying them against the shock their faith might experience when tribulation overtook them, and preparing them for it—Paul and Barnabas told them that "through many tribulations we must enter into the kingdom of God."

¶ Blessed, thrice blessed are ye, to whom your Lord has fitted your cross, as He in His righteous but tender love saw best for you. Blessed are ye, if ye but learn your blessedness, whatever cross by nature or by the order of His government He has placed upon you. Ye will not seek high things on whom the lowly cross has been bestowed. But treasure it up for yourselves in your secret hearts, there is no form of it which is not healing— bury it deep there, it will heal you first, through His precious Spirit, and, when it has healed you, will through you heal others. Only yield yourselves to His Fatherly hand who gave it to you, to do to you, in you, through you, His loving and gracious will. To be by suffering made meet for doing well, and to do well and suffer for it, and to suffer in order that we may do well, this is our calling: and if God finds in us thus, any secret resemblance to the Son of Man, He may also lift us up towards heaven, and draw men unto us by suffering.[1]

3. Barnabas and Paul were the first to venture forth into the unknown wastes of heathendom to claim the whole world for the Master. The beginning of that mighty enterprise and the epoch-making thought which suggested it were enough of themselves to give these men names which can never be forgotten. And it is not too much to say that Barnabas led the way, for the thought had its origin in his mind before it laid hold of the man who embodied it in his wider and grander labours. We are almost reminded of Luther and Melanchthon. The less-known man had the first vision of the thing that needed to be done,

[1] E. B. Pusey.

and the man of greater energy worked out the vision into act. To Barnabas the light came first, and what we may describe as "the imperial call." He knows that he belongs to those who set the pattern "how to live." Not reluctantly, but eagerly and at once, he accepts the responsibility of leadership. He is a magnetic man; men are drawn to him as flowers to the light. His voice is cheery, his words feed courage, his presence radiates comfort and gladness. He is a lovable man, lifting those around him into a higher and sunnier sphere.

Count me o'er earth's chosen heroes,—they were souls that
    stood alone,
While the men they agonized for hurled the contumelious
    stone,
Stood serene, and down the future saw the golden beam
    incline
To the side of perfect justice, mastered by their faith divine,
By one man's plain truth to manhood and to God's supreme
    design.[1]

II.

THE GOOD MAN.

He was a good man, and full of the Holy Ghost and of faith.—Acts xi. 24.

The eulogy pronounced upon Barnabas is obviously suggested by his conduct as deputy to Antioch from the Mother Church at Jerusalem, which is recorded in the passage from which the text is taken. But when we turn to the other notices of this companion of the Apostles, we find that they are consistent with this one. In all of them we recognize the same large-hearted man who here acknowledges the presence of Divine grace under forms divergent from the common and approved forms of the religious life, and extends toleration to those who have broken through restrictions long deemed essential. To each of these notices this eulogy might be appended. Barnabas is from first to last a distinctively good man, full of the Holy Ghost and of faith, a man of winning and attractive character.

[1] J. R. Lowell.

He was a good man. "Good," not in the common acceptation of the term, but in the Divine. If a man lives morally; if he pays that which he owes; if he bestows his goods to feed the poor; if he conforms to the rules of society and the forms of religion, whatever his motives for so doing, by universal consent he is denominated "a good man." Now the goodness of Barnabas involved all this. He was of the tribe of Levi; a son of exhortation, as his name signifies, and as he was surnamed by his fellow-Apostles; and so kind and charitable that he sold all his lands at Cyprus, and laid the money at the Apostles' feet at Jerusalem, that they might distribute to the necessities of the poor. But the goodness of Barnabas was Divine—the creation of the Holy Spirit. His goodness consisted in this, that "he was full of the Holy Ghost and of faith."

1. *He was full of the Holy Ghost.*—The character in which Barnabas is here presented to us is that of a person greatly rejoicing in other men's goodness. He was glad when he saw the grace of God in his brethren. This feeling is especially attributed by Holy Scripture to the sanctifying Spirit of God. So that the "charity" which "envieth not" the spiritual attainments of others, is an especial token "of the Holy Ghost and of faith."

¶ The saints of God illustrate in various ways the fulness of the Spirit. St. Barnabas shows how His illuminating grace may make an able strong man to be kindly, thoughtful and patient, self-surrendering and unobtrusive. Nothing is more beautiful in his life than the way in which the patron of St. Paul was contented to become the second figure in the first missionary journey.[1]

(1) The story in Acts xi. gives an illustration of this. Barnabas went all the way from Jerusalem to Antioch in order to ascertain the truth of the conversion of the Gentiles and to prove its character. And "when he came and had seen the grace of God, he was glad"; that is to say, he rejoiced in the results of the gospel of the grace of God even among the heathen, though it was quite a new thing in his experience. He came, he saw, he rejoiced, and therein he gave one proof of his

[1] D. Jenks, *In the Face of Jesus Christ*, 436.

spirituality and goodness in that he recognized God's work wherever he saw it. As it is a sin against the Holy Ghost to attribute to evil agency the work of God, so it is the very power of the Spirit by which we perceive that work.

Barnabas does not condemn the movement because it is new, or refuse to see its worth because it is not according to "apostolic orders." He pierces at once to the heart of things, rejoices at the proofs of the working of the grace of God in an unexpected quarter and in unforeseen ways, and, rising to the highest demands of the occasion, prepares the way for a cordial welcome by the guardians of the faith at Jerusalem of this wonderful expansion of original Christianity. That is the new fact. That is what is due to the Holy Ghost. Barnabas sees clearly and sanely; sees clearly what was altogether hidden before, and sees sanely what he saw selfishly before, for his eye is single, and his whole body is full of the Holy Ghost. We may call that "intellectual regeneration," with Chalmers, if we will, or the spiritualization of the intellect, as it might rather be described; but the fact is this, however we name it—the entrance of the whole man into a new world of thought, his emergence from the lower and darker realms of pure sense and sheer intellectualism on to the highest plane of life and thought, whence his outlook on the contents of experience and possibility makes all things new. Intellectuality and spirituality are two very different things. One man may be keenly intellectual, and yet as blind as a bat to the things of the Spirit; and another may be ignorant of litera-ture, a stranger to the kingdom of culture, and yet a master of the spiritual life. Peter and John are an offence to the ecclesi-astical statesmen of Jerusalem because they dare to initiate a revolution whilst they are "ignorant and unlearned men"; but the ages testify that they were the men who were "of the truth" and saw the truth, who knew the forces that make for progress and could wield them, and who had taken possession of and uttered the ideas that have led the life of the world. It is John Bunyan, a man who has the training of a tinker and not of a university, who has gathered at his feet as willing listeners more men, women, and children than any other teacher outside the charmed circle of the builders of the Bible. It is George Fox, a man who owes nothing to the schools, who utters truths of revelation which the

Churches have not yet fully understood, although the later years have brought us much nearer to his mind. It has been said, "The decisive movements of the world are accomplished in the intellect." That is true as it stands of material and scientific progress, but it is comprehensive of all the facts only when we speak of the intellect as quickened, regenerated, and spiritualized, as taught and swayed by the Spirit of God.

¶ In matters of this kind, everything depends upon the spirit of the deputation. Some men have not the requisite sense, because they have not the requisite senses. They have not the capacity for inquiry, because they have not acquired the proper powers of perception. "Except a man be born from above he cannot see the kingdom of God." Then why send such a man on any errand of inquiry? You would not send a blind man to the Academy. You would not send a deaf man to write a critique upon some oratorio. And in the realm of grace there are some things which the mere reporter can never report. The unequipped reporter would go to Jerusalem and he would see the happenings of Pentecost, and this would be his report: "These men are full of new wine." He would go to Wales and pass from meeting to meeting, and from town to town, and this would be the headline of his lively and flippant column: "Hysteria!" And such a man would have gone to Antioch, at the outbreak of this great revival, and he would have witnessed nothing but confusion, and he would have heard nothing but the rowdy ejaculations of an alien tongue. "Eyes have they, but they see not." Yes, we must send the right reporter. If Jerusalem would know what is doing at Antioch, everything depends upon the character and spirit of its agent.[1]

¶ "Tell me," says Dr. Arnot, "what gladdens or grieves a man and I will tell you what sort of a man he is." Christ was sorry when He saw men despising the way of peace—"O Jerusalem, Jerusalem, . . . how often would I have gathered thy children together, even as a hen gathereth her chickens under her wings, and ye would not!" Christ rejoiced when men received His Word—"I thank thee, O Father, Lord of heaven and earth, that thou didst hide these things from the wise and prudent, and didst reveal them unto babes." And St. John said, "I have no greater joy than to hear that my children walk in truth." St. Barnabas was glad too when he saw a bit of the new heaven and the new earth.[2]

[1] J. H. Jowett, in *The Examiner*, 1905, p. 506.
[2] F. Harper, *Echoes from the Old Evangel*, 59.

(2) The deeper qualities in the character of Barnabas first emerge when he comes into contact with Paul. This was soon after the wonderful transformation on the road to Damascus. When the converted persecutor went up to Jerusalem, he was at first coldly received. People could not believe that he was genuine. They thought his action a ruse, and they fought shy of him. Considering the extraordinary circumstances of the case, this is not at all remarkable. Paul had been the fiercest of the antagonists of the Christians, "breathing threatening and slaughter against the disciples of the Lord." Had he not gone on a self-chosen mission to Damascus, in order to kindle the fires of persecution in that city? To hear that such a man had suddenly become a follower of the faith which he had been hitherto living to destroy was the most unlikely news. People could not believe it. Then Barnabas came forward and took him by the hand, introducing him to the Apostles, warmly commending him for the good work he had already done in Damascus. This was a doubly generous act.

¶ There is something praiseworthy in a soul which, beholding in another the dim promise of some better, finer thing than he has yet achieved, does not hesitate to defend his cause against the suspicions of others whose goodwill he may alienate and whose judgment he may cross by his daring advocacy. This Barnabas did for Saul.[1]

(*a*) Barnabas as a Hellenist may be reckoned a member of that section of the Church to which Stephen had belonged. It does not appear that the martyrdom of Stephen was a part of a general policy of persecution, although that policy was a direct outcome of it. The provocation was found in Stephen's liberal theology. The Apostles were assiduous in their attendance at the Temple. But Stephen was thought to have spoken disrespectfully of the Temple and the ancient customs it represented. If, then, Barnabas was known to sympathize with the more liberal views, he might have been seized any day as a special object of aversion to the Jewish authorities. Paul had been consenting to the death of Stephen and taking some part in the scene. In the eyes of Barnabas, therefore, Paul would have appeared to be a very dangerous man. Yet Barnabas is the first Jerusalem

---

[1] H. S. Seekings, *The Men of the Pauline Circle*, 37.

Christian to welcome him. It is possible that he had known
Paul in those early days before the troubles arose. Cyprus is not
far from Tarsus, and there was constant communication between
the island and that part of Asia Minor where Paul had resided in
his youth. Then they were both Hellenists, both Greek-speaking
Jews, natives of Greek provinces. Previous acquaintance and
local sympathies and similarities may have rendered Barnabas
more ready than others to welcome Paul; but they are not
sufficient to account for his courageous action. This sprang from
his own noble nature. He is full of the Holy Ghost, and so he
can believe in so great a wonder as the conversion of Paul by the
grace and power of God; therefore he can believe in the genuineness of Paul's new profession of faith. The little, mean soul,
narrow in its conception of God, cold in its own relations to the
unseen, cannot believe in more than petty movements in religion.
A vast volcanic upheaval, such as had taken place in the heart of
the notorious persecutor, is wholly beyond its imagination, because
it is quite out of the range of its experience. It is the large-hearted
Barnabas who can believe in so tremendous a spiritual convulsion
as the conversion of Paul.

(*b*) Barnabas not only receives Paul and believes in his
conversion, but he does so at his own expense. There is no
reason to doubt that he recognized from the first that Paul
would to a certain extent supplant him. The beauty of his
character is seen in the gracious spirit with which he allowed
himself to be eclipsed by a younger man. There is a resemblance to the case of the two sons of Zebedee in the
change that is made with the order of their names during
the course of the history. At first the Gospels give us
"James and John his brother"; but in the account of the
martyrdom of the former we find him described as "James the
brother of John." Similarly at first we read of "Barnabas and
Paul," and this order of the names is kept up till after what we
commonly call "the first missionary journey," the preaching tour
of these two in Cyprus and Asia Minor. During the course of
this tour the genius and force of character revealed in Paul
inevitably brought him to the front, and, consequently, afterwards
we find the order reversed, and read "Paul and Barnabas," though
for once in describing a visit of the two companions to Jerusalem,

where Barnabas was so well known and so highly honoured, St. Luke reverts to the older arrangement. This recession of Barnabas, like the recession of James, cannot be accidental. But in both cases the transposition is purely relative. There is no reason to think that Barnabas lost ground absolutely; it is only that he ceased to take precedence of Paul, owing to the unique position to which the Apostle to the Gentiles attained. As far as Barnabas himself is concerned, this is not only not derogatory to him, it even helps to bring out that graciousness of spirit which is his crowning virtue.

Barnabas served Christ incomparably by taking a second place. He gave larger opportunity to the Holy Spirit, by bringing Saul from his unsuitable, if not wasteful, retirement. Few see the evidence of the Spirit of God working by them in their having assigned to them an inferior position. Very few would discover a prime condition of the growth of the Church, and the progress of the truth as it is in Jesus, in their own voluntary abandonment of a prominent position, and their equally voluntary effort to bring forward another man, who could more effectively meet the need of the time and place. This it was that Barnabas did. He must have had his heart steadily fixed on the unseen rewards prepared on high, to make him acquiesce thus joyfully in his companion, Paul, receiving so much more of the encouragement provided for apostolical men in this life. Such a mind could hardly be, without deep devotion and forgetfulness of self: such as one may see in John the Baptist, in his way of speaking of our Blessed Lord, concerning whom it was a matter of joy to him to say and think, " He must increase, but I must decrease "; such, again, as in the Old Testament, we read of in the beautiful history of Jonathan and the way in which he so gladly yielded the first place in everything to David. Such self-denial, when regularly kept up, and not indulged only now and then, out of laziness or partial affection, is one of the clearest tokens that God's Holy Spirit is with men, preparing them for eternal glory.

¶ Because he believed Saul was the man to cope with the peculiar nature of the work in Antioch he did not hesitate to bring him from Tarsus, and then he unselfishly stepped aside to allow him the unfettered exercise of his great gifts. There was discernment in that. And there was something greater than discernment; there was magnanimity. And concerning this Dr. Whyte has stated the case in a sentence which, while reading like hyperbole, is really calmest truth: "I would far rather have a little of Barnabas' grace than all Saul's genius."[1]

¶ Ten men would think themselves fit or worthy of the first place, where one would see the greater qualification of another for the honourable eminence of leadership. It needs more grace of God to enable a man to step back in order to bring forward another than to contend for, or to aim at, pre-eminence. Conceit will make a Diotrephes, but only the love of Christ can make a Barnabas.[2]

(3) We read in Gal. ii. 13, where Paul writes of the dissembling Jews, that "even Barnabas was carried away with their dissimulation." The cause of his weakness was the old controversy about the obligations of Jewish law on Gentile Christians. Paul, Peter, and Barnabas all concurred in neglecting the restrictions imposed by Judaism, and in living on terms of equality and association in eating and drinking with the heathen converts at Antioch. A principle was involved, to which Barnabas had been the first to give in his adhesion, in the frank recognition of the Antioch Church. But as soon as emissaries from the other party came down, Peter and he abandoned their association with Gentile converts, not changing their convictions but suppressing the action to which their convictions should have led. They pretended to be of the same mind as these narrow Jews from Jerusalem. They insulted their brethren, they deserted Paul, they belied their convictions, they imperilled the cause of Christian liberty, they flew in the face of what Peter had said that God Himself had showed him, they did their utmost to degrade Christianity into a form of Judaism—all for the sake of keeping on good terms with the narrow bigotry of these Judaizing teachers.

We have brought before us here the consideration of the imperfect goodness of even the best men. A good man does not mean a faultless man. Of course the power which works on a believing soul is always tending to produce goodness and only goodness. But its operation is not such that we are always

---

[1] H. S. Seekings, *The Men of the Pauline Circle*, 38.
[2] G. B. Ryley, *Barnabas*, 93.

equally, uniformly, perfectly under its influence. In Barnabas, his amiability and openness of nature, the very characteristics that had made him strong, now make him weak and wrong. How clearly, then, there is brought out here the danger that lurks even in our good! Every virtue may be run to an extreme and become a vice. Liberality is exaggerated into prodigality, firmness into obstinacy, mercy into weakness, gravity into severity, tolerance into feeble conviction, humility into abjectness. The special form of error into which Barnabas fell is worth notice. It was feebleness of grasp, a deficiency of boldness in carrying out his witness to a disputed truth.

¶ Blessed Francis was sometimes taxed with over much good nature and gentleness, and was told that this was the cause of many disorders which would not have occurred had he been more wholesomely severe. He, however, answered calmly and sweetly that he had always in his mind the words of the great St. Anselm, the glory of our Alps, among which he was born. That Saint, he observed, was in the habit of saying that if he had to be punished either for being too indulgent or being over-rigorous, he would far rather it should be for the former. He gave as his reason that judgment with mercy would be meted out to the merciful, and that God would always have more pity on the pitiful than on the rigorous.[1]

2. He was full of faith.

(1) Barnabas gave practical expression to his faith in Christ and the Christian Church by selling his land and bringing the money and laying it at the Apostles' feet. There is no preface to the mention in the Acts of the Apostles of the first most notable deed of Barnabas. Yet that first record implies much. There must have been almost from the first very fervent character and peculiarly specialized faith in Christ and love of the brotherhood in Jesus. Barnabas sold his property and gave it all for Christ. The generosity of that deed is measured not by what he gave, but by what he left. That is always so. Generosity is not a sum in addition. It is a sum in subtraction. A poor man's penny is more than a rich man's shilling. Barnabas is the man of generosity, not only because he gave much, but because that much was his all. Of course it is possible to make too much of this one act of

---

[1] J. P. Camus, *The Spirit of St. Francis de Sales*, 498.

generosity on the part of Barnabas. He will do greater things afterwards. We need not exalt him to the skies simply because this deed is recorded in the Bible, and ignore the fact that more remarkable sacrifices are told us of men in later days. Church history abounds with instances of people who gave up everything and took poverty as their bride. St. Francis not only abandoned his home and all he possessed; he took off his clothes and dressed himself only in the old garments tossed to him as a beggar. Less fantastic and vastly more self-sacrificing was his devotion of his whole life to follow in the footsteps of Christ as exactly as possible. Not less noble is the life of such a man as Francis Crossley — "the modern St. Francis" — who, though a most prosperous manufacturer, who might have amassed a fortune and lived like a prince, chose to spend a simple life among his own workpeople, devoting himself and his large business profits to the good of his fellow-men. But while there is no reason to exaggerate the importance of this one act of Barnabas, it is interesting as exhibiting at the very first the leading trait of his character, his abounding generosity. We may find it the more valuable in this way because it is a concrete action.

¶ Whilst crying, "Lord, increase my faith," see to it that you use what you have. The godly blacksmith who prays at the family altar in the morning that health and strength may be given for the day's work does not afterwards sit in his chair to wait for the strength to come. He makes for the smithy, turns up his shirt-sleeves, seizes the sledge, and every time it rings on the anvil, his muscles become more like whipcord, and his strength develops. So use your faith.[1]

(2) Another example of Barnabas' faith may be found in an incident which is generally regarded as the most regrettable fact of his history. The facts are familiar to us. When Paul and Barnabas went out on their mission, they determined to take a young man with them, to assist them, and train him for the work when they should be called away. They determined to take with them John who was surnamed Mark. When they reached Perga he became homesick. His heart failed, and he returned to his native city. A second journey was now to be undertaken, and Mark, who had repented of his former desertion from them, and

[1] J. G. Stuart, *Talks about Soul-Winning*, 89.

recovered his spirit, offered himself for the second journey, wishing to show his sorrow by the fidelity with which he would keep to the work in future. This offer was met by Barnabas and repudiated by Paul. Paul said, "He has failed me once, and I will not trust myself with him again." Barnabas said, "Let us give him one more clean page to write on, one more chance of recovering his reputation." Both thought that they were right, and neither of them would yield to the other by a hair's-breadth. Each determined to have his own way; the consequence was, "the contention was so sharp between them, that they departed asunder, one from the other."

As Christina Rossetti puts it in *St. Barnabas*:—

> Divided while united, each must run
>   His mighty course not hell should overtake;
>   And pressing toward the mark must own the ache
> Of love, and sigh for heaven not yet begun.
> For saints in life-long exile yearn to touch
> Warm human hands and commune face to face;
>   But these we know not ever met again:
> Yet once St. Paul at distance overmuch
>   Just sighted Cyprus; and once more in vain
> Neared it and passed;—not there his landing-place.

(a) It is not easy, nor is it pleasant, to apportion credit or blame in this story. Each of the Apostles may be honoured for something admirable in the conflict of judgment. Deep tenderness in one and intense earnestness in the other show themselves attractively. But without wronging Paul, it may be fairly enough wished that he had remembered how once he needed a champion and friend, and had found both comforter and advocate in Barnabas. Nor would it have been to Paul's dishonour if he had understood that when Barnabas as good as said, "Give John Mark another chance," he was doing what was, in spirit, like taking Saul of Tarsus by the hand, and justifying him before the Apostles and elders in Jerusalem. Barnabas, in this contention, is consistent with all that we know of his goodness and kindness to weak and tried brethren; Barnabas was true to the lines of his gentle and more gracious character. Under the shelter of his great charity and tenderness John Mark found a new prospect of consecration to Christ that gave him the opportunity of struggling manfully against the weakness of the past, and proving himself to be one who could "endure hardness as a good soldier of Jesus Christ." The charity that hopeth and believeth all things, of which Paul became the great exponent and example, showed its living and life-giving power in Barnabas. It made him, in this instance, the protector and helper of Mark, as once he had been of Saul. By faith he was filled with the Spirit of Christ and judged Mark not from the earthly standpoint of his inefficiency but from the standpoint of Christ, who sees the best in all of us and believes in us.

¶ The difference between the man of real Faith and other people is this, that while they judge of right and wrong by the standard of other men whom they see, the man of Faith judges of it by the standard of Christ, whom we do not see.[1]

(b) Barnabas seems at a later date to find justification for his defence of Mark, and that in the words of Paul himself. As if repenting of his former severity, Paul took pains to say a good word of Mark. To the Colossians he wrote, "Mark, the cousin of Barnabas, touching whom ye received commandment; if he come unto you, receive him." Then he writes kindly to Philemon of "Mark, my fellow-worker." And in the last lines he ever wrote, we find the great Apostle still eager to make amends for that old wrong: "Take Mark," he writes to Timothy; "and bring him with thee, for he is profitable to me for the ministry." Thus the man he would not have at the outset, he was glad to have at the close. It is a beautiful proof of how we may outgrow past errors, and become strong in that which is weakest. And it is more beautiful still as showing that Paul had outgrown his early quarrel, and that they were now one in heart. But it is most beautiful of all as an indication that Barnabas was right in his estimate of Mark, and that he was justified in his generosity.

(c) The friendship between Barnabas and Paul was not entirely broken. Barnabas did not become a Judaizer, or in any way discountenance the work of Paul. In the Acts of the Apostles he is not again mentioned. Whether he confined his mission work to his native island, to which he almost immediately sailed with Mark, or whether, as seems to be implied by the allusion in the Epistle to the Corinthians, he extended it more widely, he

[1] *Literary Churchman* (1871), 217.

certainly continued to work on the same principles as before.
And though, so far as they erred, the Apostles suffered for their
error, God overruled evil for good. Henceforth they were engaged in two spheres of missionary action instead of one, and
henceforth also the bearing and the views of Paul were more free
and vigorous, less shackled by associations, less liable to reaction.
Hitherto his position in the Church of Jerusalem had depended
much upon the countenance of Barnabas. Henceforth he had to
stand alone, to depend solely on himself and his own Apostolic
dignity, and to rely on no favourable reception for his views,
except such as he won by the force of right and reason.

¶ Tradition tells us that after, in St. Mark's company, St.
Barnabas had returned to his native Cyprus, he once more
quitted that island; and rejoining St. Paul was sent by him, with
Titus, to Corinth. He has moreover been styled the Apostle of
Milan, as of a city where he preached Christ. Nevertheless as
the doves to their windows, so did this tender dove-like saint
return to his first home; and being full of years put on his
martyr's crown where he had dwelt with his father and his mother.
In Cyprus his discourses, his miracles, his daily life, set forth the
Gospel and won souls to the faith. Thus was God glorified, the
Church edified, Satan discomfited. Thus also were certain unbelieving Jews, beforetime his persecutors in Syria, exasperated.
These came to Cypriot Salamis, and there stirred up the great men
against the apostle. Then was he seized, roughly beset, insulted,
tormented, stoned. And anon the mob gazed upon an aged body
slain by a defacing death, and the Church bewailed her nursing
father taken from her head that day, and holy Angels praised
God for a sanctified soul new-born into glory, and even as one
whom his mother comforteth the Son of Consolation was
comforted.[1]

> Crowned with immortal jubilee
> 　　This day, thy soul set free,
> From earth to Heaven thou didst pass,
> 　　O holy Barnabas.
>
> He, for whose sake, at whose dear call,
> 　　Thou gavest up thine all:
> He shall thine all, thy treasure be
> 　　Lasting eternally.

[1] C. G. Rossetti, *Called to be Saints*, 150.

'Mid fasting, prayer, and holy hands,
　Lo! 'mid the saints he stands,
The Spirit's high behest to bear,
　Christ's Heav'n-sent messenger.

Thou hast with Paul in labours stood,
　Blest bond of brotherhood!
One, in the mandate sent from high;
　And one, in charity.

To what barbaric shores away
　Did ye that light convey,
When from God's chosen race ye turn'd,
　Who faith's glad message spurn'd?

Lord, when to us an offer'd Guest
　Shall come that Spirit blest,
Let not our hearts Heaven's bounty slight
　Deeming our darkness light.[1]

[1] Isaac Williams.

JOHN MARK.

I.

HIS EXPERIENCE OF LIFE.

LITERATURE.

Boyd, A. K. H., *The Graver Thoughts of a Country Parson*, ii. (1865) 72.

Gould, E. P., *A Critical and Exegetical Commentary on the Gospel according to St. Mark* (1896).

Hammond, J., *The Boys and Girls of the Bible*, ii. (1898) 245.

Hutton, W. H., *A Disciple's Religion* (1911), 160.

Hyde, T. D., *Sermon-Pictures for Busy Preachers*, i. (1892) 215.

Lindsay, T. M., *The Gospel according to St. Mark* (1883).

Lock, W., *The Bible and Christian Life* (1905), 215.

Luckock, H. M., *Footprints of the Apostles as traced by Saint Luke in the Acts*, ii. (1905) 61.

Maclaren, A., *Christ's Musts* (1894), 297.

„ „ *Expositions* : The Acts of the Apostles xiii.–end (1907), 91.

Maurice, F. D., *The Acts of the Apostles* (1894), 185.

Moffatt, J., *The Second Things of Life*, 1.

Morison, J., *A Practical Commentary on the Gospel according to St. Mark* (1882).

Newbolt, W. C. E., *Words of Exhortation* (1900), 92.

Ramsay, W. M., *The Church in the Roman Empire* (1893), 59.

„ „ *St. Paul the Traveller* (1895), 70.

Robertson, A., *Venetian Sermons* (1905), 59.

Seekings, H. S., *The Men of the Pauline Circle* (1914), **43**.

Skrine, J. H., *Saints and Worthies* (1901), 8.

Swete, H. B., *The Gospel according to St. Mark* (1902).

Vaughan, J., *Sermons* (Brighton Pulpit), xix. (1880), No. 1149.

Vince, C., *The Unchanging Saviour* (1875), 263.

Young, D. T., *Neglected People of the Bible* (1901), 182.

Christian World Pulpit, lxxvii. (1910) 264 (S. Kirshbaum).

Dictionary of the Bible, iii. (1900) 245 (F. H. Chase).

His Experience of Life.

John, whose surname was Mark.—Acts xii. 12.

1. THE Hebrew name of this companion of the Apostles was John; it appears without addition in Acts xiii. 5, 13. To it the Roman prænomen Marcus was added, just as the Roman cognomen Paulus was added to the Hebrew name Saul. The name Marcus was that by which its bearer was commonly known among those for whom the Acts was written. As a change of name always corresponds with a crisis in life, and as in this case the name laid aside, John, was Jewish, and the name assumed or bestowed upon him, Mark (Marcus), was Roman, it is probable that the change marked his conversion from Judaism to Christianity, or his devoting himself to the propagation of his new faith among the Gentiles. The change of appellation coincides with the fact that so many of the allusions which we have to him represent him as sending messages of Christian greeting across the sea to his Gentile brethren. And it further coincides with the fact that his Gospel is obviously intended for the use of Gentile Christians, and, according to an old and reliable tradition, was written in Rome for Roman Christians. All these facts just indicate two things—that the more a man has real operative love to Jesus Christ in his heart, the more he will rise above all limitations of his interests, his sympathy, and his efforts, and the more surely will he let himself out, as far as he can, in affection towards and toils for all men.

This change of name, though it is a mere trifle, and may have been adopted as a matter of convenience, may also be taken as reminding us of a very important truth, and that is, that if we wish to help people, the first condition is that we go down and stand on their level, and make ourselves one with them, as far as we can. And so Mark may have said, "I have put away the name that parts me from these Gentiles, for whom I desire to work, and whom I love; and I take the name that binds me to them."

¶ It is the very same principle, in a small instance—just as a raindrop that hangs on the thorn of a rosebush is moulded by the same laws that shape the great sphere of the central sun—it is a small instance of the great principle which brought Jesus Christ down into the world to die for us. You must become like the people that you want to help. "Forasmuch as the children were partakers of flesh and blood, he also himself likewise took part of the same, that he might deliver them." And so, not only the duty of widening our sympathies, but one of the supreme conditions of being of use to anybody, is set forth in the comparatively trifling incident, which we pass by without noticing it, that this man, a Jew to his finger-tips, finally found himself—or, rather, finally was carried, for it was no case of unconscious drifting—into the position of a messenger of the Cross to the Gentiles; and, for the sake of efficiency in his work, and of getting close by the side of people whom he wanted to influence, flung away deliberately that which parted him from them. It is a small matter, but a little window may show a very wide prospect.[1]

2. The father of Mark is not mentioned in the New Testament or by any reliable tradition. His mother bears the common Hebrew name Mary (Acts xii. 12). She appears as a woman of some wealth, the possessor of a house with a porch, and with a room large enough to contain many, the mistress, it would seem, of a household, the duty of one παιδίσκη [slave girl] bearing a Greek name being to keep the door. Her house is one of the centres of the life of "the brethren" at Jerusalem. Peter goes there as a matter of course directly he has escaped from prison, and is well known there (v. 14). It is a natural conclusion that "the house of Mary" had become the home of Peter, and that the guest was in a sense the head of the household.

John Mark is not mentioned in this narrative, except for the purpose of distinguishing his mother Mary from others of the same name; but it is reasonable to suppose that he was present, and that he was already a believer, and intimate with Peter and the heads of the Church at Jerusalem.

In Col. iv. 10 Mark is spoken of as "the cousin" of Barnabas,

[1] A. Maclaren, *Christ's Musts*, 300.

the Joseph Barnabas of Acts iv. 36 f., of the tribe of Levi, born in Cyprus, a man of substance, and from almost the earliest days a leader among "the brethren." It is not improbable, in view of the later history, that Mark too was by birth or previous residence connected with the Jewish colony in Cyprus; and, if we may assume that the cousins were the sons of two brothers, we learn that he was a Levite. There is every reason to think that he, like Saul, was a "Hebrew of Hebrews."

I.

HIS LOST OPPORTUNITY.

John Mark was at Jerusalem during the famine of 45–6 A.D., when Barnabas and Saul visited the city for the purpose of conveying to the Church the alms of the brethren at Antioch; and on their return they took him back with them to Syria (Acts xii. 25). He may have attracted them as the son of a leading member of the Church at Jerusalem, and possibly also by services rendered during the distribution of the relief fund which revealed in him a capacity for systematic work. If we assume his identity with the Mark of St. Paul's Epistles, there was doubtless another reason. Barnabas was still leader of the Christian body at Antioch; he had been sent there by the mother Church (Acts xi. 22), and Saul's position in the Antiochian brotherhood was as yet evidently subordinate. It was for Barnabas to seek fresh associates in the work, and John was a near relative of Barnabas. Whether the father of John had been uncle to Joseph of Cyprus, or the mother his aunt, is unknown; but the relationship accounts for the persistent favour which Barnabas extended to Mark.

1. John Mark is described as the "minister" or "attendant" of the Apostles. In the account of the journey he is brought before the reader's notice in a curiously incidental way. He was not essential to the expedition; he had not been selected by the Spirit; he had not been formally delegated by the Church of Antioch; he was an extra hand, taken by Barnabas and Saul on their own responsibility.

The general character of his duties is expressly stated; it was personal, not evangelistic, service to which he was called. Blass defines this service too strictly when he comments "velut ad baptizandum"; Mark may have been required to baptize converts, but his work would include all those minor details which could safely be delegated to a younger man, such as arrangements for travel, the provision of food and lodging, conveying messages, negotiating interviews, and the like.

Dr. Chase has suggested another meaning for the term "minister." It is the word which was used of the synagogue attendant. It might thus be John's official title, and the meaning of the verse would be, "And they had with them also John, the synagogue minister." If this interpretation is the true one, we have an important fact about Mark which reveals how close his ties with Judaism were. Among his fellow-Jews he was known as Ἰωάνης ὑπηρέτης, John minister.

> Since service is the highest lot,
> And all are in one body bound,
> In all the world, the place is not
> Which may not with this bliss be crowned.
>
> The little child, in trustful glee,
> With love and gladness brimming o'er,
> Many a cup of ministry
> May for a weary veteran pour.
>
> The lonely glory of a throne
> May yet this lowly joy preserve;
> Love may make that a stepping-stone,
> And raise "I reign" into "I serve."
>
> This, by the ministries of prayer,
> The loneliest life with blessings crowds,
> Can consecrate each petty care,
> Make angels' ladders out of clouds.
>
> Since service is the highest lot,
> And angels know no higher bliss,
> Then with what good her cup is fraught
> Who was created but for this!

2. It is not stated that the Holy Spirit prescribed the details of the route. How then should Paul and Barnabas proceed? To leave Syria they must go first to Seleucia, the harbour of Antioch, where they would find ships going south to the Syrian coast and Egypt, and west either by way of Cyprus or along the coast of Asia Minor. The western route led towards the Roman world, to which all Paul's subsequent history proves that he considered himself called by the Spirit. The Apostles embarked in a ship for Cyprus, which was very closely connected by commerce and general intercourse with the Syrian coast. After traversing the island from east to west, they must go onward. Ships going westward naturally went across to the coast of Pamphylia, and the Apostles, after reaching Paphos, near the west end of Cyprus, sailed in one of these ships, and landed at Attalia in Pamphylia.

Pamphylia was the natural continuation of the work that had been going on, first in Syria and Cilicia for many years, and next in Cyprus. They went to Pamphylia to preach there, and, as they did not actually preach there, something must have occurred to make them change their plan. Further, the reason for this change of plan must have been merely a temporary one, for they preached in Pamphylia on their return journey.

¶ If you will carefully consider what it is that you have done most often during this day, I think you can hardly avoid being drawn to this conclusion : that you have really done nothing else from morning to night but *change your mind.* You began by waking up. Now that act of waking is itself a passage of the mind from an unconscious to a conscious state, which is about the greatest change that the mind can undergo. Your first idea upon waking was probably that you were going to rest for some time longer; but this rapidly passed away, and was changed into a desire for action, which again transformed itself into volition, and produced the physical act of getting up. From this arose a series of new sensations ; that is to say, a change of mind from the state of not perceiving or feeling these things to the state of feeling them. And so afterwards.[1]

3. This change of plan is connected in Acts with something which happened at Perga. John Mark left the Apostles there, and returned alone to Jerusalem. It is characteristic of St. Luke

---

[1] W. K. Clifford, *Lectures and Essays,* i. 79.

that he very rarely gives reasons for the facts that he speaks of, so that we are left to conjecture what the motive may have been which prompted the desertion. Several motives have been suggested.

(1) John, who had been converted by Peter, and had left his mother at Jerusalem, where he knew she was liable to persecution, may have been disappointed about Paul's evident intention to make the Gentiles the main object of his care, and pleading filial duty as an excuse, determined to return home. Perga, as the entrance of one of the great highways to the important Galatian centres of trade and commerce, would be frequented by merchantmen, and it may be the presence in the harbour of a vessel bound for Joppa proved irresistible, and he took his passage home. Such an explanation accounts for the fact that Barnabas was divided in his feelings towards the deserter. His relationship to and sympathy with the mother of John would lead him to appreciate the motives for his cousin's return; while in the eyes of Paul he was without excuse.

¶ Mark's motives may well have been the same as those which prompted exactly the opposite line of action on the part of Thomas Oliver. At John Oliver's death there were seven young children to provide for, six being unable to earn anything on account of age. Little "Tommy," seeing the difficulty his mother was put to in providing for them all—it was a poverty that could be felt—took the matter in hand with regard to himself, and went to seek his own living without consulting anyone, going from one place to another in search of a job of work. So he became a little "runaway" on purpose to help her, not at all realizing the difficult position she would be placed in by not knowing of his whereabouts. For, besides her own anxiety, she was worried and interviewed by officials as to what had become of him.

It is curious how he that had thus unwittingly caused her so much anxiety should have become in later years a real comfort and help to her,—before his mother passed away, she lovingly said to him, in gratitude for his thoughtful kindness: "I have had many children, but I have only one son." [1]

(2) It was due to cowardice. If Paul had kept to the Cilician coast, there would have been no danger, but to penetrate into the interior was a most perilous enterprise. Between Perga

[1] Jessy L. Mylne, *Holding up the Standard*, 4.

and Pisidian Antioch the country was inhabited by a wild and lawless people, given up to violence and brigandage, for which the rugged mountain passes offered a favourable opportunity. There were, in addition, dangers from swollen rivers and torrents. His courage failed him, and little wonder that it did, when he realized the nature of the country Paul and Barnabas were about to traverse. It is to the hardships suffered in that region that Paul refers in the eleventh chapter of his Second Epistle to the Corinthians, where he speaks of being "in journeyings often" —he had to travel long distances on foot along rough roads; "in perils of rivers"—he had to ford wild bridgeless mountain torrents; "in perils of robbers"—the mountains were the haunts of brigands; "in perils from my countrymen"—as at Iconium, where, we read, "the unbelieving Jews stirred up the Gentiles," and "there was an assault made both of the Gentiles, and also of the Jews with their rulers, to use them despitefully, and to stone them," which threats were carried out at Lystra, the evangelists' next stopping-place, whither their persecutors followed them. Such sufferings and dangers might well daunt the timid mind of Mark.

¶ I remember talking once with a brave general who had fought through our war. He was telling me about an officer whom he had rebuked upon the field of battle for cowardice. " I did not blame the man for being a coward," he said; "he could not help that. He was born so. It was no more disgrace to him to be afraid than it was credit for me not to yield to the temptation which I never felt. What I blamed him for was simply that, having found out that physically he was a coward, he yet allowed himself to occupy a place where cowardice could do such mischief. So I degraded him." That was treating physical courage as if it were a thing entirely apart from reason and from a man's own control. And so it is to a large extent as it concerns the individual.[1]

¶ Life is too great for us or too petty. . . . We must die daily on the levels of ignoble compromise or perish tragically among the precipices. On the one hand is a life—unsatisfying and secure, a plane of dulled gratifications, mean advantages, petty triumphs, adaptations, acquiescences and submissions, and on the other a steep and terrible climb, set with sharp stones and bramble thickets.[2]

[1] Phillips Brooks, *Essays and Addresses*, 322.
[2] H. G. Wells.

(3) John Mark was willing to come into Pamphylia with them, but not willing to go on into the country north of Taurus, and therefore he evidently considered that the latter proposal was a departure from the original scheme. Cyprus and Pamphylia were countries of similar situation to Cilicia and Syria, and in the closest possible relations with them, whereas it was a serious and novel step to go into the country north of Taurus. We need not therefore suppose that John Mark was actuated solely or mainly by cowardice; the facts of the situation show that he could advance perfectly plausible arguments against the change of plan, which was to carry their work into a region new in character and not hitherto contemplated by the Church. It seems no unwarrantable addition, but a plain inference from the facts, to picture the dissension as proceeding on lines like these; and it relieves John Mark from a serious charge which is not quite in keeping with his boldness in originally starting on this first of missionary journeys.

No reason is given for this sudden change of plan. Ramsay explains it by supposing that Paul was stricken at Perga with malarial fever, and it was necessary for him to leave the enervating climate of Pamphylia for the high lands of the interior, and that Antioch, which was 3600 feet above the sea, was chosen for this reason. This would also explain Paul's statement that it was by reason of physical infirmity that he first preached the gospel to the Galatians, and his personal sensitiveness to the desertion of John Mark.

4. By and by Paul and Barnabas, having completed their missionary tour in Asia Minor, in which they often "hazarded their lives for the name of our Lord Jesus Christ," returned to Antioch and Jerusalem, and, having "rehearsed all that God had done with them, and how he had opened the door of faith unto the Gentiles," they were ready to start again. Mark was present on this occasion, and heard the story of their missionary adventures, part of which he had shared, and he offered to go with them. He had failed once, but now he felt confident that he would not do so a second time. Barnabas was anxious to take him, but, we read, Paul opposed it—"Paul thought not good to take him with them, who departed from

them from Pamphylia, and went not with them to the work."
Barnabas, however, was "determined to take him." And then,
we read, "the contention was so sharp between them, that they
departed asunder one from the other: and so Barnabas took
Mark, and sailed unto Cyprus," his native place.

It may sound absurd to talk of nepotism in men who could
only promote their relatives to stripes and imprisonments; but
the principle which Barnabas sanctioned, when he would have
taken John Mark with them after he had deserted them on
the former journey, was the same as that which has wrought so
much evil in all ages of the Church, though the material rewards
were so different. He was preferring to a post of danger a man
who might turn his back upon the enemy just when it behoved
him to fight. Paul may have been very sharp in rebuking
what must have struck him as unfaithfulness to their cause and
their invisible Captain. His righteous indignation may have
passed, like the mildness of Barnabas, into the evil which is akin
to it.

No fault can be found with either of them for the motives by
which they were influenced. Barnabas was a man of a mild, conciliatory character, and of much natural affection. We can
almost hear him pleading his cousin's cause, attributing his
former wavering to his thoughtlessness and the inconsistency of
his untried youth; and it may be that he was ready with his
illustrations to prove that no man ought to be condemned for a
single failure. Even Peter himself had had his commission
renewed; and Mark's desertion and cowardice were as nothing
in comparison with his. Then there was at the bottom of all
his arguments the natural longing to see a near kinsman approving himself as a faithful minister in the great missionary cause.
On these grounds Barnabas was quite justified in wishing to give
his cousin another trial.

Paul, however, looked at the case with other eyes. He
was a man of a stern, unbending sense of duty, of unflinching
courage, of a whole-hearted devotion to anything that he took in
hand. He knew too, by a hard experience, what tremendous
difficulties confronted those who undertook to preach the gospel
in heathen lands; and he felt that this was just a case where his
Master's verdict must be rigidly enforced: "no man, having put

his hand to the plough, and looking back, is fit for the kingdom of God." With such an estimate as this of the all-exacting nature of the work before him, no one can condemn Paul's decision.

¶ "And so Barnabas took Mark, and sailed unto Cyprus." If as the shores of Asia lessened upon his sight, the spirit of prophecy had entered into the heart of the weak disciple who had turned back when his hand was on the plough, and who had been judged, by the chiefest of Christ's captains, unworthy thenceforward to go forth with him to the work, how wonderful would he have thought it, that by the lion symbol in future ages he was to be represented among men ! how woful, that the war-cry of his name should so often reanimate the rage of the soldier, on those very plains where he himself had failed in the courage of the Christian, and so often dye with fruitless blood that very Cypriot Sea, over whose waves, in repentance and shame, he was following the Son of Consolation ! [1]

> "Tell us young ones, you gray old man,
> What is your secret, if you can.
> We have a ship as good as you,
> Show us how to keep our crew."
>
> So in his ear the youngster cries;
> Then the gray Boatswain straight replies:—
> "All your crew be sure you know,—
> Never let one of your shipmates go.
>
> "If he leaves you, change your tack,
> Follow him close and fetch him back;
> When you've hauled him in at last,
> Grapple his flipper and hold him fast.
>
> "If you've wronged him, speak him fair,
> Say you're sorry, and make it square;
> If he's wronged you, wink so tight,
> None of you see what's plain in sight.
>
> "When the world goes hard and wrong,
> Lend a hand to help him along." [2]

5. Say, if you like, that this contention between Apostles was a flaw on the way towards a more perfect development of char-

---

[1] Ruskin, *The Stones of Venice*, vol. ii. chap. iv. § 1.
[2] O. W. Holmes, *The Old Cruiser*.

acter. It may have been so; but it was a beautiful protest at the same time on the part of two men who both believed themselves to be right, and who both *were* right in their different estimates of the same situation.

"I will not take a man," says Paul, "with me to the work who has shown that he has no staying powers." "I will not abandon a man," says Barnabas, "who has good stuff in him, and whom some day you will learn to value."

It is the old exhibition of δικαιοσύνη and ἐπιείκεια, of justice and equity. Paul represents justice, sternly right on a matter of principle. Barnabas represents the modifying, qualifying considerations, which prevent justice from becoming a disabling sternness. But they both felt the extreme importance of a matter of principle. Barnabas did not say, "My dear Paul, I think you are hard, but still, for the sake of peace, I will let Mark go his way, and shift for himself." St. Paul did not say, "My dear Barnabas, I think you are unduly lenient, and we shall live to repent it; still, rather than make a scandal, we will take him." No, they separated, and each made his protest.

> Alas! how light a cause may move
> Dissension between hearts that love!
> Hearts that the world in vain had tried,
> And sorrow but more closely tied;
> That stood the storm when winds were rough,
> Yet in a sunny hour fall off.[1]

(1) It teaches us first that there will be differences: "it must needs be that offences come." They came in the first and golden age of Christianity; can we hope to escape them? This is a calming reflection; it helps us to keep our heads and to keep our temper and to escape from panic.

(2) It teaches the very, very old truth that there may be much reason on both sides of a disagreement. Paul was right in insisting on taking none but true men and tried into action: Barnabas was right (thank God) in believing that a man may fail in duty once and yet prove a good man, as we know Mark did. And so to-day they are right who insist on the value of sacraments and exalt the corporate life of the Church and assert the

[1] Moore.

sacred value of it: but they too are right who insist on "experiential religion" and the reality of direct intercourse between God and the single soul: but both are wrong when they deny, or fail to accept, the truth for which the others contend.

(3) It teaches that when Christian teachers differ, the right thing to do is to go and work in separate fields; not to abuse the other on platforms or in the press, still less to mob the churches or meetings of a differing party, but to see if there be not in this wide world, so well supplied still with people who are without Christianity of any sort or colour, room for the separate, unconflicting energy of that part of the truth which each sees most clearly. Barnabas did not go to Asia Minor and get in the way of Paul: he went to Cyprus. And any modern Christian can find a Cyprus that will absorb his energies, if only he will look for one.

¶ Although a difference in opinions or modes of worship may prevent an entire external union, need it prevent our union in affection? Though we cannot think alike, may we not love alike? May we not be of one heart, though we are not of one opinion? Without all doubt we may. Herein all the children of God may unite, notwithstanding these smaller differences. These remaining as they are, they may forward one another in love and in good works. . . . I dare not presume to impose my mode of worship on any other. I believe it is truly primitive and apostolical. But my belief is no rule for another. I ask not therefore of him with whom I would unite in love, Are you of my church? Of my congregation? Do you receive the same form of church-government, and allow the same church officers with me? Do you join in the same form of prayer wherein I worship God? I inquire not, Do you receive the supper of the Lord, in the same posture and manner as I do? Nor, whether in the administration of baptism, you agree with me in admitting sureties for the baptized, in the manner of administering it, or the age of those to whom it should be administered. Nay, I ask not of you (as clear as I am in my own mind) whether you allow baptism and the Lord's Supper at all. Let all these things stand by: we will talk of them, if need be, at a more convenient season. My only question at present is, Is thine heart right as my heart is with thy heart? If it be, give me thine hand. I do not mean, Be of my opinion. You need not. I do not expect or desire it. Neither do I mean, I will be of your opinion. I cannot. It does not depend on my choice: I can no more think than I can see or hear as I will. Keep you your opinion, I mine: and that as steadily as ever. You need not even endeavour to come over to me, or bring me over to you. I do not desire you to dispute those points, or to hear or speak one word concerning them. Let all opinions alone on one side and on the other. Only give me thine hand.[1]

¶ "I've often thought that those three men—father, Mr. Fermor, and the Vicar—although they may differ about small things, think very much alike about great things. Each has lived and loved and worked, and—this is the supreme test—not one of them is afraid to die."[2]

II.

HIS SECOND CHANCE.

1. Mark stands before us as a type of the recovery of character, of the way in which one who has lost his self-respect may recover it. His position was a *very* difficult one. It is difficult enough to recover a true self-respect, when a man is wounded only in his own conscience, when only he himself witnesses against himself of some act of cowardice, or theft, or underhandness, which is not known to others; such an one goes about like a wounded man with a bullet inside him, not knowing where it may work out or what mischief it may work within: there is a loss of perfect straightforwardness, a weakened power to help others; his self-consciousness weakens his powers of sympathy and of service.

But Mark's position was worse than that: his cowardice had been branded by Paul and made known to the whole Church of Antioch; Paul had written "unworthy" across his name; he had departed with no "bene discessit"; churches had been warned against him; he was to go down to all ages as the man who had failed at a great crisis. What a crushing position to have to face! how great the temptation to despair and apostatize from this new hard religion! But Mark did not despair, did not apostatize; he boldly faced his position. It was not his now to play the part which would have brought him most before

---

[1] John Wesley.
[2] H. A. Vachell, *The Other Side*, 103.

the eyes of the world and to be the companion of the great missionary, so he would accept the humbler rôle; he would go back to his old home of Cyprus, he would stay with his relative Barnabas, and he would do such work as was possible there. Thence, later on, we find him advanced to higher work; he becomes the follower, the interpreter, the favourite pupil, "the son" of his mother's friend Peter; he follows him to Rome; he makes notes of his preaching; he interprets it to his Latin hearers; he prepares the Gospel; and probably while he was there the reconciliation came with Paul.

How long it took we do not know, but the cure was thorough. The man who had shrunk from possible dangers and disagreeables in Asia became brave enough to stand by Paul the prisoner, and not be "ashamed of his chain." So far had he won his way to Paul's renewed confidence, and made himself indispensable by service and sweetness, that the lonely Apostle, with the headsman's sword in prospect, feels that he would like to have him at hand once more, and bids Timothy bring Mark with him, "for he is useful to me for ministering"; he can do a thousand things that a man like me cannot do for himself, and he does them "all for love and nothing for reward." So he wants Mark once more. Not only Paul's generosity but Mark's patient effort had pasted a clean sheet over the page that told of his desertion, and he became useful for the very service which he had petulantly and with cowardice flung up.

¶ Some men have even made their future out of failure. Could anything seem more hopeless than to be a convicted forger, to be torn from wife and children and sent to penal servitude? Yet a man redeemed that black episode in his life. He wrote a book called *Five Years of Penal Servitude*, which contained, not the expression of regret for the past and recognition of the justice of his sentence, but certain hints of how to make prison life more beneficial to the criminal in a moral sense and less savage in some of its aspects. The man was asked to come and help to carry out his reforms. He even became a prominent prison official, and doubtless many a poor hardened wretch would feel there was a strange note of sympathy in the words of that official and know how past experiences of punishment had produced softening. Good in that case came out of evil.[1]

[1] F. Hastings.

> Have ye look'd
> At Edyrn? have ye seen how nobly changed?
> This work of his is great and wonderful.
> His very face with change of heart is changed.
> The world will not believe a man repents:
> And this wise world of ours is mainly right.
> Full seldom doth a man repent, or use
> Both grace and will to pick the vicious quitch
> Of blood and custom wholly out of him,
> And make all clean, and plant himself afresh.
> Edyrn has done it, weeding all his heart
> As I will weed this land before I go.
> I, therefore, make him of our Table Round,
> Not rashly, but have proved him everyway
> One of our noblest, our most valorous,
> Sanest and most obedient.[1]

2. We do not hear that John Mark ever tried to do any work in the way of preaching the gospel. His business was a very much humbler one. He had to attend to Paul's comfort. He had to be his factotum, man of all work; looking after material things, the commissariat, the thousand and one trifles that some-one had to see to if the Apostle's great work was to be done. And he did it all his life long. It was enough for him to do thoroughly the entirely "secular" work, as some people would think it, which it was in his power to do. That needed some self-suppression. It would have been so natural for Mark to say, "Paul sends Timothy to be bishop in Crete; and Titus to look after other churches; Epaphroditus is an official here; and Apollos is a great preacher there. And here am I, grinding away at the secularities yet. I think I'll 'strike,' and try to get more conspicuous work." Or he might perhaps deceive himself, and say, "more directly religious work," like a great many of us that often mask a very carnal desire for prominence under a very saintly guise of desire to do spiritual service. Let us take care of that. This "minister," who was not a minister at all, in our sense of the word, but only in the sense of being a servant, a private attendant of the Apostle, was glad to do that work all his days.

That was self-suppression. But it was something more. It was a plain recognition of what we all ought to have very clearly

[1] Tennyson.

before us, and that is, that all sorts of work which contribute to one end are one sort of work; and that at bottom the man who carried Paul's books and parchments, and saw that he was not left without clothes, though he was so negligent of cloaks and other necessaries, was just as much helping on the cause of Christ as the Apostle when he preached.

Mark as he stood by Peter when the shadows closed around him; Mark, the old, sturdy, eager Apostle's "son," has upon him at the last just that cordon of faithful service—to have been profitable. To hold firmly to truth as you see it—not to surrender the treasure committed to you for the sake of peace—not to yield it even to those whose honesty you know to be sound as your own, whose powers perhaps you know to be higher, whose leadership it seems almost a disloyalty to reject—that is the claim on us, that is the sacrifice we may have to offer to the highest.

Such in outline was the story of this man "of like passions with ourselves"; this Evangelist, this writer (for such he was) of our wonderful oldest Gospel, yet also this poor frail man, more than restored by the loving power of God. Shall not his experience of self, and of grace, cheer us about others now? Shall it not cheer us about ourselves?

¶ "Useful to me for ministering"—that is a striking commendation and one which anyone of us would be proud to have earned—εὔχρηστος εἰς διακονίαν—readily used for acts of service, a "handy man," quietly adequate for all emergencies, prompt, alert, willing, loyal, efficient—in Dante's phrase "a noble soul that makes not excuse, but makes its will of the will of another"; it reminds one of the praise which the Commander-in-Chief gave to Henry Havelock and his soldiers in the Indian Mutiny—"Call out Havelock's saints; they are always sober and can be depended on and Havelock himself is always ready."[1]

¶ One day an accident happened in the laboratory of the celebrated chemist Faraday. A workman knocked a silver cup into a jar of strong acid. In a very short time the cup entirely disappeared, being dissolved in the liquid. One after another the workmen gathered around and regretfully watched the melting of the beautiful cup. All said that it was utterly lost, that no particle of the silver could be recovered. But Faraday, being informed of the accident, brought some chemical mixture and poured it in the

[1] W. Lock, *The Bible and Christian Life*, 215.

jar. Gradually every particle of the silver was precipitated to the bottom and at length the great chemist drained off the acid and took out the silver, now a shapeless mass. He sent the lump of metal to the silversmith who had made the cup, and in a few days it came back restored to its former shape, a wonder and delight to those who had watched its apparent destruction.[1]

> Once like a broken bow Mark sprang aside:
> Yet grace recalled him to a worthier course,
> To feeble hands and knees increasing force,
>   Till God was magnified.

> And now a strong Evangelist, St. Mark
> Hath for his sign a Lion in his strength;
> And thro' the stormy water's breadth and length
>   He helps to steer God's Ark.

> Thus calls he sinners to be penitents,
> He kindles penitents to high desire,
> He mounts before them to the sphere of saints,
>   And bids them come up higher.[2]

[1] J. Buckham, *The Heritage of Life.*
[2] Christina G. Rossetti, *Poetical Works*, 174.

JOHN MARK.

II.

HIS GOSPEL AND TRADITIONS.

LITERATURE.

Allen, W. C., *The Gospel according to St. Mark* (1915).

Chadwick, G. A., *The Gospel according to St. Mark* (Expositor's Bible) (1877).

Gould, E. P., *A Critical and Exegetical Commentary on the Gospel according to St. Mark* (1896).

Haweis, H. R., *The Story of the Four* (1886), **3**.

Jones, J. D., *Elims of Life* (1904), 239.

Keble, J., *Sermons for the Christian Year* : Saints' Days (1877), 207.

Lindsay, T. M., *The Gospel according to St. Mark* (1883).

Morison, J., *A Practical Commentary on the Gospel according to St. Mark* (1882).

Robertson, A., *Venetian Sermons* (1905), 59.

Swete, H. B., *The Gospel according to St. Mark* (1902).

Church Pulpit Year Book, iv. (1907) 97.

Dictionary of the Apostolic Church, ii. (1916) 8 (J. Dow).

Dictionary of the Bible, iii. (1900) 245 (F. H. Chase).

Expositor, 5th Ser., vi. (1897) 268 (H. B. Swete).

Interpreter, i. (1905) 164.

Journal of Theological Studies, **vi.** (1904) 121 (V. Bartlet).

His Gospel and Traditions.

The beginning of the gospel of Jesus Christ, the Son of God.— Mark i. 1.

FOR the closing scenes of St. Mark's life we have to fall back upon tradition, which, though having no canonical authority, had an early and widespread ecclesiastical sanction. He is supposed, while with St. Peter, to have acted as his interpreter, secretary, or amanuensis; and to have settled ultimately at Alexandria in Egypt, where he became its first Bishop. In that position he is said to have gained the friendship of Philo, the Jewish philosopher and Greek scholar.

I.

St. Mark and St. Peter.

1. With very few exceptions, early writers connect St. Mark the Evangelist with St. Peter rather than with St. Paul. The single reference in 1 Peter v. 13 seems to have thrown into the shade the entire history of John Mark's connexion with St. Paul, which is to be found in the Acts and the Pauline Epistles. From Irenæus downwards, St. Mark is the disciple of St. Peter.

2. It is certain, moreover, that St. Peter was, from a very early period, on terms of the greatest intimacy with St. Mark and his mother—see Acts xii. 11-17. Not unlikely it might be by his preaching on the Day of Pentecost, or subsequently, that both the lady and her son became acquainted with the true career and character of the Saviour. And this probably accounts for the peculiarly endearing manner in which St. Peter refers to the Evangelist, at the conclusion of his First Epistle, "The church that is at Babylon, elected together with you, saluteth you; and *so doth Mark my son.*"

¶ Dr. Pusey did what he alone could do, for he looked round on the crowd of undergraduates and spoke to them as his "sons" with a fulness of feeling that was authority. For it made every rough lad there present understand that one of the most historical persons he had ever seen claimed him, cared for him, and bade him repent and be clean, and hold fast by the Faith.[1]

3. The ten or twelve years which elapsed between the last mention of St. Mark in the Acts and St. Paul's reference to his co-operation in Rome were probably the period in which St. Mark accompanied St. Peter. It may well be that the help which he rendered to the Apostle when the latter first worked among Greek-speaking people gained for him the title of "the interpreter of Peter." There is no reason why we should infer that, at least at the end of his life, St. Peter could not speak Greek, still less that he could not write a Greek letter. Moreover, it must be remembered that the word "interpreter" may have been used in reference to Latin rather than to Greek.

The word is ambiguous; the ἑρμηνεύς or ἑρμηνευτής (*interpres*) may be either the expositor who brings to light the veiled meaning of his master's words, or the translator who renders them into another tongue. But the literal sense prevails in later and Biblical Greek, and it suits the manner of Papias and agrees with his context. The phrase ἑρμηνευτής points to an office which Mark had fulfilled at a time previous to the writing of the Memoirs. He had once been St. Peter's interpreter or dragoman, and Papias mentions the circumstance in order to show that he was qualified to report accurately the teaching which he not only had heard but had at the time translated from Aramaic into Greek. That St. Peter had employed an interpreter in his intercourse with Western Churches seems to have been a recognized fact.

II.

ST. MARK'S GOSPEL.

What was the relation of John Mark to the Gospel which bears his name?

[1] R. St. J. Tyrwhitt, *Hugh Heron*, 187.

1. We read the pages of St. Mark and are struck with its crisp and graphic narrative. Picture after picture passes before our eyes, each quickened with a vivid touch which carries us to the heart of the event. There are the animated scenes caused by the early miracles of Jesus—the crowds who hasten and gather in their joyful excitement, and eagerly bear their sick to His healing touch; and we are made actually to feel the fear of the disciples as they follow their Lord on His journey to Jerusalem. Some of the descriptive expressions are of great value from a chronological point of view; for example, when the hungry villagers are fed by their compassionate Teacher, the narrator informs us that "they sat upon the *green* grass." Grass is green only at the Passover, and the artless remark affords an important clue when it is our task to compare the first three Gospels with the Fourth. Ere we close the book we are forced to the conclusion that the writer tells no borrowed tale, but had seen the things whereof he writes. The question now presents itself: Who was this man whose memory was a storehouse of sacred scenes? Tradition points to St. Peter.

2. Papias tells us, on the authority of a certain John, who was an elder of the Church, and either a disciple of the Lord or of one of His Apostles, that Mark committed to writing the oral Gospel of Peter. He says of the elder: " And the Presbyter said this. Mark, having become the interpreter of Peter, wrote down accurately whatsoever he remembered. It was not, however, in exact order that he related the sayings or deeds of Christ. For he neither heard the Lord nor accompanied Him. But afterwards, as I have said, he accompanied Peter, who accommodated his instructions to the necessities [of his hearers], but with no intention of giving a regular narrative of the Lord's sayings. Wherefore Mark made no mistake in thus writing some things as he remembered them. For of one thing he took especial care, not to omit anything he had heard, and not to put anything fictitious into the statements." Papias, it is said, died about the year 163. He was a hearer of the Apostle John, and knew many who had known Jesus and His Apostles. He tells us that Mark's Gospel was made by committing to writing what the author remembered of the fragmentary history of Jesus, which was the oral Gospel of

Peter. Other early writers repeat in different terms the same tradition, until Tertullian was almost justified in saying, as he did, that " the Gospel of Mark is maintained to be Peter's, whose interpreter he was"; and we may believe that this Gospel contains the cycle of representative facts which formed the basis of apostolic teaching, enriched with the additions which the Apostle Peter was wont to make from his personal knowledge of Jesus.

> In splendour robed for some court-revelry
> A monarch moves when eve is on the wane.
> His faithful lieges flock their prince to see,
> And strive to pierce the gathering shade—in vain.
> But lo, a torch! And now the brilliant train
> Is manifest. Who may the bearer be?
> Not great himself, he maketh greatness plain.[1]

3. If we compare St. Mark's Gospel with the rest, we shall find that it presents on the whole the completest picture of our Blessed Lord's doings as He went on from day to day, from His baptism to His resurrection. It seems to keep most exactly to the order of time, and to mention most of the minute circumstances of what He did, how He looked, how others with whom He was behaved themselves. It is less abundant in discourses and conversations, and more abundant in exact relation of miracles, and other actions of our Lord. And thus it comes to pass that, while the other Gospels seem, each of them, to have their particular object—St. Matthew, to prepare the way for our Lord's Kingdom, and explain the nature of it, to the Jews more especially; St. Luke, to set Him before us as a Priest, and to invite the Gentiles to Him; St. John, to set forth His Eternal Godhead, and put unbelievers of all times to shame, and encourage His worshippers by recording especially those words and deeds of His by which from time to time He silenced His enemies in His own holy city Jerusalem—St. Mark, on the other hand, seeming to write merely for the sake of showing us our Lord as He was, by His deeds rather than His words, leads on his reader to the most distinct and hearty acceptance of Jesus Christ come in the flesh as our only helper and healer. We feel more and more as we read the truth of what St. Peter, St.

[1] E. C. Lefroy, *Sonnets.*

Mark's own teacher, expresses in those memorable words, "Neither is there salvation in any other: for there is none other name," no other power or virtue, "under heaven given among men, whereby we must be saved," or healed.

4. Mark's Gospel was evidently written for Gentile readers, as it contains explanations of Hebrew terms and customs. Tradition says that it was written after the death of Peter and Paul. There is one decisive mark of time in the Gospel itself. In the eschatological discourse attention is called to the sign given by Jesus of the time of the destruction of Jerusalem, which leads us to infer that the Gospel was written before that time, but when the event was impending. This would fix the time as about 70 A.D.

So far as historical testimony pronounces on the question of the *place* in which this Gospel was written, it is in favour of Rome. To this effect are the statements made by Clement of Alexandria, Eusebius, Jerome, Epiphanius, and others. And there is a certain support given to this by the use of Latin words peculiar to this Gospel.

¶ One of Dean Burgon's best-known works was "The Last Twelve Verses of St. Mark." This Gospel had always been his favourite book in the New Testament. He spent years in collecting materials for a volume which should vindicate the genuineness of these verses. As he was closing the two dissertations for the Divinity School at Oxford which afterwards appeared in book form, his sister passed away. In the poem, "L'Envoy," which he appended to the work, these words occur:—

> Open those lips, kind sister, for my sake,
> In the mysterious place of thy sojourn, . . .
> And tell the Evangelist of thy brother's toil;
> Adding (be sure!) he found it his reward,
> Yet supplicates thy blessing and thy prayers,
> The blessing, saintly Stranger, of thy prayers,
> Sure at the least unceasingly of mine!

It is related of the Dean's brother-in-law, Mr. Higgins, that when lying on his death-bed he said to Burgon: "I suppose, Johnny, you will inquire for St. Mark immediately—won't you?" "What? In Paradise, do you mean?" "Yes, to be sure," he rejoined, raising his head slightly from the pillow to smile and nod.

About five minutes before the Dean's death in 1888, he said to his niece, "Give me a pencil." She gave it. "*And now St. Mark*," he whispered. "I held the New Testament before him, and was turning the page to find which passage he wanted, when quite suddenly the breathing changed, and the end came immediately." [1]

III.

TRADITION.

1. Two personal traditions may be mentioned.

(1) The remembrance of a personal deformity survives in an epithet well known at Rome early in the third century. According to Hippolytus he was known as "the stump-fingered." Three explanations of this epithet have been suggested : (*a*) It is said to signify a natural deformity. (*b*) The preface to the Vulgate states that Mark himself, after his conversion, amputated one of his fingers, in order to disqualify himself for the Jewish priesthood. This is probably due to an inference that Mark, like Barnabas, was a Levite. (*c*) An attempt was made by Dr. Tregelles to show that the word is used by Hippolytus as an equivalent for "deserter," in reference to Mark's departure from Perga. But this account of the matter can hardly be regarded as satisfactory ; it is far-fetched at the best, and so offensive a nickname is not likely to have attached itself to the Evangelist in Roman circles, where he was known as St. Paul's faithful colleague. The word itself determines nothing as to the cause of the defect, or its extent ; it may have been congenital, or due to accident ; it may have affected both hands or all the fingers of one hand or one finger only. Dr. Chase suggests that the word may refer to some mutilation or malformation of the *toes*, resulting in lameness—an infirmity which would be more likely to attract attention than a deformity of the hand.

Such a defect, to whatever cause it was due, may have helped to mould the course of John Mark's life ; by closing against him a more ambitious career, it may have turned his thoughts to those secondary ministries by which he has rendered enduring service to the Church.

[1] J. T. Stoddart, *The New Testament in Life and Literature*, 116.

¶ To incapacitate ourselves for wrong is the only way some of us can attain to virtue.[1]

¶ We saw a deep trench dug around some olive trees, and it was suggested that this was preparatory to their being felled and their roots torn up. Yet it was not so, for the trench was made to hold the manure which would make the olives live more vigorously and fruitfully. Many an affliction has seemed to threaten a good man's destruction; but it has turned out to be a special means of grace, by which he has been greatly blessed.[2]

(2) Some people have supposed that St. Mark is to be identified with the young man mentioned in Mark xiv. 51, who followed Jesus when He was arrested, clad only in a linen cloth which he had hastily caught up, and who, when the mob suspected his sympathies and seized his garment, left it in their hands and fled from them naked. The very triviality of the incident seems to point to St. Mark as the young man concerned. This incident has little or no bearing upon the story. It does not affect Christ's fortunes in the least. But if Mark was the young man concerned, it was far from being trivial to him. The act that brought him into contact with Jesus Christ would be, to him at any rate, of supreme interest and importance. Further, the minuteness of the story inevitably suggests that the Evangelist is here giving us a bit of his own history. Read the two verses, and you will find they are full of minute and vivid touches that make the picture live before us. We can see it all: the young man's hurried rush, lightly clad, into the street; his indignant interference, his sudden flight. But the minuteness comes out specially clearly in the Greek word translated "linen cloth." The Evangelist specifies a particular kind of linen cloth—a *sindon,* a fine and very costly web, so called because woven in Scinde, in India. It was a kind of linen cloth greatly valued, possessed only by the rich, and made use of by them especially as "winding sheets." That the writer should specify in this way, should be so minute and exact, and should crowd so much detail into the account—all this suggests that he is writing of what happened to himself.

¶ Superficial observers have often considered personal trivialities beneath the dignity of Scripture. The trifling is subjective; it is

[1] G. Temple Thurston, *The Antagonists.*
[2] C. H. Spurgeon.

not objective. It is their criticism that lacks dignity. "Eyes have they, but they see not." The microscopic is often as eloquent and as revealing as the majestic. Divinity often trembles in a dewdrop. A trifling incident may reflect a tremendous principle.[1]

2. As to the time and manner of St. Mark's death we have no trustworthy information. Jerome fixes his death in the eighth year of Nero, at Alexandria; but the statement seems to be merely an unsound inference from the Eusebian date for the succession of Annianus. The Paschal Chronicle assigns to Mark the crown of martyrdom, but the story cannot be traced back further than the fourth or fifth century, when it is found in the *Acts of Mark*, an apocryphon of Alexandrian origin. No reference is made to the fact in the prefaces to the Vulgate, or by Jerome, though he relates that Mark was buried at Alexandria.

3. St. Mark has a special connexion with Venice. It is said that while he was bishop of Alexandria he evangelized the coast of Dalmatia and founded the church in Aquileia. Driven by a storm amongst the lagoons of Venice, it was revealed to him in a vision that a city would one day be built on that spot, where he would be held in great honour. In 829 the body of St. Mark was brought from Alexandria to Venice, and it was then that the famous historic connexion between the saint and the city began—the Church of St. Mark was built to receive his body; the city was dedicated to his honour, thus supplanting St. Theodore as its patron saint; his symbol of the Winged Lion became the arms of the city, and the national standard; and his name became for ever linked with the fortunes of the great Republic.

The body of St. Mark was first deposited in a tower of the original Ducal Palace, where it remained three years, from 829 to 832, when it was removed to the first St. Mark's Church, completed that latter year to receive it. The tower is still standing, having been utilized to form part of the treasury of the present church, doubtless because of its connexion with St. Mark. When this earliest church was burned in 976, the body was lost, and recovered only in 1094. It was then deposited in the crypt of the present church. This crypt, or rather the mausoleum in it,

[1] F. W. Boreham, *The Luggage of Life*, 46.

which contained St. Mark's body, was called *la confessione* (the confession), not because it was a place where confessions were made, but because it contained the remains of a martyr, of one who had "witnessed a good confession." In this place it remained till 1811—that is, for the long period of 717 years—when it was taken up into the church, as, at high tide, the crypt was frequently full of water. Before placing it under the high altar of the church, where it now is, the sarcophagus was opened by order of the Italian Government, and in the presence of its representatives. It enclosed a coffin of wood, which was found to contain the chief parts of a human skeleton, a box of balsam, some coins, and a plate stating, "In the year of the incarnation of Jesus Christ, 1094, in the 8th day of the current month, October, in the reign of the Doge Vital Falier, this mausoleum was made." On the inner side of the stone corner of the sarcophagus were the letters, rudely cut, S. MA.

¶ I have sometimes thought that St. Mark, in this lesson of his life, out of weakness becoming strong, very appropriately prefigured the Venetians, with whom he has been so intimately united. He was their prototype. They too, "out of weakness, became strong." When they came to settle in these lagoons they were poor fugitives flying before their enemies, who had driven them from their mainland homes, to which, burned and in ashes, they could never return. They were weak, but they became strong. The very hardships and struggles they had to endure ennobled them. They conquered nature. They found the soil of Venice shifting mud and sand, but a little way raised above the flowing tide, and fitted but to bear the weight of wooden huts. They changed it into stable ground, on which, as on a basis of rock, they raised their marble palaces, the beauty and the endurance of which are the admiration of the world. Conquering nature under their feet, they conquered it in their own hearts. They took the Bible as their charter, writing it in the words of a universal language, that of colour and design, on the walls of St. Mark's Church, and writing it also on the fleshy tablets of their hearts. From being weak fugitives, they became conquerors, and heroes, and princes in the earth.[1]

¶ O God our God, who having no pleasure in the death of him that dieth bestowest that grace by which sinners turn and live ;— who having once called St. Mark, didst afterwards recall him ; and

[1] A. Robertson, *Venetian Sermons.* 81.

having first blessed him with a believing mother, didst bestow upon him in later life a holy spiritual father, unto the confirmation of his faith and the perfecting of his works; and allottedst unto him for vocation service with Apostles, and for renown the name of an Evangelist: grant us such grace, I implore Thee, that having put our hands to the plough we may not look back: yet, good Lord, if we look back, let mercy excel mercy, and reclaim, renew, restore us. Make our penitence holier than our former sanctity, and our last works more than our first, and our latter end better than our beginning. For His all-prevailing sake who alone fell not nor stumbled, who alone wandered not nor wavered, our Lord Jesus Christ Thy Son. Amen.[1]

> To Mark the second place; that Mark who erst
> Was kin to Barnabas and friend of Paul,
> And reckoned it an easy thing and small
> To be their yoke-fellow through lands accurst,
> Preaching deliverance to the tribes dispersed;
> Yea, and was helpful ere his faith had fall;
> Then taking fearfulness for Heaven's recall,
> Went back and walked not with them as at first;
> And so was lost to Paul, but not to God;
> Who bore him gently as a tender child,
> Strengthened and blest him; till with feet new-shod
> Again he ventured on the pagan wild,
> Carried the Light of lights from shade to shade,
> Travailed, and suffered, and was not afraid.[2]

[1] Christina G. Rossetti, *Called to be Saints*, 200.
[2] E. C. Lefroy, *Sonnets*.

SILAS.

LITERATURE.

Baring-Gould, S., *A Study of St. Paul* (1897), 197.

Binney, T., *St. Paul: His Life and Ministry* (1866), 201.

Conybeare, W. J., and J. S. Howson, *The Life and Epistles of St. Paul*, i. (1877) 268.

Gaebelein, A. C., *The Acts of the Apostles*, 271.

Haweis, H. R., *The Picture of Paul* (1887), 100.

Holden, J. S., *Redeeming Vision* (1908), 101.

Howson, J. S., *Scenes from the Life of St. Paul* (1909), 116.

Knowling, R. J., *The Acts of the Apostles* (Expositor's Greek Testament) (1900), 326.

Lefroy, E. C., *The Christian Ideal* (1883), 60.

Lewin, T., *The Life and Epistles of St. Paul*, i. (1875) 163.

M'Garvey, J. W., *New Commentary on Acts of Apostles*, ii. (1892) 75.

Maclaren, A., *Expositions*: The Acts of the Apostles xiii.–end (1907), 114.

„ „ *The Victor's Crowns*, 104.

„ „ *Christ's Musts* (1894), 270.

Marsh, F. E., *Flashes from the Lighthouse of Truth*, 11.

Peloubet, F. N., *The Teachers' Commentary on the Acts of the Apostles* (1901), 211.

Rackham, R. B., *The Acts of the Apostles* (1901), 256.

Seekings, H. S., *The Men of the Pauline Circle* (1914), 75.

Selwyn, E. C., *St. Luke the Prophet* (1901), 3.

Stalker, J., *The New Song* (1888), 168.

Thorne H., *Notable Sayings of the Great Teacher*, 115.

Trench, R. C., *Sermons Preached for the Most Part in Ireland* (1873), 142.

Zahn, T., *Introduction to the New Testament*, i. (1909) 215.

SILAS.

Sylvanus our faithful brother.—1 Pet. v. 12.

SYLVANUS is, beyond all reasonable doubt, the same man who is known to us in the Acts of the Apostles by the name of Silas. A double name was very common among Jews whose vocations brought them into close connexion with Gentiles. You will find other instances of it among the Apostles: in *Paul* himself, whose Hebrew name was *Saul*; *Simon* and *Peter*; and probably in *Bartholomew* and *Nathanael*. And there is no reasonable doubt that a careful examination of the various places in which the names Silas and Sylvanus are mentioned shows that they were borne by one person.

Silas glides about in the dim background of the Acts. He is named only when some circumstance arises which makes it necessary, and he is never mentioned save in company with some one else. He is apparently a secondary character, playing a subordinate part in the stupendous endeavour to evangelize the Gentile world. Yet his is by no means an expressionless personality, and his work as an edifier of his brethren lifts him out of the group of the unknown, and makes him something more to us than simply a name.

¶ It is horribly vexatious to be next door to greatness. An old proverb tells us that a miss is as good as a mile; but, like most proverbs, it is as false as false can be. A mile is ever so much better than a miss.[1]

¶ Janet was one of those rare women who are efficient performers on that useful instrument known as "the second fiddle." It is a great gift. They make the sweetest music in the world. There are no more essential performers in the orchestra than they.[2]

[1] F. W. Boreham, *Mushrooms on the Moor*, 188.
[2] Ellen Thorneycroft Fowler, *In Subjection*.

¶ Blessed the man and woman who is able to serve cheerfully in the second rank—a big test.[1]

I.

CHIEF AMONG THE BRETHREN.

1. Before he met with Paul, Silas had "proved his soul." Certain men who came from Jerusalem had brought a disturbing element into the Church at Antioch. To the consternation of the Gentile believers, their message was, "Except ye be circumcised after the manner of Moses ye cannot be saved." They announced themselves teachers of authority.

Paul and Barnabas, however, detected the subtle work of the enemy. The gospel preached by Paul had nothing to do with the law or with circumcision. It was determined that they both, with certain other of them, should go up to Jerusalem to discuss the question. There Paul gained his point, and made a friend; for "it pleased the apostles and elders, with the whole church, to send chosen men of their own company to Antioch with Paul and Barnabas; namely, Judas, surnamed Barsabas, and Silas, *chief men among the brethren.*" They further commissioned these men to carry a message to the brethren of the Gentiles in Antioch, Syria, and Cilicia. The letter was a most wonderful document, brief and extremely tactful.

These two disciples were possessed of that power of "prophecy" which was one of the forms in which the Holy Spirit made His presence known: and the Syrian Christians were "exhorted and confirmed" by the exercise of this miraculous gift. The minds of all were in great tranquillity when the time came for the return of these messengers "to the Apostles" at Jerusalem. Silas, however, as has been stated, either remained at Antioch or soon came back. He was destined, as we shall see, to become the companion of Paul, and to be at the beginning of the second missionary journey what Barnabas had been at the beginning of the first.

[1] *Mary Slessor of Calabar*, 298.

"Behold the holy man! Behold the Seer!
    Him who hath spoken with the unseen Lord!"
He to his heart with large embrace had taken
    The universal sorrow of mankind,
And, from that root, a shelter never shaken,
    The tree of wisdom grew with sturdy rind.
He could interpret well the wondrous voices
    Which to the calm and silent spirit come;
He knew that the One Soul no more rejoices
    In the star's anthem than the insect's hum.
He in his heart was ever meek and humble,
    And yet with kingly pomp his numbers ran,
As he foresaw how all things false should crumble
    Before the free, uplifted soul of man:
And, when he was made full to overflowing
    With all the loveliness of heaven and earth,
Out rushed his song, like molten iron glowing,
    To show God sitting by the humblest hearth.
With calmest courage he was ever ready
    To teach that action was the truth of thought,
And, with strong arm and purpose firm and steady,
    And anchor for the drifting world he wrought.
So did he make the meanest man partaker
    Of all his brother-gods unto him gave;
All souls did reverence him and name him Maker,
    And when he died heaped temples on his grave.[1]

2. As soon as the company arrived the multitude of Christians came together for a general meeting. The letter was then read and the result was great joy. It was a great consolation to them to receive such a loving message. But Judas and Silas had been enjoined to tell them "the same things by mouth." They now discharged their commission. They were both prophets, and exhorted the brethren with many words. The gift of a prophet is here described. It is exhortation and speaking for the edification of God's people. Through these exhortations the assembly was confirmed, that is, more fully established. No doubt their chief exhortation must have been "to keep the unity of the Spirit in the bond of peace." They abode in Antioch for some time and then, perhaps after another assembly gathering, they were permitted to return to the Apostles in Jerusalem in peace, or rather, *with peace.*

[1] J. R. Lowell.

¶ "To prophesy," in the language of the Scripture, is "to speak the words of God," as opposed to speaking our own words from our own devices. Prophecy, according to Paul, convinces, judges, makes manifest the secrets of the heart; and at last urges the hearer of it to give himself up to God, and acknowledge that what he hears has God's authority.[1]

II.

THE COMPANION OF ST. PAUL.

1. Silas was on the one hand a man who enjoyed the confidence of the Mother Church, and on the other hand was in sympathy with the progress of the Gentile mission up to this time. Both things were important for St. Paul, and probably decided him, after his break with Barnabas, to choose Silas of Jerusalem as his companion on the second missionary journey, instead of some one of the other teachers at Antioch.

Silas was apparently a Hebrew by birth, but a Roman citizen, like Paul, and this Roman side of him rendered him one who might be useful to the great Apostle in his further travels and mission work.

¶ I was travelling on a ship the other evening. I was strolling on the port side of the deck; I noticed another minister strolling on the starboard side. Here we were—one and one. Presently we introduced ourselves to each other, and spent the evening in delightful comradeship. Some of the thoughts suggested by our chat that night will cling to me to my dying day. Inspirations visited the two of us together that could never have come to either of us singly. In his *Life of Nathaniel Hawthorne*, too, Henry James makes the casual remark that "every man works better when he has companions."[2]

2. Silas remained in Antioch, although his co-deputy went back to Jerusalem; and the attraction of Paul—the great mass of that star—drew this lesser light into becoming a satellite, moving round the greater orb. So, when the unfortunate quarrel broke out between Paul and Barnabas, and the latter went away by

---

[1] T. Arnold, *Sermons*, 213.
[2] F. W. Boreham, *The Golden Milestone*, 163.

himself with John Mark, Paul chose Silas and set out upon his second missionary tour.

It is in his association with Paul that Silas is seen to best advantage. Though chosen by the Apostle for the arduous task of the second missionary journey, it must not be understood that he consented blindly and impulsively. His response was rather that of his own quiet and deep conviction, and it was perfectly voluntary. And when they set out together, their purpose was one that lay near to his heart. They desired to confirm the churches and gain new trophies for the cross. And as they journeyed and laboured, the range of the work so grew that they set aside their earlier plans and, in obedience to the will of God, carried the gospel into Europe. The rapid movements of Acts xv. 40–xvi. 12 make it impossible for the reader to grasp the greatness of this undertaking unless the places mentioned are closely followed by the aid of a map. That tour through Asia Minor which is dismissed in a verse or two was no easy matter. What patience and endurance and devotion to the will of God are hinted at in the swiftly moving record! Had it pleased St. Luke to be more explicit, what revealings might we not have had of that eventful journey! But he is eager to get the feet of Paul upon European soil, and in his haste he contents himself with the simple statement that " as they went on their way through the cities, they delivered them the decrees for to keep, which had been ordained of the apostles and elders that were at Jerusalem. So the churches were strengthened in the faith, and increased in number daily." But even in this, however impatient he may be, St. Luke does not overlook the significant thing in all that journeying—the edification of the churches.

¶ Man must go. It is not a question of whether we will go or not go, that is determined for us—we *must* go. Every man is accomplishing a journey, going through a process. No man is standing still. The infant is going on towards youth ; youth is advancing towards the stature and strength of manhood ; and man, in the summer of his prosperity and honour, is going on towards the sere leaf, and towards a land of darkness as darkness itself. Men must go on, then. The only question is—*How?* Man may go either with God or without Him.[1]

[1] Joseph Parker.

3. Silas was Paul's companion when the first European antagonism to the gospel showed itself. They had incurred the anger of the magistrates of Philippi. They had roused to hostility the masters of a certain damsel who possessed a spirit of divination; these in turn stirred up the multitude, and the multitude dragged the Apostles to the judgment-seat. There seems to have been no trial and little investigation. The charge indeed was not very definite: "These men, being Jews, do exceedingly trouble our city, and teach customs, which are not lawful for us to receive, neither to observe, being Romans." But it was enough for the magistrates. They "rent off their clothes, and commanded to beat them. And when they had laid many stripes upon them, they cast them into prison, charging the jailor to keep them safely: who, having received such a charge, thrust them into the inner prison, and made their feet fast in the stocks." It was not a case of ordinary imprisonment. They were treated as criminals of no common kind. Mere thieves or ruffians would have enjoyed the comparative freedom of the outer jail; but Paul and Silas had offended the prejudices of a whole city, and must be kept like murderers in the dark recesses of the inner cell.

During the night, while the Apostles were singing hymns, an earthquake shook the prison; the doors flew open, and the chains which were stapled into the walls fell down. For these birds could sing in a darkened cage. The jailor's treatment of them after his conversion shows what he had neglected to do at first. They had no food; their bloody backs were unsponged; they were thrust into a filthy hole, and put in a posture of torture. No wonder that they could not sleep! But what hindered sleep would, with most men, have sorely dimmed trust and checked praise. Not so with them. God gave them "songs in the night." We can hear the strains through all the centuries; and they bid us be cheerful and trustful, whatever befalls. Surely Christian faith is never more noble than when it triumphs over circumstances, and brings praises from lips which, if sense had its way, would wail and groan. "This is the victory that overcometh the world." The true anæsthetic is trust in God. No wonder that the baser sort of prisoners—and base enough they probably were—"were listening to them," for such sounds had never been heard there before.

Blest is the man who with the sound of song
    Can charm away the heartache, and forget
The frost of Penury, and the stings of Wrong,
    And drown the fatal whisper of Regret!
        Darker are the abodes
            Of Kings, tho' his be poor,
        While Fancies, like the Gods,
            Pass thro' his door.

Singing thou scalest Heaven upon thy wings,
    Thou liftest a glad heart into the skies;
He maketh his own sunrise, while he sings,
    And turns the dusty Earth to Paradise;
        I see thee sail along
            Far up the sunny streams,
        Unseen, I hear his song,
            I see his dreams.[1]

4. The First Epistle to the Thessalonians was written shortly after the arrival of Timothy and Sylvanus in Corinth, under the stimulus of the good news which Timothy brought back from Macedonia.

In the first division we have a review of the founding of the Church by the preaching of the writers, Paul and Sylvanus and Timothy, and of everything which, since their departure from Thessalonica, had manifested their loving interest in the growth of the Church and in the continuance of its pleasant relations with its founders.   In this review a prominent place is given to statements about the persecutions which the readers had endured at the beginning, and in the face of which they had since maintained their faith.

¶ A young Christian Hindoo, who, when up on the hills for a time, joined my Bible class, had undergone most cruel treatment as a lad, for expressing a desire to become a Christian.   His heathen parents tied him fast by ropes for five days in a room, from which he could not escape, and starved him all the time. They then put pepper in his eyes, and tried by every means to induce him to renounce his Christianity.

All the devices, however, proved fruitless, and they at last released him from his torture; soon afterwards he managed to escape to the Mission House.   There he was instructed carefully, and after a time, finding him truly sincere, he was baptized.

[1] Frederick Tennyson.

Some time afterwards, going with the missionary to preach in his native village, a tumult was made, the missionary's cart was surrounded by roughs, and the lad was captured. It was with much difficulty and some danger, that he was at last rescued, the missionary refusing to return without him. He is now studying with other lads at the High School at Palamcottah, and we trust that a useful career is before him. He is a true Christian, and the persecutions he has endured seem to have strengthened his character, and given him a stability and a firmness of purpose which otherwise he might have lacked. He is a bright, good-looking lad, but is slightly built and delicate in appearance. We hope he may be spared to be a blessing to his people.[1]

5. The rest, so far as Silas is concerned, is soon told. From Philippi they pass to Thessalonica, where a riot brings their labours prematurely to a close. They go on to Berœa, where a threatening of further trouble necessitates the departure of Paul; but Silas remains in the company of Timothy until after Paul's experience at Athens, when they both join him at Corinth. From that point Silas disappears from the Acts.

A great genius, a wise philosopher, an eloquent preacher, a statesman, a warrior, poet, painter? No! "A faithful brother." He may have been a commonplace one. We do not know anything about his intellectual capacity. He may have had very narrow limitations and very few powers, or he may have been a man of large faculty and acquirements. But these things drop out of sight; and this remains—that he was *faithful*. No doubt the eulogium is meant in both senses of the word. The one of these is the root of the other; for a man that is full of faith is a man who may be trusted, is reliable, and will be sure to fulfil all the obligations of his position, and to do all the duties that are laid upon him.

¶ "Surely the Captain may depend on me" may not be the best thing to say before others, but, rightly meant, it is a noble self-commitment. Dependable people!—their price is above rubies. The world would be a dreary place if there were not some Christians who need no prodding or watching; who can be told, and then trusted.[2]

---

[1] H. S. Streatfeild, *Glimpses of Indian Life*, 146.
[2] M. D. Babcock, *Thoughts for Every-Day Living*, 5.

LYDIA.

LITERATURE.

Adeney, W. F., *Women of the New Testament* (1899), 221.

Baker, E., *The Revivals of the Bible* (1906), 174.

Davidson, T., in *Biblical Character Sketches* (1896), 198.

Elder, R., *The Redeemer's Cry* (1892), 101.

Howson, J. S., *The Companions of St. Paul* (1874), 31.

Lewis, H. E., in *Women of the Bible* : Rebekah to Priscilla (1874), 31.

Luckock, H. M., *Footprints of the Apostles as traced by Saint Luke in the Acts*, ii. (1905) 125.

McGarvey, J. W., *Sermons* (1894), 145.

Maclaren, A., *The Acts of the Apostles* (Bible Class Expositions) (1894), 203.

Minifie, W. C., *The Mask Torn Off* (1901), 46.

Noble, F. A., *Typical New Testament Conversions* (1901), 51.

Norton, J. N., *Old Paths* (1880), 390.

Raleigh, A., *From Dawn to the Perfect Day* (1883), 265.

Stokes, G. T., *The Acts of the Apostles* (Expositor's Bible), ii. (1892) 271.

Dictionary of the Apostolic Church, i. (1915) 726 (W. F. Boyd).

Dictionary of the Bible, iii. (1900) 176 (G. Milligan).

Twentieth-Century Pastor, xxix. (1911) 407 (A. B. Gardner).

LYDIA.

A certain woman named Lydia, . . . one that worshipped God, heard us.—Acts xvi. 14.

ABOUT twenty years after the death and resurrection of Christ there was still no Christianity at all in Europe, except so far as a few scattered Jews, travelling for purposes of trade—or here and there a Greek sailor or Roman soldier—might have in their hearts the seeds of Divine truth, sown there by the words and work of Christ in Judæa, or elsewhere by some followers of Christ. No doubt in this way some preparation was going on for the great Christian community of Rome; but still, on the whole, it may be said with truth that Europe at this moment was heathen from one end to the other.

1. The significance of the events which turned Paul's steps to Europe is more clearly seen to-day than at the time. By Divine leading the Apostle's course was blocked in Asia. At Troas he was on the edge of Asia, with Europe on the opposite shore. At this place he had a vision, in which a man of Macedonia stood on the other side of the water and beckoned for aid. Coupled with the closed door in Asia, this was accepted as indicating an open one in Europe. And Paul, with Timothy, Silas, and Luke immediately started for the new field.

2. After a prosperous voyage of two days, the Apostle and his companions landed at Neapolis, a Macedonian harbour, and then travelled ten miles inland to Philippi.

Philippi was a city built by King Philip, the father of Alexander the Great. After the conquest of Macedonia by the Romans, it became famous as the scene of the great battle between Brutus and Cassius on the one hand, and Mark Antony and Augustus on the other, a battle which decided the fate of the Empire and influenced the course of the world's history as few other battles have done. Augustus made Philippi into a colony, erecting a triumphal arch to celebrate his victory over Brutus, and placing there a large settlement of his veterans who had secured for him this important outpost.

3. What day the Apostles landed we do not know. But as a few days elapsed before the Sabbath came round, it is clear they arrived early in the week. Whilst it was useless to look round for a Christian cause, it was not an unreasonable thing for them to endeavour to discover a Jewish place of worship. Their practice had always been to go to their own nationality first. But there was no synagogue in Philippi. Wherever ten wise men could be found in a city, the rule of the Jews allowed for the establishment of a synagogue. These ten were not in evidence in the Macedonian centre. Not only did the Apostles discover no synagogue during those first few days, but they observed no Jewish features among the crowds that thronged the streets, for when the Sabbath day came round they were not sure that there was even a place of prayer for a few. "On the Sabbath we went forth without the gate by a river side, where we supposed there was a place of prayer." They had not got beyond supposition when the Sabbath morning dawned.

In the absence of a synagogue there was frequently an enclosure, sometimes open to the sky, outside the city boundaries, where a few worshippers would assemble every Sabbath. For such a spot Paul and his companions looked. They found one, but it was occupied only by women. To this little gathering Paul spoke. He sat down and talked to them. The first gospel sermon in Europe was conversational. It was not rhetorical. There was nothing about it to dazzle. It was an earnest talk for the purpose of winning a few to Christ, and not for the sake of gaining a reputation for the preacher. And the first convert in Europe was gained at this service. That convert was Lydia.

Drink: the immortal waters quench the spirit's longing.
Art thou not now, bright one, all sorrow past, in elation,
Made young with joy, grown brother-hearted with the vast,
Whither thy spirit wending flits the dim stars past
Unto the Light of Lights in burning adoration.[1]

[1] A. E., *The Divine Vision*, 32.

I.

LYDIA'S READINESS.

1. Lydia was born at Thyatira, in the province of Asia, and probably spent most of her life there. It was business that brought her to Philippi. Her native city was famous for its dye-works. Purple was a favourite colour with the ancients. This included shades ranging all the way "from rose-red to sea-green or blue." The dye which yielded this colour was procured from a certain shell-fish. This woman, who was "a seller of purple," may have been disposing of the dye, or the cloth which had passed through the colouring process.

It is doubtful whether "Lydia" was her proper name, since it may well be a designation of her nationality. She was certainly a Lydian, since Thyatira was in Lydia; and it is scarcely probable that so ambiguous a word should have been given as a name.

Lydia would seem to have been a widow, and must have been a woman of some position, for she was able to entertain the Apostle and his company as soon as she embraced the faith and felt its exceeding preciousness.

2. Lydia was a Jewish proselyte. Evidently devout by nature and habit, she was walking with God up to the full measure of her knowledge, and doing her best to serve Him. Born outside the ranks of the chosen people, and without direct share in the truths and traditions which had come down from Abraham and Moses and the long line of the prophets, she yet accepted the faith of Israel—most likely as soon as it was brought to her attention—and was living a religious life and developing and illustrating a religious character.

She had adopted the Hebrew faith, she worshipped one God; but she was not content. Like the Ethiopian eunuch, she cherished longings that could scarcely be expressed in words—a hunger of love created by the very pureness of the law which she had accepted as her rule of life. She followed the ceremonies of her new religion faithfully: the many washings were duly observed, the prayers were duly prayed; but there was still an

aching void. That morning brought about for her a spiritual
crisis.

¶ Emotion and the inward contact with God are the explanation of our hunger and our striving; for the Spirit of God gives
chase to our spirit, and the closer the contact the greater the
hunger and the striving. This is the life of love in its highest
development, above reason and higher than all understanding; for
in such love reason can neither give nor take away, for our love
is in touch with the divine love. And I think that once this
point is reached there will be no more separation from God.[1]

> Of all the myriad moods of mind
>   That through the soul come thronging,
> Which one was e'er so dear, so kind,
>   So beautiful as Longing?
> The thing we long for, that we are
>   For one transcendent moment,
> Before the Present poor and bare,
>   Can make its sneering comment.
>
> Still, through our paltry stir and strife,
>   Glows down the wished Ideal,
> And Longing moulds in clay what Life
>   Carves in the marble Real;
> To let the new life in, we know,
>   Desire must ope the portal;—
> Perhaps the longing to be so
>   Helps make the soul immortal.
>
> Longing is God's fresh heavenward will
>   With our poor earthward striving;
> We quench it that we may be still
>   Content with merely living;
> But, would we learn that heart's full scope
>   Which we are hourly wronging,
> Our lives must climb from hope to hope
>   And realize our longing.[2]

3. There are two things worth noting in connexion with
Lydia's readiness to receive the truth.

(1) First, *she kept the Sabbath day holy.*—In this heathen
town of Philippi, and all over the world, the Sabbath day was

---

[1] M. Maeterlinck, *Ruysbroeck and the Mystics*, 149.   [2] J. R. Lowell.

unknown, except among the Jews and the proselytes of the Jewish religion. We find Lydia here, then, engaged in business, and in a line which was pursued, most probably, by many others in the city of Philippi. When the Sabbath day dawned did she keep her shop open, in order to maintain competition with other dealers who knew nothing of the Sabbath? Many a man who professes to be a Christian, in our cities and all over our land, in all the different lines of business, labours through the Lord's day like any other day, when it is customary for men in his line to do so, claiming that he is compelled to do it in self-defence. Lydia was not a woman of an indiarubber conscience. When the Sabbath day came, her house of business was closed. She and the women whom she had employed with her in the business could not be found there. They had left home, and left the town, and gone outside the city to spend the Sabbath.

> Ah! ev'ry day mid bring a while
> O' eäse vrom all woone's ceäre an' tweil,
> The welcome evenèn, when 'tis sweet
> Vor tired friends wi' weary veet,
> But litsome hearts o' love, to meet:
> An' yet while weekly times do roll,
> The best vor body an' vor soul
> 'S the church an' happy Zunday.
>
> Vor then our loosen'd souls do rise
> Wi' holy thoughts beyond the skies,
> As we do think o' Him that shed
> His blood vor us, an' still do spread
> His love upon the live an' dead;
> An' how He gi'ed a time an' pleäce
> To gather us, an' gi'e us greäce,—
> The church an' happy Zunday.[1]

¶ Nearly a hundred years ago, eleven young Scotsmen met together in New York. They had recently landed from a voyage of several weeks' duration. It was a fine Sunday morning, and one of them announced his intention of going to church. The others demurred. They had been shut up on board ship so long, and on their first Sunday in the new country they intended to go for a walk. The first speaker stood firm. He said, "My father said to me when leaving the pier, 'Now, my

[1] William Barnes.

boy, wherever you go, Remember the Sabbath day to keep it holy,' and I am not going to break my father's last command."

His companions ceased urging him. He went to church ; they said they would go next Sunday. The name of the one who went to church was Thorburn Grant. He rose to be a wealthy and influential man. At the age of eighty he wrote the story of his life, and stated that the other ten young men, who put off going to the house of God, got into bad company that very first Sunday, and never fulfilled their purpose. He had traced the career of every one of them, and found that all went astray and wasted their lives.[1]

(2) Secondly, *Lydia was at the place of prayer.*—She was away from her native place, but she was worshipping. The faith that had come to her at Thyatira was not left behind with that city. The habit of worship acquired there was continued at Philippi. She was in a city without churches and ministers, but she was worshipping. She did not wait for a lead. She was not spiritually helpless. In material matters she had learned to look after herself. The spirit of self-help, so strong there, she applied to the needs of her soul.

Eleazer, the servant of Abraham, tells how, being in the way, the Lord led him. That is the principle illustrated by Lydia's case. Worshippers are " in the way." Those who make a habit of gathering to worship God put themselves in the way for God to deal with them.

> I know a spot where budless twigs
> 　Are bare above the snow,
> And where sweet winter-loving birds
> 　Flit softly to and fro ;
> There with the sun for altar-fire,
> 　The earth for kneeling-place,
> The gentle air for chorister,
> 　Will I adore Thy face.[2]

II.

The Divine Influence.

1. Lydia had a nature highly sensitive to religious influences; and appeals made to her spiritual faculties, or to her spiritual

[1] Helen S. Dyer, *The Ideal Christian Home*, 126.　　　[2] Alice Brown.

hungerings, met a quick response. She had a clear perception that this life is not all, and that loyalty to one's own soul means loyalty to things invisible and immortal. But beyond this she came under the special illumination of the Spirit of the Lord whom Paul was preaching, and her mind was quickened to understand the truth, and her heart was made willing and even eager to receive the grace of God in Christ.

"The Lord opened her heart." For such as Lydia it is not His way to use violent means, forcing the locks of the heart. He may deal so with a rebellious spirit like that of Saul of Tarsus—the preacher for that day. But for his hearer no such violence was necessary : she went forth to meet God, tremblingly : her heart was opened by consent and preparation of her will.

¶ The most fundamental phenomenon of the religious life in all Churches and Creeds is weariness, not to say sickness, of self, and a passionate desire to find some new centre of life— a " not-ourselves," as Mr. Arnold would say—which can renovate the springs and purify the aims of the soiled and exhausted nature. Now this craving, so far from being confined to those who have led a life of vice or self-indulgence, is perhaps even more powerfully exhibited in men of strong self-control and highly-disciplined nature, provided their spiritual affections be also deep and warm.[1]

2. Immediately on hearing the truth from the lips of the Apostle, Lydia applied it to her own soul. She gave " heed unto the things which were spoken by Paul." She did precisely what everybody who finds his way into the faith and fellowship of the Son of God has to do sooner or later—she called her own will into action, and by deliberate choice set herself over on the side of Him who came to announce a Divine love for all and to be a universal Redeemer. It would have been all in vain for her to be present at this river-side prayer-meeting, and to listen never so intently to the truth brought to her attention, had she formed no opinion and taken no steps for herself. It would have been all in vain, too, to have her heart opened by the Spirit, had she not brought her will into accord with the will of the Spirit and accepted Christ.

¶ " 'Tis in thy power to think as thou wilt." And were the cheerful, sociable, restorative beliefs, of which Marius had read so

[1] R. H. Hutton, *Contemporary Thought and Thinkers*, i. 372.

much, that bold adhesion, for instance, to the hypothesis of an eternal friend to man, just hidden behind the veil of a mechanical and material order, but only just behind it, ready perhaps even now to break through :—were they, after all, really a matter of choice, dependent on some deliberate act of volition on his part ? [1]

¶ Respecting what is called the Christian's experience, it is certain that we have no reason, from the mere contemplation of the operations of our own minds, to ascribe them to an intrinsic agent, because they arise from their proper causes, and are directed to their proper ends. Scripture informs us that it is "God that worketh in us, both to will and to do, of his good pleasure"; which passage, while it asserts the reality of God's influence, points out also the manner of His acting, for He works in us to will before He works in us to do. [2]

III.

THE DISCIPLE OF CHRIST.

1. Lydia put the sincerity and earnestness of her confession of Christ in evidence in two ways.

(1) In the first place *she received baptism*—"And when she was baptized, and her household." Not necessarily in an ostentatious manner, but in a way to make the fact known to all who had a right to know, and to all, no doubt, who would be made the better by knowing it, she walked through the open door of baptism into membership in the Holy Catholic Church. This "seller of purple" seems to have given not so much as a passing thought to the effect on her business of this step she was taking. She did not ask whether it would be likely to increase or decrease her popularity. She accepted Christ; and she wanted to be baptized into the name of the Father and the Son and the Holy Spirit. Considering all the circumstances, this was a remarkable exhibition of devotion and courage.

With her they also baptized her household—either her children, or the workers in her business, and perhaps her domestic servants. It was understood that the proselyte to Judaism took over his household with him. The same was sometimes done in the case

<hr>

[1] Walter Pater, *Marius the Epicurean*, ii. 48.
[2] J. Sargent, *Life and Letters of Henry Martyn*, 31.

of the earlier converts to Christianity. Thus the jailor of this same city of Philippi was baptized " with his household."

But may we not, without overdoing hypothesis, see more in the baptism of Lydia's household than " the feeling of solidarity in an ancient family " ? The whole narrative, so modestly, so chastely coloured, suggests a picture of modesty and gentleness which wield their own authority. Her character recommended her faith ; her piety was persuasive—as it too often is not. She did not shut the gate of Christ's Kingdom in passing through, making it harder for others to follow. A woman who could beseech with such grace might well have learnt to command with equal grace.

(2) In the second place *she was forward to extend Christian hospitality* to those to whom she felt so greatly indebted for the new light and life brought to her. This was one of the first forms of service open to her, and she entered upon it without question or hesitation. "She besought us, saying, if ye have judged me to be faithful to the Lord, come into my house, and abide there. And she constrained us."

When the quiet riverside scene and service came to be followed by violent persecutions, we lose sight of Lydia. But we may take it that her faithfulness was not shaken ; for when Paul and Silas came out of prison they " entered into the house of Lydia." We cannot be far wrong in judging that during those stormy hours she betook herself with her household to prayer and intercession. She would continue worthy of her guests, whether God would vouchsafe to let them return to her or not. Had she proved unfaithful, they would not have re-entered her house ; had her love chilled, there would have been no open door for them. In sunshine and wild storm she had earned the right of repeating, " If ye have judged me to be faithful to the Lord, come into my house, and abide there."

The dream of the world and the wheel of our dreaming,
　The glow and the glory, the love and the strife :
These too are His making, for through them are streaming
　The infinite forces that fashion all life.

But lo ! as they break us and thwart us and bend us,
　A touch through the whirring, the curve of a line,
When life is at darkest is felt to befriend us,—
　A touch that is human, yet wholly Divine !

Then, deep in the furnace of torments infernal,
    The rapture of Heaven we know and we feel:
His touch that we see not, untiring, eternal,
    That yearns to our yearning, is guiding the wheel.

O Love, the indwelling, by Thee are we shriven,
    Ineffable Comforter, Lord of delight!
To those who are born of Thy Spirit, is given
    The quickening of peace in the thick of the fight.

Thou comest, and swift, through the doorways of dulness,
    Come joy and vitality, glory and grace!
Who loves Thee will serve Thee with life in its fulness,
    Or die at his post with Thy joy on his face.[1]

¶ The family consisted of an old grey-bearded man and his wife, with five or six sons and sons-in-law, and their several wives, and a joyous genealogy out of them.

They were all sitting down together to their lentil-soup, a large wheaten loaf was in the middle of the table, and a flagon of wine at each end of it promised joy through the stages of the repast; 'twas a feast of love.

The old man rose up to meet me, and with a respectful cordiality would have me sit down at the table; my heart was set down the moment I entered the room; so I sat down at once, like a son of the family; and, to invest myself in the character as speedily as I could, I instantly borrowed the old man's knife, and, taking up the loaf, cut myself a hearty luncheon; and, as I did it, I saw a testimony in every eye, not only of an honest welcome, but of a welcome mixed with thanks that I had not seemed to doubt it.

Was it this? or tell me, Nature, what else it was that made this morsel so sweet; and to what magic I owe it, that the draught I took of their flagon was so delicious with it, that they remain upon my palate to this hour.

If the supper was to my taste, the grace which followed it was much more so.[2]

2. Lydia was one who combined the virtue of practical common sense with those of a generous heart and an open mind. She was not ashamed to work for her living. She was not one of those women who consider a life of languid idleness to be the most enjoyable kind of existence. She followed an honest trade,

[1] Annie Matheson, *Maytime Songs*, 16.   [2] Sterne.

and apparently was a person of considerable independence of spirit.

We have already noted her courage and her devotion to duty. To these she added a noble hospitality and a fine humility. She considered opportunities of kindness to be God's *rewards*, not His burdens. Charity was a privilege, to be won through faithfulness of service. There is womanly tact too in the way in which she words her invitation to Paul, " If ye have judged me to be faithful to the Lord." It would be hard to refuse what she presented as a proof that Paul believed her to be sincere in her faith. She gracefully covers over the benefit to Paul, and makes out herself to be the obliged party. " Unless you come to my house, it will look as if you were not sure of me." How could that kindly though transparent artifice be resisted ?

Her charity was not a solitary star in the sky of the Philippian Church. Her spirit touched all the rest: " Now ye Philippians know also, that in the beginning of the gospel, when I departed from Macedonia, no church communicated with me as concerning giving and receiving, but ye only." May we not fairly infer that this mother in Israel, first-named convert on European soil, had affected the whole of the little Church that gathered round her, and that as it continued to grow, her influence still remained strong ? For we must remember that in the house of Lydia was cradled the Philippian Church—that Church which St. Paul afterwards described as his " joy and crown."

¶ One who knows what he wills and wills what he knows is a moral character. The ideal of his life is his firm possession, and he himself has become a conscious organ of this ideal. One who consciously experiences and wills to experience the sovereignty of God, and who consciously subjects and wills to subject himself to it in faith and love is a Christian character. The Christian character is the Christian life-ideal. The Christian character is the highest form of a moral personality.[1]

3. We have all a direct interest in the story of Lydia; and the fact that the earliest convert on European soil was a woman may be looked upon almost as a significant prophecy of what the gospel was destined to accomplish for woman among the most advanced peoples of the world. In that fact we have the pledge

---

[1] R. Seeberg, *The Fundamental Truths of the Christian Religion*, 324.

and actual beginning of her elevation. She is no longer to be drudge, slave, plaything to man. She is to enter the Kingdom by his side. Lydia was the herald of the best kind of "new woman."

¶ St. Luke's story leaves Lydia in the place where every woman's life should be at its best—in her home. Lydia the hostess is perhaps the highest type of Christian woman. Her own table ought to be her highest place of honour; the family is her throne. What she is there, society will be in her time, and in the after-time. Every woman ought to covet the title of lady in its old acceptation—"breadgiver"—to her own folk first, and then to strangers.[1]

"Strange" with the glow of a wakened soul,
　　And "new" with the purpose of large endeavour,
She turned her face to the higher goal—
　　To the higher goal it is turned for ever.
Trade and science and craft and art,
　　Have opened their doors to the call of woman;
And greater she grows in her greater part,
　　More tenderly wise, and more sweetly human.

The woman wonder with heart of flame,
　　The coming man of the race will find her.
For petty purpose and narrow aim,
　　And fault and flaw she will leave behind her.
He grown tender, and she grown wise,
　　They shall enter the Eden by both created;
The broadened kingdom of Paradise,
　　And love, and mate, as the first pair mated.[2]

[1] R. W. Barbour, *Thoughts*, 47.
[2] E. Wheeler Wilcox, *Poems of Experience*, 13.

PRISCILLA AND AQUILA.

LITERATURE.

Adeney, W. F., *Women of the New Testament* (1899), 236.

" " in *Women of the Bible*: Rebekah to Priscilla (1904), 247.

Baring-Gould, S., *A Study of St. Paul* (1897), 243.

Burrell, D. J., *The Unaccountable Man* (1901), 262.

Connell, A., *The Endless Quest* (1914), 52.

Conybeare, W. J., and J. S. Howson, *The Life and Epistles of St. Paul* (1870), 299, 330.

Deane, A., *Friends and Fellow Labourers of St. Paul* (1906), 72.

Farrar, F. W., *The Life and Work of St. Paul* (1897), 317.

Gaebelein, A. C., *The Acts of the Apostles*, 310.

Goodman, J. H., *The Lordship of Christ* (1901), 131.

Goulburn, E. M., *The Pursuit of Holiness* (1870), 221.

Howson, J. S., *The Companions of St. Paul* (1874), 243.

" " *Scenes from the Life of St. Paul* (1909), 135.

Luckock, H. M., *Footprints of the Apostles as traced by Saint Luke in the Acts*, ii. (1905) 156.

Mackay, W. M., *Bible Types of Modern Women* (1912), 258.

Maclaren, A., *Expositions*: St. Paul's Epistle to the Romans (1909), 357.

" " *Leaves from the Tree of Life* (1899), 74.

Maurice, F. D., *The Acts of the Apostles* (1894), 293.

Moule, H. C. G., *The Second Epistle to Timothy* (1905), 177.

Neander, A., *History of the Planting and Training of the Christian Church* (tr. J. E. Ryland), i. (1880) 197.

Robertson, F. W., *Expository Lectures on St. Paul's Epistles to the Corinthians* (1873), 1.

Seekings, H. S., *The Men of the Pauline Circle* (1914), 97.

Young, D. T., *Neglected People of the Bible* (1901), 224.

British Congregationalist, Sept. 17, 1908 (J. H. Jowett).

Christian World Pulpit, lxv. (1904) 363 (F. Paget); lxxxiv. (1913) 425 (H. Jeffs).

Dictionary of the Apostolic Church, i. (1915) 87 (J. E. Roberts).

Dictionary of the Bible, i. (1898) 129 (G. Milligan); iv. (1902) 102 (A. C. Headlam).

PRISCILLA AND AQUILA.

Salute Prisca and Aquila my fellow-workers in Christ Jesus.—Rom. xvi. 3.

THE connexion of Corinth with the life of St. Paul and the early progress of Christianity is so close and eventful that no student of the Bible ought to be satisfied without obtaining as correct and clear an idea as possible of the circumstances.

The reasons which determined him to come to Corinth (over and above the discouragement he seems to have met with in Athens) were probably twofold. In the first place, it was a large mercantile city, in immediate connexion with Rome and the west of the Mediterranean, with Thessalonica and Ephesus in the Ægean, and with Antioch and Alexandria in the east. The gospel, once established in Corinth, would rapidly spread everywhere. And, again, from the very nature of the city, the Jews established there were numerous. Communities of scattered Israelites were found in various parts of the province of Achaia —in Athens, in Argos, in Bœotia and Eubœa. But their chief settlement must necessarily have been in that city, which not only gave opportunities of trade by land along the isthmus between the Morea and the Continent, but received in its two harbours the ships of the Eastern and Western seas. A religion which was first to be planted in the synagogue, and was intended to scatter thence its seeds over all parts of the earth, could nowhere find a more favourable soil than among the Hebrew families at Corinth.

The efficiency of Paul's ministry at Corinth was doubtless much promoted by his meeting with a friend and zealous advocate of the gospel, at whose house he lodged, and with whom he obtained employment for his livelihood—the Jew Aquila from Pontus, who probably had a large manufactory in the same trade as that by which Paul supported himself. Aquila appears not to have had a fixed residence at Rome, but to have taken up his abode, at different times, as his business might require, in various large cities situated in the centre of commerce, where he found himself equally at home. But at this time he, with many others, was forced to leave Rome against his will, by a mandate of the Emperor Claudius, who found in the restless, turbulent spirit of a number of Jews resident at Rome (the greater part freed-men), a reason or a pretext for banishing all Jews from that city.

Think of the complicated chain of circumstances, one end of which was round Aquila and the other round the young Pharisee in Jerusalem. It steadily drew them together until they met in that lodging at Corinth. Claudius, in the fulness of his absolute power, said, "Turn all these wretched Jews out of my city. I will not have it polluted with them any more. Get rid of them!" So Priscilla and Aquila were uprooted, and drifted to Corinth. We do not know why they chose to go thither; perhaps they themselves did not know why; but God knew. And while they were coming thither from the west, Paul was coming thither from the east and north. He was "forbidden of the Holy Ghost to speak the word in Asia"; and, driven across the sea against his intention to Neapolis, hounded out of Philipp and Thessalonica and Berœa, and turned superciliously away from Athens, he at last found himself in Corinth, face to face with the tent-maker from Rome and his wife. Then one of the two men said, "Let us join partnership together, and set up here as tent-makers for a time."

¶ *Why does the swallow migrate?* How does the swallow know when to turn its face to the ocean? How does it know in which direction to go? I do not know. And, what is more, the swallow does not know! Yes, that is the beauty of it—the swallow does not know. You tell me that the swallow knows *instinctively.* But what is instinct? You do not explain a thing, or lessen its mystery, by giving it a name.

> A fire mist and a planet,
>   A crystal and a cell,
> A jelly-fish and a saurian,
>   And a cave where the cave-men dwell;
> Then a sense of law and beauty,
>   A face turned from the clod—
> Some call it Evolution,
>   And others call it God.

It is better—far better—to call it God and be done with it. And, in exactly the same way, there is this wondrous force that guides the swallow:

> Some people call it instinct,
> And others call it God.

It is better, I repeat, to call it God. Far better. Now at this point the study of the swallow becomes of vast importance to me. For in many respects I am very like the swallow. I move through life guided by a force that I cannot explain. By what strange impulse was I impelled to follow this profession—this and no other? By what freak of fate did I marry this wife—this and no other? By what stroke of fortune did I settle in this land—this and no other? Looking back on life, it seems almost like a drift; we seem to have reached this position by the veriest chance. And yet it has all turned out too well to be the result of chance. The fact is that like the swallow we acted instinctively. And that instinct was God! We say with Browning's Paracelsus:

> I see my way as birds their trackless way.
> I shall arrive! What time, what circuit first,
> I ask not: but unless God send His hail
> Or blinding fireballs, sleet or stifling snow,
> In some time, His good time, I shall arrive:
> He guides me and the bird. In His good time![1]

I.

PREPARATION.

1. It is open to question, whether Priscilla and Aquila were Christians when they left Rome; and seeing that Aquila is still called a Jew, the weight of authority appears to be on the negative side. The inference, however, is precarious, inasmuch as a Jew who became a Christian would still be regarded politically as a Jew. Race and not faith would determine the matter. Still, one inclines to the view that it was in Corinth that, through the preaching of Paul and the testimony of his life, Priscilla and Aquila came to embrace Christianity. By whatever means they were led to the faith it matters little, but it is beyond dispute

[1] F. W. Boreham, *The Golden Milestone*, 42.

that, having accepted it, they adorned it with singular grace; and among the group of Paul's helpers, while many have been more illustrious, few were more consistent or more timely with their aid.

2. Aquila came from Pontus, a remote Roman province, by the shores of the Euxine. Priscilla is not traced back to that distant province. Her name, appearing sometimes in its shorter form, as Prisca, is often met with in monuments at Rome.

¶ One of the oldest of the catacombs at Rome, situated outside the Porta Salaria, is known as "the burial-place of Priscilla" (*Coemeterium Priscillae*). The name Prisca has been found in association with an aristocratic family, the Acilian *gens*, some members of which were buried in this catacomb. From these facts it has been inferred that Priscilla was a member of this high family, and that has been taken as the reason why, of the six places where she and her husband are mentioned in the New Testament, four have the wife's name first. If she "married beneath her," it is supposed the difference of rank might be indicated by this exceptional precedence. The primitive Church may not have been socialistic or communistic with regard to property; but certainly it was a great leveller of distinctions with reference to persons. It refused to "respect persons," knew no precedence of rank. Besides, is it likely that a high-born Roman lady would have married a Jewish artizan and travelled about with him, working with her hands at the rough toil of tent-making? If she had made so exceptional a sacrifice, should we not have met with some reference to the fact? That this working woman, wife of a working man, was a lady of the blue blood of Rome's proud aristocracy, a member of a Patrician house, is most improbable. But Priscilla does not need the poor worldly distinction to gain our respect. She stands high among the honourable women of the primitive Church on much more solid grounds.[1]

3. "They were tent-makers." Paul's association with them began in a purely commercial partnership. But as they abode together and worked at their trade, there would be many earnest talks about the Christ, and these ended in both husband and wife becoming disciples.

Many a time would the needles become still and silent as Paul told the story of Nazareth, and Calvary, and Olivet, and his

[1] W. F. Adeney.

own solemn experiences on the way to Damascus, until at last the tent-makers' house became a sanctuary, and all three were on their knees together in adoration of a common Lord.

¶ Many of the earliest churches were " house-churches." The believers frequently met in the house of some prominent member, and, until the fellowship grew too large for it, the meetings were held, and the common meal was eaten, in the large family room of a private house.[1]

¶ Memory goes back to the little room, where, the day's toil done, a few men and women met together to hold a simple service. The one candle stuck in a bottle and placed on the mantelpiece, and the pail with its pennyworth of coal at the fireside ready for use, were the pathetic touches, among the little things which the gentle old woman had done to make her room comfortable. And, as the neighbours entered, bringing their chairs, and in the half-light hymns were sung, verses repeated, and prayer ascended, one felt that surely it was just in such gatherings of the " two or three," that Jesus had promised to be " in the midst."[2]

4. Such a couple, and a couple in which the wife took the foremost place, was an absolute impossibility in heathenism. They are a specimen of what Christianity did in the primitive age, all over the Empire, and is doing to-day, everywhere—lifting woman to her proper place. These two, yoked together in "all exercise of noble end," helping one another in Christian work, and bracketed together by the Apostle, who puts the wife first, as his fellow-helpers in Christ Jesus, stand before us as a living picture of what our sweet and sacred family life and earthly loves may be glorified into, if the light from heaven shines down upon them, and is thankfully received into them.

¶ Marius felt, felt amid the stirring of some wonderful new hope within himself, the genius, the unique power of Christianity. The nature of the family, for which the better genius of old Rome itself had sincerely cared, of the family and its appropriate affections—all that love of one's kindred by which obviously one does triumph in some degree over death—had never been so felt before. Here, surely ! in its genial warmth, its jealous exclusion of all that was opposed to it, to its own immaculate naturalness, in the hedge set around the sacred thing on every side, this de-

[1] R. M. Jones, *Studies in Mystical Religion*, 22.
[2] J. Goodfellow, *The Print of His Shoe*, 38.

velopment of the family did but carry forward, and give effect to, the purposes, the kindness, of nature itself, friendly to man.[1]

II.

SERVICE.

1. We have no record of the conversations that took place over the sewing of the coarse goat's-hair canvas, as the three craftsmen talked together on the subjects that lay nearest their hearts. But the result of it was that Aquila and his wife were both so fully equipped that they could undertake the training of others in the larger truths of the gospel.

Some time after, Paul determined to go to Ephesus. Priscilla and Aquila resolved to break up their business and go with him. In that city they did a great work for God. Having probably a larger house than most of the early Christians, they began that "church in the house" which they seem to have continued wherever they went, for we hear of their doing the same thing at Rome also.

2. While Priscilla and Aquila were still at Ephesus, Apollos, an eloquent preacher and "mighty in the scriptures," arrived from Alexandria. He had, however, a serious defect. The only Jesus he knew was an ethical Jesus, that is, Jesus as a preacher of righteousness, the Jesus of the Sermon on the Mount, Jesus as prophet, but not as priest and king. He declaimed passionately against sin; called on men to repent and turn to Jesus. But when you asked what turning to Jesus meant, he was very vague and left you in the mist.

Priscilla and Aquila listened with pleasure, mingled with great pain. He was so gifted, so earnest; but so long as he preached mere morality they felt he would do little good. But how guide him? It was a delicate thing to tell a gifted preacher, fresh, perhaps, from the University of Alexandria, that his preaching was radically defective. Yet they must do it; so one night we may imagine Priscilla inviting him to their house after the sermon, and, when supper was over, beginning the

[1] Walter Pater, *Marius the Epicurean*, ii. 82.

delicate task. They expounded unto him the way of God more perfectly. Fed as they were on Paul's "strong meat," we need have little doubt as to what that instruction would be. It would begin with atonement through the blood of Christ. It would go on to salvation through faith in that blood. And it would close with the fruits of holy living, due to the Presence of Christ in the believer, through the baptism of the Holy Ghost.

As they dwelt with glowing hearts on these precious truths, Apollos forgot to be offended. His candid mind received the truth as a little child, and he who before knew only the baptism of John, knew now the baptism of the Holy Ghost.

3. It does not appear that, after their stay in Ephesus, these two were closely associated with Paul, and certainly they were not among what we may call his evangelistic staff. Nor do they appear to have met him again after that time. Their gipsy life was probably forced on them by the exigencies of Aquila's trade. When he had made tents in Ephesus for a while, he moved on somewhere else, looking for work. Yet Paul continues to call them his "fellow-workers in Christ Jesus." No matter whether it was in Corinth or in Ephesus or in Rome, these two carried Jesus Christ with them where they went, and while they were plying their trade were also preaching Christ.

4. After this we meet with the two evangelists on two other occasions, both probably at Ephesus. The first is of thrilling interest, tantalizing us with a passing allusion that makes us long to know more. It occurs in the sixteenth chapter of the Epistle to the Romans, which, there is good reason to suppose, is a misplaced fragment of an epistle to Ephesus. There we read, "Salute Prisca and Aquila my fellow-workers in Christ Jesus, who for my life laid down their own necks." Then they had risked their lives to save the Apostle's life — when and in what circumstances we do not know. Possibly it was during the riot at Ephesus. Thus we see that they had the true ring of Christ's heroes, the genuine martyr spirit; they were ready to take up the cross. At the same time they showed the spirit of staunch friendship. They were willing to die for Paul. But then Paul was worth dying for. All the Gentile Churches, who

looked up to Paul as their leader, must have honoured them for this.

> For we must share, if we would keep
> That good thing from above;
> Ceasing to give, we cease to have—
> Such is the law of Love.[1]

5. The last reference to Priscilla and Aquila is when the Apostle, on the further edge of life, looked back over it all; and, whilst much had become dim, and some trusted friends had dropped away, like Demas, he saw these two, and waved them his last greeting before he turned to the executioner—"Salute Prisca and Aquila." Paul's Master is not less mindful of His friends' love, or less eloquent in the praise of their faithfulness, or less sure to reward them with the crown of glory. "Whosoever shall confess me before men, him will I confess also before my Father which is in heaven."

¶ Faithfulness unto death is God's standard for human life. On this He bases His judgments. As we apply this standard, our views on many things undergo a radical change. We come to see that the thing of value is not speed but endurance. The real hero is not he who makes the fastest schedule but he who lasts the longest. There are those who go up like a rocket and come down like a stick. It is the power to hold on that wins. Great Britain's most famous general once said that the difference between the soldiers of his country and those of another was not that the English soldier was braver than other soldiers, but that he was brave five minutes longer. It is endurance that wins the crown.

The thing of value is not achievement but fidelity. It is not what we accomplish but the way we accomplish it. It is our ideals, our principles. It is not success that God looks at, but the struggle. Success is a cheap thing, it is merely relative; but struggle is an affair of eternity, it is a spiritual asset.[2]

6. Paul's letters always seem to run into doxology when he is writing of men and women who have suffered on behalf of Christ. But he never wrote to them in sympathy; it was always in congratulation. He did not look upon them as the bearers of

---

[1] R. C. Trench, "The Law of Love."
[2] J. I. Vance, *Tendency*, 229.

burdens, but rather as the privileged children of the Highest. "Unto you it is given in the behalf of Christ, not only to believe on him, but also to suffer for his sake." And so Priscilla and Aquila were chivalrous disciples in the service. And what were the fruits of it? What the fruits always are. Holy boldness has the key to many a secret door. The disciple who bears much discovers much. The Kingdom of Heaven is taken by force. If we risk a personal loss, if we risk contumely, if we risk disaster and defeat, we shall find the Lord of glory on the road. Along these roads, at any rate, something ventured is something won.

¶ Every chain is a ray of light, and every prison is a palace, and every loss is the purchase of a kingdom, and every affront in the cause of God is an eternal honour, and every day of sorrow is a thousand years of comfort, multiplied with a never-ceasing numeration; days without night, joys without sorrow, sanctity without sin, charity without stain, possession without fear, society without envying, communication of joys without lessening; and they shall dwell in a blessed country, where an enemy never entered, and from whence a friend never went away.[1]

> All thy old woes shall now smile on thee
> And thy pains sit bright upon thee;
> All thy suff'rings be divine.
> Tears shall take comfort, and turn gems
> And wrongs repent to diadems.
> Even thy Death shall live; and new
> Dress the soul that erst they slew.
> Thy wounds shall blush to such bright scars
> As keep account of the Lamb's wars.[2]

[1] Jeremy Taylor.   [2] Richard Crashaw.

APOLLOS.

LITERATURE.

Cone, O., *Paul* (1898), 112.

Davidson, S., *An Introduction to the Study of the New Testament*, i. (1868) 39, 255.

Deane, A., *Friends and Fellow Labourers of St. Paul* (1906), 20.

Farrar, F. W., *The Early Days of Christianity* (1891), 136.

Howson, J. S., *The Companions of St. Paul* (1874), 76.

Lightfoot, J. B., *Notes on Epistles of St. Paul* (1895), 153.

Ramsay, W. M., *St. Paul the Traveller* (1895), 267.

Rankin, J., *The First Saints* (1893), 300.

Roberts, H., *The Spiritual Mind* (1902), 8.

Seekings, H. S., *The Men of the Pauline Circle* (1914), 107.

Stevens, G. B., *The Theology of the New Testament* (1899), 483.

Weizsäcker, C. von, *The Apostolic Age of the Christian Church*, i. (1897) 320.

Wright, A., *Some New Testament Problems* (1898), 309, 318.

Young, D. T., *Neglected People of the Bible* (1901), 245.

Christian World Pulpit, lii. (1897) 318 (G. H. Dubbink).

Clergyman's Magazine, 3rd Ser., vii. (1894) 33.

Dictionary of the Apostolic Church, i. (1915) 81 (J. E. Roberts).

Dictionary of the Bible, i. (1898) 124 (J. H. Bernard).

Expositor, 1st Ser., i. (1875) 329, 409 (E. H. Plumptre).

Expository Times, vii. (1896) 243, 564 (F. Blass); ix. (1898) 8 (A. Wright).

Hermathena, xxi. (1895) 233 (G. Salmon).

Journal of Theological Studies, vii. (1905) 16 (J. H. A. Hart); xvi. (1915) 241 (B. T. D. Smith).

Preacher's Magazine, ix. (1898) 272 (J. C. Nattrass).

APOLLOS.

A certain Jew named Apollos, an Alexandrian by race, a learned man.—
Acts xviii. 24.

THE name Apollos is contracted from either Apollonius or
Apollodorus, probably the former.   So at least it is written in full
in Codex D (Acts xviii. 24), and the variation seems to point to
some very early tradition.   Apollos was an Alexandrian, and the
name Apollonius was common in Alexandria, probably owing to
the fact that the first governor left by Alexander in his African
province was so called.

I.

HIS PREPARATION.

The first thing to be taken into account in estimating any
man who has played an important part in life is the influence to
which he was exposed in his early days.   The associations of his
youth, the place of his training, the manner of his education,—
these things have usually much to do with the career which follows.

1. Now we know what Alexandria was.   Even in the Acts of
the Apostles we see it in its relations to the religious life of the
Jews in Jerusalem, and to the world-wide commerce of heathen
Italy.   This city was a most remarkable meeting-place of East
and West, and was characterized alike by mercantile and by
mental activity.   Even the memory of Alexander, its great
founder, would tend to produce breadth of view among the
Alexandrians, to make them tolerant and less disposed than others
to lay stress on national distinctions.   Moreover, there was no
place where greater advantages of education were enjoyed in the

age of the Apostles, among which may be reckoned the greatest
library of the ancient world.

¶ Alexandria was founded by the wise foresight of the great
conqueror of the ancient world, as the place where his Greek
power could be brought to bear most easily on Egypt, and which,
therefore, was best suited for the Greek capital of that land of
mystery and wonder. It is not probable he had in view any
especial adaptation of the city as that centre of the world's
intellectual life which it afterwards became; and yet its admirable facilities for communication with every part of the then
known world, and the impress he left upon it by the munificence
and wisdom of his dispositions in reference to its structure, were
the conditions which gave it the possibility of this future
eminence.[1]

¶ In America there is a Yankee type everywhere visible; in
Russia there is a Muscovite type; and everywhere, from the
Mississippi to the Volga, there is a certain uniformity of face, or
at all events of dress. But here, in Alexandria, each face seems
to stand alone. There are eyes and foreheads, noses and beards,
colours of skin, peculiarities of expression—the sly, the dignified,
the rascally, the ignorant, the savage, the refined, the contented,
the miserable,—giving each face its own distinct place in the
globe. And there is, if possible, a greater variety in costume.
Every man seems to have studied his own taste, or his own whim,
or, possibly, his own religion, in the shape, colour, and number of
his garments. The arms, whether dirk or dagger, single pistols or
half a dozen, modern or as old as the invention of gunpowder,
sword, gun, or spear—all have their own peculiar form and
arrangement, so that every Eastern has to a Western a novelty
and picturesqueness that is indescribable. And the motley crowd
presses along: fat, contented, oily Greek merchants, or majestic
Turks, on fine horses splendidly caparisoned, or on aristocratic
donkeys, who would despise to acknowledge as of the same race
the miserable creatures who bray in our coal-carts; bare-legged
donkey boys, driving their more plebeian animals before them;
Arabs from the desert, with long guns and gipsy-like coverings,
stalking on in silence; beggars, such as one sees in the pictures of
the old masters—verily "poor and needy, blind and naked";
insane persons, with idiotic look, and a few rags covering their
bronzed bodies, seeking alms; Greek priests, Coptic priests, and
Latin priests; doctors of divinity and dervishes.[2]

[1] J. F. Garrison.
[2] N. Macleod, in *Good Words*, 1865, p. 37.

2. A Jew born in Alexandria at that time would find himself living in the midst of a community of his own countrymen in a separate quarter of the city, and yet subject to the manifold influences of Greek culture. If he belonged to the class that set a high value on that culture, he would learn grammar and rhetoric from Greek teachers; he would become acquainted with at least the terms and main ideas of the forms of Greek philo-. sophy then dominant, and would read at least selected portions of Greek dramatists and poets. Even as a Jew, his education and his worship would differ materially from that of his brethren in Jerusalem. Though still exulting in the old name of Hebrew, the speech of his fathers would be comparatively strange to him. A few etymologies of proper names, more or less accurate, often glaringly inaccurate, would be impressed upon him by his teachers, and, in proportion to his ignorance of the language as a whole, would be treasured up by him as precious. But when he read the Sacred Books of his fathers, it would be in what we have learnt to call the Version of the Seventy. His ignorance of the speech of Palestine would render him unable to correct its numerous errors. It would keep him also from studying the traditions of the elders, the casuistic disputes of Pharisees and Sadducees, of Hillel and of Shammai, in the schools of Jerusalem. The temple at Leontopolis would probably for him take the place of that at Jerusalem.

3. Pre-eminent among the influences at work on the mind of a young and thoughtful Alexandrian Jew at this period would be that of the teaching of Philo. We know but little of the personal history of that illustrious teacher, but it is clear that he must have been the leader of Jewish thought in that city, the founder of a new school of interpretation. He was, so far, the forerunner of the great masters of the Catechetical school for which the Church of Alexandria was afterwards famous. Clement and Origen would hardly have been what they were if Philo had not preceded them. While Paul was sitting at the feet of Gamaliel, growing into the strictest Pharisaism, we may think of Apollos as drinking in new knowledge and wider thoughts from the lips of Philo. Every page of the Sacred Records became full of new meanings. The arithmetic, geometry, astronomy of the

Greeks were brought to bear upon the history of the Creation in Gen. i., till it was made to read like a page from the *Timæus* of Plato. The literal meaning disappears, and an allegory is found at every step. Paradise is no garden upon earth, but the supreme element of the soul; the trees of which it was full were the ten thousand thoughts that fill the mind of man; the tree of life was godliness, that of the knowledge of good and evil was the "neutral understanding" which hovers on the border-land of vice and virtue. The serpent was but the symbol of pleasure, with its grovelling lusts, crawling on the ground and eating dirt. The four rivers were but the four great virtues of the Greek schools— Prudence, Temperance, Fortitude, Justice. With a winning eloquence, he leads his hearers on to these and a thousand like interpretations, as that which would complete their training and raise them out of the state of children, in which they had been governed by rule and precept taken in their literal meaning, to that of full-grown men, who were capable of a higher knowledge. It was obvious that this attempt to make the records of the remote past of the patriarchal age speak the thoughts of the schools of Greece involved the risk of the obliteration of what had been most characteristic in them. The Messianic hopes, which among the Jews of Palestine were growing into ever-clearer distinctness, were almost, if not altogether, absent from those of Alexandria.

Such mutual relations of Jews and Gentiles in this place were among the providential preparations for the spread of Christianity. In the midst of these influences Apollos was brought up; and the accomplishments thus acquired were of essential service to him in his future work. Even if we consider Alexandria only as a school of high education, a resort of learned men, and a place affording opportunities, if rightly used, for the training of the mind, it is instructive to observe how God made use of such opportunities in preparing His servant for his appointed task.

¶ It was to Emerson that Lowell's debt was particularly great. This he has himself acknowledged in his essay on "Emerson the Lecturer": "To be young is surely the best, if the most precarious, gift of life; yet there are some of us who would hardly consent to be young again, if it were at the cost of our recollection of Mr. Emerson's first lectures during the consulate of Van Buren. We used to walk in from the country to the Masonic Temple (I think it was), through the crisp winter night, and listen to that thrilling voice of his, so charged with subtle meaning and subtle music, as ship-wrecked men on a raft to the hail of a ship that came with unhoped-for food and rescue. Cynics might say what they liked. . . . At any rate, he brought us life, which, on the whole, is no bad thing. . . . The delight and the benefit were that he put us in communication with a larger style of thought, sharpened our wits with a more pungent phrase, gave us ravishing glimpses of an ideal under the dry husk of our New England; made us conscious of the supreme and everlasting originality of whatever bit of soul might be in any of us; freed us, in short, from the stocks of prose in which we had sat so long that we had grown well-nigh contented in our cramps. . . . To some of us that long-past experience remains the most marvellous and fruitful we have ever had. Emerson awakened us, saved us from the body of this death. It is the sound of the trumpet that the young soul longs for, careless what breath may fill it. Sidney heard it in the ballad of Chevy Chase, and we in Emerson. Nor did it blow retreat, but called to us with assurance of victory."[1]

II.

HIS PREACHING AT EPHESUS.

1. We first hear of Apollos at Ephesus. Ephesus, one of the most celebrated cities of Ionia in Asia Minor, was situated on the river Cayster, not far from the sea-coast, between Smyrna and Miletus. After falling into the hands of the Romans, it became the metropolis of pro-consular Asia; and was famous as a place of great commerce; still more so as the chief seat of the worship of the goddess Artemis, whose splendid temple stood not far from the harbour Panormus. Having been burnt by Herostratus on the night when Alexander the Great was born (B.C. 355), a new and more magnificent structure was reared, which was reckoned one of the seven wonders of the world. The Apostle Paul visited the place on his second missionary journey, as he returned from Corinth with Priscilla and Aquila. He did not, however, remain

[1] W. H. Hudson, *Lowell and his Poetry*, 30.

in it, but left Aquila and Priscilla. On his third journey, he revisited the city and abode there two years and three months, preaching first in the synagogue, and then in the school of Tyrannus.

It was in the interval between St. Paul's visits that Apollos came to Ephesus.

¶ Ephesus was the seat of that form of corrupted Christianity which we find so often alluded to in the Acts of the Apostles as "science falsely so called," "vain philosophy," etc. Here let us make a distinction; confuse not the philosophy of those days with that of the present day; they are alike in name alone. The science of these days is a reverent investigation of the laws of God, and it is marvellous how men can fail to gain from it something of the love of God; but the philosophy of those days was simply the craving of the intellect for amusement and enjoyment in the things of God. And let it be remembered that religion's self may become a mere matter intellectual, and men may examine the evidences respecting the being of a God, or the proofs of immortality, with the same apathy and coldness with which we consider the evidences of the existence of some volcanic crater or of some distant nebula.[1]

2. Now, what brought Apollos to Ephesus? The most obvious answer is, the claims of business. But if this is true, those claims had a very slight hold upon him, for as soon as occasion arose he was ready to pass on to Corinth for a definitely religious work. In the absence of any positive statement, the opinion may be advanced that he came to Ephesus with an equally religious purpose in view. Ephesus possessed attractions likely to appeal to this learned and zealous Jew, and with all the passion of a teacher and an apologist in his soul he made his way thither, intent upon proving to the Jews that in Jesus their own Messianic prophecies had received their fulfilment. It was a noble mission, and it had as its object the enthronement of that Lord he so imperfectly understood.

¶ His intention was beyond criticism, but his equipment was incomplete. How reminiscent of Wesley's comment on his missionary endeavours in Georgia, "I who went to America to convert others was never myself converted to God," especially in the light of the later note, "I am not sure of this!" Apollos

---

[1] F. W. Robertson, *The Human Race*, 179.

went to Ephesus to teach others, and he learned that he himself stood in need of a teacher.[1]

> Spirit of Light! do Thou impart
> Majestic truths, and teach my heart;
> Teach me to know how weak I am,
> How vain my powers, how poor my frame;
> Teach me celestial paths untrod,
> The ways of glory and of God.[2]

III.

His Qualification for the Work.

1. St. Luke suddenly introduces Apollos in Acts xviii. 24, where he describes him as "an eloquent man (or *a learned man*— R.V.) and mighty in the scriptures." Then in the next verse he says, "This man had been instructed in the way of the Lord; and being fervent in spirit, he spake and taught carefully the things concerning Jesus, knowing only the baptism of John." The precise character of his religious knowledge is not easily determined from these few words. It has been generally held that Apollos' instruction in "the way of the Lord" was such as any well-educated Jew might have gathered from teaching like that of the Baptist based on the Messianic prophecies.

Dean Farrar expresses the common view of this passage when he says that Apollos must have been very imperfectly acquainted with the doctrines of Christianity if he did not know any baptism but that of John. And when it is stated a few verses farther on that St. Paul found at Ephesus, after the departure of Apollos, twelve men who were baptized into John's baptism, it has been freely believed that they were converts whom Apollos had made, and that he had actually told them nothing of Jesus, but left them disciples of the Baptist. That belief, however, is contradicted by the narrative itself. For, as Dr. Blass points out, these men are called "disciples," an expression which, standing by itself, is never used except of Christians. They are also said to have "believed," another word which is appropriated to faith in Christ.

---

[1] H. S. Seekings, *The Men of the Pauline Circle*, 111.
[2] Crabbe.

And then, the way in which St. Luke speaks of Apollos himself, that "he taught carefully the things concerning Jesus," is unintelligible if Apollos did not know or did not teach anything beyond the preaching and the baptism of John.

Accordingly, Dr. Blass suggests that Apollos did know accurately the story of our Lord's life, and taught it; but that he was unacquainted with any other *baptism* than John's. Whereupon the interesting inquiry arises, How did Apollos acquire the knowledge which he possessed? Was it from a book, or from *viva voce* intercourse with Christians? Surely, if he had been converted by a Christian missionary, he would have been taught by him the necessity for Christian baptism. But if he learned from a written Gospel, it might have been one as full in its account of our Lord's words and deeds as Mark's or Luke's, and yet have said no more than these do about Christian baptism.

¶ If this suggestion could be accepted, it would certainly have an interesting bearing on the date of the publication of the Gospels. To know that a written Gospel had found its way to Alexandria at so early a date as the conversion of Apollos is with one stroke to settle some of the keenest controversies of our day.

But the word translated "instructed" ($\kappa\alpha\tau\eta\chi\epsilon\tilde{\iota}\sigma\theta\alpha\iota$) is that which is specially employed of oral instruction. Almost unknown outside the New Testament till the early Church seized it to signify that course of instruction which converts underwent before they were admitted to baptism—(the word "catechumen" is simply its present participle), it is used there for a report that is carried from mouth to mouth, or for teaching that is derived "from *viva voce* intercourse with Christians." And the Revised Version actually reminds us of this, by explaining in the margin that the Greek for "instructed" is "taught by word of mouth."

Dr. Wright's solution of the problem is as follows:—Apollos had been baptized by John. He had been taught to expect the Messiah at once. Possibly Jesus had been pointed out to him as such. He then, according to the Western text of Acts xviii. 25, returns to Alexandria, where rumours would reach him from time to time of what was happening in Palestine. He would hear of our Lord's ministry, of His mighty works, His rejection, crucifixion, and resurrection. For a long time report would give him only the broad outlines of the facts, but in the course of twelve or fifteen years one of those catechists whom the Church of Jerusalem sent out in large numbers visited the metropolis of Egypt. This itinerant was neither apostle, evangelist, nor preacher. He had learned by heart, and was anxious to teach others, "the facts concerning Jesus," and he formed a class for that purpose. Apollos became one of the pupils, and, like Theophilus, was "orally instructed" in the way of the Lord, until he became perfect and was able to teach others also. For when he came to Ephesus, "being fervent in spirit," he could not keep silence, but "repeated by rote, and taught accurately the facts concerning Jesus."[1]

2. Among his hearers were Priscilla and Aquila, who discovered that the preacher's knowledge of "the way" was imperfect. Accordingly, when Priscilla and Aquila had heard him in the synagogue, "they took him unto them and expounded unto him the way of God more carefully." These two Jewish Christians— as we learn from the early part of the chapter—were "tentmakers," with whom St. Paul had made acquaintance at Corinth, and whom he had left at Ephesus a short time previous to the arrival of Apollos. They became the religious instructors of this Alexandrian stranger, who in their hands was a most willing learner. Thus here we have an eloquent man, a learned man, a fervent man, not unwilling to be taught, and taught too by plain and homely people who were engaged in business. One of these teachers, moreover, was a woman. In making this observation we are certainly not justified in suggesting that Scripture throws any contempt on learning or scholarship. We have seen the very contrary in the case both of this Jew of Alexandria and of St. Paul himself. Still the fact is as stated here. The secular training of Apollos came from a very distinguished source, his high religious training from a very lowly one. How frequently has this been the case since! Those who have been eminent in University honours have often learnt their best lessons of religion even from the poor, and often from women, in the retired hours of domestic life. By such methods God's Providence brings all parts of a man's experience into harmony, and causes all to bear upon the one point of active service. Those men who produce great religious results on the minds of others have usually drawn their own teaching from very various sources. Many things are made tributary to that stream of wide influence, which in the end flows full and strong. There must, however, be a teachable spirit

[1] *The Expository Times*, vii. 243.

if the benefits are to be fully realized. We must become children, if we are to be high in the Kingdom of Heaven.

It would seem probable, though the fact is not stated, that Apollos received baptism at the hands of Priscilla and Aquila, as his followers in a like case did at the hands of St. Paul.

¶ You cannot, as the Sophist proposed to do (that was part of his foolishness), take and put truth into the soul. If you could, it might be established there, only as an " inward lie," as a mistake. " Must I take the argument and literally insert it into your mind ? " asks Thrasymachus. " Heaven forbid," answers Socrates.[1]

IV.

His Corinthian Ministry.

After some stay in Ephesus, Apollos determined to go to Corinth, an invitation to do so having come to him, according to the Western text, from certain Corinthians who were in Ephesus at the time. They gave him letters of commendation, and when he arrived in Corinth " He helped them much which had believed through grace : for he powerfully confuted the Jews and that publicly, shewing by the scriptures that Jesus was the Christ."

1. He could not have chosen a place more suitable for his work. St. Paul had established a branch of the Church in Corinth, but it was a city where gross idolatry and immorality were conspicuous. Further, it was a place where Apollos's talents would have a peculiar usefulness. It was a centre of commerce ; it was a town also of great intellectual activity. And in both these respects it resembled Alexandria, with whose inhabitants Apollos was so familiar. From his early experience he knew precisely what methods would avail best, both with the merchants and with the philosophers. Within a short time he gained a position of great influence.

¶ " The gods sell anything and to everybody at a fair price," says Emerson ; and he might have added that they give nothing away. Whatever a man secures in the way of power or fame he pays for in preliminary preparation ; nothing is given him except his native capacity ; everything else he must pay for.[2]

[1] Walter Pater.   [2] H. W. Mabie, *Essays on Work and Culture*, 102.

2. But the very success of his work had an unexpected and unfortunate result. Against his wish, he was made to figure as the rival of St. Paul. To many of the educated thinkers of Corinth the lofty eloquence of Apollos seemed greatly superior to St. Paul's simple and unpolished manner of speech. Thus there grew up an Apollos-party and a Paul-party in the Corinthian Church. We may be quite sure that the admirers of Apollos lost no occasion of telling him how much they preferred him to his predecessor, and nothing would have pleased them more than if he had proclaimed himself the head of this party, and St. Paul's avowed rival.

The First Epistle to the Corinthians was occasioned by internal conditions in the Church which arose shortly after St. Paul's departure from Corinth for Ephesus, and was written from the latter city, when he was contemplating a visit to them. He had received information as to the situation from various persons. Some dependents of " the house of Chloe" had told him of " contentions" (1 Cor. i. 11). Stephanas, Fortunatus, and Achaicus had visited him (1 Cor. xvi. 17), and Apollos had come, and was with him when the Epistle was written (1 Cor. xvi. 12).

¶ Unable to persuade himself that parties are even indifferent means to useful ends, Stanley felt that all, especially in religion, are combined of truth and falsehood, and that to join any is to accept the evil as well as the good. He believed that "the man who loves Christianity better than truth is on the highroad to love his own sect better than Christianity, if not to love himself better than either." He detested the principle of party, as the great rival in the minds of men to the love and pursuit of that truth which was " to be sought, above all things, for itself, and not for any ulterior object." [1]

3. The question at issue may have been only the relative importance of St. Paul and Apollos in the founding of the Corinthian Church ; but it seems likely that there was also a difference in the manner in which the gospel was presented by each ; and it may be (though for this there is no proof) that some doctrinal differences appeared after the lapse of years. The teaching of Apollos's followers may, *e.g.*, have degenerated into Antinomian Gnosticism. However that may be, the Corinthian

[1] R. E. Prothero, *The Life of Dean Stanley*, i. 376.

Church was agitated by bitterly opposed factions as late as the time of Clement of Rome. But it is unlikely that there was any personal disagreement between St. Paul and Apollos. It has indeed been suggested that in 1 Cor. ii. 1, St. Paul has the eloquent Apollos in his mind, and again in 2 Cor. iii. 1, where he declares that he at least needed no commendatory letters; and it is curious that Apollos is not mentioned at all as one of the founders of the Christian society at Corinth in 2 Cor. i. 19. But, however we explain these passages, they do not prove anything like serious estrangement.

¶ General Grant had been for several months in front of Petersburg, apparently accomplishing nothing, while General Sherman had captured Atlanta, and completed his grand " march to the sea." Then arose a strong cry to promote Sherman to Grant's position as lieutenant-general. Hearing of it, Sherman wrote to Grant, " I have written to John Sherman (his brother) to stop it. I would rather have you in command than any one else. I should emphatically decline any commission calculated to bring us into rivalry." Grant replied, " No one would be more pleased with your advancement than I; and if you should be placed in my position, and I put subordinate, it would not change our relations in the least. I would make the same exertion to support you that you have done to support me, and I would do all in my power to make your cause win." [1]

4. Now the question arises—and in estimating his character it is quite essential to answer the question—whether this party-spirit which was developed at Corinth was in any way the fault of Apollos, and whether, when it was developed, he encouraged it at all. Here another passage from the latter part of the same Epistle presents itself to our attention, and supplies the answer. The Apostle writes: " As touching our brother Apollos, I greatly desired him to come unto you with the brethren; but his will was not at all to come at this time; but he will come when he shall have convenient time."

It is not hard to see the reason of Apollos's refusal, which was simply his fine sense of loyalty to St. Paul. He knew only too well the present temper of the Corinthian Church, and he was sure that his presence in Corinth at this juncture would

---

[1] O. S. Marden, *Architects of Fate*, 448.

do more harm than good. His arrival would cause the party feeling to break out again with fresh vigour, and St. Paul's detractors would once more become active. With equal unselfishness, St. Paul bade him disregard any such fears and go, but Apollos was firm in his refusal. To preach in Corinth might be to make some converts, and certainly it would add to his reputation; but it would tend also to lessen the authority of St. Paul. Therefore he would not return until length of time had allowed this spirit of faction to die down. Then, according to the tradition preserved by St. Jerome, he did revisit Corinth, becoming bishop of that city.

> Weary of all this wordy strife,
>   These notions, forms, and modes, and names,
> To Thee, the Way, the Truth, the Life,
>   Whose love my simple heart inflames,
> Divinely taught, at last I fly,
> With Thee and Thine to live and die.
>
> Forth from the midst of Babel brought,
>   Parties and sects I cast behind;
> Enlarged my heart, and freed my thought,
>   Where'er the latent truth I find,
> The latent truth with joy to own,
> And bow to Jesu's name alone.[1]

V.

HIS LATER LIFE.

In the year 67, when St. Paul wrote his letter to Titus, Apollos was expected in Crete during the course of a missionary journey. This is the last mention of him in the New Testament.

While no writings have come down to us under the name of Apollos, there is a widely accepted opinion, first suggested by Luther, that he may have been the author of the Epistle to the Hebrews. There is no external evidence or authority for this view. It rests entirely upon the internal characteristics of the book.

[1] Charles Wesley.

The principal consideration in favour of the authorship of Apollos is that he is described in the Acts as a cultured and rhetorical Alexandrian, who was well versed in the Greek Old Testament. This fact might account for the elaborate style, the Alexandrian cast, the kinship with Philo and the Book of Wisdom, and the copious use of the Septuagint in the Epistle, while the fact that Apollos had come under the influence of St. Paul might be regarded as explaining its kinship to St. Paul's thought. On the other hand, Apollos was not a disciple of the primitive Apostles, as the author of Hebrews seems to have been (ii. 3). The argument carries us only thus far: The author, if not Apollos, was some such man as Apollos was — a literary Hellenist, familiar with the philosophical ideas which were current at Alexandria and practised in the argumentative use of the Septuagint.

The apocryphal book called the Wisdom of Solomon has also been attributed to Apollos.

VI.

HIS CHARACTER.

1. All that we know of the history of Apollos may be summed up in a few verses, but the lessons of his life endure. Gifted with great natural ability, he enhanced it by years of patient toil. Above all other literature he prized the Word of God—whereas in our own day the number of educated people who could be termed "mighty in the Scriptures" is lamentably small. Wholly free from the pride of intellect, he was alert to welcome fresh truth, however unexpected its form and source. He applied himself to his ministry with fervour, courage, and success. Yet success had no evil effect upon his character. To the end he cared much for the welfare of the Church, much for the honour due to his fellow-labourer, and nothing at all for his personal fame. A strenuous toiler, a profound scholar, a loyal companion —such was Apollos; such is a type of man needed by the Church in every age.

¶ Men of achievement crown loyalty as one of the first of the virtues. Charity must be a divine gift indeed if it is greater than

faithfulness. The soldier's worth is in his adherence to duty.
The test of the jurist is loyalty to the client. The test of the
pupil is loyalty to his master. The two great books in ancient
literature are the *Iliad* and the *Odyssey*. The *Iliad* exposes the
fickleness and disloyalty of beautiful Helen, whose infidelity
turned a city into a heap. The *Odyssey* celebrates the loyalty of
Penelope, who kept her palace and her heart. Young man, scorn
the very thought of disloyalty to your employer. If you can't
work with him, resign. But flee the very thought of disloyalty
as you would flee from the edge of the precipice. Disloyalty
belongs to the serpent that bites, the wolf that rends, and the lion
that slays. To be disloyal is to join hands with the devil himself.
Pride yourself on your loyalty. Learn to follow, that you may be
worthy to lead. Life may bring you gold, office, and honour, but
it will bring you nothing comparable to the happiness that comes
from the consciousness of having been loyal to your ideals. And
when it is all over, let this be men's judgment upon you: "He
was faithful unto death."[1]

2. Probably Apollos is not much more than a name to the
average reader of the New Testament, yet his character is one
which well deserves our admiring study. That it is possible to
include him among the friends of St. Paul is a tribute alike to his
greatness and to the power of Christian love. It would not have
been surprising had he proved, at one stage of his life, St. Paul's
most dangerous opponent, and at another his avowed rival. In
the first instance, he was saved by the inherent nobility of his
character. From the second risk he escaped through the thorough-
ness with which he accepted the fulness of the new teaching,
bringing its doctrines of love and fellowship to bear upon the
practice of his life. And so Apollos has a double claim upon our
regard: both intellectually and morally he was a great man.
Remarkable as were St. Paul's mental attainments, and profound
as was his acquaintance with the literature of the Old Testament,
it is doubtful whether in these respects he was the superior of
Apollos. In eloquence and the power of impressing the educated
men of Corinth, Apollos was unmistakably the more gifted. But,
had it not been united to moral greatness, his intellectual greatness would have thwarted in place of furthering the growth of
the Christian faith. Exceptional gifts seem always to carry with

[1] N. D. Hillis, *The Contagion of Character*, 202.

them the penalty of exceptional temptations, and the very fact that his intellectual powers were so remarkable might easily have made Apollos either impatient of instruction or intolerant of a subordinate position in the Church. We may feel quite certain that those temptations presented themselves to him in full force. But he overcame them, and remained to the end St. Paul's loyal comrade and fellow-worker.

¶ Cowden Clarke has left us a very pleasant record of one curious feature in the intercourse between the two friends [Leigh Hunt and John Keats]. From time to time they would challenge one another to poetic effort in the composition of verses written in amicable rivalry on some given theme. On one occasion, when the talk had run "on the character, habits, and pleasant associations with that reverent denizen of the hearth, the cheerful little grasshopper of the fireside," Hunt proposed to Keats that they should compose, "then and there and to time," a sonnet each on the grasshopper and the cricket. "No one but myself was present," says Clarke, "and they accordingly set to," Keats being the first to complete his task. Then came "the after-scrutiny," which, says Clarke, "was one of many such occurrences which have riveted the memory of Leigh Hunt in my affectionate regard and admiration for unaffected generosity and perfectly unpretentious encouragement." And he goes on to speak of Hunt's "sincere look of pleasure" on reading out the first line of Keats's poem: "The poetry of earth is never dead." "Such a prosperous opening," he exclaimed. And when he came to the tenth and eleventh lines—

> On a lone winter evening, when the frost
> Has wrought a silence . . .

"Ah, that's perfect! Bravo, Keats!"[1]

> If the wide world stood row on row,
> And stones at you began to throw,
> I'd boldly out with them to fight,
> Saying they were wrong and you were right.

> If every bird on every tree,
> With note as loud as loud could be,
> Sang endlessly in your dispraise,
> One graceless thought it would not raise.

[1] W. H. Hudson, *Keats and his Poetry*, 25.

If all the great, and wise and good,
Upon your sins in judgment stood—
They'd simply waste their valued breath,
For I'm your friend through Life and Death.

If I were wrong, and they were right,
I'd not believe (for all their might),
Not even if all they said were true,
For you love me and I love you.[1]

¶ Dean Stanley writes: To make sure of "Apollos's name being enrolled in no calendar, however apocryphal," I wrote to Ward from Norwich to ask, but got no answer till this morning, forwarded from Norwich. Fortunately, it coincided with what I had said; he had put the question to the Roman Catholic divines at Ware, and they had said that it had never struck them before, but that certainly it was a remarkable fact that Apollos was nowhere called Saint or Doctor.[2]

[1] D. Mountjoy, *The Hills of Hell*, 26.
[2] R. E. Prothero, *The Life of Dean Stanley*, 368.

GALLIO.

LITERATURE.

Ainger, A., *The Gospel and Human Life* (1904), 241.

Banks, L. A., *Paul and his Friends* (1898), 97.

Burrell, D. J., *God and the People* (1899), 330.

Buss, S., *Roman Law and History in the New Testament* (1901), 285.

Farrar, F. W., *Seekers after God* (1891), 16.

Maclaren, A., *Expositions* : The Acts of the Apostles xiii.–end (1907), 165.

Norton, J. N., *Old Paths* (1880), 418.

Potter, H. C., *Sermons of the City* (1880), 66.

Ramsay, W. M., *St. Paul the Traveller* (1895), 257.

Seekings, H. S., *The Men of the Pauline Circle* (1914), 211.

Smellie, A., *In the Hour of Silence* (1899), 61.

Stokes, G. T., *The Acts of the Apostles* (Expositor's Bible), ii. (1892) 325.

Vaughan, C. J., *Sundays in the Temple* (1871), 20.

Christian World Pulpit, xlix. (1896) 52 (F. C. Spurr).

Dictionary of the Apostolic Church, i. (1915) 439 (J. E. Roberts).

Dictionary of the Bible, ii. (1899) 105 (H. Cowan).

GALLIO.

And Gallio cared for none of these things.—Acts xviii. 17.

GALLIO, the proconsul of the Roman province of Achaia, has been subjected, like many other characters of history, to certain marked changes in public estimation. He has been over-abused and over-praised, over-attacked and over-defended. It has been, perhaps, to the accident of the use of a particular word in the English translation that his ordinary reputation has been due. "He cared for none of these things" is an ambiguous phrase, including, no doubt, the indifference of a sceptic as well as the impatience of a judge towards matters over which he has no jurisdiction. There is nothing in the Greek words to exclude either interpretation. But then there is nothing to decide for one rather than for the other; and it is hard upon the Roman judge that the epithet "careless," so easily formed out of the phrase "cared nothing," should have become so associated with his name that he has become almost a byword for the most unfavourable view that can be taken of his character.

It is only too easy to jump to a popular conclusion without investigating the case in question, but in doing so may we not be guilty of that very carelessness with which we charge Gallio— a carelessness of justice and of truth? Let us see if we can form a just estimate of this man from what we know of him in contemporary history and literature, and from St. Luke's narrative in the Acts.

I.

GALLIO IN CONTEMPORARY HISTORY.

1. Gallio was born at Cordova in Spain. His father was a Roman knight; his mother was a Spanish lady remarkable for

her fine intellect and for the nobility and sweetness of her mind. As a young child Gallio left Spain and came with his father to Rome.

His true name was Marcus Annæus Novatus: but when he was adopted into the family of Lucius Junius Gallio, he assumed the name of Junius Annæus Gallio. He was the brother of Seneca, the Stoic philosopher. Lucan, the poet, was his nephew, being the son of his brother Mela. Another poet, Statius, was his friend.

Under Claudius, Gallio became proconsul of Achaia, probably through the influence of Seneca, who was Nero's tutor, and also perhaps, as Renan suggests, on account of his "haute culture hellénique." He entered on office at Corinth during St. Paul's first visit to the city, c. A.D. 52–53. An attack of fever, which he attributed to the climate, led to his departure, and to a sea-voyage for his health (Sen. *Ep.* 104); eventually he returned to Rome.

In his later years he was involved in political complications. His brother Seneca had been in exile in Corsica for eight years, and on his recall in A.D. 49 was appointed prætor. Gallio himself, probably after he left Achaia, had risen to be consul. His life was in danger in A.D. 65, when Seneca was sentenced by Nero to put himself to death. He begged for his own life, which was spared by Nero for the time; but soon afterwards he and his brother Mela, the father of Lucan, were sentenced to death.

2. Gallio seems to have acquired both among his friends and among strangers the epithet of "dulcis," "the charming or fascinating Gallio": "This is more," says the poet Statius, "than to have given Seneca to the world, and to have begotten the sweet Gallio." "No mortal man is so sweet to any man as he is to all mankind," his brother Seneca writes of him. And again, "Even those who love my brother Gallio to the very utmost of their power yet do not love him enough."

> All, that he came to give,
> He gave, and went again:
> I have seen one man live,
> I have seen one man reign,
> With all the graces in his train.

As one of us, he wrought
Things of the common hour:
Whence was the charmed soul brought,
That gave each act such power;
The natural beauty of a flower?

Magnificence and grace,
Excellent courtesy:
A brightness on the face,
Airs of high memory:
Whence came all these, to such as he?

Like young Shakespearian kings,
He won the adoring throng:
And, as Apollo sings,
He triumphed with a song:
Triumphed, and sang, and passed along.

With a light word, he took
The hearts of men in thrall;
And, with a golden look,
Welcomed them, at his call
Giving their love, their strength, their all.

No man less proud than he,
Nor cared for homage less:
Only, he could not be
Far off from happiness:
Nature was bound to his success.

Weary, the cares, the jars,
The lets, of every day,
But the heavens filled with stars,
Chanced he upon the way:
And where he stayed, all joy would stay.[1]

¶ If one looks closely at life, one sees the same quality (charm) in humanity, in men and women, in books and pictures, and yet one cannot tell what goes to the making of it. It seems to be a thing which no energy or design can capture, but which alights here and there, blowing like the wind at will. It is not force or originality or inventiveness; very often it is strangely lacking in any masterful quality at all; but it has always just the same wistful appeal, which makes one desire to understand it, to take

[1] Lionel Johnson.

possession of it, to serve it, to win its favour. It is as when the child in Francis Thompson's poem seems to say, "I hire you for nothing." That is exactly it: there is nothing offered or bestowed, but one is at once magically bound to serve it for love and delight. There is nothing that one can expect to get from it, and yet it goes very far down into the soul; it is behind the maddening desire which certain facts, hands, voices, smiles excite—the desire to possess, to claim, to know even that no one else can possess or claim them, which lies at the root of half the jealous tragedies of life.

Some personalities have charm in a marvellous degree, and if, as one looks into the old records of life, one discovers figures that seem to have laid an inexplicable hold on their circles, and to have passed through life in a tempest of applause and admiration, one may be sure that charm has been the secret.[1]

II.

GALLIO IN ST. LUKE'S NARRATIVE.

1. St. Paul was at Corinth, the capital of the province of Achaia. He had been in Corinth at least eighteen months, working at his own trade, and preaching every Sabbath day in the synagogue, making many converts. His success made the Jews who remained unconverted furious—so much so that when Crispus, the ruler of the synagogue, became a convert to the Faith, they endeavoured to find some way of retaliation. And so it happened that when Gallio came fresh into the proconsulship they, hoping to take advantage of his inexperience, and assuming his willingness to gain their favour at the price of unfairness to a defenceless man, drew up a cleverly disguised charge against Paul, and forcibly brought him forward for judgment.

The charge against St. Paul was that he was "teaching men to worship God contrary to the law." Now, as Judaism was a *religio licita*, this accusation might be regarded as serious. It was a charge similar to that brought against Christ before Pilate's tribunal. The two judges were very different in character. Pilate was apt to be severe: at times he was ruthless, and prone

---

[1] A. C. Benson, *Escape*, 89.

to shed blood. Yet the Jewish priests had their way with him.
After alternate bluster and conciliation, he gave way. A much
more easy victory might be expected before the mild Gallio.

But they had miscalculated. Gallio could be firm when
occasion required.

We infer, from his reply to the plaintiffs, that he made a
preliminary examination; and finding that no crime or civil
wrong (ἀδίκημα), nor even a misdemeanour or reckless act of
levity (ῥᾳδιούργημα πονηρὸν), had been committed by the defendant,
he came without hesitation to the conclusion that it was a comparatively trifling question of their own law, relating to words
and names, and interpretation of the utterances of the Jewish
prophets. It was a matter with which the Roman law had
nothing to do. Paul may have given enough offence to the Jews,
but he had kept within the law of the Empire; no breach of
Roman law could be brought against him. It was purely a
Jewish question, and Gallio peremptorily refused to deal with it.
He would not even listen to the defence. None was needed.
And when the accused was about to open his mouth, he bade
him be silent. He would not be a judge in such matters. The
Jews must look to it themselves. His decision, in fact, is precisely the same as that at which Pilate first arrived, when he
said, "Take ye him, and judge him according to your law."
Pilate was overborne by the clamours of the priests; but Gallio
refused to alter his decision, and drove the accusers from his
judgment-seat.

¶ We see Cicero resigning his high station to Cato, who, with
half his abilities, little foresight, and no address, possessed that
first requisite for a statesman—firmness.[1]

¶ "The most valuable thing I learnt at Rossall," said Edmund
Garrett, "was sticking to my guns."[2]

¶ You may love warmly, but what is your love worth if you
presently forget all about it, and do the very thing which will
wound the one whom you profess to love? What is your love
worth, if when you are away you are at the mercy of every sharp
temptation that assails you? What is your love worth in best, if
it cannot be trusted as soon as you have been out of sight for a
little while? You may repent with much sorrow; but what is

---

[1] A. Whyte, *Newman: An Appreciation*, 228.

[2] E. T. Cook, *Edmund Garrett*, 10.

your sorrow or your repentance worth if the fault is presently to be repeated? You may resolve nobly and enthusiastically; but what is your enthusiasm and your resolution worth, if it cannot uphold you when you come to action? The one thing which all men will ask of you before they can have much to do with you will be, where and how far you may be trusted. Till they know that, they cannot admit you to any confidence at all. As far as they know that, they can be on friendly terms, perhaps more, on terms of friendship. If you cannot be trusted at all, you are worse to your fellow-creatures than a wild beast. So, too, is it in our relations with God. If you are to be His in any sense, you must learn to be trustworthy. You must learn to obey the bidding of duty even when you are left entirely to yourself. You must learn to care for His will even when you are strongly tempted to disregard it, and when no punishment seems likely to follow your disregard. You must learn to think about His will even when it seems quite impossible that disobedience should be detected. You must learn to obey in little trifles which no one will notice, and all the more because no one will notice them.[1]

2. But this was not the end. The Greeks had sympathized with Paul. Whether they accepted his teachings or not, they seem on this occasion to have believed in the right of free speech, and, like a great many other champions of free speech, they proceeded to proclaim their sympathies by an act of personal violence. "And they all laid hold on Sosthenes, the ruler of the synagogue, and beat him before the judgement-seat." Sosthenes was presumably the leading man among Paul's opponents, and the Corinthian idlers present were so delighted to see him baffled that they could not refrain from mobbing him, with kicks and cuffs, in the very presence of the judge. And it is at this point in his narrative that St. Luke chooses to insert the memorable remark, "And Gallio cared for none of these things."

III.

GALLIO'S CHARACTER.

Gallio has been blamed for two kinds of indifference—indifference to religion, and indifference to the concerns of others.

[1] Archbishop Temple.

The first indictment has been based chiefly upon the fact that "when Paul was about to open his mouth" the proconsul refused to hear his defence, and upon the summary manner in which he dismissed the case. The second has been founded upon Gallio's not interfering to stop the attack upon Sosthenes, and upon the words with which St. Luke concludes his narrative—"And Gallio cared for none of these things."

1. With regard to the first charge we must remember that Gallio was present in that court merely as a judge, and that as a judge he is to be commended for his alertness of mind and loftiness of principle. Gallio as an example of unstained honour in the discharge of public duty is not unworthy of a place in the pages of the New Testament. He would not pander to prejudice, neither would he stoop to meanness nor swerve from right. And when expediency clashed with principle, and when to be unjust was all too easy, he would not willingly commit a wrong.

¶ The virtue of impartiality is not immediately or easily acquired. To do justly between man and man can appear a simple matter only to an unsophisticated intelligence. Once perceive the intricacy of social connexions, and the difficulty of the task becomes obvious. Solomon's drastic solution of a complicated situation may commend itself to those who prefer the method of the bludgeon when confronted with rival claimants to a disputed property, but can hardly be recommended for general observance. Nor may we take refuge in the decision of the worthy magistrate who declared that he would be guilty neither of partiality nor impartiality in the conduct of his office.[1]

2. And yet we often err in our judgments of character by supposing that only one class of motives is at work in certain circumstances. It may be the case with Gallio that he honestly fulfilled his judicial duty in these circumstances, and that at the same time he did not pretend to conceal his contempt for the whole class of questions brought under his notice. He may have been an upright judge as to the merits of the case before him, and yet have been a notable instance of sceptical indifferentism. Perhaps he was both, and St. Luke may have wished to accentuate both.

[1] A. C. Hill, *The Sword of the Lord*, 110.

We cannot help feeling it is a thousand pities that, as a man, Gallio did not allow St. Paul to speak. As a man of affairs, familiar with the religious controversies of his time, he must have known about the disputed claims of Jesus. It was twenty-two years since the crucifixion, yet the dispute concerning the Man of Nazareth had gone on continuously ever since. Would His spectre never be laid? Never! This question must be confronted and settled by every man.

The blame of Gallio in refusing to consider the claims of Jesus as the Christ must be measured by circumstances. He probably regarded this as a matter of mere provincial importance, not knowing that his own salvation was in the balance. He had doubtless discussed many questions in the forum and in philosophic halls, but never one so intensely personal as this: "Is Jesus the Christ?" To him St. Paul's preaching and the Jews' passionate denials of it seemed only a squabble about "words and names." How little Gallio knew of what a possibility was opened out before him! Angels were hovering unseen, and he was unaware of their presence. He was a man who lost his opportunity.

If thou hadst known in those far-distant days,
Which now lie buried with the long-dead past;
If thou hadst known how wistful was the gaze
Love turn'd on thee, oh! wouldst thou then have cast
One swift responsive glance, and thus have seen
Life's possibility?—It might have been!

If thou hadst known how, through the long, long years,
One aching heart would yearn for thee in vain,
Wouldst thou in that far time have dried the tears
With tender answering touch, had all been plain?
Ah, who can tell! Thy lonely grave is green;
Thy memory still lives on. It might have been!

It might have been! and yet, perchance, may be,
In some glad day, when nought shall be concealed;
The cramp'd and longing spirit will be free,
And all its hidden beauty be revealed;
Then drawn aside, the once-dividing screen—
No more life's dreary moan—It might have been![1]

[1] Una, *In Life's Garden*, 68.

3. There seems to be some foundation for the other charge, that Gallio was indifferent to the concerns of others. He was a Stoic and had no doubt the Stoic's philosophic contempt for the outside world and its business, the sayings and doings, the joys and the sorrows of the puny mortals who fume and strut and fret their lives away upon this earthly stage. Moreover, the position of St. Luke's words, even more than the words themselves, does seem to give colour to the popular view of Gallio. In the first place, it seems to follow the mention of the violence of the Gentile crowd, as if some explanation would be expected as to why Gallio did not interfere to protect the Jewish prosecutor. It seems as much as to say, "The mob used Sosthenes very roughly, but the proconsul took no notice." And perhaps this was the case.

And why did Gallio not interfere? Many people are of the opinion that as the representative of law and order he ought to have intervened. There are two possible reasons for his line of conduct.

(1) He was probably not altogether displeased that the Jews, fanatical and troublesome here as in other places, should be taught a rough and ready lesson by the operation of a kind of lynch law.

(2) He was a man of amiable character and he probably disliked fuss. It was no concern of his. Let them fight it out among themselves. May it not have been his contempt for petty squabbles that influenced him here as well as at the judgment-seat? He would take no part in the machinations of the Jews, neither would he mix himself up with the brawlings of a mob.

Gallio may have been indifferent; he may even, in this case, have been culpably indifferent; but his indifference was rather the noble indifference of the man who has schooled himself to rise superior to the little frets and quarrels of daily life than the selfish apathy of one who heartlessly ignores the troubles of his fellows because he is too much bound up in his own concerns to care about them.

¶ We cannot indeed overcome our affections, nor ought we if we could, but we may repress them within due bounds, and avoid coaxing them to make fools of those who should be their masters.[1]

---

[1] *Sir Walter Scott's Journal*, 34.

I touch my strings
　　To melodies rare;
Whether God looks after things
　　I know not, neither care;
I never think of the black pit,
Or if I do, I laugh at it.

My notes are borne
　　Through infinite space,—
Are your limbs all bruised and torn?
　　And in a losing race?
I take no heed of all your pain—
My fingers of the harp are fain.

Though all men be
　　Full stricken in grief,
What are little men to me?—
　　Their days and woes are brief;—
But I for ever touch my strings,
Remote from perishable things.[1]

4. It is interesting to note that Gallio's decision seems to have greatly influenced St. Paul's future line of conduct.

Gallio being governor of Achaia, his judgment would become a precedent and would have far-reaching influence. It gave St. Paul a new idea of the protection he could gain from the Roman law. Although Judaism was a *religio licita*, evidently the Imperial Government did not consider Christian preaching illegal. This amounted to a declaration of freedom in religion of immense value to Christians. From this point of view, Gallio's treatment of the Jewish complaint was a landmark in St. Paul's missionary labour, and did a great deal to confirm his confidence in Roman protection for his preaching.

¶ My conviction is, that this great subject of religious freedom is not to be dealt with as one of the ordinary matters in which you may, with safety or with honour, do to-day and undo to-morrow. This great people, whom we have the honour to represent, moves slowly in politics and legislation; but, although it moves slowly, it moves steadily. The principle of religious freedom, its adaptation to our modern state, and its compatibility with ancient institutions, was a principle which you did not adopt

---

[1] J. Drinkwater, *Poems of Men and Hours*, 3.

in haste. It was a principle well tried in struggle and conflict. It was a principle which gained the assent of one public man after another. It was a principle which ultimately triumphed, after you had spent upon it half a century of agonising struggle. . . . Show, I beseech you—have the courage to show that England too, as well as Rome, has her *semper eadem*; and that when she has once adopted some great principle of legislation, which is destined to influence the national character, to draw the dividing lines of her policy for ages to come, and to affect the whole nature of her influence and her standing among the nations of the world—show that when she has done this slowly, and done it deliberately, she has done it once for all; and that she will then no more retrace her steps than the river that bathes this giant city can flow back upon its source.[1]

[1] Speech against the "Ecclesiastical Titles Bill," in Morley's *Life of Gladstone*, i. 412.

FELIX.

LITERATURE.

Burrell, D. J., *God and the People* (1899), 62.

    „   „   *A Quiver of Arrows* (1904), 172.

Buss, S., *Roman Law and History in the New Testament* (1901), **373**.

Chapman, J. W., *Bells of Gold*, 42.

Church, R. W., *Village Sermons*, i. (1892) 231.

Fraser, J., *University Sermons* (1887), 118.

Gibbon, J. M., *The Vision and the Call* (1894), **33**.

Goodwin, H., *Parish Sermons*, ii. (1861) 179.

Hiley, R. W., *A Year's Sermons*, iii. (1897) 105.

Hobhouse, W., *The Spiritual Standard* (1896), 130.

Howson, J. S., *The Companions of St. Paul* (1874), 145.

Little, W. J. K., *The Journey of Life* (1893), 65.

McFadyen, J. E., *The City with Foundations* (1909), 221.

M'Garvey, J. W., *Sermons* (1894), 172.

Maclaren, A., *The Acts of the Apostles* (Bible Class Expositions) (1894), 262.

    „   „ *Expositions* : The Acts of the Apostles xiii.-end (1907), 281.

Mills, B. R. V., *The Marks of the Church* (1901), 198.

Morrison, G. H., *The Footsteps of the Flock* (1904), 362.

Pierson, A. T., *Dr. Pierson and his Message* (ed. J. K. Maclean), 206.

Price, A. C., *Fifty Sermons*, iv. (1886) 17.

Seekings, H. S., *The Men of the Pauline Circle* (1914), 227.

Smellie, A., *In the Hour of Silence* (1899), **393**.

Smith, Gipsy, *As Jesus Passed by* (1905), 139.

Trench, R. C., *Westminster and Other Sermons* (1888), **32**.

Vaughan, J., in *Anglican Pulpit Library*, ix. 97.

Whyte, A., *Bible Characters* : Stephen to Timothy (1901), 48.

Church of England Pulpit, xlii. (1896) 139 (T. B. Naylor).

Dictionary of the Apostolic Church, i. (1915) 405 (G. P. Gould).

Dictionary of the Bible, ii. (1899) 1 (A. Robertson).

Literary Churchman, xxxi. (1885) 471 (J. H. Buchanan).

Twentieth Century Pastor, xxxii. (1913) 181 (N. D. Hillis).

FELIX.

And as he reasoned of righteousness, and temperance, and the judgement to come, Felix was terrified, and answered, Go thy way for this time; and when I have a convenient season, I will call thee unto me.—Acts xxiv. 25.

THE career of Felix corresponded in one sense with his name. He *ought* to have been a happy man, for he was eminently a successful one.

Felix and his brother Pallas were originally slaves, and then freedmen, in the house of a noble Roman lady, Antonia, mother of the Emperor Claudius. Pallas became the favourite, and subsequently minister, of the emperor. He procured for his brother Felix the important post of procurator of Judæa about A.D. 52. The historian Tacitus writes of Felix as one who, trusting to his brother's powerful influence at court, knew he could commit any wrong with impunity. He was notoriously avaricious, cruel, and licentious, but withal a man of great energy and talent, wielding, however, as Tacitus tells us, "the power of a tyrant with the temper of a slave." According to Josephus, he was one of the most corrupt and oppressive governors ever despatched from Rome to rule over Judæa.

He married three wives, each one of royal birth. The name of one of his wives is unrecorded: the other two were both named Drusilla. There was the Drusilla of Acts xxiv. 24, who was the daughter, the sister, and the wife of a king; the daughter of Agrippa I., the sister of Agrippa II., and the wife of Azizus, king of Emesa. It is almost past belief that a princess so connected could have condescended to a union with an enfranchised slave. The other Drusilla was a daughter of Juba, king of Mauritania, and a granddaughter of Antony and Cleopatra.

As procurator of Judæa Felix ruled with vigour and ability, upon which he was complimented by Tertullus; but his servile origin was perceptible in all his deeds. During the whole of his term of office, the province was in a disturbed condition, torn to pieces by false prophets, robbers, sicarii, and other disorderly characters. In the suppression of these disorders he did good service, justifying to some extent the complimentary address of Tertullus, "by thee we enjoy much peace, and by thy providence evils are corrected for this nation." St. Paul more wisely contented himself by saying, "I know that thou hast been of many years a judge unto this nation"; for, in fact, his ruthless massacres of Galilæans, Samaritans, and Jews had altogether failed to bring peace to the distracted land.

> But vain the sword and vain the bow,—
> They never can work war's overthrow;
> The hermit's prayer and the widow's tear
> Alone can free the world from fear.[1]

I.

THE ROMAN OFFICIAL.

1. Claudius Lysias, finding nothing worthy of death or of bonds in St. Paul's case, sent him on to Felix with a courteously worded letter, after reading which the governor said, "I will hear thee when thine accusers are also come."

After being five days at Cæsarea, St. Paul was brought before Felix.

Now we must remember that the attitude of the Roman law towards the infant Church was by no means hostile. Persecutions sprang up at an early date, and before the close of the first century the Empire and the Church were at deadly war. But the first generation of Christians were more often protected than oppressed by the State. It was much more for protection than for punishment that St. Paul was sent by Lysias to Cæsarea. It is quite a mistake to suppose that magistrates like Pilate and Felix were types of Roman officials. On the contrary, they were strongly condemned by the authorities as soon as their misdeeds came to light, and it is satisfactory to know that both these official miscreants met with the disgrace they deserved. Felix was the

---

[1] W. Blake, "The Grey Monk."

more inexcusable, as he seems to have known about the Christian religion, and to have been quite aware that this was a matter altogether beyond his jurisdiction. His obvious duty was to release St. Paul at once.

> It isn't the thing you do, dear,
>   It's the thing you leave undone,
> Which gives you a bit of a heart-ache
>   At the setting of the sun.
> The tender word forgotten,
>   The letter you did not write,
> The flower you might have sent, dear,
>   Are your haunting ghosts to-night.[1]

2. The case against St. Paul was conducted by Tertullus, who was as unscrupulous as he was eloquent.

It was after the Apostle had answered the charges which Tertullus had preferred against him, by denying the accusations of sedition, and desecration, and by confessing devotion to the cause of Christ, that Felix really failed in the discharge of his duty. St. Paul had made it clear that he was no heretic, by showing that the religious movement to which his life was committed—the faith which was finding its way everywhere, and was stirring the hearts of men with a new life and inspiring them with a new ideal—was the spiritual fulfilling of that Messianic hope which every normal Jew claimed to hold. Unless his judgment was altogether warped, Felix could scarcely avoid seeing that the whole matter on the part of St. Paul's accusers was personal and malicious, and that the proper course for him was that which Gallio had previously adopted, the more so as he had what Gallio did not possess, " a more exact knowledge concerning the way."

¶ Better a just unbeliever than a believing tyrant.[2]

3. But the legal side of Felix's association with the Apostle is of so little real importance that, were it not for one arresting phrase, it might be passed over without comment. That phrase reflects the very soul of Felix, and it is therefore significant. It

---

[1] Margaret Elizabeth Sangster.
[2] Jami. in *A Little Book of Eastern Wisdom*, 44.

reveals the mind which lies behind the act and gives it being. It is the soul emerging to the surface; it is the defining mark of individuality. The act hinted at by the simple clause which terminates the trial scene helps us to understand Felix. It prepares the way for the more famous saying which is ever associated with his name. "Felix deferred them," is of the same nature, though not of the same far-reaching importance, as "Felix answered, Go thy way for this time; and when I have a convenient season, I will call thee unto me."

His plea for delay was conveniently indefinite. When was Lysias coming? His letter said nothing about such an intention, and took for granted that all the materials for a decision would be before Felix. Lysias could tell no more. The excuse was transparent, but it served to stave off a decision, and to-morrow would bring some other excuse. Prompt carrying out of all plain duty is the only safety. The indulgence given to St. Paul, in his light confinement, only showed how clearly Felix knew himself to be doing wrong; but small alleviations do not patch up a great injustice.

¶ "'But how do you know that there is any Christ? You never saw Him?' said poor Augustine St. Clare, the slave-owner, to Uncle Tom, the slave.

'I feel it in my soul, mas'r—feel Him now! Oh, mas'r, the blessed Lord Jesus loves you!'

'But how do you know that, Tom?' said St. Clare.

'I feels it in my soul, mas'r; oh, mas'r, the love of Christ that passeth knowledge.'

'But, Tom, you know that I have a great deal more knowledge than you; what if I should tell you that I don't believe your Bible? Wouldn't that shake your faith some, Tom?'

'Not a grain, mas'r!' And St. Clare felt himself borne, on the tide of Tom's faith and feeling, almost to the gate of heaven.

'I like to hear you, Tom; and some time I'll talk more.'" [1]

¶ It is hard to admit that we are wrong. How easy to say, "The woman, the serpent, my temperament, my circumstances!" Few things more surely reveal our self-love and pride than this instinctive, automatic excuse-making. We thoroughly understand the lawyer who asked the question, "And who is my neighbour?" wishing to "justify himself." There is little hope for our growth

---

[1] F. W. Boreham, *Mushrooms on the Moor*, 112.

in virtue, unless we make up our minds frankly to admit the truth about ourselves, no matter how it hurts.[1]

4. In part Felix was doubtless prompted by a merely sordid and selfish motive. He wished to gain time, and to avoid giving a decision. If he did his duty, and released St. Paul, he would become unpopular with his subjects, who had many ways of making themselves disagreeable. If he condemned the prisoner illegally—and he could not condemn him legally—he ran the risk of detection and disgrace by the Emperor. And no doubt he waited in the hope of a bribe from St. Paul for his release, for the offering and acceptance of bribes from accused persons was only too common when magistrates like Felix were concerned.

¶ Indecision, cowardice, ought to be branded legal crimes. When we have done our best to determine, no matter how near to evenness reasons for and against may be balanced, it is an imperative duty to act, and inaction may be a sin worse than the action which follows the lighter scale.[2]

II.

The Slave.

Tacitus describes Felix as, "exercising in each form of cruelty and lust the jurisdiction of a monarch in the spirit of a slave." From our point of view, his was an entangled life, and we are concerned with those snares which caught his soul and made him the slave we know him to have been. "And after certain days, when Felix came with his wife Drusilla, which was a Jewess, he sent for Paul, and heard him concerning the faith in Christ."

1. What Felix looked for was entertainment; what he found was judgment and penalty. Because time hung heavy upon him, Felix bethought himself of Paul, the prisoner. The fame of St. Paul's eloquence had made its way even into the palace. For reasons of curiosity and motives of entertainment, soldiers were sent for the Apostle, in the hope that he might while away an hour and kill a little time.

---

[1] M. D. Babcock, *Thoughts for Every-Day Living*, 68.
[2] Mark Rutherford, *Last Pages from a Journal*, 98.

¶ There was one who went to hear Mr. Whitefield—a member of the "Hell-fire Club," a desperate fellow. He stood up at the next meeting of his abominable associates, and he delivered Mr. Whitefield's sermon with wonderful accuracy, imitating his very tone and manner. In the middle of his exhortation he converted himself, and came to a sudden pause, sat down broken-hearted, and confessed the power of the gospel. That club was dissolved. That remarkable convert was Mr. Thorpe, of Bristol, whom God so greatly used afterwards in the salvation of others. I would rather have you read the Bible to mock at it than not read it at all. I would rather that you came to hear the Word of God out of hatred to it than that you never came at all.[1]

2. Beside Felix on the seat of judgment sat Drusilla—"his wife," the sacred historian calls her; for he does not think it needful to interrupt the history by laying bare the shame and scandal of their connexion, or to bring out that, however wife in name, yet wife in deed she was not. For Felix had enticed her, the first of three queens whom he successively married, from her own husband, one of those petty princes whom the Romans endured within their empire; and in his case and hers the *names* of husband and wife did but palliate and conceal the *realities* of adulterer and adulteress.

Drusilla was the youngest daughter of King Herod Agrippa I. She was a beautiful young Jewess of some eighteen years of age. But those dark shadows lying across her path would have marred the fairest womanhood. It was not God who had made her Felix's wife.

One reading inserts in verse 24 the statement that Drusilla wished to see St. Paul, and that Felix summoned him in order to gratify her. Very probably she, as a Jewess, knew something of "the Way," and with a love of anything odd and new, which such women cannot do without, she wanted to see this curious man and to hear him talk. It might amuse her, and pass an hour, and be something to gossip about.

3. In the palace, however, St. Paul was a very different man from St. Paul in the judgment-hall. There he was on his trial, and he confined himself to the matters of the hour; but in the palace Felix was, so to say, on his trial before St. Paul, and the Apostle

---

[1] C. H. Spurgeon, *Barbed Arrows*, 41.

did not fail to probe the most sensitive point in the conscience of his hearer.

St. Paul's was a great heart-searching appeal, as courteous as courageous, direct to the soul of Felix. And Felix quailed before it. But conscience can only warn and guide, it cannot compel. In the famous words of Butler, "Had it might as it has right, had it power as it has manifest authority, it would absolutely govern the world." "Felix was terrified." It may be that Felix longed for a purer life, but the bond of his sin tightened upon his soul, and he dismissed St. Paul. He had to reckon with Drusilla, and she was unmoved by St. Paul's words.

¶ At one time Creighton had a Shakespeare reading-class for some of the young people; and he gave lectures sometimes in the evenings in the schoolroom. On these occasions he often took a play of Shakespeare and explained it, reading the most striking scenes. At one of these lectures on "Macbeth," the school was filled with an audience so attentive that they even forgot to cough; but it was almost too much for an old woman who was one of his most devout admirers. "Oh, it was too terrible," she said sadly the next day; "generally when I go home, I try to remember the vicar's sermons, but this time I tried to forget as quick as possible."[1]

4. St. Paul had succeeded in some measure in bringing the truth home to the darkened or neglected conscience of Felix, and therefore it was that he "trembled." In this second department of his reasoning, St. Paul had gone even deeper into the heart of the moral question with which man has to grapple in his mortal pilgrimage than he had in reasoning upon justice. For justice is a virtue of the understanding and the will, while temperance is more of the affections and the heart. If the understanding is the basis of character, if the will is the crown, it is the affections and the heart that are the centre. Find out that on which a man sets his heart—this is an axiom of all religious teachers, learnt from our Lord Himself—and you will know whither his character is tending. To do full justice to St. Paul's meaning, we must call the virtue "self-control" rather than "temperance." In its fullest sense it means the complete mastery of the immortal spirit over all the departments of its activity, but especially over those which

---

[1] *Life and Letters of Mandell Creighton*, i. 168.

relate to the affectionate nature, and are situated upon that border-land where flesh and spirit join.

Before he concluded his high argument, the teacher sought to lift his listener's mind to the greatest of all thoughts—"man's relation to God." He spoke of "the judgment to come"—the great external fact which is the correlative of the sense of responsibility in man. "Every one of us," says the Apostle elsewhere, "shall give account of himself to God."

¶ The timely remembrance of responsibility eventuating in judgment has ere now changed and elevated the purpose of a life. Listen! On the upper ledges of the wind-swept Apennine stand the venerable towers of Monte Casino, below stretches the purple valley, beyond the purple sea, beneath the jagged cliff winds the silvery Garigliano, beyond the dim and undulating plain stretch line on line of azure misty mountains, carved in the stately shapes, robed in the magic colours, of beautiful dreamy Italy. Thither—if Italian legend speaks truly—thither, through the ilex woods and up the tortuous mountain paths came Totila the Ostrogoth. He had crossed the Alps, had beaten the conquerors of the world, had triumphed at Faenza, swept the Mugello, carried Florence, Ravenna, almost Rome; and now he came, impelled (who can doubt it?) by a supernatural influence, to take counsel of the wisest and saintliest of living men. "What shall I do, my father?" asked the barbarian conqueror, as he stood awestricken before the aged Benedict. Calmly the saint replied in this fashion: "My son, thou shalt enter Rome." "And then?" "Then thou shalt cross the sea, shalt sweep and conquer Sicily." "And then?" "Then thou shalt reign nine years; and then," said the father, "then thou shalt die, and then *thou shalt be judged.*" We may hope, in part at least we may believe, the lesson was not lost on Totila. My brothers, have we learnt that lesson? The grave prerogative of the soul is this: life's struggle over, *then* it "shall be judged."[1]

III.

THE SINNER.

1. It is not so much Felix the corrupt magistrate as Felix the depraved man who speaks to us in the significant words— "Go thy way."

[1] W. J. Knox Little, *Our Reasonable Service*, 43.

Felix reasoned with his better self that over against justice there were other considerations which were not without weight with him. There was the claim of policy and of greed. Hence he determined to use the Apostle as a tool. Greatly as he scorned the Jews, he knew how impolitic it would be to anger them by releasing their prisoner; and beyond all that there was the hope of the offer of a bribe, which he would not hesitate to accept.

> Gold! gold! in all ages the curse of mankind,
> Thy fetters are forged for the soul and the mind:
> The limbs may be free as the wings of a bird,
> And the mind be the slave of a look or a word.
> To gain thee, men barter eternity's crown,
> Yield honour, affection, and lasting renown.[1]

2. So far as we know, the impression made upon the mind of Felix passed wholly away. He remained two years in the palace of Cæsarea, and was then deposed. His downfall seemed to begin from that time. His inaction was his ruin. People are moved to tears in the rehearsal of a tragedy, then return to the world and live as if nothing had moved them. So the religious impression at this moment may pass as a dream.

¶ If you take a bit of phosphorus and put it upon a slip of wood and ignite the phosphorus, bright as the blaze is, there drops from it a white ash that coats the wood and makes it almost incombustible. And so when the flaming conviction laid upon your hearts has burnt itself out, it has coated the heart, and it will be very difficult to kindle the light there again. Felix said, "Go thy way, when I have a more convenient season I will send for thee." Yes, and he did send for Paul, and he talked with him often—he repeated the conversation, but we do not know that he repeated the trembling. He often communed with Paul, but it was only once that he was alarmed. You are less likely to be touched by the Gospel message for every time that you have heard it and put it away.[2]

¶ Men have two short words by way of excusing themselves when they are warned to think of God. "Not now," they say; "it will be soon enough by and by." And God has two short words, too, to set against them, which He is making good each day that we live—who can tell how awfully? To man's "not

---

[1] P. Benjamin.   [2] A. Maclaren.

yet," God's answer is, "then, never." To man's "soon enough,"
He answers, "too late."[1]

Lord, what am I, that with unceasing care
Thou didst seek after me, that thou didst wait,
Wet with unhealthy dews, before my gate,
And pass the gloomy nights of winter there?
O strange delusion!—that I did not greet
Thy blest approach, and O, to Heaven how lost,
If my ingratitude's unkindly frost
Has chilled the bleeding wounds upon thy feet.
How oft my guardian angel gently cried,
"Soul, from thy casement look, and thou shalt see
How he persists to knock and wait for thee!"
And, O! how often to that voice of sorrow,
"To-morrow we will open," I replied,
And when the morrow came I answered still, "To-morrow."[2]

[1] R. W. Church, *Village Sermons*, i. 241.   [2] Longfellow.

FESTUS.

LITERATURE.

Baring-Gould, S., *A Study of St. Paul* (1897), 403, 420.

Caird, J., *Essays for Sunday Reading* (1906), 215.

Farrar, F. W., *The Life and Work of St. Paul* (1897), **323**, 504, 556.

Fox, W. J., *Collected Works*, iii. (1865) 89.

Fraser, D., *Autobiography and a Selection from his Sermons* (1892), 236.

Furneaux, W. M., *The Acts of the Apostles* (1912), 378.

Fürst, A., *Christ the Way* (1883), 179.

Hausrath, A., *A History of the New Testament Times* : The Time of the Apostles, iv. (1895) 126, 187.

Haweis, H. R., *The Picture of Paul* (1887), 219.

Howson, J. S., *Scenes from the Life of St. Paul* (1909), 194.

Hull, E. L., *Sermons preached at King's Lynn*, iii. (1874) 221.

Jones, M., *St. Paul the Orator* (1910), 221.

Luckock, H. M., *Footprints of the Apostles as traced by Saint Luke in the Acts*, i. (1905) 23 ; ii. (1905) 257.

Maclaren, A., *Expositions* : The Acts of the Apostles xiii.–end (1907), 322.

Morrison, G. H., *The Footsteps of the Flock* (1904), 364.

Parker, J., *Studies in Texts*, i. 96.

Robinson, C. S., *Sermons on Neglected Texts* (1884), 172.

Seekings, H. S., *The Men of the Pauline Circle* (1914), 239.

Smellie, A., *In the Hour of Silence* (1899), 52.

Spurgeon, C. H., *Metropolitan Tabernacle Pulpit*, xxxiv. (1888), No. 2016.

Vaughan, C. J., *University and Other Sermons* (1897), 324.

Wilson, S. L., *Helpful Words for Daily Life* (1905), 328.

Contemporary Pulpit, 2nd Ser., vi. (1891) 41 (J. M. Wilson).

National Preacher, v. (1830) 168 (E. W. Hooker) ; vi. (1831) 297 (G. A. Calhoun).

FESTUS.

The natural man receiveth not the things of the Spirit of God : for they are foolishness unto him.—1 Cor. ii. 14.

PORCIUS FESTUS succeeded Felix as procurator of Judæa. His appointment was probably in 60 A.D., and so we have here one of the few data for fixing the chronology of the Acts. His tenure of office was brief, as he died in the year 62. It was marked by the dispersion of the *sicarii*, and by the dispute concerning the wall of the Temple, which was put up to interrupt the view of its courts from the new wing of Agrippa's palace.

I.

THE MAN OF GOOD INTENTION.

1. In personal character Festus seems to have been a great improvement upon his predecessor. The portrait given in the Acts is that of a high official anxious to perform the duties of his exalted position conscientiously, and with the equity and justice so characteristic of Rome and the Roman Government at their best.

Three days after his arrival at Cæsarea he went up to Jerusalem, when at once the high priest and the chief of the Jews informed him against Paul. Their resentment was kept alive by the continued diminution of the funds sent from the Hellenistic synagogues. Festus ordered the accusers to come down to Cæsarea and there lay their accusation against St. Paul.

After a stay of eight or ten days in Jerusalem, he proceeded to Cæsarea, and, on the day after his arrival, took his seat in the procurator's court and summoned the prisoner to his presence, where his accusers, who had in the meantime also arrived from

Jerusalem, repeated the charges which they had already formulated against St. Paul before Felix. Once again he was accused of being guilty of offences (1) against the law of the Jews, (2) against the Temple, and (3) against Cæsar, all of which charges he emphatically denied, and in support of which the prosecution was unable to produce any evidence. The character of the charges seemed to Festus, who showed no tendency to treat his prisoner with any degree of injustice, to be more suitable for consideration by a Jewish than by an Imperial tribunal, seeing that they were concerned principally with questions of Jewish law and religion. He therefore suggested to St. Paul that the case should be transferred to Jerusalem, where he could be tried before the Sanhedrin, while his own presence at the hearing would guarantee that justice should be done to him. It is manifest from this suggestion that he attached but slight importance to the charge of treason to the Empire, which would have been much too serious a matter to be entrusted to the decision of an inferior court.

St. Paul declined to go to Jerusalem, and appealed to Cæsar.

¶ Paul knew that Festus, honest as he might be in the intention to secure him a fair trial, would be powerless to save him from being murdered by the way, and, besides, it was altogether illegal to refer to a Jewish court a case which had been already brought under the Imperial jurisdiction, by being transferred to Cæsarea. Sent to Jerusalem, the dagger awaited him; sent to Rome, he must, as he rightly believed, be set free.[1]

¶ The root of honesty is an honest intention, the distinct and deliberate purpose to be true, to handle facts as they are, and not as we wish them to be. Facts lend themselves to manipulation. Many a butcher's hand is worth more than its weight in gold. What we want things to be, we come to see them to be; and the tailor pulls the coat and the truth into a perfect fit from his point of view.

Oh, to get life out of our sinful and selfish desires, and "walk in the light as he is in the light," not wishing merely, but "willing to live honestly!"[2]

2. Shortly after Festus had assumed the reins of government as governor of Judæa, a ceremonial visit was paid to him by

---

[1] C. Geikie, *Hours with the Bible: Life and Epistles of St. Paul*, ii. 451.
[2] M. D. Babcock, *Thoughts for Every-Day Living*, 32.

Herod Agrippa the Second, accompanied by his sister, Bernice. Festus had been placed in a somewhat awkward predicament by St. Paul's appeal to Cæsar, which necessitated the formulating of a legal statement of the case to the higher Imperial court. He had been unable, in the course of the inquiry that he had held, to discover evidence of any crime charged against the prisoner which could be construed into an offence against Roman law, and, as far as his information went, Paul's condemnation was sought by his accusers on grounds connected entirely with their own law and custom. His ignorance of all that pertained to Judaism was such that he was unable to distinguish the relevancy of the charges, and to state a case to the court of Cæsar was, therefore, a matter of considerable difficulty.

Herod, on the other hand, was a Jew by birth, and had a wide knowledge of Jewish law and custom, and was conversant with questions of Jewish theology. His official connexion with the Temple had also brought him into close contact with the ecclesiastical authorities, and gave him an opportunity of becoming acquainted with all the minutiæ of ritual and ceremonial. It would, indeed, have been difficult for Festus to meet with a person who, by position and knowledge, was better fitted to extricate him out of his present predicament. He, therefore, lost no time in laying before Herod a complete statement of St. Paul's case, explaining to him the dilemma in which he was placed by the prisoner's appeal to Cæsar, and requisitioning his assistance in the matter. The king's curiosity was aroused by the procurator's statement, and he expressed a desire to have the prisoner examined in his own presence, a request which was readily granted.

¶ There is a mean curiosity, as of a child opening a forbidden door, or a servant prying into her master's business;—and a noble curiosity, questioning, in the front of danger, the source of the great river beyond the sand,—a nobler curiosity still, which questions of the source of the River of Life, and of the space of the Continent of Heaven,—things which "the angels desire to look into." [1]

3. Festus opened the court proceedings by repeating in public what he had already explained to Herod privately, how, on his

---

[1] Ruskin, *Sesame and Lilies*, § 29.

first visit to Jerusalem, he had been assailed by the whole Jewish community, leaders and people, with accusations against St. Paul, who had been declared unfit to live. He then proceeded to describe how he himself had examined him in their presence and could discover no evidence of any crime committed against Roman law, and how, on his proposing to hand over the prisoner to the Jewish authorities to be tried on an issue having reference to Jewish law, St. Paul had appealed to Cæsar, and how to Cæsar's court he had decided to send him. He had now summoned the prisoner to give an account of himself in the presence of the king and the assembly, in order that Herod, with his intimate knowledge of all that pertained to Judaism, might assist him in framing the charge which must accompany the prisoner when he appeared before the Supreme Court. When Festus had completed his introductory address, Agrippa expressed the desire of the court to hear what the Apostle had to say for himself.

¶ It has always seemed to me, as the Saints say, that self-defence, though not advisable ordinarily, is a duty when it is a question of faith.[1]

4. As St. Paul made his defence, the patience of Festus broke down. It broke down on two points. First, he did not care for the "preaching" part of the Apostle's speech. As long as St. Paul stood on his defence, or attacked the Jews, the thing was entertaining enough; but the forgiveness of sin and the call to repentance was out of place in court circles, and sounded trivial to men of the world.

The other distasteful element in St. Paul's address was the story of a risen Jesus—visions, personal convictions, sects, prophets, and all that—such a mixture as Festus had never heard in his life; quite unintelligible and visionary—so it seemed to him. Not unkindly, or even discourteously, did he at last exclaim, hoping to bring so able an orator back to reason and common sense, "Paul, thou art mad; thy much book learning doth turn thee to madness."

With unruffled calm and dignity St. Paul brushed aside the exclamation with a simple affirmation that his words were true in themselves, and spoken by one who had full command over his

[1] W. Ward, *The Life of Cardinal Newman*, ii. **128.**

faculties; and then he turned away from Festus, who understood nothing, to Agrippa, who, at any rate, did understand a little. Indeed, Festus has to take the second place throughout, and it may have been the ignoring of him that nettled him. For all his courtesy to Agrippa, he knew that the latter was but a vassal king, and he may have chafed at St. Paul's addressing him exclusively.

¶ Oh, blessed fervour that glowed in the heart of Paul! Oh, most admirable infatuation! Oh, most wise ecstasy! A story runs of some formal old officer disparaging General Wolfe to the King, and insinuating that he was mad; on which the King shrewdly answered, "If he be mad, I wish he would bite some of my generals, that they might be mad also." If Paul was mad, I wish we were all affected with the same mania.[1]

¶ Then it seems to me as if my heart would break in pouring out one glorious song that should be the gospel of Reform, full of consolation and strength to the oppressed, yet falling gently and restoringly as dew on the withered youth-flowers of the oppressor. That way my madness lies.[2]

5. How could such an one as Festus understand a man like St. Paul? A man, Festus probably thought, of natural intellectual vigour and force of character—for his whole tone and bearing indicate that—who has permitted himself to pore over old Jewish records till his brain has been heated by some mystical visions, some contemptible vaticinations of Hebrew superstition. The healthy balance between imagination and sense, the world of thoughts, fancies, speculations, and the world of material realities, has been disturbed, and this clever man, of whom better things might have been made, has become a morbid dreamer and enthusiast.

Yet Festus has caught the point of St. Paul's gospel, as many Christians have not. Like the Athenians, who thought Anastasis a new goddess—so frequent was the mention of Resurrection in the stranger's address—Festus, too, has seen that the question between Christianity and Judaism was a certain Person's life after death, and that the real crime of his prisoner was, not an assault upon the traditions of Moses, the sanctities of the Temple, or the

---

[1] *Autobiography of the late Donald Fraser*, 242.
[2] W. H. Hudson, *Lowell and his Poetry*, 42.

prerogatives of Cæsar, but the assertion, in opposition to the ecclesiastical authorities and the religious world of his country-men, of a fact about which he was positive, in testimony of which he had suffered the loss of his all, and was prepared to endure any torture and a degrading death.

¶ Gibbon, among historians, is typical of that wisdom of this world which is blind to the spiritual facts and forces of life; his story of the Decline and Fall of the Roman Empire, brilliant and majestic in its march of events, stumbles and falters, is darkened and diminished, when it confronts the factor of Christianity in the rise and fall of men and nations. Its chapters on this new power in history are a pitiful endeavour to measure the infinite by finite standards; it is as the effort of a blind man to explain colour, of the deaf to appraise music. Sight without insight, view without vision, cannot read aright either the tale of past ages, or the scene of the present hour.[1]

> Whoso hath felt the Spirit of the Highest
> Cannot confound nor doubt him nor deny:
> Yea with one voice, O world, tho' thou deniest,
> Stand thou on that side, for on this am I.[2]

¶ Livingstone when found dead upon his knees in Central Africa, had his diary open before him, and the last entry was "My Jesus, my Saviour, my Life, my all, anew I dedicate myself to Thee."

II.

"ONE JESUS."

1. Festus evidently did not know Jesus, for he spoke of Him as "one Jesus." He mentioned the name as belonging to some obscure individual about whom he knew nothing, and cared less.

He had dismissed the resurrection of "one Jesus" as un-important: St. Paul asserted it, the Jews denied it. It was not worth while to ask which was right. The man was dead, that was agreed. If St. Paul said He was alive after death, that was only another proof of madness, and a Roman governor had

---

[1] A. Rudman, in *Notes on the Scripture Lessons*, 1916.
[2] F. W. H. Myers, *Saint Paul*, 50.

more weighty things to occupy him than investigating such obscure and absurd trifles.

¶ He is a great man who sees great things where others see little things, who sees the extraordinary in the ordinary. Ruskin sees a poem in the rose or the lily, while the hod-carrier would perhaps not go a rod out of his way to see a sunset which Ruskin would feed upon for a year.[1]

2. We cannot fail to be struck with the strange contrast between the results which that asserted fact of Christ's resurrection produced in those two men, Festus and Paul. In the Apostle, belief in it had kindled a fire of all-sacrificing devotion, and braced him with a courage which no terrors could quell. By Festus, on the contrary, that asserted fact was received with complete indifference. Had it been a question of political import touching the quietude of his province, or a question of criminal law, that keen judge would have exerted the power of his intellect to detect the truth, avert the danger, or punish the crime. But because it referred to an unseen world, he dismissed it with apparent contempt, without for a moment troubling himself to inquire whether it were false or true.

¶ Then we told them as much as we could in an hour about the great love of Jesus Christ. I was in the middle of it, and thinking only of it and their souls, when an old lady with fluffy white hair leaned forward and gazed at me with a beautiful, earnest gaze. She did not speak; she just listened and gazed, "drinking it all in." And then she raised a skeleton claw, and grabbed her hair, and pointed to mine. "Are you a widow too," she asked, "that you have no oil on yours?"[2]

¶ A nation of men blind from their birth, to whom a solitary traveller should reveal the joys of the light, would deny not only that the latter was possible, but even imaginable.[3]

3. Did Festus wince a little at the mention of St. Paul's bonds? At all events, the entertainment had taken rather too serious a turn for the taste of any of the three—Festus, Agrippa, or Bernice. If this strange man was going to shake their consciences in that fashion, it was high time to end what was, after

---

[1] O. S. Marden, *Architects of Fate*, 317.

[2] A. Wilson-Carmichael, *Things as They are in India*, 8.

[3] M. Maeterlinck, *Life and Flowers*, 42.

all, as far as the rendering of justice was concerned, something like a farce.

So with a rustle, and amid the obeisances of the courtiers, the three rose, and, followed by the principal people, went through the form of deliberation. There was only one conclusion to be come to. St. Paul was perfectly innocent. So Agrippa solemnly pronounced, what had been known before, that he had done nothing worthy of death or bonds, though he had "these bonds" on his arm; and he salved the injustice of keeping an innocent man in custody by throwing all the blame on St. Paul himself for appealing to Cæsar. But the person to blame was Festus, who had forced St. Paul to appeal in order to save his life.

¶ There's folk's 'ud stand on their heads and then say the fault was i' their boots.[1]

4. The calm secured by the firm action of Festus, on his arrival in his province, was of short duration. In the spring of 62 A.D., Rome suffered a humiliating defeat at the hands of the Parthians. Triumph over Rome seemed to be coming, and the hopes of the turbulent zealots of Judæa were once more kindled. A general rising was indeed impossible, thanks to the measures of Festus, nor would it have been prudent, so long as the legions of Corbulo lay on the north-east borders of the Empire. But it was clear that the first defeat he suffered would see the Jews, and probably the Arabs, in full revolt.

Things might have gone more peacefully had there been a party among the Jews from whom the Romans could have obtained reliable counsel. Instead of this, Agrippa, the Jewish king, who was the official adviser of the procurator, in the distracting intricacies of religious affairs, was himself the source of endless trouble. He rebuilt the old palace of the Maccabees on the western hill of Jerusalem, and thus had a view over the whole city and neighbourhood; the Temple grounds, with their constant crowds, lying, amidst all else, under his eyes, as he rested on his couch. The eminently religious Ishmael and Ananias, however, seeing the opportunity of revenging themselves on him, declared that it was against the law that the courts of the Temple should be overlooked, and forthwith raised a huge wall to shut out the

---

[1] George Eliot.

king's view, bending its course so that, in addition, it shut out the view of the courts from the fortress Antonia. Such audacity roused both the king and the procurator. St. Paul had been saved from the fury of the mob at the Pentecost of the year 59 by the Romans overlooking the grounds, and it had often been of equal value in similar disturbances. Festus therefore ordered the wall to be thrown down, but the Jews at once appealed to Rome and, through the influence of Poppæa, who favoured the Jewish faith, obtained the victory. Festus died during or shortly after this settlement.

¶ Many a man knoweth full well what is just or unjust, and yet neither is nor ever will become a just man. For he loveth not justice, and therefore he worketh wickedness and injustice. If he loved justice, he would not do an unjust thing; for he would feel such hatred and indignation towards injustice wherever he saw it, that he would do or suffer anything that injustice might be put an end to, and men might become just. And he would rather die than do an injustice, and all this for nothing but the love of justice. And to him, justice is her own reward, and rewardeth him with herself; and so there liveth a just man, and he would rather die a thousand times over than live as an unjust man.[1]

[1] *Theologia Germanica*, 157.

AGRIPPA.

LITERATURE.

Farrar, F. W., *The Herods* (1898), 205.

Goodman, J. H., *The Lordship of Christ* (1901), **156.**

Grandpierre, J. H., in *Foreign Protestant Pulpit*, ii. (1870) 243.

Hausrath, A., *A History of the New Testament Times* : The Time of the
    Apostles, ii. (1895) 16.

Jones, M., *St. Paul the Orator* (1910), 221.

Luckock, H. M., *Footprints of the Apostles as traced by Saint Luke in the
    Acts*, ii. (1905) 264.

Maclaren, A., *Christ's Musts* (1894), 187.

    ,,   ,, *Expositions* : The Acts of the Apostles xiii.-end (1907),
        337.

Mathews, S., *A History of New Testament Times in Palestine* (1899), 181.

Morrison, G. H., *The Footsteps of the Flock* (1904), 362.

Rackham, R. B., *The Acts of the Apostles* (1901), 455.

Stevens, W. B., *Sermons* (1879), 63.

Stokes, G. T., *The Acts of the Apostles* (Expositor's Bible), ii. (1892) 422.

Trench, R. C., *Sermons Preached for the Most Part in Ireland* (1873), 11.

Church Pulpit Year Book, 1915, p. 26.

Contemporary Pulpit, 2nd Ser., x. (1893) 239 (A. Maclaren).

Dictionary of the Apostolic Church, i. (1915) 564 (D. Frew).

Dictionary of the Bible, ii. (1899) 353 (A. C. Headlam).

AGRIPPA.

King Agrippa, believest thou the prophets? I know that thou believest. And Agrippa said unto Paul, With but little persuasion thou wouldest fain make me a Christian.—Acts xxvi. 27, 28.

A UNIQUE interest centres round this "the last of the Herods." It has been said indeed that justice has hardly been done to him, taking into consideration the circumstances of his birth, and the difficult part he had to play in the stormy times which preceded the great national catastrophe.

1. At the time of his father's death, Agrippa II. was resident in Rome, and but seventeen years of age. Claudius, the Emperor, had he not been dissuaded from his purpose by his freedmen and counsellors, would at once have granted him the succession to the Jewish kingdom. It was urged that he was too young to guide the destinies of the stormy province of Judæa, so Claudius re-transformed it into a Roman province. About six years afterwards, however, the Emperor bestowed on him his uncle Herod's kingdom of Chalcis as well as the rights which he had possessed of supervising the Temple and choosing the high priest. Later, Claudius added to Agrippa's dominions the tetrarchies of Philip and Lysanias (see Luke iii. 1), and conferred on him the coveted title of King; and in 56 A.D. Nero, who had meanwhile succeeded to the throne and expected Agrippa's aid against the Parthians, added to his kingdom the regions of Tiberias and Tarich, with Julias, a city of Peræa and several villages in its vicinity. Agrippa showed his gratitude by changing the name of his capital from Cæsarea Philippi to Neronias, in honour of the Emperor.

2. It was natural that Agrippa should be strongly attached to the Empire which had adopted him, and to that family which never seemed to weary of showing him kindness and considera-

tion. A Roman at heart, and devoted by education and circumstances to the Roman influence, he endeavoured to bring the customs of his people into conformity with those of the Gentiles. At the same time, he evinced an occasional interest in the Jewish religion, and sought to win over the Pharisees to his projects. In the final struggle between the Jews and Rome, which he did his utmost to avert, he, however, maintained his loyalty to the Imperial power, and at the close of the war was rewarded with considerable enlargement of his territories.

I.

AGRIPPA AS JUDGE.

1. Shortly after Festus had assumed the reins of government as governor of Judæa, Agrippa the king and Bernice came down to Cæsarea to pay him their respects. Now, Agrippa was on the one side a real Jew and held an authoritative position in the Jewish religious policy. He was therefore fully conversant with Jewish customs and theology. When at Rome, he had on two occasions used his influence with Claudius on behalf of his countrymen with success. Against one governor, Cuspius Fadus, he had secured for the Jews the custody of the high priest's vestments; he also procured for them the condemnation of another governor, Cumanus. On the other side, like all the Herods and their partisans the Herodians, he was thoroughly Roman in tastes and sympathies. He had been educated at Rome and before his accession had hardly seen Judæa.

2. This double character of Agrippa made Paul also the more ready to make his defence before him. Agrippa would thoroughly understand the points at issue, and at the same time was no bigot; rather, his actual relations to the high priests would dispose him to give Paul an impartial hearing. Accordingly the Apostle made a great effort and delivered the speech which is evidently intended by St. Luke to form a climax in his work. The solemnity of the occasion is marked by its elaborate setting, and the repetitions which it involves. Three times over we read the account of Festus' dealings with the Jews; and thereby three times is the

Apostle's innocence insinuated. For the third time we hear the story of Paul's conversion. That famous episode is now told by the Apostle in a scene of pomp and before a distinguished audience of Jewish and Gentile magnates, before a Roman governor and a Jewish king—in a word "before the Gentiles and kings and the children of Israel."

The request to give his assistance fell in with Agrippa's own desire. Like his sister Drusilla, he also had been curious to see Paul and "had intended" to ask Festus for an opportunity of "hearing the man"—a somewhat contemptuous expression when compared with the more polite word (for *man*) used by Festus in verses 5 and 14.

¶ Extract from Bishop Hannington's Diary, written while in prison in Busoga :—

"*Afternoon.*—To my surprise my guards came kneeling down, so different to their usual treatment, and asked me to come out. I came out, and there was the chief and about a hundred of his wives come to feast their eyes on me in cruel curiosity." [1]

3. Festus decided to make Paul's "hearing" an occasion for a compliment to the king. In compensation for their loss of liberty and real power, the dependent princes and wealthy provincials found scope for their ambition in the outward show of dress and ceremonial, of decorations and grand titles. So Festus gave the young Herodian prince the opportunity of making a public display with the semblance of power; for he conceded to him (it would seem) the judge's seat. Agrippa permits Paul to speak, takes precedence of the governor in rising from his seat, and pronounces the final verdict. The scene was to be in the palace; not in its basilica or hall of justice, but in the auditorium or hall of hearing. This would be the hall devoted to matters of public ceremonial, oratorical displays, and similar shows, thus corresponding to the "schools" and "porches" in the public gymnasia. Agrippa and Bernice accordingly came to the palace in royal state, with much splendour of apparel and escort; and then, together with the procurator and the chief captains of the Roman garrison, the chief men of the city, both Jews and Syrians, and the notables who had accompanied them from the province,

[1] E. C. Dawson, *James Hannington*, 436.

they entered the audience-chamber and took their seats. Then Paul was brought in, still wearing his chain, and Festus presented him to the king and assembled magnates.

The scene was one well calculated to call out Paul's characteristic courage and boldness of speech; and, inspired by the comfort of the Holy Ghost, he stretched forth his arm, with the chain hanging from it—as it were to call God to witness—and began his *apologia*.

¶ It is often said that every Christian is a missionary : it is no less true that every Christian is an apologist, a defender of the faith ; and if St. Francis Xavier was right in saying that of all the means for extending the faith, none could compare with a holy life, the same is true of the various means by which men try to defend Christianity against attack. And here the duty is the same for all. The difference between priest and layman in the Christian Society is a difference of function. We have each our several duties to do for God, but there is one duty which rests upon us all simply because we are Christians, and that is the duty of so living that people may "take knowledge of us that we have been with Jesus."[1]

4. Festus could make little of Paul's speech, but he was startled by its enthusiasm : he was so affected as to cry out—"Paul, thou art mad." For support Paul turned to Agrippa, but again his enthusiasm carried him into his characteristic boldness of speech. He was convinced that his story appeared perfectly sane to the king; for the facts of the crucifixion and the growth of the Church had happened, not in an obscure corner, but in broad daylight before all the Jews at Jerusalem ; and his theology was taken out of the Jewish Scriptures. At this personal address Agrippa probably showed some sign of discomfort. St. Paul, whose charity believed and hoped all things, may have taken it for the dawning of faith ; and he drove the charge home by a direct appeal. Agrippa must assent, for he believed the Scriptures. "King Agrippa, believest thou the prophets? I know that thou believest." This was too much. As it was, the young king had no doubt found the practice of Judaism irksome enough in the scoffing society of Rome, and it was too much to expose him to the astonishment of the Roman governor and the

[1] Aubrey Moore.

distinguished audience by extorting from him the patronage, if not the profession, of this new faith. His courtly breeding was equal to the occasion, and he passed it off by a piece of raillery : " A little more persuasion and you will make me too a Christian." Agrippa uses the term by which the followers of " the Christ " (verse 23) were known to the Gentile world. At once St. Paul falls back into his soberness, but with intense earnestness he takes up the king's word: " I would to God that, whether with little or with much, not only thou, but also all that hear me this day, might become such as I am, except these bonds."

¶ Agrippa is half amused and half angry at the Apostle's presumption in supposing that so easily or so quickly he was going to land his fish. " It is a more difficult task than you fancy, Paul, to make a Christian of a man like me." That is the real meaning of his words, and I think that, rightly understood, they yield lessons of no less value than those that have been so often drawn from them as they appear in our Authorized Version.[1]

¶ Far be it from us to say, that solemnity is an essential of greatness ; that no great man can have other than a rigid vinegar aspect of countenance, never to be thawed or warmed by billows of mirth ! There are things in this world to be laughed at, as well as things to be admired ; and his is no complete mind, that cannot give to each sort its due. Nevertheless, contempt is a dangerous element to sport in ; a deadly one, if we habitually live in it. The faculty of love, of admiration, is to be regarded as the sign and the measure of high souls : unwisely directed, it leads to many evils ; but without it there cannot be any good. Ridicule, on the other hand, is indeed a faculty much prized by its possessors ; yet, intrinsically, it is a small faculty. It is directly opposed to Thought, to Knowledge, properly so called ; its nourishment and essence is Denial, which hovers only on the surface, while Knowledge dwells far below. Moreover it is by nature selfish and morally trivial ; it cherishes nothing but our Vanity, which may in general be left safely enough to shift for itself. Little " discourse of reason," in any sense, is implied in Ridicule : a scoffing man is in no lofty mood, for the time ; shows more of the imp than of the angel.[2]

[1] A. Maclaren.
[2] Carlyle, *Miscellaneous Essays*, ii. 133.

II.

A Judge in Chains.

1. While in the political world Agrippa was only a petty potentate, socially he represented a great influence. The Herodian family stand out conspicuous for their intimate connexion with the family of the Cæsars, and this gave them a leading position in Roman society.   Agrippa II., as we have already seen, had been brought up at the court of Claudius.   Now we see Paul brought before him.   As Christ stood before Herod Antipas, so Paul stands before Herod Agrippa II.   St. Peter also had the honour of being arrested by a Herod : and the pomp of this scene is an evident counterpicture to the ostentatious display made at Cæsarea by the first Agrippa.   Of all these Herods, Agrippa II. comes out best.   The Lord would not open His lips before Antipas; nor would Paul give an exposition of his faith before Drusilla.   But before Agrippa II. the Apostle made his most elaborate *apologia* ; he bore witness to the Jewish faith ; he had even hopes of winning him to Christianity.

He would have Agrippa a fellow-citizen with him in the city of God, a brother heir in his glorious hopes, but without the chain, and the sorrow, and the persecution which in his, Paul's, case had accompanied his profession of Christianity.   "Such as he," beauti- fully writes Plumptre, "pardoned, at peace with God and man, with a hope stretching beyond the grave, and an actual present participation in the power of the eternal world—this is what he was desiring for them.   If that could be effected, he would be content to remain in his bonds, and to leave them upon their thrones."

> Brothers and sisters, careworn, pale,
>   Before your time,
> O wanderers, weary, footsore, frail,
>   From every clime,
>
> Come, take my hands : could you but know
>   My longing heart,
> Opprest with tears that wait to flow,
>   Pride would not part

Our souls, nor subtle doubt which bars
    The love that seeks,
And here, beneath the patient stars,
    Feels, yearns, and speaks:—

I do not judge, I claim no height
    Of wise or good
To pity, only the human right
    Of brotherhood,

The right to claim my kindred, know
    The worst and best,
And fold the shapes that come and go
    Against my breast.[1]

2. Paul's arm was chained; he himself was free. But Agrippa, as he sat on the judgment-seat, was bound by chains which nothing short of Almighty power could break. He had certainly a legitimate indebtedness to Rome. Rather than offend the Emperor of Rome, whose creature he was, he suffered himself to take up arms against his compatriots; and he feared that if he became a Christian he would entirely lose the favour of the man whom in reality he hated. Agrippa loved the world, and the vanities of the world: the Jews reported of him that he wept bitterly when he believed himself excluded from the crown, and St. Luke's account reveals the attraction that outward pomp and magnificence had for him. In short, he was a slave to his passions. It was widely reported that he had entered into an illicit connexion with Bernice his sister, and to embrace the Christian faith, he knew that it would be necessary for him to crucify the flesh with its lusts.

Of the poor bird that cannot fly
Kindly you think and mournfully;
For prisoners and for exiles all
You let the tears of pity fall;
And very true the grief should be
That mourns the bondage of the free.

The soul—*she* has a fatherland;
Binds *her* not many a tyrant's hand?

[1] J. W. Taylor, *The Doorkeeper*, 58.

And the winged spirit has a home,
But can she always homeward come?
Poor souls, with all their wounds and foes,
Will you not also pity those?[1]

¶ On another occasion, when I had shown over-much relish
for some dish, my father reminded me that it was a poor thing to
be a slave to any appetite or practice. Blushing to the roots of
my hair, I ventured to retaliate, saying, "Well, father, how is it
that the snuff-box is brought to you every day at the end of
dinner?—you always take out a big pinch." For a moment he
was silent, and then made me fetch the box, and while in the act
of tossing it into the fire he said, "There goes the box, and that is
the end of that bit of slavery."[2]

3. Agrippa listens to Paul; Bernice listens; Festus listens.
And what comes of it? Only this, "And when they were gone
aside, they talked between themselves, saying, This man doeth
nothing worthy of death or of bonds." We might translate into
a modern equivalent: And when they were gone aside, they
talked between themselves, saying, "This man preached a very
impressive sermon," or, "This man preached a very wearisome
sermon," and there an end. Agrippa and Bernice went their
wicked way, and Festus went his, and none of them knew what a
fateful moment they had passed through.

The Herods were magnificent, clever, beautiful. But they
were of the earth, earthy. Agrippa said indeed to Paul, "With
but little persuasion thou wouldest fain make me a Christian."
But it was not for souls like his that the gospel message was
intended. The Herods knew nothing of the burden of sin or the
keen longing of souls desirous of holiness and of God. They were
satisfied with the present transient scene, and enjoyed it thoroughly.
Agrippa's father, when he lay dying at Cæsarea, consoled himself
with the reflection that though his career was prematurely cut
short, yet at any rate he had lived a splendid life. And as the
parent had been, such were the children. King Agrippa and
his sister Bernice were true types of the stony-ground hearers,
with whom "the care of the world, and the deceitfulness of riches,
choke the word." And they choked the word so effectually in his

[1] G. MacDonald, *Poetical Works*, ii. 255.
[2] *The Life of Cardinal Vaughan*, i. 26.

case, even when taught by St. Paul, that the only result upon Agrippa, as St. Luke reports it, was this: "Agrippa said unto Festus, This man might have been set at liberty, if he had not appealed unto Cæsar."

¶ I chose for the students of Kensington, two characteristic examples of early art, of equal skill; but in the one case, skill which was progressive—in the other, skill which was at pause. In the one case, it was work receptive of correction—hungry for correction; and in the other, work which inherently rejected correction. I chose for them a corrigible Eve, and an incorrigible Angel.

And the fatal difference lay wholly in this. In both pieces of art there was an equal falling short of the needs of fact; but the Lombardic Eve knew she was in the wrong, and the Irish Angel thought himself all right. The eager Lombardic sculptor, though firmly insisting on his childish idea, yet showed in the irregular broken touches of the features, and the imperfect struggle for softer lines in the form, a perception of beauty and law that he could not render; there was the strain of effort, under conscious imperfection, in every line. But the Irish missal-painter had drawn his angel with no sense of failure, in happy complacency, and put red dots into the palm of each hand, and rounded the eyes into perfect circles, and, I regret to say, left the mouth out altogether, with perfect satisfaction to himself.[1]

¶ When Josephus published his *Wars of the Jews* he sent a copy to Agrippa. The king had given him much information, and wrote him a friendly and approving letter in return for his book, congratulating him on his accurate knowledge of the events. Altogether, Josephus boasts, he had received no less than sixty-two letters from the king. Agrippa seems to have attained a peaceful old age, living inglorious and unnoticed at Rome.[2]

[1] Ruskin, *Sesame and Lilies*, § 124 (*Works*, xviii. 172).
[2] F. W. Farrar, *The Herods*, 215.

BERNICE.

LITERATURE.

Adeney, W. F., *Women of the New Testament* (1899), **249.**

Bird, R., *Paul of Tarsus* (1900), 452.

Buss, S., *Roman Law and History in the New Testament* (1901), **262.**

Conybeare, W. J., and J. S. Howson, *The Life and Epistles of St. Paul* (1870), 621.

Farrar, F. W., *The Herods* (1898), 207.

    „   „   *The Life and Work of St. Paul*, ii. (1879) 352, 598.

Hausrath, A., *A History of the New Testament Times* : The Time of the Apostles, iv. (1895) 97, 194.

Howson, J. S., *Scenes from the Life of St. Paul* (1909), 182.

Johnston, C. N., *St. Paul and his Mission to the Roman Empire* (1909), 160.

Josephus, *Antiquities of the Jews*, xix. v. 1, xx. vii. **3.**

    „   *Jewish War*, ii. xv. 1, xvi. **3.**

Lewin, T., *The Life and Epistles of St. Paul*, ii. (1875) 109, 174.

Luckock, H. M., *Footprints of the Apostles as traced by Saint Luke in the Acts*, ii. (1905) 266.

Maclaren, A., *Expositions* : The Acts of the Apostles xiii.–end (1907), 322.

Mathews, S., *A History of New Testament Times in Palestine* (1899), 197.

Milman, H. H., *The History of the Jews*, ii. (1866) 183.

Morrison, G. H., *The Footsteps of the Flock* (1904), 364.

Pounder, R. W., *Saint Paul and his Cities* (1913), 196, 202.

Robertson, A. T., *Epochs in the Life of St. Paul* (1909), 250.

Schürer, E., *A History of the Jewish People in the Time of Jesus Christ*, I. ii. (1890) 195.

BERNICE.

Now when certain days were passed, Agrippa the king and Bernice arrived at Cæsarea, and saluted Festus. So on the morrow, when Agrippa was come, and Bernice, with great pomp, and they were entered into the place of hearing, with the chief captains, and the principal men of the city, at the command of Festus Paul was brought in.—Acts xxv. 13, 23.

And the king rose up, and the governor, and Bernice, and they that sat with them.—Acts xxvi. 30.

WHEN Agrippa I. died in agony at Cæsarea, while celebrating the games there in honour of the Emperor Claudius, on his return from the conquest of Britain, he left four children— Agrippa the younger, his only son, and three daughters, Bernice, Mariamne, and Drusilla. Agrippa was at that time seventeen years of age, and was in detention as a kind of hostage at Rome, at the court of Claudius, who took charge of his education. Bernice was sixteen, and a little before had married her paternal uncle, Herod of Chalcis. Mariamne at her father's death was only ten years of age, and Drusilla was six. The latter grew up to be one of the most celebrated beauties of the day. The young Agrippa had learnt the vices of the age at the Imperial Court, but profligacy is the only charge that history has recorded against him. He is described by Josephus as a man of extraordinary accomplishments. His three sisters were all of them but indifferent characters, and, indeed, the single favourable trait mentioned of any one of them is, that at the commencement of the Jewish war Bernice, as the representative of her family, in the absence of her brother Agrippa, had the courage and patriotism to present herself barefooted as a suppliant before the tribunal of Gessius Florus, the tyrannical procurator, to intercede for the lives of her countrymen, whose blood he was then recklessly shedding.

Bernice was the Lucrezia Borgia of the Herodian family. She was beautiful, like all the princesses of her house, but she was one of the most profligate women of a profligate age, exceeding even Cleopatra in her sensuality and shamelessness. It is not a pleasant career to contemplate.

¶ Satan said to the Almighty, "I wish for a subtle snare wherein to entrap men"; God showed him silver and gold and horses;

Satan said, "Yes, these are good," but did not seem satisfied.

Then God showed him mines full of jewels, but he said, "Give me more, O Generous One." Then He showed him costly cloths and silks and wines; but he said, "I require more than these, for men can break these chains." Then He showed him the beauty of women, which deprives men of reason and self-control. Satan began to dance with joy and said, "Give me that! now I shall succeed!"[1]

I.

BERNICE'S EARLY LIFE.

Agrippa the younger, who, at the death of his uncle, had reached the age of twenty-one, was now invested with the kingship of Chalcis, a high-sounding title, but conferring little extent of territory, and a very moderate income. Agrippa, therefore, still remained at the Imperial Court, and Bernice his sister, the widow of Herod of Chalcis, seems to have joined him at Rome, and to have resided at his house.

Her beauty, her rank, the splendour of her jewels, the interest and curiosity attaching to her race and her house, made her a prominent figure in the society of the capital; and a diamond, however lustrous and valuable, was enhanced in price if it was known that it had once sparkled on the finger of Bernice, and had been a present to her from her brother. The relations between the two gave rise to the darkest rumours, which gained credence because there was nothing to contradict them in the bearing or character of the defamed persons.

Such scandal was caused by her conduct, that even Rome, the Paris of the first century, began to cry, "Shame." And it was arranged that she should contract a third marriage. A husband

---

[1] Jalaluddin Rumi, in *A Little Book of Eastern Wisdom*, 62.

was found without difficulty, in Polemo II., king of Cilicia, the last independent prince in Asia Minor. She was still young and beautiful, and, what seemed more to the purpose in the estimation of Polemo, she was wealthy. With some still lingering remnant of religious feeling, she insisted upon her husband submitting to the outward rite of the Jewish religion, which he was quite willing to do, and accordingly became nominally a Jew, though St. Paul, writing a few years after, and bearing such cases in mind, would have said, " He is not a Jew, which is one outwardly; neither is that circumcision, which is outward in the flesh" (Rom. ii. 28). It is possible that Polemo and Bernice were in Asia Minor about the year 52, when St. Paul was travelling in the same region.

The union, however, did not last for any length of time, for Polemo was a man of inferior talents, and Bernice, through mere wantonness, craved for a life of greater excitement. She accordingly deserted her husband, and went back to her brother.

Bernice, in her various marriages and other connexions, was but one woman out of many. She had learned those evil ways from the "smart" ladies in the corrupt society at Rome, where such women as Messalina and Agrippina shone as brilliant stars in a black sky of deepest hue. The profligacy of women at that time was incredible. Luxury and extravagance, combined with immorality, were so rife, that marriage itself became discredited. Divorce indeed was easy, but marriage had become hateful. The holy associations of home, as they had existed under the ancient republic, had disappeared from society.

> What does our country need? . . .
> Not jewelled dolls with one another vying
>   For palms of beauty, elegance, and grace.
>
> But we want women, strong of soul, yet lowly,
>   With that rare meekness, born of gentleness,
> Women whose lives are pure and clean and holy,
>   The women whom all little children bless.
> Brave, earnest women, helpful to each other,
>   With finest scorn for all things low and mean;
> Women who hold the names of wife and mother
>   Far nobler than the title of a Queen.

Oh, these are they who mould the men of story,
  These mothers, oft-times shorn of grace and youth,
Who, worn and weary, ask no greater glory
  Than making some young soul the home of truth;
Who sow in hearts all fallow for the sowing
  The seeds of virtue and of scorn for sin,
And, patient, watch the beauteous harvest growing
  And weed out tares which crafty hands cast in.

Women who do not hold the gift of beauty
  As some rare treasure to be bought and sold,
But guard it as a precious aid to duty—
  The outer framing of the inner gold;
Women who, low above their cradles bending,
  Let flattery's voice go by, and give no heed,
While their pure prayers like incense are ascending;
  These are our country's pride, our country's need.[1]

II.

BERNICE AND ST. PAUL.

The only mention of Bernice in the New Testament is the fact of her presence with her brother Agrippa at the examination of St. Paul at Cæsarea.

¶ Cæsarea on the Sea is, next after Jerusalem, the most prominently mentioned city in the pages of the New Testament. It was indeed less ancient than Corinth or Ephesus, or even than Antioch or Thessalonica. Only about twenty years before the Christian era it was built and named in honour of the Roman emperor on a part of the coast of Palestine where merely a tower and a poor village had existed before. But the new city rapidly grew to be a place of large population and of no inconsiderable renown. Its magnificent harbour became the usual place of approach and departure for travellers to and from the Holy Land (Acts xviii. 22, xxv. 1, xxvii. 1, 2). The seat of government (Acts xxiii. 23, 33, xxv. 13), and the place where the largest military force of the country was quartered (Acts x. 1, xxv. 23), it was connected by good roads with Jerusalem and the interior (Acts xxiii. 31–33) and also (along the coast-line) with Ptolemais and all the north in one direction (Acts x. 5, 8, 23, 24). The

---

[1] E. W. Wilcox, *Maurine and other Poems*, 205.

greatness, however, of Cæsarea decayed almost as rapidly as it rose. In the course of a very few centuries it passed altogether out of the field of history; and now that city which in St. Paul's day was the most eminent and magnificent in Palestine is a mere collection of utter ruins on a desolate shore. It might seem as if these buildings had been raised up to be the scene of impressive Biblical histories. All their chief interest is connected with the family of the Herods, and with those Roman governors under whom the Jews were provincials.[1]

1. Felix had been about a year in office, as procurator of Judæa, when Agrippa the younger, who had continued at Rome, and was now about twenty-six, received from the Emperor, 53 A.D., an accession of dignity. He was removed from the kingdom of Chalcis, which he had held for four years, and was promoted to the tetrarchy of Herod Philip, comprising Trachonitis, Gaulanitis, Batanaea, and Ituraea, with the addition of Abilene. These yielded him an income of one hundred talents, or about £25,000 per annum, a moderate sum for royalty, but not so contemptible if we take into account the high value of money at that day. Agrippa now took leave of the Emperor, and embarked for his kingdom. He fixed his ordinary residence at Cæsarea Philippi, the capital, but he had also a palace, the patrimony of his family, at Jerusalem, on the brow of Sion, opposite the Temple, and he frequently made his abode there, particularly at the celebration of the principal festivals. It seems that Bernice also accompanied her brother Agrippa from Rome, and scandal, whether justly or not, still followed her into her own country.

2. It was during the procuratorship of Felix that St. Paul was arrested at Jerusalem and sent down to Cæsarea, for trial. Bernice's youngest sister, Drusilla, was now the wife of Felix, and in this way was destined, like her sister, to come into contact with the Apostle.

For two years Felix kept St. Paul in prison at Cæsarea in the hope that he would tire him out, and so at last force him to seek his liberation by means of a bribe. During all this time Felix would often send for his captive and hold conferences with him. St. Luke significantly informs us that Drusilla the wife of Felix

---

[1] J. S. Howson, *Scenes from the Life of St. Paul*, 138.

was a Jewess, connecting this statement with the fact that the
Roman governor "sent for Paul, and heard him concerning the
faith in Christ Jesus." The implied suggestion is that the nationality of the wife of Felix prompted his interest in his prisoner.
Perhaps Drusilla was drawn to the Apostle at first only from the
idle motive of curiosity. We have no information as to any impression he may have made on her. Since her dissolute husband
was deeply affected by the Apostle's trenchant words on the great
moral principles of temperance and righteousness, and alarmed to
trembling at the warnings he heard of coming judgment, it can
scarcely be that they meant nothing to Drusilla. And yet no
permanent effect was left on Felix, and we have no ground for
supposing that his wife yielded to the truth in which she had
shown some interest.

3. About the year 60, Felix was recalled, and was succeeded
in the governorship by Porcius Festus. Festus seems to have
been a better ruler, and probably he was a better man, than
Felix, but he cared little for religion, and could not understand
religious earnestness. He was perplexed about this Jewish
prisoner; it occurred to him that he might try the case at
Jerusalem; and it was then that St. Paul, apprehending the
danger he was in, took the great step of appealing to Cæsar.

Only a day or two had elapsed after the appeal, when
Agrippa II. and his sister came down to Cæsarea to pay their
respects to the new procurator. It was a compliment which they
could never safely omit, and we find that they paid similar visits
to each procurator in succession. The regal power of Agrippa,
such as it was, depended on no popular support, but simply and
solely on the will of the Emperor. As a breath had made him
king, first of Chalcis, then of the tetrarchy of Philip, and finally
of various other cities, so on any day a breath might unmake him.
He was not, like his father, "the king of the Jews," and therefore
St. Luke, with his usual accuracy in these details, calls him only
"the king"; but as he had succeeded his uncle Herod of Chalcis
in the guardianship of the Temple, with its sacred robes, and the
right of nomination to the high-priesthood, he practically became
a mere gilded instrument to keep order for the Romans, and it
was essential for him to remain on good terms with them. They

in their turn found it desirable to flatter the harmless vanities of a phantom royalty.

4. Festus received Agrippa and Bernice very graciously, and mutual hospitalities soon established an intimacy. In the course of conversation, Festus alluded to a subject which he rightly conceived would not be uninteresting to his guests. One may imagine the languid air of the palace when the conversation flagged, and Festus, for lack of other topics and because his guests were Jews, "laid Paul's case before the king." He relates the story (finely preserved by St. Luke) with an air of nonchalance and a tone of superiority to St. Paul and Jesus natural to this Roman governor of easy manners and morals. He stands for his adherence to Roman usage in the matter of the request at Jerusalem, and expresses his surprise at the pettiness of the Jewish charges against St. Paul, merely "certain questions against him of their own religion, and of one Jesus, who was dead, whom Paul affirmed to be alive."

"There is a certain man," he said, "left in bonds by Felix; about whom, when I was at Jerusalem, the chief priests and the elders of the Jews informed me, desiring to have judgment against him. To whom I answered, It is not the manner of the Romans to deliver any man to die, before that he which is accused have the accusers face to face, and have licence to answer for himself concerning the crime laid against him. Therefore, when they were come hither, without any delay on the morrow I sat on the judgment seat, and commanded the man to be brought forth. Against whom when the accusers stood up, they brought none accusation of such things as I supposed; but had certain questions against him of their own superstition, and of one Jesus, which was dead, whom Paul affirmed to be alive. And because I doubted of such manner of questions, I asked him whether he would go to Jerusalem, and there be judged of these matters. But when Paul had appealed to be reserved unto the hearing of Augustus, I commanded him to be kept till I might send him to Cæsar." Agrippa expressed a desire "to hear the man" himself. Next day, at Festus' commandment, Paul was brought forth.

5. It was not, as is commonly represented, a new trial. That

would have been, on all grounds, impossible. Agrippa was without judicial functions, and the authority of the procurator had been cut short by the appeal. It was more of the nature of a private or drawing-room audience—a sort of show occasion designed for the amusement of these princely guests, and the idle aristocracy of Cæsarea, both Jewish and Gentile. Festus ordered the auditorium to be prepared for the occasion, and invited all the chief officers of the army, and the principal inhabitants of the town. The 5th, 10th, and 15th legions or regiments of the line, besides five cohorts or auxiliary corps, with accompanying squadrons of cavalry, were usually stationed at Cæsarea, and the gleaming armour and gay attire of the great captains of the Roman army of Judæa, with the furred gowns and flowing robes of the municipal authorities, must have presented a most imposing spectacle, well calculated to stimulate the energies of the Christian advocate.

The Herods were fond of show, and Festus gratified their humour by a grand processional display. He would doubtless appear in his scarlet paludament, with his full attendance of lictors and bodyguard, who would stand at arms behind the gilded chairs which were placed for himself and his distinguished visitors. We are expressly told that Agrippa and Bernice went in state to the Prætorium, she, doubtless, blazing with jewels, and he in his purple robes, and both with the golden circlets of royalty around their foreheads, and attended by a suite of followers in the most gorgeous apparel of Eastern pomp. It was a compliment to the new governor to visit him with as much splendour as possible, and both he and his guests were not sorry to furnish a spectacle which would illustrate at once their importance and their mutual cordiality.

It was before this notorious brother and sister that St. Paul was now to present his case, as he had previously done before the younger sister Drusilla.

6. In their private conversation Festus had told the king that the main charge against him turned upon the fact that "one Jesus, which was dead," was affirmed by St. Paul to be alive. If Agrippa's heart had not been hardened, the bare mention of the Name would have stirred unpleasant memories. Did he think of

his great-grandfather Herod, and the massacre of the innocents? of his great-uncle Antipas, and the murder of John the Baptist? Did he realize how closely, but unwittingly, the faith in that "one Jesus" had been linked with the destinies of his house? It was James, an Apostle of Jesus, whom his father had beheaded; it was Peter, another Apostle of the same Jesus, whom he had cast into prison; and immediately after those two events he had gone down from Judæa to Cæsarea, and there, probably in the very hall where they were then assembled, while he was making an oration to the people, "immediately the angel of the Lord smote him, because he gave not God the glory: and he was eaten of worms, and gave up the ghost." The persecution of the followers of Jesus and the first Agrippa's death had been, we should imagine, inseparably linked together in history.

7. St. Paul had now before him one whose moral responsibility was greater than that of Festus, and to whose conscience a direct path was open through the remembrance of early religious impressions. Thus turning to him abruptly, after the brief dialogue with Festus, he exclaimed, "King Agrippa, believest thou the prophets? I know that thou believest."

Here it is that Agrippa uttered the words which are popularly understood as an acknowledgment that, under the pressure of this appeal, he was "almost persuaded to become a Christian"; and it is with reluctance that we deviate from this interpretation, remembering how often it has been used to point a most serious moral. But we really gain more than we lose by the correct translation, which may be given thus on the highest authority: "What? In so short a space, and on so slight a summons to become a Christian—to forfeit perhaps fortune and rank, and to become the brother and the fellow of an outcast like thee—to part with all, as the result of listening, in a casual visit, to a poor prisoner's self-defence—such changes are not for me!" It was a scornful retort, either uttered to disguise his real feelings, or the true expression of a cold heart; and derisive smiles from Festus and Bernice very probably accompanied the words.

The substance of the Apostle's reply, intensely earnest, but tenderly delicate, may be given on the same authority. "Well! be it sooner or later; be it on the sudden or on long reflection;

be it by my brief words, or by any other process which God may see fit in His wisdom and in His mercy to employ; my heart's desire and prayer is that thou, with all that hear me, mightest become such as I am, except these bonds." What a royal courtesy, what a commanding dignity, is in these memorable words! The true king here was the manacled and suffering prisoner, not the monarch seated in state by the side of the Emperor's representative and surrounded by all the pomp of office.

8. Now Bernice was present throughout this memorable scene. She heard the Apostle's thrilling account of his conversion; she heard his declaration about Christ; she heard him speak of the resurrection. What an utterly different world this Jew lived in from that in which she had been brought up! What an entirely new range of ideas he was setting before her! For a moment the golden gates were opened, and she looked into a realm of the very existence of which she had previously had no conception. It was her first introduction to the spiritual world. Like Balaam, she saw the star afar off. Faint and dim must have been her conception of it. We do not know whether it dwelt much with her. Yet she could not easily forget so impressive a scene. We may suppose it not unlikely that in rare quiet moments the memory of this inspired Jew and his startling message would float back into her mind and perhaps stir some slumbering thoughts of better things than she ever saw in her daily life at court.

¶ You have had such visions of Christ as have caused you to overflow with love. You have felt love within you as a river that has burst its banks and deluged your very nature. It was by the ministry of the Holy Ghost. Your glimpses, your visions, you wished them to abide there; but no, they passed on, and yet after they had gone, their very memory was to you inspiration, strength, and heaven in pledge.[1]

III.

BERNICE IN THE JEWISH WAR.

It is some years later, in the spring of 66 A.D., that we find Bernice in Jerusalem, influenced apparently by some revival of

[1] J. Parker.

womanly feeling. She had undertaken a vow, probably the vow of a Nazirite, under the stress of sickness; and for thirty days she went barefoot, and at the end of the period sacrificed the locks of her head. While this vow was in progress, the Jewish war had broken out, through the high-handed action of Florus, the last of the procurators of Judæa.

1. The war began at Cæsarea. The Syrian Greeks in that city did everything in their power to insult the Jews. They all but blocked up the entrance to the chief synagogue by buildings erected in its immediate vicinity, and Florus, while he calmly pocketed the immense bribe of eight talents given him by John the tax-gatherer to secure his interference, went away to Sebaste and did nothing. Collisions daily occurred between the wanton Greeks and the hot-headed young Jews. One Sabbath day a Greek placed an earthen pan near the entrance of the synagogue, and ostentatiously sacrificed small birds on the bottom of it. This was intended as a mockery of the Jewish rites for the purification of a leper, and was understood as a contumelious reference to the pagan scandal that the nation had been driven out of Egypt as a nation of lepers. John went with the chief Jews to implore the interference of Florus; but in spite of the huge bribe which he had received, the procurator simply threw them into prison.

The news of this outrage and injustice spread to Jerusalem. The city was in a state of violent excitement. It was the deliberate purpose of Florus to drive the people to insurrection, both that all inquiry into his former oppressions might be drowned by the din of war, and that he might have better opportunities for plunder. He seized this critical moment to demand seventeen talents from the sacred treasury under pretence of Cæsar's necessities. The people assembled around the Temple with the loudest outcries. The name of Florus was passed from one to another with every epithet of hatred and contempt. Some carried about a basket, entreating alms for the poor beggar, Florus

Florus entered Jerusalem with a large force, and refusing to be appeased by the submission of the people, gave the order for his troops to plunder the upper market and put to death all they met. The soldiery were but too ready instruments of his cruelty. They cleared the market, then broke into the houses, pillaged them, and put to death the inhabitants. The narrow streets were crowded with fugitives; many who escaped the sword were trampled to death. Unoffending citizens were seized, carried before Florus, scourged and crucified. Of men, women, and children—for neither age nor sex was spared—there fell that day 3600. Florus paid no regard to the sacred rights of Roman citizenship; some freedmen of the first distinction—for many of the Jews had attained even the equestrian rank—were scourged and executed with their meaner countrymen.

2. It was then that Bernice did the one redeeming act recorded in her infamous career. She and the principal Jews sent an embassy to Cestius to complain of the iniquities of the procurator. Horrified at the massacres and tortures of her countrymen, she herself, in all her beauty and misery, went before the brutal Florus with dishevelled tresses and naked feet to offer her weeping intercession. He heeded her so little that even in her presence Jews were scourged and murdered. She fled back to her palace, and even there she felt that her scanty bodyguard was so insufficient for her personal protection that she lived in the most intense alarm, her heart torn by pity for the monstrous wrongs and cruelties which she was compelled to witness and was impotent to restrain. Cestius decided to visit Jerusalem, and sent before him the centurion Neapolitanus. Agrippa met Neapolitanus at Jamnia, and they proceeded on their way together.

About seven or eight miles from Jerusalem, Neapolitanus and Agrippa were met by a mournful procession. The people were preceded by the wives of those who had been slain. The women, with wild shrieks and outcries, called on Agrippa for protection, and recounted to Neapolitanus all the miseries they had undergone from the cruelty of Florus. On the entrance of the king and the Roman into the city, they were led to the ruined market-place, and shown the shops that had been plundered, and the desolate houses where the inhabitants had been massacred. Neapolitanus, having passed through the whole city, and found it in profound peace, went up to the Temple, paid his adorations there in the court of the Gentiles, exhorted the people to maintain their loyal demeanour, and returned to Cestius.

Agrippa added his own entreaties. He summoned the people to meet him in the Xystos, the royal colonnade, which overlooked the city, and, seating himself on a lofty throne with Bernice by his side, he harangued the Jews at length, and held out to them the hope that, in this the extremity of their misery, Nero would send them a milder and juster procurator, and their miseries would be at an end. He pointed out to them the utter madness of a revolt against the Romans, who had subdued so many nations and kingdoms. He warned them that so hopeless an insurrection could have no possible result except the obliteration of their city and their religion and the desolation of their loved land. As he closed his harangue he burst into tears, and remained weeping, while Bernice stood weeping at his side. The people, moved by his eloquence, and the thought of their hopeless present misery and imminent peril, wept with them, and promised to pay the tribute. As a sign of their renewed allegiance, they agreed to restore the passage from the Castle Antonia to the Temple, their destruction of which was, as Agrippa pointed out to them, little short of an open declaration of war.

They began the work at once, and for one moment it might have seemed as if Jerusalem were saved. Agrippa and Bernice did their utmost to encourage them; but, in another harangue, Agrippa, while commending their repentance, urged them to continue their allegiance to Florus until Nero should send another procurator. The maddening name of Florus was too much for this strange, excitable people. They broke out into open maledictions. From curses on the name of Florus they passed to insults against Agrippa himself, his sister, his whole house. From insults they proceeded to stone-throwing, and passionately ordered him to leave the city. He did so, with a feeling of indignation and despair.

¶ The slightest passion in most people upsets their judgment.[1]

If thou examine things with hell-fire in thy heart,
How canst thou see distinct the good and bad apart?
Seek by degrees to drown that fire in holy light,
So shalt thou, sinner, soon thy weakness change for might.[2]

[1] Mark Rutherford, *Last Pages from a Journal*, 260.
[2] Jalaluddin Rumi, in *A Little Book of Eastern Wisdom*, 111.

3. In the riots which followed, the insurgents burned the palaces of the high priest, Agrippa, and Bernice, and then set fire to the public archives and all bonds in order to cancel all debts.

Throughout the rest of the war Agrippa and his sister were on the side of the Romans. In 75 A.D. he went to Rome, where he lived with his sister, with whom, in spite of her dubious reputation, Titus was so madly in love that, but for the open murmurs of the Romans, he would have made her his Empress. Finding in 79 A.D. that Titus, when he became Emperor, took no further notice of her, she retired to Palestine, and we hear no more about her. On her way she stopped at Athens, where an inscription in her honour still exists.

4. It is difficult for us to read the stories of these four queens —Herodias, and her daughter Salome, and the two sisters Bernice and Drusilla, all of them adulteresses, two of them guilty of foulest murder—and not set them apart from their sex as beneath the nature of womankind. There is no reason to minimize their crimes. We cannot compare them with the poor, miserable, outcast women whom Jesus treated so mercifully because those women, "sinners" as they were called, had become penitents, and probably throughout had been crushed down by poverty and ill-usage. These gay queens had no excuses to plead in defence of their shameless careers of crime. And yet there is much in heredity, and more in the influence of example. The royal sinners had never known a pure home life. They had been cradled in wickedness. We regard them as monsters of sin; but we must remember that there was something monstrous about the circumstances with which they had been surrounded from their childhood. It would have been a miracle if ever a virtuous woman had appeared in the family of the Herods.

Father is a townsman, mother from the far
Green southern uplands where wealthy pastures are:
My kith and my kindred are prosperous and sleek,
Who feed well and work well and thrive all the week.

But somewhere and sometime, many a year ago,
There was a gypsy woman, that right well I know,
A wild dark woman from the moor and wold,
Who bare me an ancestor in days of old.

They hushed up her memory, hid her name away,
Thought they had done with her for ever and a day—
Yet hath she left a heritage that none else shall win,
Whereunto my wandering feet have entered in.

For surely when the dead leaves scatter down the street,
With a rush and rustle, like little flying feet,—
When the sou'-west wakens, and with scared looks askance
The townsfolk hasten from the storm's advance,—

My whole soul sickens with a fierce desire,
Stress of sudden longing sets my blood on fire,
For the wind on the hill-top in a lonely place,
And the cold, soft raindrops blowing on my face;

For the steep-hung hedges of the winding road,
And the forest pathway by the stream o'erflowed;
For the storm-swept heather where the blackcock whirs,
And the salt wind whistles through the stunted firs;

For the brown wood-water, and the brown field's smell,
And the wide sea-marshes where the curlews dwell:
For the moorland black against the last red light,
And the sunk reef's breakers brawling to the night.

Hide within your houses with your glaring gas!
Mine shall be the peat-smoke in the beech-roofed grass:
Count your sordid silver, tell your grimy gain—
Mine shall be the treasures of the wind and rain![1]

[1] May Byron, *The Wind on the Heath*, 83.

PHŒBE.

LITERATURE.

Adeney, W. F., *Women of the New Testament* (1899), 217.

Conybeare, W. J., and J. S. Howson, *The Life and Epistles of St. Paul* (1870), 342, 497.

Edmunds, L., *Sunday by Sunday* (1903), **233**.

Garvie, A. E., *Romans* (Century Bible) (1901), 300, 315.

Howson, J. S., *The Companions of St. Paul* (1874), 126.

Maclaren, A., *Expositions* : St. Paul's Epistle to the Romans (1909), 352.

Moule, H. C. G., *The Epistle of Paul the Apostle to the Romans* (Cambridge Bible) (1881), 245.

„   „   *The Epistle of St. Paul to the Romans* (Expositor's Bible) (1894), 422.

Redlich, E. B., *St. Paul and his Companions* (1913), 264.

Sanday, W., and A. C. Headlam, *A Critical and Exegetical Commentary on the Epistle to the Romans* (International Critical Commentary) (1902), 416.

Dictionary of the Apostolic Church, ii. (1916) 231 (T. B. Allworthy).

Dictionary of the Bible, iii. (1900) 855 (A. C. Headlam).

PHŒBE.

I commend unto you Phœbe our sister, who is a servant of the church that is at Cenchreæ.—Rom. xvi. 1.

I.

The Church and Women.

1. It may be said with perfect truth that the religious service of women is characteristic of Christianity itself, and that we see this most clearly in connexion with St. Paul and his companions. That the gospel has raised woman to a higher point than any which she ever occupied before, we will admit. The place of woman among the Jews was indeed free and honourable as compared with her position either in Greece or in Rome, but in none of them was she placed on the level of man, or regarded mainly in the aspect of an equal possessor of the same life of the Spirit. But a religion which admits her to precisely the same position of a supernatural life as is granted to man necessarily relegates to a subordinate position all differences of sex as it does all other natural distinctions. Historically the emancipation of one half of the human race is the direct result of the Christian principle that all are one in Christ Jesus.

¶ Amongst the heathen *woman* is the down-trodden slave of man. She is kept working hard, and bears all the heavier burdens, while he walks by her side with musket, club, or spear. If she offends him, he beats or abuses her at pleasure. The girls have to toil and slave in the village plantations, to prepare all the materials for fencing these around, to bear every burden, and to be knocked about at will by the men and boys.

Oh, how sad and degraded is the position of Woman, where the teaching of Christ is unknown, or disregarded though known! It is the Christ of the Bible, it is His Spirit entering into

Humanity, that has lifted Woman, and made her the helpmate and the friend of Man, not his toy or his slave.[1]

2. The elevation of women through the coming of Him, who was Himself "born of woman," has left with them henceforward a peculiar power of efficient ministration. Such ministrations began even in the earliest gospel days, during the sojourn of our Saviour on earth. In fact all the great principles of the Christian life and the Christian Church, and this principle among the rest, were foreshadowed in the records of that biography. We may omit, if we will, the mention of Anna, the pious prophetess "of the tribe of Aser," as belonging rather to the end of the Old Dispensation than to the beginning of the New; and also of Mary, the mother of our Lord, and "her cousin Elisabeth," as standing apart in a sphere of their own. But when we turn beyond the period of Christ's infancy and youth, to the beginning of His active work, we find Him punctually aided by the devoted sympathy and service of women. They followed Him from place to place; they practised self-denial for His sake; they found their happiness in diminishing His toil and supplying His wants. No word is recorded in the New Testament as ever having been spoken against our Lord by a woman; many a man, but never a woman.

When St. Luke describes our Lord as going "throughout every city and village, preaching and shewing the glad tidings of the kingdom of God," he proceeds to say not merely that "the twelve were with him," but likewise "certain women." Three are specified; and it is added that there were "many others," who, with those three, "ministered to him of their substance." This was in Galilee, the scene of numerous journeys and of much active work. From thence "many of them" followed Him into Judæa, at a time when the Apostles were full of fear, and still the description given of them at the cross is that they were "ministering." From the cross to the grave they "followed" Him, and even at the grave itself we see in them the same spirit of serving. It might have been supposed when the great stone was placed at the door of the sepulchre, and when evening came on, that all occasion, all possibility, of "ministering" was over. But such was not the view of these women. When they went away from

[1] *John G. Paton: An Autobiography*, i. 146.

the sepulchre, it was still to do Him honour. They bought and prepared sweet spices for the embalmment of the body. Can we fail to see in this an anticipation and prophecy of that service by women which became a distinguishing mark of the Christian Church ?

¶ The idea and place of woman have been slowly and laboriously elevated by the Gospel: and their full development has constituted the purest and most perfect protest, that the world has ever seen, against the sovereignty of force. Now it is nowhere written in Holy Scripture that God is knowledge, or that God is power, while it is written that God is love : words which appear to set forth love as the central essence, and all besides as attributes. Woman then holds of God, and finds her own principal development in that which is most Godlike. Thus, therefore, when Christianity wrought out for woman, not a social identity, but a social equality, not a rivalry with the function of man, but an elevation in her own function reaching as high as his, it made the world and human life in this respect also a true image of the Godhead.[1]

3. If we turn to the Book of Acts, with the illustrations of it supplied by the Epistles, we find this service appearing in a more systematic form. As regards the women mentioned already, even they are seen once more, just after the Ascension, in company with the Apostles. And when they are lost to view, others become prominent in efficient ministrations.

It is in connexion with the life of St. Paul that we should expect the fullest notices of such ministrations by women as were characteristic of the earliest Church. With St. Paul everything takes a wider range; and we begin to see more clearly the place which women are destined to occupy in relation to the social life of Christendom. Lydia, Priscilla, the daughters of Philip, all did useful service in the Church. Damaris might fairly be adduced as an example of bold confession of the faith, such as women have often made when men have faltered. Chloe and Appia, Euodia and Syntyche, are mentioned by name among the women who were directly or indirectly associated with St. Paul in promoting the cause of the gospel at places as widely separated as Corinth, Colossæ, and Philippi. And in the Epistle to the Romans we find a catalogue of names of women which almost startles us, when

[1] W. E. Gladstone, *Studies on Homer*, ii.

we think of the early period to which this document belongs. The salutations in the sixteenth chapter, incidental as they are, give us much information as to the facts of the case. The number of female fellow-workers who are mentioned there by name, and with a distinct reference to their Christian co-operation, is remarkable.

¶ "What Nature originally decreed," Meredith said once, "men are but beginning to see, namely, that women are fitted for most of the avenues open to energy, and by their entering upon active life they will no longer be open to the accusation men so frequently bring against them of being narrow and craven."[1]

¶ However strong may have been the prejudice against a woman becoming captain, and taking her place upon the bridge, nobody could object to her becoming first mate; and it is as first mate that woman has rendered the most valuable service. A few, like Fanny Burney and Jane Austen and Charlotte Brontë and George Eliot, may have become skippers; but we could better afford to lose all the works of such writers than lose the influence which women have exerted over captains whom they served in the capacity of first mate. It was a saying of Emerson's that a man is entitled to credit, not only for what he himself does, but for all that he inspires others to do. To no subject does this axiom apply with greater force than to this. It would be a fatal mistake to suppose that the contribution of women to the republic of letters begins and ends with the works that bear feminine names upon their title-pages. Our literature is adorned by a few examples of acknowledged collaboration between a man and a woman, and only in very rare instances is the woman the minor contributor. But, in addition to these, there are innumerable records of men whose names stand in the foremost rank among our laureates and teachers, yet whose work would have been simply impossible but for the woman in the background. From a host of examples that naturally rush to mind we may instance, almost at random, the cases of Wordsworth, Carlyle, and Robert Louis Stevenson.[2]

> The woman singeth at her spinning-wheel
> A pleasant chant, ballad, or barcarole:
> She thinketh of her song, upon the whole,
> Far more than of her flax; and yet the reel
> Is full, and artfully her fingers feel
> With quick adjustment, provident control,
> The lines, too subtly twisted to unroll,

[1] J. Moffatt, *George Meredith*, 40.
[2] F. W. Boreham, *Mushrooms on the Moor*, 193.

Out to a perfect thread. I hence appeal
To the dear Christian Church—that we may do
Our Father's business in these temples mirk,
Thus swift and steadfast,—thus, intent and strong;
While, thus, apart from toil, our souls pursue
Some high, calm, spheric tune, and prove our work
The better for the sweetness of our song.[1]

II.

PHŒBE'S WORK AND PLACE.

Among the women who took a prominent place in the Early
Church was Phœbe—" a servant of the church " at Cenchreæ. As
regards both her direct association with St. Paul and the exact
account of her character and work, she must always demand our
special attention in connexion with this general subject.

St. Paul commends Phœbe to the Roman Church and bespeaks
for her a kind reception and assistance in whatever matter she
may have need of them. " Letters of commendation " played a
very large part in the organization of the Church, for the tie of
hospitality, implying also the reception to communion, was the
great bond which united the separate local Churches together, and
some protection became necessary against imposture.

1. Phœbe is introduced to his readers by St. Paul in Rom.
xvi. 1, 2, presumably as the bearer of the letter. The Imperial
post was not available for private correspondence, and such a
letter could be sent only by special messenger or by a trusted
friend who happened to be travelling. Phœbe was about to visit
Rome, and the Apostle, hearing of her projected journey, seized
the opportunity of writing and despatching his letter.

Phœbe is not mentioned again in the New Testament, and
nothing further is known of her than may be gathered from this
reference. The name is that of the moon-goddess, the sister of
Phœbus (Apollo). It is interesting to notice that a Christian
woman in the Apostolic Age did not think it necessary to discard
the name of a heathen deity. That Phœbe was evidently preparing to travel alone suggests that she was a widow. She could not

[1] E. B. Browning.

(according to Greek manners) have been mentioned as acting in the independent manner described, either if her husband had been living or if she had been unmarried.

¶ Women played no part in social intercourse at Athens. There were but few occasions when the girls left the close confinement of the women's apartments for any kind of publicity. And as the door which separates the women's apartments from the rest of the house is the boundary set for a maiden, so the door which shuts the house off from the street must be the boundary for the wife.

Women of the better classes only went out attended by a servant or slave, and then but seldom. A respectable woman stayed at home as much as possible; in fact, the symbol of domestic life was a tortoise, a creature which never leaves its home, and was regarded as an attribute of Aphrodite Urania.[1]

2. Phœbe's Christian associations were with the Church at Cenchreæ of which little Christian community nothing further is known. Cenchreæ was the port of Corinth, on the Saronic Gulf, looking eastward towards Ephesus, and therefore the place through which all the traffic of the Achaian capital with Asia passed to and fro. Here St. Paul once tarried for a while when he had shorn his head, according to Jewish custom, to mark the expiration of a vow. Its position would afford an excellent opportunity for the exercise by Phœbe of the special duties of hospitality.

If again we take into account the hideous immoralities of Corinth we shall count it probable that the port, with its shifting maritime population, was, like most seaports, a soil in which goodness was hard put to it to grow, and a church had much against which to struggle. To be a Christian at Cenchreæ can have been no light task. Travellers in Egypt are told that Port Said is the wickedest place on the face of the earth; and in Phœbe's home there would be a like drift of disreputables of both sexes and of all nationalities. It was fitting that one good woman should be recorded as redeeming womanhood there.

> A youth is a madcap, and time is a churl,
>   Pleasure calls and remorse follows after;
> The world hustles on in its pitiless whirl,
>   With its kisses, its tears, and its laughter.

[1] H. Blümner, *The Home Life of the Ancient Greeks*, 133, 150.

But there's one gentle heart in its bosom of white—
  The maid with the tender eyes gleaming—
Who has all the wealth of my homage to-night,
  Where she lies in her innocent dreaming.
And a watch over her my spirit shall keep,
  While the angels lean down to caress her,
And I'll pledge her again in her beautiful sleep—
  The woman that's good—God bless her!

Ah, Bohemia's honey is sweet to the sip,
  And the song and the dance are alluring!
The mischievous maid with the mutinous lip
  Has a charm that is very enduring!
But out from the smoke wreaths and music and lace
  Of that world of the tawdrily clever,
There floats the rare spell of the pure little face
  That has chased away folly forever.
And I drain my last toast ere I go to my rest—
  O, fortunate earth to possess her—
To the dear, tender heart in the pure, white breast
  Of the woman that's good—God bless her!

3. Now look at the way in which Phœbe is spoken of.

(1) She is first described as "our sister." Thus a member of the Christian community is designated in the affectionate simplicity of primitive times. In using the plural "our," the Apostle may be including the two or three fellow-missionaries who accompanied him on his travels, or he may be writing in the name of the Church at Corinth with the associated branch Church at Cenchreæ.

(2) Then Phœbe is called "a servant of the church that is at Cenchreæ," and the word translated "servant" is the Greek *diaconos*, from which our word "deacon" is derived. Hence it has been inferred that Phœbe was a deaconess. On the other hand, we must not forget that the Greek word was used in a very general sense in early times, quite apart from official relations. It does not appear as the title of an official before the Pastoral Epistles—unless the case before us may be cited for that usage earlier. And further, it is not the feminine deaconess (*diaconissa*), but the masculine, which will serve for either sex, but which seems to imply that it does not stand for a definite feminine office. If it must be assigned to some church function here we should

conclude that this was one open to men and women alike. But nothing of the kind was known in the primitive Church. By the time of the Pastoral Epistles the "widows" seem to have been organized into an order. Thus St. Paul writes, "Let none be enrolled as a widow under three-score years old," etc.; and yet the limit of age points to eleemosynary purposes rather than to service. You would not require a woman to be old before electing her for some work in the Church. Still there must have been women to do certain things for their own sex, such as attending on them at their baptism. We are too much inclined to think these services were relegated to definitely appointed officials from the first. In the simple family life of the Early Church this would not be thought of. The ministry preceded the office; and later the office grew out of the ministry. In the primitive Church much was made of service, little of office. Methods were free and elastic; fluidity had not yet been followed by crystallization. Before long, we know, there was a definite order of deaconesses in the Church. This was so in Bithynia at least, in the reign of Trajan; for Pliny writes that he obtained his information concerning the Christians by torturing "two hand-maidens" (*ancillæ*), whom the Christians call "servants" (*ministræ*). Notice that the technical word *diaconissa* is not employed here. Later the so-called "Apostolical Constitutions" refer to the deaconess, who must be "a chaste virgin." On the other hand, Tertullian writes of "widows" and "mothers" being in the order. We must not assume that Phœbe was a deaconess in the full later sense of the word; but that her position was analogous to that of the later deaconesses seems most probable.

¶ The word "minister" is Latin, and the word "deacon" is Greek; but they both mean the same thing, a "servant." As "ministers" and "deacons"—distinctively so called—we may have different duties to fulfil; but we are all "ministers" in the wider sense of the word. Our offices are offices of ministry—of service. We are all called to serve Christ by serving in a special manner the Church of Christ.[1]

(3) St. Paul further describes Phœbe as "a succourer of many." This phrase is very beautiful: and, even in the English, it means a great deal. But the English phrase fails to express

---

[1] T. C. Finlayson, *Essays, Addresses, and Lyrical Translations*, 276.

the whole sense of the original. "Succour" may be given in various ways; but the term here employed would seem to indicate one who had stood forth as the patroness of the unprotected and despised. There is no doubt that the Christians were objects of contempt at this time in Achaia; and even if this were not the case, the Greek word would in itself imply moral courage, generous bounty, and large sympathy. Phœbe had been a devoted and it would seem particularly *a brave* friend of converts in trouble. Perhaps in the course of her visits to the desolate she had fought difficult battles of protest, where she found harshness and oppression. Perhaps she had pleaded the forgotten cause of the poor, with a woman's courage, before some neglectful richer " brother."

Among the Jews the Greek word here translated "succourer' meant also the wealthy patron of a Jewish community; such an one was the Roman centurion who built a synagogue for the Jews in Capernaum. There seems good reason, therefore, for supposing that Phœbe was a person of some rank and substance. We might place her in comparison with the "great woman" of Shunem, dwelling "among her own people," who showed hospitality to Elisha; and certainly the Apostle's feeling finds expression in language very similar in tone to that used by the Prophet: "Behold, thou hast been careful for us with all this care; what is to be done for thee?" In a special degree, made possible by her circumstances, she discharged the duties of "communicating to the necessities of the saints" and of "pursuing hospitality," which belonged to all Christians alike.

> I know a woman
> Who lives life with a childlike zest
> And has a heart for all things human;
> And well she loves the world, and best
> Whatever in the world is loveliest;
> Yet cannot wholly scorn the rest—
> Vice, dirt,
> And poverty, and helplessness, and pest.
> Not hers to avert
> From the prone wretch beneath the wayside palm
> The virtuous Levite skirt:
> She asks not, What is his desert?
> But, Is he hurt?

That found,
She pours her cunning oils into the wound
And tends the wastrel with the costliest balm.
For this she made
Herself a Good Samaritan by trade;
Cloaked her large heart
And bounteous feeling
Behind the faculty and art
Of healing:
That ofttimes those whom she relieves
Give, kneeling,
Thanks for that day they fell among the thieves.[1]

(4) Phœbe had been not only "a succourer of many" but of St. Paul himself. It has been conjectured that the personal reference ("and of mine own self") may be to an illness in which Phœbe ministered to St. Paul at Cenchreæ, and that his recovery was the occasion of his vow. Certainly we may assume that she received him into her home when he visited or passed through Cenchreæ, and that she "mothered" him as did the mother of Rufus. The house in which the Apostle stayed naturally became a centre for the community, and if it was also used as the meeting-place of the Church, the owner must have been looked up to as a kind of "president," to whom the term "patron" might suitably be applied. In some such way as this Phœbe devoted herself and her means to the service of the Church.

¶ "It is told me," writes Li Hung Chang in his diary, "that of all those fair women who have been mistresses of the Executive Mansion at Washington, Mrs. Cleveland is one of the most lovable. This I can readily believe, for I do not know when or where I have seen a face and form more pleasing to the eye. I would call her the Mother of Graciousness and the Sister of Heavenly Love. As the Chief Lady of the United States she is an ornament to her sex, and a glory to womankind the world over."[2]

¶ Do you ask how your work may be truly effective? I answer you in the words of the text, "He took the damsel by the hand." There must be an intensity of human sympathy, and there must be an indwelling of Divine power. The lesson of the miracle which I have taken for my starting-point involves

[1] E. Garrett, *A Woman Doctor.*
[2] *Memoirs of Li Hung Chang,* 179.

both these ideals. The current of womanly sympathy must flow
out deep, and strong, and clear. Is not this the typical meaning of Christ's action in the text. The touch of His warm hand
restores the circulation and revives the life in those pale, motion-
less, death-like limbs. We find sympathy here, sympathy first,
and sympathy last—sympathy reflecting, however faintly, Christ's
own boundless compassion and love. The cold, mechanical
formalism of the relieving officer will not suffice; the haughty
assertion of superiority, the condescending patronage of the fine
lady will be worse than nothing. You must be a sister to your
sisters, treading in the footsteps of your Brother, Jesus Christ.[1]

4. Phœbe, then, is about to set out for Rome, and the Apostle
follows her with his gratitude. The letter which she carries is
a record of what he owes to her; and this obligation is made
the ground of an appeal to the Roman Christians, to enforce the
duty of their receiving her with confidence and respect, and of
aiding her to the utmost of their power.

They are to "receive her in the Lord, worthily of the saints,"
and to "*assist*" her in whatsoever matter she may have need." Each
of these clauses merits a separate and careful attention. "In the
Lord" is a customary phrase with St. Paul. It denotes in such
a passage as this community of interest under Christ, and points
to the fact that all the persons in question, and all their concerns,
belong to Him. But it means even more than this. It suggests
the thought of co-operation in the same kind of religious work.
We might compare what is said here to the Romans of Phœbe
with what is said to the Corinthians of Timothy: "If Timothy
come, see that he be with you without fear; for he worketh the
work of the Lord, as I also do";—or with what is said to the
Philippians of Epaphroditus: "Receive him in the Lord with all
gladness; and hold such in honour: because for the work of
Christ he came nigh unto death." As to the phrase, "worthily
of the saints," it may be difficult to decide whether the meaning
is that Phœbe is to be received in such a manner as she herself
deserves, or in such a manner as would be a matter of course with
the Roman Christians if they were what they professed to be.
We may be quite content to leave this point indeterminate, and
to consider that the phrase includes both meanings.

[1] J. B. Lightfoot.

And, further, they were not only to give her a friendly and worthy reception, but to furnish her with all the assistance she needed for the errands on which she was sent. Such a request was clearly most reasonable. St. Paul is here asking help for one who herself had been a helper of "many." What Phœbe's business at Rome was, is quite unknown to us. It may have concerned property, and involved inquiries and directions about law. Or it may have been (though less probably) religious business.

¶ La Bruyère, that philosopher, always accessible, even in the deepest studies, who tells you to come in, for you bring him something more precious than gold or silver, *if it is the opportunity of obliging you.*[1]

5. Whether Phœbe at last laid down her life as did St. Paul and so many of the early Christians, we know not; whether she always stayed on at Rome, we cannot tell. But many there were who could rise up and bless her for her goodness and sympathy, and practical help. She went to her rest and her reward many centuries ago, and two verses tell us what we know of her. St. Paul commended her, and no doubt St. Paul's Master also commended her when her day's work was done in the world. By us Phœbe might well be commended as setting forth the most womanlike ideal. Her ministry was a ministry of help; and surely such gentle ministry is that which most befits the woman's heart and comes most graciously to the woman's fingers. In this world of woe and need, there is ever a cry, even in apparently successful lives, for help and a helper. Man's clumsy hand is but too apt to hurt where it strives to soothe, and nature itself seems to devolve on the swifter sympathies and more delicate perceptions of woman the joy of binding up wounded spirits.

¶ You women are so kind, and in your kindness have such wise perception, you know so well how to be affectionate and full of solicitude without appearing to be; your gentleness of feeling is like your touch—so light and easy that the one enables you to deal with wounds of the mind as tenderly as the other enables you to deal with wounds of the body.[2]

[1] Sainte-Beuve.　　　　[2] Charles Dickens.

In the darkest path of man's despair,
Where War and Terror shake the troubled earth,
Lies woman's mission; with unblenching brow
To pass through scenes of horror and affright
Where men grow sick and tremble: unto her
All things are sanctified, for all are good.
Nothing so mean, but shall deserve her care:
Nothing so great, but she may bear her part.
No life is vain: each hath his place assigned:
Do thou thy task, and leave the rest to God.[1]

[1] *The Life and Letters of Lewis Carroll*, 356.

TERTIUS.

LITERATURE.

Banks, L. A., *The Great Saints of the Bible* (1902), **317.**

Deissmann, G. A., *Bible Studies* (1901), 21.

Farrar, F. W., *The Life and Work of St. Paul* (1897), 452.

Gregory, C. R., *Canon and Text of the New Testament* (1907), 300, 302.

Maclaren, A., *Expositions* : St. Paul's Epistle to the Romans (1909), 395.

Milligan, G., *St. Paul's Epistles to the Thessalonians* (1908).

    ,,   ,, *The New Testament Documents* (1913), 241.

Moule, H. C. G., *The Epistle of Paul the Apostle to the Romans* (Cambridge Bible) (1881), 254.

    ,,   ,,   *The Epistle of St. Paul to the Romans* (Expositor's Bible) (1894), 435.

Redlich, E. B., *St. Paul and his Companions* (1913), 58, 278.

Sanday, W., and A. C. Headlam, *A Critical and Exegetical Commentary on the Epistle to the Romans* (International Critical Commentary) (1902), lx. 431.

Weiss, B., *A Manual of Introduction to the New Testament*, ii. (1888) 403.

Christian World Pulpit, xlvi. (1894) 230 (W. J. Henderson).

Contemporary Pulpit, 1st Ser., vi. (1886) 221 (A. Maclaren).

Homiletic Review, xx. (1890) 154 (H. J. Parker).

TERTIUS.

I Tertius, who write the epistle, salute you in the Lord.—Rom. xvi. 22.

1. St. Paul on whom was laid as a daily burden, "anxiety for all the churches," found quickly that he could keep in touch with the communities he had founded only by means of letters or epistles. And there can be little doubt that those writings of his which have come down to us are only part of a large correspondence which he carried on in order to confirm and develop the work that had been begun in the course of his missionary journeys.

He did not write his letters with his own hand. Thus history repeats itself. The older men of to-day grew up at a time at which most men wrote for themselves what they wished to entrust to paper. To-day, however, everyone is eager to have an assistant with a writing machine, or to tell his thoughts to a gramophone and hand that over to his typewriting clerk. So was it in St. Paul's day. Even men who could write were in the habit of having scribes to do the drudgery of writing for them. If a man was not rich, he might have a young friend or a pupil who was ready to wield the pen for him. It comports less with the dignity of age in the East to write. St. Paul had a good reason for using another's hand, if his eyes were weak. It was Tertius who wrote the Epistle to the Romans, if the sixteenth chapter belongs to it. Timothy and Lucius, and Jason, and Sosipater were probably all sitting round Paul and Tertius, at Corinth, when Tertius wrote their greetings in xvi. 21, and added his own before he went on to name Gaius.

¶ The letters were written on papyrus. The costlier pergament, which was used for copies of the Old Testament books, was not only beyond the Apostle's slender means, but would have been out of keeping with the fugitive and occasional character he himself ascribed to his writings. And he would naturally fall back upon a material which was easily procurable, and whose use for the purposes of writing had already a long history behind it.

In itself papyrus is derived from the papyrus-plant (*Cyperus papyrus*, L.), and was prepared for the purposes of writing according to a well-established process, of which the elder Pliny (NH. xiii. 11–13) has left a classical account.[1]

2. In speaking of St. Paul's amanuensis, we must think, not of a professional scribe, but rather of some educated friend or companion who happened to be with the Apostle at the time (cf. Rom. xvi. 21). The writing would then be of the ordinary, non-literary character, though doubtless more than the usual care would be taken in view of the importance of the contents. The words, in accordance with general practice, would be closely joined together. Contractions, especially in the way of leaving out the last syllables of familiar words, would be frequent. And, as a rule, accents and breathings would be only sparingly employed. The bearing of these facts upon the various readings that crept later into the Pauline texts is at once obvious. But for our present purpose it is more important to ask, How much was St. Paul in the habit of leaving to his amanuensis? Did he dictate his letters word for word, his scribe perhaps taking them down in some form of shorthand? Or was he content to supply a rough draft, leaving the scribe to throw it into more formal and complete shape? It is true that to these questions no definite answer can be given. In all probability the Apostle's practice varied with the special circumstances of the case, or the person of the scribe whom he was employing. But, in any case, the very fact that such questions can be put at all shows how many of the difficulties regarding the varied style and phraseology of the different Epistles might be solved if only we had clearer knowledge of the exact conditions under which they were severally written.

¶ What hired amanuensis can be equal to the scribe who loves the words that grow under his hand, and to whom an error or indistinctness in the text is more painful than a sudden darkness or obstacle across his path? And even these mechanical printers who threaten to make learning a base and vulgar thing —even they must depend on the manuscript over which we

---

[1] G. Milligan, *The Epistle to the Thessalonians*, 122.

scholars have bent with that insight into the poet's meaning which is closely akin to the *mens divinior* of the poet himself; unless they would flood the world with grammatical falsities and inexplicable anomalies that would turn the very fountain of Parnassus into a deluge of poisonous mud.[1]

¶ Dean Stanley's Commentary was crowded with typographical errors. For these anyone acquainted with Stanley's handwriting might be fully prepared. One instance is quoted by him in writing to Professor Jowett. "'The Horn of the Burning Beast.' What Apocalyptic mystery do you conjecture is veiled beneath these words? 'The thorn of the burning Bush.'"[2]

I.

TERTIUS THE AMANUENSIS.

1. In a room, then, in the house of Gaius, a wealthy Corinthian Christian, Paul the Apostle, having at his side his amanuensis, Tertius, addresses himself to write to the converts of the mission at Rome. We enter in spirit the Corinthian citizen's house, in the sunshine of the early Greek spring, and find our way, invisible and unheard, to where Tertius sits with his reed-pen and strips of papyrus, and where St. Paul is prepared to give him (shall we say?), word by word, sentence by sentence, this immortal message. Perhaps the corner of the room is heaped with hair-cloth from Cilicia and the implements of the tent-maker. But the Apostle's host is a man whose means enable him to be "the host of the whole church"; so we may rather think that for the time this manual toil is intermitted. The Lord speaks through His servant. Tertius, the scribe, is busy with his pen, as the message of Christ is uttered through the soul and from the lips of St. Paul.

¶ When God would do anything among men He chooses and uses a man. When He wanted to grow a nation that would stand for the highest ideals of revealed religion, even as later Greece stood for letters, and Rome for the power of organization, He chose a man up in the Euphrates Valley. And about this man,

---

[1] George Eliot, *Romola*.
[2] R. E. Prothero, *The Life of Dean Stanley*, i. 475.

Abraham, He began slowly to build up that strange people which has had the greatest influence of any upon the nations of the earth. When that nation, not yet fully born as a nation, was in sore danger of being throttled in its birth, He took a man, Moses, chosen from his birth, graduate in the highest learning of earth's best schools, who has left the indelible marks of his native gifts and special training upon that people, and upon the life of the whole race.

With deepest reverence be it said, when God would redeem a world He sent a Man.[1]

> " 'Tis God gives skill,
> But not without men's hands: He could not make
> Antonio Stradivari's violins
> Without Antonio." [2]

2. A Christian, thinking of the pretty editions of the Bible that we have, would say that Tertius, when he wrote St. Paul's letter to the Romans, must surely have used those large and fine letters which we call uncials. But those who know what people at that day were likely to write would say no. It was a letter that Tertius was writing, even if it was a very large letter. It was an essay, a treatise, an article; but it was the habit then, as it often has been since, upon occasion, to write such an essay in the form of a letter. And such a letter would be written, not in the formal stiff capitals, but in the running hand. A running hand was just what the name says, handwriting written at a run, written in a hurry, as so many people write to-day. The letters were at first, we might say, just like those capital letters. But the swiftness of the strokes had impaired the form of the letters. If we look at many a handwriting that we see to-day and ask how much a *d* or an *m* or a *u* looks like the printed form of those letters or like the forms given in copy-books, we may understand that in the same way the writing that Tertius wrote in all probability contained many strange-looking letters. The letters will often have been written close together, and all joined together without respect to the division between words. We cannot at all tell how well Tertius was able to write. We do not know whether he wrote a clear hand or whether he wrote a bad hand. The

---

[1] S. D. Gordon, *Quiet Talks on Personal Problems*, 81.
[2] George Eliot, *Stradivarius*.

chances are that he wrote well. That may be the reason why he, and not Timothy or Lucius or Jason or Sosipater, who were all there at the time, was asked to do the writing.

¶ Ruskin very rarely dictated, but it was one of the duties of his personal servant—successively "George," Crawley, and Baxter—to make fair copies of his rough drafts; a task often undertaken in later years by Mrs. Severn.[1]

3. One would like to know whether Tertius appreciated the Epistle to the Romans. Doubtless he did, as well as one could then. But he could not value it as we do after these centuries, during which it has instructed and warned and chided and comforted hundreds of thousands of Christians.

Judging by his name, he was probably a Roman, and possibly had some connexion with Italy, but clearly he was a stranger to the Church in Rome. We do not know whether he was a resident in Corinth, where he wrote this Epistle, or one of St. Paul's travelling companions. Probably he was the former, as his name never recurs in any of St. Paul's letters. One can understand the impulse which led him for one moment to come out of obscurity and to take up personal relations with those who had so long enjoyed his pen. He would fain float across the deep gulf of alienation a thread of love which looked like gossamer, but has proved to be stronger than centuries and revolutions.

But all that we really know of Tertius who wrote the Epistle is that he wrote it. He ventures, however, in closing it, to add his salutations to those to whom the Apostle had directed him to write. He appears here for a moment and is gone, just as a star sometimes for an instant emerges from a cloud, shines brightly and is swallowed up again by the darkness. This one utterance, however, gives him an immortality.

¶ Probably he did not know a single Christian in Rome. All those people were strange to him, and they did not know there was such a man. But Tertius, lonely, homesick for love and fellowship, puts in his little love note on the margin, saying, in substance, "I Tertius, Paul's amanuensis, who wrote down this epistle from his holy lips, I, too, am a Christian, and I salute you in the Lord. You don't know me, and I don't know you, but we both know the Lord, and I think you will like to know when you

[1] E. T. Cook, *The Life of Ruskin*, i. 366.

read these words of Paul that it was a faithful Christian hand which wrote them down for you." [1]

¶ Tradition reckons Tertius one of the Seventy and as having become Bishop of Iconium. The same traditions are stated in the *Menologium Basilianum*, where he is commemorated on November 10, together with Olympas, Rhodion, Sosipater, Erastus, and Quartus, and in the *Acta Sanctorum*, where he is commemorated on June 20, together with Jesus Justus and Artemas (June, vol. iv. pp. 7 and 8).[2]

II.

THE SALUTATION OF TERTIUS.

"I Tertius, who write the epistle, salute you in the Lord." He wanted the Romans to know that they owed something of their instruction even to him. He liked to think there would be some kind of bond of mutual affection if they did.

¶ Tertius writing "in the Lord" aids an Apostle to get his thoughts circulated throughout the world. The dependence of the great upon the small, how common that is and how impressive! The artist asks the guidance of a rustic; poets, philosophers, statesmen are indebted to lowly craftsmen for the publication of their fancies, speculations, and plans. The great admiral is rowed by a common sailor to the ship which is to lead the fleet to victory. The soul of Paul utilizes the skill Tertius acquired in his pre-Christian days—a fact reminding us that the employment of common powers is almost or quite as necessary as the exercise of distinguished ability.[3]

1. We can discern in Tertius' words a little touch of what we may call pride in his work. No doubt he knew it to be subordinate, but he also knew it to be needful; and no doubt he had put all his strength into doing it well. No man will put his best into any task which he does not undertake in such a spirit. It is a very plain piece of homely wisdom that "what is worth doing at all is worth doing well." Without a lavish expenditure of the utmost care and effort, our work will tend to be slovenly and

---

[1] L. A. Banks, *The Great Saints of the Bible*, 318.

[2] E. Basil Redlich, *St. Paul and his Companions*, 278.

[3] W. J. Henderson.

unpleasing to God, and to man, and to ourselves. We may be sure there were no blots and bits of careless writing in Tertius' manuscript, and that he would not have claimed the friendly feelings of his Roman brethren, if he had not felt that he had put his best into the writing of this Epistle. The great word of King David has a very wide application. "I will not take that which is thine for the Lord, nor offer burnt offerings without cost."

> For me—to have made one soul
>   The better for my birth:
> To have added but one flower
>   To the garden of the earth:
> To have struck one blow for truth
>   In the daily fight with lies:
> To have done one deed of right
>   In the face of calumnies:
> To have sown in the souls of men
>   One thought that will not die—
> To have been a link in the chain of life:
>   Shall be immortality.[1]

¶ J. D. Brash came to Manchester. His mother came to live with him, and while attending the church in which he was minister, gave her heart to God. Her son asked her to attend his society class, but her Scotch reserve made her insist upon a promise being given by him that he would never call upon her to speak. To this he assented, but said that he would tell the story of her conversion. At the first class-meeting he began to tell the story, but he had not travelled far before his mother very excitedly said, "You are not telling it right, Jack," and forthwith speedily poured forth the story of her new-found love. He often told this to prove that when the most timid soul is aglow with love, there is something which makes it claim a share in the spiritual conversation of the class-meeting.[2]

2. Is Tertius to be censured as intrusive for making mention of himself? The appearance of the personal element is valuable, and sometimes it may even be conspicuous without offence to humility. As a witness it is never impertinent. It is proper for Tertius the scribe to show himself, for he is an instance in point, and has something to say which is important to a right decision. He has a right to lift his head and say, "Amen!"

---

[1] E. Hatch.   [2] *Love and Life: The Story of J. Denholm Brash*, 42.

¶ Sir Joshua Reynolds painted a picture of the famous Sarah Siddons in the character of the Tragic Muse. The portrait was a great success, and pleased both the artist and the public. The soul of the theme was so embodied on the canvas, and the poetry so incarnated in pose and expression, that many persons were strongly affected in contemplating it. The great artist assured the gifted Mrs. Siddons that the colours would remain unfaded as long as the canvas would hold together, and gracefully and gallantly added, "And to confirm my opinion, here is my name; for I have resolved to go down to posterity on the hem of your garment." Accordingly, his name appears on the border of the drapery. So Tertius comes down to us from the past, and will go on to the future, so long as the Bible is loved and honoured among men, on the margin of Paul's letter to the Romans.[1]

3. Here, as we seem to discern the scene, there is indeed a pause, and what might look like an end. Tertius lays down the pen. The circle of friends breaks up, and St. Paul is left alone—alone with his unseen Lord, and with that long, silent letter; his own, yet not his own.

> Yes, without cheer of sister or of daughter,
> Yes, without stay of father or of son,
> Lone on the land and homeless on the water
> Pass I in patience till the work be done.
>
> Yet not in solitude if Christ anear me
> Waketh Him workers for the great employ
> Oh not in solitude, if souls that hear me
> Catch from my joyaunce the surprise of joy.
>
> Hearts I have won of sister or of brother
> Quick on the earth or hidden in the sod,
> Lo every heart awaiteth me, another
> Friend in the blameless family of God.[2]

[1] L. A. Banks, *The Great Saints of the Bible*, 317.
[2] F. W. H. Myers, *Saint Paul*.

PHILEMON.

LITERATURE.

Ainger, A., *The Gospel and Human Life* (1904), 256.

Bonar, H., *Light and Truth* : The Lesser Epistles (1870), 204.

Brown, H. S., *Manliness and Other Sermons* (1889), 257, 273.

Deane, A., *Friends and Fellow Labourers of St. Paul* (1906), 54.

Drury, T. W., *The Prison-Ministry of St. Paul* (1911), 123.

Henson, H. H., *Light and Leaven* (1897), 236.

Hiley, R. W., *A Year's Sermons*, iii. (1897) 305.

Hole, S. R., *Hints to Preachers* (1880), 105.

Lightfoot, J. B., *Saint Paul's Epistles to the Colossians and to Philemon* (1879), 303.

Maclaren, A., *Colossians and Philemon* (Expositor's Bible) (1887), 417.

Parker, J., *The City Temple*, i. (1870) 405.

Seekings, H. S., *The Men of the Pauline Circle* (1914), 117.

Thorne, H., *Notable Sayings of the Great Teacher*, 223.

Vincent, M. R., *A Critical and Exegetical Commentary on the Epistles to the Philippians and to Philemon* (International Critical Commentary) (1897), 157.

Witherow, J. M., *Grapes of Gold* (1914), 13.

Dictionary of the Apostolic Church, ii. (1916) 212 (H. Cowan).

Dictionary of the Bible, iii. (1900) 622 (W. Lock), 832 (J. H. Bernard).

Expositor, 3rd Ser., v. (1887) 138 (F. Godet).

PHILEMON.

Paul, a prisoner of Christ Jesus, and Timothy our brother, to Philemon our beloved and fellow-worker, and to Apphia our sister, and to Archippus our fellow-soldier, and to the church in thy house: Grace to you and peace from God our Father and the Lord Jesus Christ.—Philem. i.

OUR only source of information about Philemon in the New Testament is the short letter addressed to him by St. Paul. He was most probably a native of Colossæ (cf. Philem. 1 with Col. iv. 17); and in Theodoret's time his house was pointed out in that city. Tradition speaks of him as bishop of Colossæ; and the *Menœa* of November 22 record his martyrdom there, by stoning, in company with Apphia, Archippus, and Onesimus, in the reign of Nero. In the case of such facts as these, local tradition may generally be regarded as trustworthy; and here it falls in with the documentary evidence, for the idea that Philemon was of Laodicea is a mere guess.

From the letter, brief as it is, we gain a vivid impression of the character of the man to whom it was written.

I.

THE MAN.

1. In the city of Colossæ, in the beautiful basin of the Lycus in Phrygia, there lived a rich citizen named Philemon. This man, as we gather from the Epistle, had been brought by St. Paul himself to the knowledge of Christ; and as St. Paul had never visited the churches of the district in which Colossæ was (Col. ii. 1), we must conclude that the rich Phrygian burgher had been converted by the Apostle at Ephesus during a visit which he paid to that capital.

Like Epaphras he had visited Ephesus from Colossæ, had

listened to St. Paul's message during the three years' ministry in that city, and may well have found his spiritual birthplace in the "school of Tyrannus" where the Apostle taught.

The wife of Philemon, we find from the second verse of the Epistle, was named Apphia, and as St. Paul mentions immediately afterwards in the same verse the name Archippus, it is highly probable that this third personage was no other than their son. Chrysostom indeed speaks of Archippus as a friend of the house, and Theodoret supposes him to have been a Christian teacher receiving the hospitality of Philemon; but these suppositions are not so natural. It seems more probable that Archippus, as a young Christian and the son of Philemon, should have been entrusted (in the absence of Epaphras, who had gone to Rome to see St. Paul) with the care of the Church at Colossæ, and that it was in order to make him feel the responsibility resting upon him that in the Epistle to the Colossians St. Paul wrote these words: "Say to Archippus, Take heed to the ministry which thou hast received in the Lord, that thou fulfil it."

A fourth member in the family group is the most interesting to us, as we know more of his romantic story. Philemon had in his employ a worthless slave called Onesimus. His name means literally "profitable," but he belied his name, for a more *unprofitable* piece of property could hardly be imagined. He robbed his master, escaped from Colossæ, and fled to Rome. But though lost to his old home, God's eye was upon him, and somehow or other he came under St. Paul's influence, and was converted to Christ. "Whom," says the Apostle, "I have begotten in my bonds."

2. St. Paul thought very highly of Philemon. He calls him his beloved fellow-worker.

(1) The virtue which in an especial manner St. Paul ascribes to Philemon is hospitality. Such a characteristic might be inferred from the fact that the Church met in his house. There was no small measure of hospitality in that arrangement. Unless that Church was very unlike most others, there would be some rather disagreeable people in it, some very ignorant, some of very uncultivated manners; and probably a considerable proportion of them were slaves. But Philemon cordially welcomed them all in his faith toward the Lord Jesus, and his love to all saints. He

appears to have been a man well to do in the world, and there is good reason to suppose that he was generous in his bounty to the poor. "Their bowels were refreshed" by him. They found in him a sympathizing friend, whose religion consisted mainly in doing good to such as were in need. He was not a Jew; he had not been instructed and trained in those Old Testament Scriptures which extol so highly the virtue of almsgiving; he had not been brought up among people accustomed to kind actions. He was a Gentile; he had never before his conversion to Christ had any idea of hospitality or kindness beyond the extension of them to intimate friends. And the change wrought in him by his conversion must have led some of his heathen neighbours to reflection, and must have been a better and more moving testimony to the gospel than anything Philemon could have preached, however eloquent he might have been.

¶ W. B. Brash writes of his father: He invited the strangers and the outcasts to meals, and my mother made ready for the feast. She always lived on the eve of domestic surprises, for it was ever impossible to tell how many and whom my father would bring in with him. He had read that little noted parable of our Lord, in which He speaks about asking to meals those who can never invite you to their tables; and having grasped its meaning, such was his childlike faith that he dared to apply it. Often we were sent out, unknown to our many and varied visitors, to replenish the insufficient larder. Sometimes my mother would protest, "You should have told me that you intended to bring six in to supper"; and yet she cherished in her heart nothing but pride in her generous husband, and hoped that he would never reform. How delighted we are that he never did, and that to the end of his days he was unrepentably hospitable. He was greatly pleased by the remark of a friend, who said, "Your house is the easiest to get into and the hardest to get out of that I know." This consciously played a part in his ministry, for hospitality was to him as true to the gospel as preaching.[1]

(2) Philemon was an active member of the Church. The private abodes of Christians were probably the places in which the Christian churches of that age most frequently met. The Church of Colossæ met in the house of Philemon, the Church of Laodicea in the house of Nymphas, the Church of Philippi in the house of Lydia, the Church of Rome in the house of Aquila and

---

[1] *Love and Life: The Story of J. Denholm Brash*, 42.

Priscilla. Those whose houses were thrown open for such a purpose were probably the wealthier members of the Church, or members who for some other reason occupied rather extensive premises. It is worthy of notice that there is no example of any building being dedicated to the sole purpose of Christian worship before the third century. The climate of those countries in which the gospel was then preached did not demand such buildings, and the number of Christians in each place was small. When they were too numerous to be accommodated in one house, they probably met in several. Perhaps the disadvantages were great, the inconveniences many, but the Church continued for more than two hundred years to get on without any edifice of a public character consecrated to its work.

Here we see something of Philemon's value as a fellow-worker, which quite agrees with St. Paul's description of him. Perhaps he could not preach, could not even trust himself to make audible prayer in the assembling of the Church, but he threw open to the Church the doors of his house.

> If you cannot on the ocean
>   Sail among the swiftest fleet,
> Rocking on the highest billows,
>   Laughing at the storms you meet,
> You can stand among the sailors,
>   Anchored yet within the bay,
> You can lend a hand to help them,
>   As they launch their boats away.
>
> If you are too weak to journey,
>   Up the mountain steep and high,
> You can stand within the valley,
>   While the multitudes go by.
> You can chant in happy measure,
>   As they slowly pass along;
> Though they may forget the singer,
>   They will not forget the song.

II.

THE LETTER.

1. With one exception, all the Epistles of St. Paul which we possess belong, so to speak, to his official correspondence. They were written as a part of his ordinary work, enabling him to keep in touch with the churches under his charge.

But there is, as has been said, a remarkable exception to the general rule. In one instance, that of the Epistle to Philemon, we have a letter which does not belong to the official correspondence of the Apostle, but is entirely personal and private. It contains no doctrinal instruction or spiritual exhortation; it is wholly taken up with a request of a very delicate kind—a request arising out of a particular circumstance. The other Epistles were intended to be read aloud to the churches, and St. Paul, we may think, would not have been greatly surprised at their being used still in this way many years after his death. But he would have been astonished indeed to know that this private letter of his, intended only for the eye of its recipient, would be preserved through nineteen centuries and included in the Church's lectionary. In fact, such writers as Chrysostom and Jerome had to defend the canonicity of the Epistle to Philemon against those who argued that a private letter of this sort had no place in the Bible.

¶ Jerome tells us that the Epistle to Philemon was rejected by many writers. From the absence of any approach to doctrinal teaching in this Epistle, they concluded that it was not by St. Paul, or that, if it was his, it did not belong to the canon, since it contained nothing by which the Church might be edified. This decision arose out of a narrow view of the canon, and the primitive Church, as a whole, did not ratify the verdict. Preserved at first as a precious relic in the family of Philemon, this apostolic document was subsequently placed among the archives of the Church at Colosse, in the house of one of its elders. We find the first mention of it, as forming part of the Pauline collection, in the writings of Marcion, son of the Bishop of Sinope in Pontus, who about the year 140 went to Rome from Asia Minor. Soon after this it finds a definite place in the Canon of Muratori, in the fragment found at Milan in the middle of the last century, which dates from about the year 170, and contains a list of the writings received and publicly read at that time in one of the Western churches, either that of Italy, or more probably that of Africa.

We observe, moreover, that the Epistle to Philemon formed part of the Western canon, included in the old Latin translation, usually called *Itala*, and that in the Church most remote from this, the Church of Syria, it also found a place in the authorized translation of the Scriptures, the *Peshito*, in the latter part of the second century.[1]

2. In many ways this document is of interest and value. It throws fresh light upon the character of the Apostle who wrote it, as well as incidentally upon the character of the man to whom it was written. It is almost as great a credit to Philemon as it is to St. Paul. What a tribute, only to have had such a letter addressed to one! A man's nature, it has been said, is shown as much by the letters which he receives as by those which he writes. And St. Paul, with his swift perception of character, with his adaptability to become all things to all men, would have used the tender language of this Epistle, appealing to the highest motives, only in the case of one with whom, as he felt sure, this line of argument would prevail. It was simply the sweetness and loving-kindness of Philemon's nature that encouraged St. Paul to address him with these persuasions, and to trust that he would do what was right and loving in this difficulty.

¶ There is a letter of the younger Pliny's (a generation later than St. Paul), the 21st in the ninth book of his Letters, written to his friend Sabinian, asking him to forgive an offending freedman. Its subject is akin to that of our Epistle, and the two have often been compared. It reads as follows:

"Your freedman, who so greatly displeased you, as you told me, has come to me, fallen at my feet, and clung to them as if they were your own; he wept much, begged much, was much silent too, and in brief guaranteed to me his penitence. I think him really reformed, for he feels that he has sinned. You are angry, as I know; justly angry, as I also know; but clemency wins its highest praise when the reasons for anger are most just. You have loved the man, and I hope you will yet love him again; in the interval (*interim*) you are only asked to let yourself be brought to forgive. You will be quite free to be angry again if he deserves it; and this will have the more excuse if now you

[1] F. Godet, in *Expositor*, 3rd Ser., v. 139.

yield. Allow something for his youth, something for his tears, something for your own indulgence (of him); do not put him to torture, or you may torture yourself too. For tortured you are when you, kindliest of men, are angry. I fear I may seem rather to insist than entreat, if I join my prayers to his. But I will join them, the more fully and without reserve as I chid him sharply and severely, adding a stern warning that I could never beg him off again. This for *him*, for I had to frighten him; but I take another tone with *you*! Perhaps I shall entreat again, and win again; so the case is one in which I may properly entreat, and you may properly bestow. Farewell."

It is a graceful, kindly letter, written by a man whose character is the ideal of his age and class; the cultured and thoughtful Roman gentleman of the mildest period of the Empire. Yet the writer seems somewhat conscious of his own epistolary felicity, and his argument for the offender is much more condescending than sympathetic. His heart has not the depth of Paul's, nor are his motives those of the Gospel, which taught Paul to clasp Onesimus in his arms, and to commend him to Philemon, as a friend in God for immortality. From the merely literary view-point, a perfect freedom of style, along with a delicate tact of manner, easily gives the letter to Philemon the palm over that to Sabinian.[1]

3. The letter also shows the spirit in which St. Paul faced one of the most difficult social problems of his time. And, if for no other reason, its inclusion in the New Testament is justified by the fact that it gives us an example of applied Christianity. Elsewhere St. Paul lays down for others the principles of Christian conduct; here, all unconsciously, he shows how he himself translated them into practice. Our religion should influence each detail of our daily life. How it swayed St. Paul in so small a matter as the writing of a friendly note is apparent from the Epistle to Philemon.

> Lo! this one preached with fervent tongue;
>   The world went forth to hear;
> Upon his burning words they hung,
>   Intent, with ravished ear.
>
> Like other lives the life he led,
>   Men spake no word of blame:
> And yet, unblest, unprofited,
>   The world went on the same.

[1] H. C. G. Moule.

Another came, and lived, and wrought,
    His heart all drawn above;
By deeds, and not by words, he taught
    Self-sacrificing love.

No eager crowds his preaching drew;
    Yet one by one they came;
The secret of his power they knew,
    And caught the sacred flame.

And all around, as morning light
    Steals on with silent wing,
The world became more pure and bright
    And life a holier thing.

Ah! Pastor, is thy heart full sore
    At all this sin and strife?
Feed with the Word, but ah! far more
    Feed with a holy life.[1]

III.

THE REQUEST.

1. The sole and simple object of this letter to Philemon is to entreat him to receive back his fugitive slave, now a Christian; to forgo all such penalties and claims as he might otherwise justly have enforced against the runaway; to blot out the past, and to admit this former servant into the new relation of friend and fellow-worker in the cause they now had equally at heart. On the mere statement of the facts, any one can see how difficult and delicate a task St. Paul was undertaking; for Philemon had clearly suffered a wrong. The legalized relations between master and servant had been violated by that servant—for what cause, or with what circumstances of excuse, we are not told; and in addition to the loss of the slave's services, there had been other outstanding debts due from slave to master. At least St. Paul seems to hint at something of the kind in verse 18: "If he hath wronged thee, or oweth thee ought, put that on mine account." The master, Philemon, had unquestionably a grievance; for had

[1] W. W. How.

he been in the first instance to blame, had he been a hard or unjust master, we can have no doubt that the Apostle would have rebuked as boldly as he here pleads and exhorts; and nothing had occurred in the interval that had elapsed to heal or to remove this grievance. But the offending servant had undergone a change through becoming the disciple of St. Paul—a change which transformed him as a man. This change had given him so new and sacred a relation to the Apostle that the latter calls it by the most endearing of all relations: "I beseech thee for *my son* Onesimus, whom I have begotten in my bonds."

¶ O My Saviour Christ, Christ my Saviour! who will grant that I may die rather than again offend Thee! Christ my Saviour, O my Saviour! Lord, let a new manner of life prove that a new spirit hath descended on me; for true penitence is new life, and true praise unremitted penitence, and the observation of a perpetual Sabbath from sin, its occasions, fuel, and danger. For as penitence destroys old sins, so do new sins destroy penitence.[1]

2. It is difficult for us to realize adequately the degradation of Onesimus' position. In the eyes of the ancient world a slave was a mere chattel, outside the ordinary rules of humanity. "Any act is lawful towards a slave," wrote Seneca, and history supplies us with ample evidence that this maxim was generally accepted as a matter of course, even by the most enlightened pagans. Cruelty of the most repulsive kind was viewed as the merely normal and ordinary treatment of a slave : while the precepts of the Rabbis on this point scarcely differed from the laws of paganism. Onesimus, however, was not merely a slave, but a criminal slave, who had robbed his master and escaped. If he were caught, a quite normal penalty would be crucifixion. In any case he would be put to the torture and branded as a runaway with a red-hot iron. Such, then, was the miserable creature who came to St. Paul. And never did the Apostle show more clearly the fulness with which he had received his Master's teaching than by his kindness towards Onesimus. There was no pride of Roman citizenship, there was no shrinking from this criminal outcast. Underneath the degraded and sin-stained exterior, St. Paul saw the possibilities of goodness; he showed the love which believeth all

[1] Bishop Andrewes.

things, the Divine optimism so perfectly exemplified by Christ. He preached the gospel to this wretched slave; he taught him to hate sin instead of merely dreading sin's consequence; he baptized him—and the slave became a member of the Body of Christ and the Apostle's "dear son." For St. Paul's confidence was well founded. The better qualities of Onesimus were still alive, and, quickened by Divine grace, they transformed his character.

¶ For disobedience, in short for anything which in the private court of the *dominica potestas* was a crime in his master's eyes, the slave might be privately executed, with any and every cruelty. In the reign of Augustus, the noon of Roman culture, one Vedius Pollio, a friend of the Emperor's, was used to throw offending slaves into his fish-pond, to feed his huge electric eels (*murœnœ*). He was one day entertaining Augustus at table, when the cupbearer broke a crystal goblet, and was forthwith sentenced to the eels. The poor fellow threw himself at the Prince's feet, begging, not to be forgiven, but to be killed in some other way; and Augustus, shocked and angered, ordered the man's emancipation (*mitti jussit*), and had Pollio's crystals all broken before him, and his horrible pool filled up; but he did not discard his friend. "If," says Horace (*Satires*, I. iii. 80), "a man is thought mad who crucifies his slave for having filched something from . . . the table, *how much more mad* must he be who cuts his friend for a trifling offence!" In brief, the slave in Roman law is a thing, not a person. He has no rights, not even of marriage. To seek his good is in no respect the duty of his master, any more than it is now the duty of an owner to improve his fields *for their own sake*.[1]

3. Perhaps some one will say: But surely Philemon was the greater wrongdoer of the two? What right had he, a Christian, to have any slaves at all? And why does St. Paul not bluntly tell him he was dishonouring his Lord in keeping in bondage any man for whom Christ died?

This is a fair question, and the answer is very interesting. It opens up the whole relation of Christianity to social institutions. The Lord Jesus and His Apostles lived in a time when the institutions of social order were intertwined with grave injustice. Yet they never utter a word that could fairly be construed as an

[1] H. C. G. Moule.

attack on social order or as in the accepted sense inciting to revolution. They saw concubinage, they saw tyranny, they saw slavery. But they denounced none of these things. What they did was, they undermined them. They enunciated new principles of a new social order which was certain in the end to make the older one obsolete and to displace it. Christianity did not attempt all at once to abolish an institution which was so deep rooted as slavery in Roman social life, however inconsistent it was with the religion of the Incarnation. Indeed, the revelation of the brotherhood of men in Christ made it especially necessary to emphasize (as the Apostle did) the fact that social differences were not thereby obliterated. Even if (which is doubtful) St. Paul was so much in advance of his age as to have grasped the idea that no man has a right to *own* another, to have proclaimed the iniquity of slavery to a world which was not prepared for it would have exposed society to the frightful dangers of a *bellum servile*, on the one hand, and would, on the other, have done more to arouse the hostility of the Roman imperial authorities than any other proclamation could have effected. Christians had to show at the very outset that Christianity was not inconsistent with good citizenship, and that the reforms which it hoped to promote in social life would not be imposed violently from without, but would be the outcome of the development of the national conscience, in which the seed of the gospel was to grow and fructify, secretly but surely, as the leaven spreads in the meal.

¶ Dolling, writing of the evils of overcrowding, concludes: But when statesmen have spoken their last word the Christian has still a word to speak. Create within the respectable poor the longing for all these things; stir the soul till it is utterly discontented with and abhors its present surroundings; make the father and mother realize that all duty to their children is impossible as things are. The task seems well-nigh impossible. The truth is we have not got the vigour of body or the keenness of mind to care about these things. We have always lived in them; we feel we cannot alter them. And nothing but Christian enthusiasm can alter them—ay, Christian enthusiasm could alter even the loafer and his slum. And so, while we must do our best to insist upon present legislation being put into force and future legislation being created, Christianity must labour on in making the heart and conscience of the man right, and then he will insist upon an environment which will be possible for himself and his fellows.[1]

4. Here is the secret of the gospel's power to destroy slavery, that it teaches the slave-owner to regard his slave as his brother—his brother in Christ. So far as this doctrine was recognized by the slave-owner—and the acceptance of the gospel was an impossibility without the acceptance of this principle—so far as this principle was accepted, slavery, of course and of necessity, ceased to exist. The slave-owner's bondsmen became his brethren.

¶ Lowell labours to open the eyes of his readers to the eternal sanctities of love, and to make them share with him in that comprehensive passion of brotherhood to which nothing is common or unclean, nothing in all nature too small to have its divine meaning and mission.[2]

¶ A touching little story is told of Tolstoy; he moves out one day, and meets a poor peasant; and being asked to give a coin, puts his hand in his pocket but finds it empty; then with compassionate love he looks into the eyes of the peasant and says: "Brother! I am sorry I have nothing to give." And the poor peasant tells Tolstoy: "Say not, you have nothing: you have given me much: you called me brother!"[3]

¶ While running along the road with hoop and stick, Catherine Booth saw a drunkard being dragged to the lock-up by a constable. A jeering mob was hooting the unfortunate culprit. His utter loneliness appealed powerfully to her. It seemed that he had not a friend in the world. Quick as lightning Catherine sprang to his side, and marched down the street with him, determined that he should feel that there was at least one heart that sympathized with him, whether it might be for his fault or his misfortune that he was suffering.[4]

5. What happened to Onesimus we cannot know certainly. Tradition, as usual, has been active in filling the void places of history, and has woven much legend around his name, but we know nothing certainly. We may, however, agree with Bishop Lightfoot, that "it is reasonable to suppose that Philemon would not belie the Apostle's hopes; that he would receive the slave as

---

[1] C. E. Osborne, *The Life of Father Dolling*, 244.
[2] W. H. Hudson, *Lowell and his Poetry*, 47.
[3] T. L. Vasvani, *The Path of Service*, 13.
[4] *The Life of Mrs. Booth*, i. 77.

a brother; that he would even go beyond the express terms of the Apostle's petition and emancipate the penitent."

But even if he did not go so far, he and Onesimus were in a new relationship—master and man they might still continue, but above that there was a common bond of brotherhood, of disciples and followers of Jesus the Saviour of men. If they lived together for years as master and man, how would their days be spent? Onesimus would go about his work, and Philemon would still be the gentleman employing him, but they would daily talk to each other of Jesus their crucified Lord, of Paul the Apostle, of the judgment to come, of the future home in store for the servants of God. They would join in worship together; they would comfort each other on the pilgrimage of life; and when one of them came to his journey's end, the other would close his eyes in the sure and certain hope of a resurrection to eternal life, where they should meet again.

> Oh from the hush and dying of the splendour
> Take thou a patience and a comfort then!
> Oh let thine eyes be satisfied and tender
> Knowing the common brotherhood of men!
>
> Children of God! and each as he is straying
> Lights on his fellow with a soft surprise,
> Hearkens, perchance, the whisper of his praying,
> Catches the human answer of his eyes.
>
> Then having met they speak and they remember
> All are one family, their sire is one,
> Cheers them with June and slays them with December,
> Portions to each the shadow and the sun.
>
> Therefore His children hold to one another,
> Speak of a hope and tarry till the end,
> Strong in the bond of sister and of brother,
> Safe in the fellowship of friend and friend.[1]

[1] F. W. H. Myers, *Poems*, 94.

TIMOTHY.

LITERATURE.

Davies, T., *Expositions on the Epistle to the Philippians* (1895), 135.

Deane, A., *Friends and Fellow Labourers of St. Paul* (1906), 89.

Hasell, E. J., *Bible Partings* (1883), 351.

Hervey, A. C., *I Timothy* (Pulpit Commentary) (1887), p. i.

Howson, J. S., *The Companions of St. Paul* (1874), 266.

Humphreys, A. E., *The Epistles to Timothy and Titus* (Cambridge Bible) (1895), 57.

Luckock, H. M., *Footprints of the Apostles as traced by Saint Luke in the Acts*, ii. (1905) 160, 313.

Macduff, J. R., *Saint Paul in Rome* (1871), 90, 155.

Maclaren, A., *Expositions* : II Cor. Gal., etc. (1909), 295.

Martineau, J., *Hours of Thought*, i. (1896) 86.

Matheson, G., *The Representative Men of the New Testament* (1905), 319.

Milligan, G., in *Men of the New Testament* : Matthew to Timothy (1905), 337.

Noble, F. A., *Typical New Testament Conversions* (1901), 151.

Paget, F., *The Spirit of Discipline* (1891), 162, 174.

Plummer, A., *The Pastoral Epistles* (Expositor's Bible) (1888), 19.

Simpson, J. G., *Christian Ideals* (1908), 127.

Stock, E., *Plain Talks on the Pastoral Epistles* (1914), 12.

Stokes, G. T., *The Acts of the Apostles* (Expositor's Bible), ii. (1892) 261.

Christian World Pulpit, lxxi. (1907) 60 (H. S. Seekings) ; lxxxvi. (1914) 198 (H. Jeffs).

Dictionary of the Bible, iv. (1902) 767 (W. Lock).

Expositor, 5th Ser., ii. (1895) 223 (E. Medley).

TIMOTHY.

And he came also to Derbe and to Lystra : and behold, a certain disciple was there, named Timothy. . . . The same was well reported of by the brethren that were at Lystra and Iconium.—Acts xvi. 1, 2.

AMONG the friends of St. Paul there is no one who appeals more to our interest and sympathies than Timothy. For not only was he associated with the Apostle during a longer period than any of his other companions, but he was evidently regarded with an altogether peculiar affection and esteem. Following the example of the fourth Evangelist, Timothy might have called himself "the disciple whom Paul loved." He shared his spiritual father's outward labours and intimate thoughts. He was with him when the Apostle could not or would not have the companionship of others. He was sent on the most delicate and confidential missions. He had charge of the most important congregations. When the Apostle was in his last and almost lonely imprisonment it was Timothy whom he summoned to console him and receive his last injunctions. All, therefore, that we can learn regarding Timothy is significant for the light it throws upon the character alike of the pupil and of the master.

I.

WITH LOIS AND EUNICE.

1. The early home of Timothy was at Lystra, and owing to the general Græcizing tendency of the district, we are not surprised to learn that while his mother was a Jewess, his father was a Greek. We do not, however, know even the latter's name; and as there is no further reference to him in the Acts or the Epistles, it is probable that he died during his son's infancy.

It was to his mother, Eunice, and his grandmother, Lois, that Timothy owed the moulding of his character. St. Paul in his Second Epistle to Timothy speaks with warm appreciation of their faith, and "from a babe" the boy was instructed by them in the sacred writings of the Old Testament. There was never a time in his whole experience when the majestic words, the wonderful cadences, of psalmist and of prophet were unfamiliar to the ear. The Book was no less a part of the growing lad's daily life than the sky above him and the earth beneath his feet. He was in living touch with grace as with nature before the ripening intelligence had learned to harmonize the messages that fell upon the attentive ear. The wistful eyes looked up into the loving face of her who taught, and lo! the words of Scripture on the lips of the believer became, as is their wont, a sacrament of the love of God, and the faith of Eunice, the faith of the aged Lois, passed as through an open door to the heart of their little son.

> Happy he
> With such a mother! faith in womankind
> Beats with his blood, and trust in all things high
> Comes easy to him; and tho' he trip and fall,
> He shall not blind his soul with clay.

It was so with Timothy. He had inherited the religious instinct from Eunice, and through her influence he remained true to it.

¶ "We must make up our minds," said Mrs. Booth, "that our children shall not be wicked"; but the misery of to-day is that, in so many cases, it is left to the children to make up their minds, while father and mother look helplessly on. There are mysteries in human character, and sometimes after real care and patience, there are outburstings of passion which baffle all a mother's hope. Temptations, against which nothing could guard, lay hold of some element in a boy's inheritance, and carry him away; but even then the case may not be lost. George Meredith, in one place, says very nobly, "My boy, if he fall, will fall from an actual region of purity. He dare not be a sceptic as to that. Whatever his darkness, he will have the guiding light of a memory behind him; so much is secure." [1]

¶ Lowell's boyhood was spent in an atmosphere of refinement and culture. His father's library of nearly four thousand volumes included, besides theological treatises, an excellent representative

---

[1] W. M. Macgregor, *Some of God's Ministries*, 46.

selection of literary classics, ancient and modern, and among these he was allowed to browse at his will. This early miscellaneous reading laid the foundations of the remarkably broad and sound scholarship of his later life. It also gave that distinctively bookish bias to his mind which, amid all the distracting crowd of other interests, he never afterwards lost.[1]

2. St. Paul visited Lystra in the course of his first missionary journey. A work of healing which he wrought so impressed the people that they wished to worship him and Barnabas as Zeus and Hermes. But before long St. Paul's bitter enemies pursued him from Antioch and Iconium; they turned the fickle crowd against the Apostles, a riot ensued, and St. Paul was stoned and left for dead. To the surprise, however, of his friends, he quickly recovered, and, as further work in Lystra would be impossible, left on the next day for Derbe. Although no mention is made of them, it seems certain that Eunice and Timothy were converted and baptized during this first visit, and it is interesting to put together the evidence for this point. In writing his First Epistle to the Corinthians, St. Paul declares that he can address them as " my beloved children." " For though ye should have ten thousand tutors in Christ, yet have ye not many fathers; for in Christ Jesus I begat you through the gospel." In other words, he limits the use of " children " to describe those of whom he is the spiritual father, who owe their conversion directly to him. Immediately afterwards he adds : " I have sent unto you Timothy, who is my beloved and faithful *child* in the Lord." This seems to imply quite clearly that Timothy also was converted by the Apostle himself. But when did it happen ? Not during St. Paul's second visit to Lystra, for when he arrived Timothy was already a disciple " well reported of by the brethren." Wherefore the evidence seems to show that the conversion of Timothy and Eunice must have been among the unrecorded events of St. Paul's first visit to Lystra. Again, it is probable that Timothy was an eye-witness of St. Paul's stoning in that city. Many years later St. Paul appeals to him by his remembrance of " what things befell me at Antioch, at Iconium, at Lystra "; and indeed the scene would make a lasting impression upon this sensitive youth. In bygone days St. Paul as a youth had witnessed the stoning of Stephen ; now he

[1] W. H. Hudson, *Lowell and his Poetry*, 17.

himself was stoned, while another young man, destined also to work nobly in the ministry of the Church, stood by.

¶ One of Millais' freshest and most delightful pictures is termed " The Boyhood of Sir Walter Raleigh." An adventurer who has sailed and fought in the Spanish Main is recounting his travels and exploits in the West. The animation in his face and his dramatic action show that he is calling into service the powers of a vivid imagination. His audience is composed of two boys, one of whom is the youthful Raleigh, who has ceased now to listen to the sailor's romance and is gazing down the "vistas of a dream." His heart leaps within him, and his youthful fancy conjures up a glowing picture of romance. "He sees El Dorado, and the palaces of the Aztecs and Incas, temples of the Sun where the sun's face burns in gold, hidden treasures, fair Indian captives, and the fountains of eternal youth." The call has come to him ; the little old-fashioned toy which, before it came, constituted his world, now lies neglected in the corner. In an hour he has grown into youth, and has put childish things away for ever. The end of it all he does not see—the scaffold and the axe—but if he did they would not appal him. He has heard the call, and he must " go out, not knowing whither he goeth." [1]

3. Timothy was a lad of about fifteen when St. Paul converted him at Lystra, in or near 45 A.D. Seven years later St. Paul, on his second missionary journey, came again to Lystra. He had just passed through the crisis of his separation from Barnabas, and, while Silas served as a faithful travelling-companion, he was not an intimate friend, as Barnabas had been. The Apostle must have regarded it as a direct gift of Providence that, while thus bereaved, he came once more upon Timothy. For he chose him as his comrade, with the result that the loss of Barnabas was felt no longer. The Apostle had lost a brother, but he gained a son. His personal good opinion of Timothy was strengthened by the testimony of those who knew him well—his fellow-Christians in Lystra and Antioch. So " him would Paul have to go forth with him."

The conduct of the Apostle of the Gentiles on this occasion has sometimes excited surprise. St. Paul, the great proclaimer of the abrogation of the Law by the Gospel, circumcised the young evangelist. The inconsistency is more apparent than real. It was an instance of his becoming " all things to all men " for the salvation of souls, and of his sacrificing his own convictions in

---

[1] J. Burns, *Illustrations from Art*, 60.

matters that were not essential, rather than cause others to offend. Timothy's father had been a Gentile, and the son, though brought up in his mother's faith, had never been circumcised. To St. Paul circumcision was a worthless rite. The question was whether it was a harmless one. That depended upon circumstances. If, as among the Galatians, it caused people to rely upon the Law and neglect the Gospel, it was a superstitious obstacle with which no compromise could be made. But if it was a passport whereby preachers who would otherwise be excluded might gain access to Jewish congregations, then it was not only a harmless but a useful ceremony. In the synagogue Timothy as an uncircumcised Jew would have been an intolerable abomination, and would never have obtained a hearing. To free him from this crippling disadvantage, St. Paul subjected him to a rite which he himself knew to be obsolete.

¶ It is respectful to bow to the King of England, it is disrespectful to bow to the King of France; it is the rule to curtsy to the Emperor; and the prostration of the whole body is required by Eastern Monarchs. These are established ceremonies, and must be complied with; but why they were established, I defy sense and reason to tell us. It is the same among all ranks, where certain customs are received, and must necessarily be complied with, though by no means the result of sense and reason. As for instance, the very absurd, though almost universal custom of drinking people's healths. Can there be any thing in the world less relative to any other man's health, than my drinking a glass of wine? Common sense, certainly, never pointed it out; but yet common sense tells me I must conform to it. Good sense bids one be civil, and endeavour to please; though nothing but experience and observation can teach one the means, properly adapted to time, place, and persons. This knowledge is the true object of a gentleman's travelling, if he travels as he ought to do. By frequenting good company in every country, he himself becomes of every country; he is no longer an Englishman, a Frenchman, or an Italian; but he is an European; he adopts, respectively, the best manners of every country; and is a Frenchman at Paris, an Italian at Rome, an Englishman at London.[1]

4. Then followed the ordination, performed with great solemnity by the laying on of the hands of all the elders of the congregation. This we learn, not from the Acts, but from St.

---

[1] Chesterfield, *Letters to his Son*, iii. 353.

Paul's Epistles to Timothy. The Book of Acts simply says of Timothy, "Him would Paul have to go forth with him." But then when we turn to the Epistles written to Timothy, we find that it was not as an ordinary companion that Timothy was taken. He went forth as St. Paul himself had gone forth from the Church of Antioch, a duly ordained and publicly recognized messenger of Christ. Every circumstance of that day lived in the memory of St. Paul; many years later it is by the remembrance of the gift bestowed by the laying on of hands, by the good confession witnessed, by the prayers and prophecies of the assembled Church, that he appeals to Timothy in his letters.

> Spirit of Remembrance, come,
>   Quickening Spirit, strong and wise,
>   Bid the slumbering soul arise,
> Wake to speech the conscience dumb.
>
> Bring to mind the dreams of youth,
>   Ere the world our tempter proved;
>   Show again the things we loved,
> And the vows we meant in truth.[1]

II.

By the Side of St. Paul.

The young evangelist now leaves his home and his mother, and goes forth with Paul and Silas to preach the gospel. The parting from her son would be a sore trial to the widowed Eunice. He had been so much to her: she, stronger tie of love still, had done so much for him. Nor could she shut her eyes to the hardships and perils which now lay before him. But, like Hannah of old, she recognized an even higher call than that of earthly affection: "I have lent him to the Lord; as long as he liveth he shall be lent to the Lord."

1. The progress of the three missionaries through Asia Minor is traced in Acts xvi. 4–8, till at Troas they stand on the seashore and look across the Ægean Sea towards Europe; and the vision of the "man of Macedonia" calls them thither. They have now

---

[1] W. G. Tarrant, *Songs Devout*, 32.

become a party of four, as we find by the word "we" occurring for the first time (verse 10), showing that they had been joined by Luke, the beloved physician, who writes the narrative. But he is with them only a little while. The "we" occurs again at Philippi (verse 16), but after that we find "they" as before. Only Paul and Silas are mentioned by name, but Timothy is with them, as we find a little later; and a passage in the Epistle to the Philippians, written years after, reveals Timothy's presence at Philippi on this first occasion: "I hope . . . to send Timothy shortly unto you . . . Ye know the proof of him, that, as a child serveth a father, *so he served with me* in furtherance of the gospel."

At Philippi St. Paul and Silas were imprisoned. At Thessalonica a fierce attack was made upon the house in which the travellers lodged. Their enemies followed them to Berœa, whence St. Paul left for Athens. Timothy and Silas remained for a while, but their companionship was much needed by their leader, who sent word that they should come to him with all speed. But no sooner did Timothy arrive than he was sent away again on an important errand. For the first time in his experience as a Christian missionary he was given independent work. The persecution of the Church in Thessalonica had not ceased with St. Paul's departure, and its members were in sore need of encouragement. Of course St. Paul, as his urgent message had shown, longed for the companionship of Timothy in Athens. Yet his spirit of unselfishness triumphed. Hearing of the state of things in Thessalonica, to use his own words, "we could no longer forbear"; "we thought it good to be left behind at Athens alone; and sent Timothy, our brother and God's minister in the gospel of Christ, to establish you, and to comfort you concerning your faith; that no man be moved by these afflictions." In this task Timothy was successful, and was able to bring back good news. "But when Timothy came even now"—*i.e.* immediately before the writing of the First Epistle to the Thessalonians—"unto us from you, and brought us glad tidings of your faith and love . . . for this cause, brethren, we were comforted over you."

On his return from Thessalonica Timothy found St. Paul at Corinth. At Corinth, as at Lystra, Iconium, and Philippi, Timothy became prominent for his zeal as an evangelist; and then for about five years we lose sight of him. We may think of him as generally at the side of St. Paul, and as always working with him; but of the details of the work we are ignorant.

> Yes, while on earth a thousand discords ring,
> Man's fitful uproar mingling with his toil,
> Still do thy sleepless ministers move on,
> Their glorious tasks in silence perfecting;
> Still working, blaming still our vain turmoil,
> Labourers that shall not fail, when man is gone.[1]

2. We next meet with Timothy at Ephesus, in that long period of "three years" during which St. Paul worked in that great city. From here he is sent, with a companion, Erastus, into Macedonia, where he would no doubt visit the Churches of Philippi, Thessalonica, and Berœa. He is also to go on to Corinth. His mission to the last place was evidently a very delicate one, and, fearful of the result, St. Paul bespoke for his envoy a kindly welcome, in a letter in which he explained the object of his coming. "I have sent unto you," so he writes to the Corinthians, "Timothy, who is my beloved and faithful child in the Lord, who shall put you in remembrance of my ways which be in Christ, even as I teach everywhere in every church." And in a later passage in the same Epistle he earnestly calls upon the Corinthians to respect Timothy's timidity, and to set him forward again on his journey in peace. Timothy was evidently of a shy and sensitive disposition, and St. Paul, whom "anxiety for all the churches" never made forgetful of the courtesies of everyday life, desired that nothing should be done to wound or annoy him. But the appeal, so kindly meant, would seem to have been in vain, if, as many scholars hold, we are to identify Timothy with the wronged sufferer of 2 Cor. vii. 12. His mission was not successful; he brought back news which caused St. Paul great anxiety and necessitated a mission of Titus.

When St. Paul wrote 2 Corinthians from Macedonia later in the year, Timothy was again with him, for his name is coupled with St. Paul's; and he was still with him when the Apostle wrote to the Romans from Corinth, for he joined in sending salutations to the Roman Christians.

[1] Matthew Arnold.

3. From Corinth Timothy crossed over to Troas, where, along with other brethren, he awaited the arrival of St. Paul, who had been making the longer circuit through Macedonia. But we are left uncertain whether he accompanied the Apostle from thence on his last visit to Jerusalem. We do not know what he was doing during St. Paul's two years' imprisonment at Cæsarea; but he joined him during the first imprisonment at Rome, for the Epistles to the Philippians, the Colossians, and Philemon are written in the names of Paul and Timothy. From certain passages in Philippians we may conjecture that Timothy went to Philippi and returned again before the Apostle was released. At the close of the Epistle to the Hebrews we read, " Know ye that our brother Timothy hath been set at liberty." It is possible that the imprisonment to which this notice refers was contemporaneous with the first imprisonment of St. Paul, and that it is again referred to in 1 Timothy (vi. 12) as " the good confession " which he confessed " in the sight of many witnesses."

III.

ALONE IN EPHESUS.

1. The few additional facts respecting Timothy are given us in the two letters to him. Some time after St. Paul's release the two were together in Ephesus; and when the Apostle went on into Macedonia he left his companion behind him to warn and exhort certain holders of erroneous doctrine to desist from teaching it. There were tears, on the younger friend's side at any rate, to which St. Paul alludes at the opening of the Second Epistle; and they were natural enough. The task imposed upon Timothy was no easy one; and after the dangers and sufferings to which the Apostle had been exposed, and which his increasing infirmities continually augmented, it was only too possible that the friends would never meet again.

2. It is worth while trying to conceive to ourselves the situation at Ephesus, the atmosphere in which Timothy was called upon to discharge his Christian ministry, for the evidence goes to show that his was a nature likely to be keenly sensitive to the conditions under which his work had to be done.

To begin with, Ephesus was the seat of the worship of Diana; her temple was a magnificent building dominating the entire city, and on it wealth and taste had lavished their utmost. Everything was done to attract the eye, to inspire with awe and wonder. Its courts were daily thronged with worshippers from every quarter of the Roman Empire. Perhaps it was under the shadow of the great temple, and in the presence of all this splendid pageantry of worship, that Timothy had to shepherd the flock of Christ, to lead the unadorned worship, and to administer the austerely simple ordinances of the primitive Church. It must have required a firm courage, an eye undimmed for spiritual things, for a man with Greek blood in his veins, and trained from childhood to think with reverent delight of the Temple at Jerusalem, to hold on unabashed, and not sometimes to be visited with a sort of undefined wish that in some way or other he might be able to blend together the body of a splendid ritual with the soul of a spiritual Christian service. One can imagine him, not exactly ashamed of Christ, but feeling like a dissenter in a cathedral city. He believes himself to be right, but he wishes that he had not to breathe so much of the chilling air of social contempt. Perhaps his position might find a modern parallel in that of a native Christian teacher, whose work shall lie, say in Benares, the metropolis of Hinduism, if the supposition be added that India were not under British but under native rule.

If this was the condition outside the body of Christian disciples, there were elements at work inside that body with which Timothy had to reckon. Oriental speculation had its chosen home at Ephesus, and the Judaizing tendency, which had been rampant in Galatia, was not wholly absent. These two influences, apparently so diverse, conspired against the simplicity that is in Christ. It was beginning to be a cherished dream with certain minds that a sort of eclectic religion might be developed out of a union of philosophic speculation, Jewish ritualism, and the gospel of Christ. These people did not mean to deny the gospel, but only to enrich it; they would rid it of its barrenness, and, in a non-apostolic sense, adorn the doctrine of God their Saviour.

In addition to these religious, or quasi-religious, elements of

Ephesian life, we may be sure that there was, ever present, the abounding licentiousness which distinguished populations in which the Greek and the Oriental mingled; the darker vices of the Asiatic were partly veiled by the flashing splendours of the Greek imagination, and, becoming less repulsive, were the more dangerous.

Timothy seems to have been by nature one to whom opposition would always mean distress and pain, to whom firmness would often be difficult and expensive. He was not a man who, when things seemed to be going against him or getting into confusion, could shrug his shoulders and refuse to be harassed. Rather, he seems one to whom antagonism, insolence, isolation, would mean sharp suffering; one whose heart might grow sick as he looked at a gathering storm of hostility and danger; one on whose courage and constancy such a storm would break with a severe if not a staggering shock. His was a character deficient somehow in that useful sort of obstinacy which is an element in some men's power of endurance, and stands them in good stead in hard times. The traits of moral beauty on which St. Paul elsewhere lays stress, in speaking of Timothy, are such as might well consist with this deficiency; they are the attractions likeliest to be wrought by the grace of God in such a nature. Eminent unselfishness; the capacity for generous self-devotion; warmheartedness and loyalty in personal affection; a spiritual sense which made the care for others' welfare seem instinctive; —these are the features which, as we read the First Epistle to the Corinthians and the Epistle to the Philippians, appear to supplement the impression of Timothy's character which we get from the Pastoral Epistles. There is often in such men an unfailing charm of delicacy and gentleness; they seem as though there had been more summer than winter in their lives; while, with some characteristics which may be misnamed effeminate, there is in them a really womanly power of patience and self-sacrifice. Surely, if we may form any such idea of Timothy, we cannot wonder at St. Paul's intense affection for him, as a constant presence of tenderness and sympathy in the midst of much antagonism and disappointment and anxiety. We cannot wonder that St. Paul should have trusted him largely, and believed that he would rightly bear his high charge as Apostolic delegate over the Church of Ephesus; nor yet can we wonder that, as the Apostle thinks of him in the isolation, the perils, the tangled difficulties of his position, as he thinks of the subtlety of error, the restlessness of idle talk, the malignity of moral corruption, the brutality of persecution, all besetting, or likely to beset, that sensitive temperament, a fear should be continally haunting him lest the strain prove too great.

¶ We may say of Newman, as he said of himself, that he had a "morbidly sensitive skin," and this is about as bad an equipment for active life in a world of struggle as nature can bestow. That a pre-eminently sensitive man tastes more keenly than others the choice delights of life is probably true, but it is certain that he suffers a thousand miseries which tougher natures never feel. An acute sensitiveness may be allied with, though it is by no means a synonym for, keen sympathy with the sorrows of others, and so may gather round a man a band of grateful admirers; but it will never disarm an opponent, or turn a foe into a friend. Still less will it enable a man to force his way through clenched antagonisms, or to crush resistance as he marches towards his end. Then again a sensitive nature is

Wax to receive, and marble to retain.

It may forgive, but it cannot forget, slights and injuries, buffets and bruises. Forgetfulness of injuries is the blessed lot of those who have inflicted them.[1]

3. It was to encourage Timothy in his hard task that St. Paul wrote to him the two Epistles. The First Epistle was sent from Macedonia some time after the Apostle had left Ephesus. Fearing that his return may be delayed he writes this letter to press his original charge more solemnly on Timothy, to encourage him in his work, to guide him in his teaching and dealing with various classes in the Church, and to regulate certain points of Church order which needed organization without delay. The Second Epistle was written from Rome when the aged Apostle was imprisoned for the second and last time. In the interval between the letters the sky had darkened. The Neronian persecutions had broken out and the Church was threatened by a new danger. St. Paul knew that his own days were numbered, and in his loneliness

---

[1] G. W. E. Russell, *Selected Essays on Literary Subjects*, 136.

his heart went out to the young evangelist who had been to him more than a son.

In both these letters, but especially in the second, St. Paul seems never tired of enforcing, with every sanction, every appeal, every encouragement that he can use, the paramount duty of unflinching steadfastness. Again and again that duty is impressed on his disciple's conscience, that it may be safe from all risks of forgetfulness or surprise: "God hath not given us the spirit of fearfulness"; "Be not thou ashamed"; "Take thy share of hardship"; "Hold fast the form of sound words"; "Be strong in grace"; "Continue, abide in the things which thou hast learned"; "Be instant in season, out of season"; "Watch thou in all things"; "Endure afflictions."

¶ When Luther was in the hall, about to be ushered into the presence of the assembly, a veteran knight, George Freundsberg, commander of the guard, touched him on the shoulder, and said kindly, "My poor monk, my poor monk, thou hast a march and a struggle to go through, such as neither I nor many other captains have seen the like of in our worst campaigns. But if thy cause be just, and thou art sure of it, go forward, in God's name, and fear nothing! He will not forsake thee!" A noble tribute from a brave soldier to the courage of the soul!

4. The authenticity of the Pastoral Epistles has been called in question: Renan, in his bold way, calls the writer of them a forger, who perhaps incorporated some authentic notes of St. Paul in his apocryphal composition; and the school of Baur, as might have been expected, gives them short shrift, rejecting the whole of them. Such criticism can be met on its own ground, but is there not another method? Forgery stumbles, not when it sets itself deliberately to delineate character, but when character is not so much carefully outlined as taken for granted, and made the groundwork (almost invisible) of the superstructure. And if we can discover in these letters a character consistent with itself and with its circumstances, if a score of delicate suggestions make us feel that we are dealing with a living man, who is being dealt with by one stronger than himself, whose words vibrate with the personal element, then we feel that we have got into that atmosphere in which the mere literary actor and the forger cannot live, and we gain a new evidence that these two letters are rightly

entitled the First and the Second Epistles of Paul the Apostle to Timothy.

5. The Second Epistle to Timothy closes with a pressing and repeated entreaty to Timothy to hasten to St. Paul. The aged Apostle was alone, save for the faithful Luke. Demas had forsaken him, Crescens and Titus had been summoned elsewhere. His friends among the Roman Christians were timorous; not one of them had dared to stand by him when he appeared to make his defence in court. Not thus, he knew, would Timothy act. And so he is entreated to come with all speed, and to bring with him Mark, whose former difference with St. Paul was now happily at an end. And then we notice the little personal touches: the homely directions to bring a cloak and some books which St. Paul needed. Perhaps they would give him some comfort in prison, perhaps he wished to give them to his friends to be kept in memory of him after his death. Above all he needs Timothy himself—Timothy, who had wept when last he parted from him. And yet, despite the repeated bidding that he should come at once, St. Paul seems to feel a presentiment that he must arrive too late. Therefore he speaks words of farewell, infinitely tender and pathetic, yet without a trace of weakness, to his " beloved child."

Whether Timothy was able to comply with St. Paul's entreaties we have no means of knowing. We like to think of the beloved disciple as comforting the last hours of his master; but, although the conjecture may be a right one, we must remember that it is conjecture and no more.

With the Second Epistle to him ends all that we really know of Timothy. Tradition and ingenious guesswork add a little more, which can be neither proved nor disproved. More than two hundred years after his death, Eusebius tells us that he is related to have held the office of overseer of the diocese of Ephesus; and five centuries later Nicephorus tells us that he was beaten to death by the Ephesian mob for protesting against the licentiousness of their worship of Artemis. It has been conjectured that Timothy may be the " Angel " of the Church of Ephesus, who is partly praised and partly blamed in the Apocalypse, and parallels have been drawn between the words of blame in Rev. ii. 4, 5, and the uneasiness which seems to underlie one or two passages in the

Second Epistle to Timothy. But the resemblances are too slight to be relied upon. All we can say is that, even if the later date be taken for the Apocalypse, Timothy may have been overseer of the Church of Ephesus at the time when the book was written.

6. In the relation of St. Paul to Timothy we have one of those beautiful friendships between an older and a younger man which are commonly so helpful to both. It is in such cases, rather than where the friends are equal in age, that each can be the real complement of the other. Each by his abundance can supply the other's want, whereas men of equal age would have common wants and common supplies. In this respect the friendship between St. Paul and Timothy reminds us of that between St. Peter and St. John. In each case the friend who took the lead was much older than the other; and (what is less in harmony with ordinary experience) in each case it was the older friend who had the impulse and the enthusiasm, the younger who had the reflectiveness and the reserve. These latter qualities are perhaps less marked in Timothy than in John, but nevertheless they are there, and they are among the leading traits of his character.

It is difficult to estimate which of the two friends gained most from the affection and devotion of the other. No doubt Timothy's debt to St. Paul was immense: and which of us would not think himself amply paid for any amount of service and sacrifice, in having the privilege of being chosen friend of such a man as St. Paul? But, on the other hand, few men could have supplied the Apostle's peculiar needs as Timothy did. That intense craving for sympathy which breathes so strongly throughout the writings of St. Paul found its chief human satisfaction in Timothy. To be alone in a crowd is a trial to most men; and few men have felt the oppressiveness of it more keenly than St. Paul. To have some one, therefore, who loved and reverenced him, who knew his "ways" and could impress them on others, who cared for those for whom St. Paul cared and was ever willing to minister to them as his friend's missioner and delegate—all this and much more was inexpressibly comforting to the Apostle. It gave him strength in his weaknesses, hope in his many disappointments, and solid help in his daily burden of "anxiety for all the churches."

While his other friends were St. Paul's "brethren in the Lord," Timothy became to the childless and wifeless Apostle his "beloved son." We are right, surely, in thinking that not Barnabas, Luke, Apollos, or any other of his companions, was quite so dear to St. Paul, or was admitted so far into his confidence.

The friendship between these two men, so unequal in years and so different in powers, is one of the most suggestive episodes in the early history of the gospel. It was apparently the one mellowing affection that toned down the impassioned vigour of St. Paul; that bound him tenderly to life, and, when he would spring to grasp the heavenly crown, recalled him with a sigh; that mingled a constant human image with his prayers and brought them trembling on his voice; that, homeless as he was, made him feel amid his wanderings, the sadness of absence and of loneliness.

¶ Friendship requires that rare mean betwixt likeness and unlikeness, that piques each with the presence of power and of consent in the other party. Let me be alone to the end of the world, rather than that my friend should overstep, by a word or a look, his real sympathy. I am equally balked by antagonism and by compliance. Let him not cease an instant to be himself. The only joy I have in his being mine, is that the *not mine* is *mine*. I hate, where I looked for a manly furtherance, or at least a manly resistance, to find a mush of concession. Better be a nettle in the side of your friend than his echo. The condition which high friendship demands is ability to do without it. That high office requires great and sublime parts. There must be very two, before there can be very one. Let it be an alliance of two large, formidable natures, mutually beheld, mutually feared, before yet they recognize the deep identity which beneath these disparities unites them.[1]

¶ In the church of San Paolo at Rome a gorgeous baldacchino surmounts the traditional tomb of Paul the Apostle. In immediate juxtaposition with it, in front of the high altar, is a shrine of more modest pretensions, on which is inscribed the one name, which tells its own touching story—

"TIMOTHEI."

Here the ashes of the Apostle Timothy are said to rest. Strong is the temptation, for once, not too exactingly to demand or

---

[1] Emerson.

scrutinise authority for the truth of a legend in itself so beautiful, that these two honoured servants of Christ, who had loved and laboured, wept and prayed, sorrowed and rejoiced together, are now resting side by side, a true " family burying-place," the father and his " own son in the faith." [1]

[1] J. R. Macduff, *St. Paul in Rome*, 90.

TITUS.

LITERATURE.

Bourdillon, F., *Our Possessions* (1904), 133.

Farrar, F. W., *The Life and Work of St. Paul* (1897), 229.

Hervey, A. C., *The Epistle to Titus* (Pulpit Commentary) (1887).

Howatt, J. R., *A Year's Addresses to the Young* (1913), 180.

Howson, J. S., *The Companions of St. Paul* (1874), 101.

    "   "   *Scenes from the Life of St. Paul* (1909), 122.

Moffatt, J., *Reasons and Reasons* (1911), 179.

Plummer, A., *The Pastoral Epistles* (Expositor's Bible) (1888), 199.

Seekings, H. S., *The Men of the Pauline Circle* (1914), 65.

Stock, E., *Plain Talks on the Pastoral Epistles* (1914), 6.

Wakinshaw, W., *John's Ideal City* (1915), 71.

Wilson, S. L., *Helpful Words for Daily Life* (1905), 240.

Dictionary of the Bible, iv. (1902) 782 (W. Lock).

    "   "   "   (Single-volume, 1909), 940 (C. T. P. Grierson).

Expositor, 1st Ser., xi. (1881) 201 (A. B. Bruce) ; 2nd Ser., v. (1883) 177, 267 (J. O. Dykes).

Homiletic Review, xxxi. (1896) 443 (M. W. Jacobus).

TITUS.

To Titus, my true child after a common faith: Grace and peace from God the Father and Christ Jesus our Saviour.—Tit. i. 4.

TITUS has been called "the most enigmatic figure in early Christian history" (Ramsay, *St. Paul the Traveller*, 284). He is never mentioned in Acts. The only references to him are in 2 Corinthians, Galatians, and 2 Timothy, and his story must be re-constructed from these and the Epistle addressed to him by St. Paul. In 2 Corinthians he is mentioned nine times. His birthplace is unknown, but he was a Gentile, and he was living at Antioch when the controversy arose about the circumcision of the Gentiles. He was brought to Christ by St. Paul, who calls him "my true child after a common faith." He may have been among the fruits of St. Paul's first great ministry in Antioch, when, with Barnabas, he followed up the preaching of the men of Cyprus and Cyrene "to the Greeks." The first mention of him is in Gal. ii. 1, where St. Paul says, "I went up again to Jerusalem with Barnabas, taking Titus also with me." This journey was undertaken in order to settle the great question of making the Jewish law binding upon the Gentiles.

The Judaistic party within the Church wished to have Titus circumcised; but the Apostle and those representing Gentile Christianity strenuously resisted, and the decision of the Church was in their favour. The case of Titus seems thus to have been the test case in this controversy. From this time we may suppose that Titus continued with St. Paul as one of his missionary companions and assistants, but we have no distinct reference to him until some ten years after the Council at Jerusalem.

I.

THE COMFORTER OF ST. PAUL.

1. In the Second Epistle to the Corinthians we are told that St. Paul came from Ephesus to Troas, expecting to meet Titus there: "Now when I came to Troas for the gospel of Christ . . . I had no relief for my spirit, because I found not Titus my brother." Why was the Apostle expecting to meet Titus, and why was he so sadly disappointed?

Titus had been sent to Corinth as the bearer of the First Epistle to the Corinthians, and had been told to rejoin St. Paul at Troas; but perhaps the precipitation of St. Paul's departure from Ephesus had brought him to that town earlier than Titus had expected, and, in the uncertain navigation of those days, delays may easily have occurred. At any rate, he did not come, and St. Paul grew more and more uneasy, until in that intolerable oppression of spirit he felt that he could no longer continue his work, and left Troas for Macedonia. There, at last, he met Titus, who relieved his painful tension of mind by intelligence from Corinth which, although chequered, was yet on the main point favourable. From Titus he learnt that his change of plan about the visit had given ground for unfavourable criticism, and that many injurious remarks on his character and mode of action had been industriously disseminated, especially by one Jewish teacher. Still, the effect of the First Epistle had been satisfactory. It had caused grief, but the grief had been salutary, and had issued in an outburst of yearning affection, lamentation, and zeal. Titus himself had been received cordially, yet with fear and trembling. The offender denounced in his letter had been promptly and even severely dealt with, and all that St. Paul had said to Titus in praise of the Church had been justified by what he saw.

2. That welcome visit from an old comrade was, we may be sure, like a gleam of sunshine on a wintry day. It exhilarated the lonely Apostle like a tonic. It was as the cool touch of a mother's hand on the hot forehead of her fevered child. "When two friends meet after a period of absence," says Edward Irving, "and exchange their various experiences, recount their dangers

past and their present condition, they are refreshed again; they open up their schemes to one another, their difficulties, and their fears; and before the good countenance and encouragement of our friend, our difficulties, like the great mountain before Zerubbabel, become a plain; we feel like new men again; and we go forth to renew the struggle in the sea of troubles wherewith we are encompassed."

¶ The incident of a friend's visit may be part of God's large providence of encouragement. Titus comes in many ways. James Smetham closes a letter with thanks to a friend for writing to him when he happened to be depressed. "Glad to get your friendly letter. It was like the coming of Titus. I think Providence in these days often sends Titus by post."[1]

¶ The late George Ensor, the first English missionary in Japan, used at C.M.S. meetings to tell the story of his first convert. Open missionary work was then impossible in Japan, but an inquirer came at night who was eventually baptized and given the name of Titus; "for God," Mr. Ensor used to say, "who comforteth the downcast, comforted me by the coming of Titus."[2]

Oh, gift of God, my friend!
　Whose face has brought th' Eternal nigh;
No sermon like thy life doth tend
　To turn my gaze toward the sky.

Oh, ray of light, my friend!
　When sorrow's gloom made life so drear,
Then comfort sweet thy words did lend,
　As if Christ spake, "Be of good cheer!"

Oh, rock of strength, my friend!
　When shifting sands beneath my feet,
And changing scenes my steps attend,
　Thy truth and constancy are sweet.

Oh, home of rest, my friend!
　When wearied with the toil and rush
My wistful gaze on thee I bend,
　Then o'er my spirit falls a hush.

[1] J. Moffatt, *Reasons and Reasons*, 185.
[2] E. Stock, *Plain Talks on the Pastoral Epistles*, 9.

I clasp thy hand, my friend!
Thank God that thou art here;
I am not worthy He should send
To me a gift so dear.[1]

II.

HIS WORK IN CORINTH.

1. From Macedonia Titus was sent back promptly with two others, as the bearer of the Second Epistle to Corinth. There is also hardly any doubt that, as already mentioned, he had been one of the bearers of the First Epistle. And if we consider the contents of these two letters, revealing, as they do, the difficult theological and practical questions which had arisen at Corinth, the factions which were disturbing and tearing its Church, the rebellious spirit of many of its members towards the Apostle, and the sanction which it gave to vice by passive acquiescence, we see at once how difficult a task was assigned to Titus, and what great qualities were required in him for the discharge of his duty.

Now this was the distinction of Titus—he was a *peacemaker*. All his other gifts lent their strength to this, and by it whatever claim to permanence he possessed must be demonstrated. He found an opportunity for the exercise of his special gifts in the critical task which fell to his hand at Corinth and Crete. Here a weaker man must have failed; and that fact alone disposes of the theory of insignificance. We are dependent upon the Second Epistle to the Corinthians for the facts which provide an insight into his character. Corinth was the Church in which St. Paul had felt a founder's pride. "I gloried on your behalf," he writes to them at a later date. That glorying, however, had been rudely disturbed. News had come from Corinth that filled him with sorrow. A shadow was resting upon the Church, and a state of affairs tending to moral chaos prevailed. Stephanas and his fellow-delegates had to report that the Church was lending countenance to wrong-doers. Faction was rife, a grave moral

[1] Una, *In Life's Garden*, 12.

scandal was being tolerated, and unseemliness had crept into the observance of the sacramental ordinance. A man wise enough to restore unity without appearing to have that object in view, and strong enough to stamp out heresy and evil, was needed; and St. Paul, who, as Thurloe said of Cromwell, "sought out men for places, not places for men," turned to Titus. And Titus went to Corinth. He went to a disorganized Church with the avowed intention of arranging a collection for the poor of the Church at Jerusalem, but with the deeper purpose of reconciling and establishing the Church at Corinth; and by his discreet and able dealing with the momentous crisis he left it in such a state that the Apostle could say, "I was not put to shame."

Accordingly the highest praise is given to Titus for his zeal and sympathy, his grief at the sight of what was evil, and his rejoicing over that which was good. "God comforted us by the coming of Titus, and not by his coming only, but by the consolation wherewith he was comforted in you, when he told us your earnest desire, your mourning, your fervent mind toward me. Yea, and exceedingly the more joyed we for the joy of Titus, because his spirit was refreshed by you all. And his inward affection is more abundant toward you, whilst he remembereth the obedience of you all, how with fear and trembling ye received him."

¶ Her own harmonious and well-balanced disposition enabled our dear "Fräulchen" (Fanny Lavater) to play the part of peacemaker among stormier natures, and her influence was ever used for good. Never in thirty years of the closest intimacy did I hear a single word fall from her lips by which I could possibly have felt hurt; and I was as ultra-sensitive and liable to take offence, as are most children, who are too harshly brought up. With others I was always looking out for blame,—a scolding seemed the natural thing to expect,—never with her! She could find fault, too, when it was needful, but with so much tact and kindness, and accompanying her criticism with reflections that took away all its bitterness and made it sound almost like indirect praise; and then when I looked up at her, half in alarm, with her soft little hand she would stroke mine and say smiling: "There was the horrid little serpent concealed beneath the roses, was it not?" She was for ever pouring oil on the troubled waters, making life better and happier for everyone.[1]

[1] *From Memory's Shrine: Reminiscences of Carmen Sylva*, 98.

2. To this we must add another service. A collection was being made at this time for the poor Christians in Judæa; and their Corinthian brethren, though at first they had made great professions of liberality, had been dilatory and flagging in providing the promised fund. This difficulty, too, Titus had faced with much moral courage. When he was first among the Corinthians he had promoted this cause with great energy (2 Cor. viii. 6), and now he willingly received the Apostle's commission; indeed he was eager of his own accord to return and urge its progress (2 Cor. viii. 16, 17). His integrity, too, was as conspicuous as his energy. The fund was large, and the Apostle took great precautions in regard to the proper care of it (2 Cor. viii. 20); and he appealed to the Corinthians themselves for a testimony that Titus in this matter had been above all suspicion (2 Cor. xii. 18). Reading all these passages attentively, we cannot well doubt that this companion of St. Paul was remarkable for a strong, vigorous, honest, fearless character, as well as for warm sympathies and excellent judgment.

¶ "When I think of Mr. Ewing's work and influence here," said Professor Drummond, "my soul fills with gratitude and enthusiasm for my friend. His concentration, it is true, was exceptional, his initiative very great, his vitality as exuberant as his hope. It is true—and how wonderful this is—that he never did anything but his work. He had no petty interests. He saw always the main stream of the kingdom of God, all currents in Church or State that make for righteousness, and he threw himself into them. But none of these things could have produced the extraordinary demonstration here on Friday last. Intellectual brilliancy could not have done it, nor ecclesiastical position, nor successful preaching power. What did it was his character, his downright, sterling, pure, strong character. Three and a half years of that—it looks very short. But character knows no calendar, for it alone of all forces is infinitely great, and cannot but do its work."[1]

III.

HIS MINISTRY IN CRETE.

1. The next reference to Titus is in the letter to him. This implies that St. Paul, after the release from his first Roman im-

[1] G. A. Smith, *The Life of Henry Drummond*, 365.

prisonment, had travelled with Titus in the East, that they had landed at Crete and had evangelized several towns, but that St. Paul had been unable to remain longer, and had therefore left Titus behind to appoint presbyters and to complete the organization of the Church.

Crete is a large island in the Greek seas with a range of high hills running through its entire length from east to west, from which fertile valleys open upon a continuous strip of flat shore round the coast line. On the north it possesses good natural harbours. In its palmy days these served as outlets for the abundant crops of wheat, wine, and oil which it then yielded to the industry of a dense population. Descended from an ancient Greek stock, its early inhabitants were employed partly as cultivators in the interior, partly as seamen on the coast. They were a somewhat rude, turbulent, and independent race, among whom the usual defects of the Greek character in its less cultured condition were very strongly marked. Of these defects, falsehood, both in the form of over-reaching and in that of treachery, has always been the foremost. To this vice there were joined, in St. Paul's time, gross forms of licentiousness and a readiness to swift insolent brawling such as has never been quite cured among the maritime Greeks of the Archipelago.

¶ The untrustworthy character of the Cretans (Acts ii. 11 A.V. Cretes, Tit. i. 12 A.V. Cretians) was proverbial. St. Paul quotes from one of their own poets, Epimenides (Tit. i. 12), who lived about 600 B.C., and is called by Plato "a divine man," that "they were always liars, evil beasts, idle gluttons." Witness to their avarice is also borne by Livy (xliv. 45) and Plutarch Æmilius (§ 23), "the Cretans are as eager for riches as bees for honey": to their ferocity and fraud by Polybius and Strabo; and to their mendacity by Callimachus, Hymn in *Jov.* 8, who begins a line with the same words as Epimenides.[1]

2. Such a population did not offer very hopeful soil for the gospel; nor had Christianity been introduced into Crete, or propagated there, under the most favourable auspices. In its seaports, as in other business centres of the Mediterranean, numbers of Hebrews were at that period to be found. It is probable that a good share of the export trade of the island was in their hands.

[1] W. Lock, in Hastings' *Dictionary of the Bible*, i. 520.

Some of these Jews of Crete had been among the motley and
polyglot audience which listened to St. Peter's first Christian
sermon at the memorable Pentecost. It is a fair presumption
that, having accepted the new gospel of the Messiah of Nazareth,
some of them would carry back the tidings to the island of their
adoption. But how it was propagated from one coast town to
another, we do not know; nor how far it succeeded in penetra-
ting the interior and winning converts among the farmers,
shepherds, and peasants, who lay more remote from Hebrew and
foreign influences. When St. Paul paid his hurried visit to the
island in the year 66 or so, it is certain that he found congregations already existing in most of the chief seats of population ; nor
were these congregations of recent origin, since he anticipated no
difficulty in selecting for office in the Church men whose families
had been trained in the Christian Faith. "Ordain elders," he
writes, "in *every city*"; men "having faithful" (that is, believing
or Christian) "children" (Tit. i. 5, 6). St. Paul's brief sojourn in
the island with Titus was probably the first serious effort to con-
solidate the young, struggling, and imperilled churches; and we
can easily imagine that it was the necessity of completing an
anxious work that compelled the Apostle reluctantly to leave his
companion behind him.

3. Titus was by this time no novice in the management of
difficult affairs. Eight or nine years had elapsed since St. Paul
entrusted him with a mission to the most unmanageable of
churches—that in Corinth—at a moment when that Church was in
its most distracted condition. Ever since then, it can hardly be
doubted, Titus must have been acquiring similar experience.
None of the band of missionaries who took their inspiration and
their guidance from the great Apostle stood higher than he for
energy, tact, and ability. Hence, although he could be ill spared,
St. Paul left him behind for a time to finish the task he had begun
of organizing the Cretan congregations.

The materials with which Titus had to build up the Cretan
Church were of the most rugged kind.

Moreover, when we consider that he was isolated and un-
supported in this position, we feel how much need there was of a
strong character for such a post. Here was a conspicuous token

indeed of the deep confidence reposed in him by his master; which implies to us much hardness endured with cheerful patience; tells of much diligence under most disheartening labours; of faith well and truly tried by works of love; of the dedication of the whole man in body, soul, and spirit to a service which he thankfully accepted from God, and executed in the true mind of Christ. We see how much is condensed into the brief expression used by the Apostle of Titus: "He is my partner and fellow-helper" (2 Cor. viii. 23). We cannot doubt that he rose to the standard set before him: "In all things shewing thyself a pattern of good works: in doctrine shewing uncorruptness, gravity, sincerity, sound speech, that cannot be condemned" (Tit. ii. 7, 8)—and we can well understand how the last words of St. Paul concerning him are an expression of sorrowful regret at Rome (as formerly at Troas) for the absence of his friend: "Titus is departed unto Dalmatia. Only Luke is with me" (2 Tim. iv. 10, 11).

¶ We have to learn to be the servants of each other, to be "true yoke-fellows" willing to give and take, and to bear and forbear; if necessary, to speak a painful truth faithfully and in love, but always to be able to hear one so spoken in a sisterly spirit.[1]

> Yet deem not, on such parting sad
> Shall dawn no welcome dear and glad:
>   Divided in their earthly race,
> Together at the glorious goal,
> Each leading many a rescued soul,
>   The faithful champions shall embrace.
>
> For even as those mysterious Four,
> Who the bright whirling wheels upbore
>   By Chebar in the fiery blast,
> So, on their tasks of love and praise
> The saints of God their several ways
>   Right onward speed, yet join at last.
>
> Companion of the saints! 'twas thine
> To taste that drop of peace divine,
>   When the great soldier of thy Lord
> Call'd thee to take his last farewell,
> Teaching the Church with joy to tell
>   The story of your love restored.

[1] W. Bradfield, *The Life of Thomas Bowman Stephenson*, 185.

O then the glory and the bliss,
When all that pain'd or seem'd amiss
  Shall melt with earth and sin away!
When saints beneath their Saviour's eye,
Fill'd with each other's company,
  Shall spend in love th' eternal day![1]

IV.

His Subsequent Life.

One sentence in the Epistle to Titus forms an apparent link
of connexion with the latest notice of the name of Titus. St.
Paul says to him: "Be diligent to come unto me to Nicopolis:
for I have determined there to winter." Now we find it stated
in the last of the Pastoral Epistles, written shortly before St.
Paul's death, that Titus was gone to Dalmatia. This was a wild
and rugged district, with a rough population, not far from
Nicopolis; and there may have been some connexion between the
two journeys. Neither tradition nor history helps us to any
details. It is just worth while to observe that this mention of a
difficult mission and an inclement season is in harmony with the
temperament and capabilities of Titus and the work which the
Apostle was in the habit of assigning to him.

It is, however, with the island of Crete that this companion
of St. Paul must be closely and permanently associated. Subsequent Church historians treated Titus as bishop of Crete and
living a celibate life to an old age in the island. An interesting
panegyric on him is found in the works of Andrew of Crete. He
says that Titus "laid the foundation of the Church in Crete, was
himself there the pillar of the Truth and the strong support of
the Faith, the unwearied trumpet of the proclamation of the
Gospel, and the clear utterance of the tongue of St. Paul."

His name is given still to churches in Crete; it was appealed
to as a battle-cry in the struggles of the Cretans with the
Venetians; his body was said to have been retained at Gortyna
for many centuries; the head was carried away by the Venetians,
and is still preserved at St. Mark's. His death is commemorated

---

[1] J. Keble, *The Christian Year.*

on 4th January in the Latin Church, on 25th August in the Greek, Syriac, and Maronite Churches.

¶ Spake we not of a communion of Saints, unseen, yet not unreal, accompanying and brother-like embracing thee, so thou be worthy? Their heroic sufferings rise up melodiously together to Heaven, out of all lands, and out of all times, as a sacred *Miserere*; their heroic actions also, as a boundless, everlasting song of Triumph. Neither say that thou hast now no Symbol of the Godlike. Is not God's Universe a Symbol of the Godlike; is not Immensity a Temple; is not Man's History, and Men's History, a perpetual Evangel? Listen, and for organ music thou wilt ever, as of old, hear the Morning Stars sing together.[1]

[1] Thomas Carlyle.

Printed by
MORRISON & GIBB LIMITED
Edinburgh